A Man of Contradictions

RICHARD OLLARD

A Man of Contradictions

A LIFE OF A. L. ROWSE

ALLEN LANE
THE PENGUIN PRESS

ALLEN LANE
THE PENGUIN PRESS

Published by the Penguin Group
Penguin Books Ltd, 27 Wrights Lane, London w8 5tz, England
Penguin Putnam Inc., 375 Hudson Street, New York, New York 10014, USA
Penguin Books Australia Ltd, Ringwood, Victoria, Australia
Penguin Books Canada Ltd, 10 Alcorn Avenue, Toronto, Ontario, Canada m4v 3b2
Penguin Books (NZ) Ltd, 182–190 Wairau Road, Auckland 10, New Zealand

Penguin Books Ltd, Registered Offices: Harmondsworth, Middlesex, England

First published 1999
1 3 5 7 9 10 8 6 4 2

Copyright © Richard Ollard, 1999

Set in 11/14 pt PostScript Monotype Sabon
Typeset by Rowland Phototypesetting Ltd, Bury St Edmunds, Suffolk
Printed in England by The Bath Press, Bath

A CIP catalogue record for this book is available from the British Library

ISBN 0-713-99353-7

To Mary
μάλιστα δέ τ' ἔκλυον αὐτοί

Contents

APPENDICES

List of Illustrations

Preface and Acknowledgments

This biography is based largely on A. L. Rowse's personal archive which he presented, two or three years before his death, to the Library of the University of Exeter. When I was invited to write his life I made two stipulations: first, that nothing I wrote on the subject should appear during his lifetime and second, that I should be granted exclusive access to all his books and papers until after my book had been published. Rowse, who had several times expressed the wish that no biography of him should be written, nevertheless agreed at once to these conditions. He further presented me with a great deal of material (he had not yet made his gift to the University of Exeter) and welcomed my visits to discuss its contents and, indeed, to range at will over his long life.

The disorder of the papers (he kept, it sometimes seems, everything, even Christmas cards, but made only fitful efforts to sort and to arrange) meant that if I was to get on with the job I could not afford to wait for what was bound to be a long undertaking. The papers had been piled into boxes and files which were numbered, so that in taking notes and transcribing I had the rough means of citation necessary for my own reference but useless to future researchers when the papers will have been properly classified and arranged. Thus to facilitate reference I have tried to indicate by date and description the documentary authority for statements deriving from this my principal source. Other sources are cited in the usual manner in the footnotes.

It will be seen that I had the advantage, unknown to a biographer whose work has been largely in the seventeenth century, of conversing with my subject. The kindness of his contemporaries and friends has been no less valuable. The late Lord Sherfield, who was Rowse's contemporary at Christ Church and was elected to a Fellowship at All Souls on the same day, and the late Sir Isaiah Berlin, elected only a few years later, both allowed me to come and question them. So did his colleagues of a younger generation, Sir Raymond Carr and Sir Michael Howard. The chaplain of the College, Professor McManners, and the ex Codrington Librarian, J. S. G. Simmons, the closest friends of his last years at All Souls, have been unfailingly helpful.

In Cornwall the hospitality of Lord and Lady St Levan at St Michael's Mount and that of David Treffry at the great house from which his family have for centuries commanded Fowey harbour introduced me to two of the County's splendours dearest to Rowse's heart. His near contemporary and sometime solicitor Mr John Pethybridge supplied me with invaluable recollections of the circumstances of Rowse's early life.

I wish to express my thanks to Tim Farmiloe and John Handford at Messrs Macmillan and to Mrs J. C. Sen at the John Rylands University Library, Manchester for searching their archives on my behalf. In America I wish to record my obligation to the Library of the University of Georgia at Athens (to which Rowse sold part of his library) where I was shown much kindness by Mary-Ellen Brooks, and to the Huntington Library at Pasadena, especially to its distinguished senior scholars, J. M. Steadman, Andrew Rolle and Robert Wark, who allowed me to profit from their memories of Rowse's visits.

In Shakespearean matters Miss Mary Edmond, Mr Stephen Freer and Professor Stanley Wells have generously put their scholarship at my disposal. Elizabeth Jenkins, in Rowse's opinion his most rewarding correspondent, has kindly supplied me with letters of hers which are not in the Rowse archive. My old friend Kenneth Rose has allowed me to quote from his Diary whose future publication is eagerly awaited.

Mr Sydney Cauveren has saved me much labour by permitting me to avail myself of his A. L. Rowse bibliography which is shortly to be published in America by the Scarecrow Press. Mr John Saumarez Smith of Heywood Hill Books, the purchaser of Rowse's library, has drawn my attention to much that I would have missed. For the assistance and considerate attention of the Exeter University Librarian, Dr Alasdair Paterson, and his staff over many months I am deeply grateful.

Finally to Rowse's oldest and closest friends, Jack Simmons, Norman Scarfe, David Treffry, and Raleigh Trevelyan my debt is limitless. Their friendship and encouragement have irradiated the writing of this book.

For permission to quote from T. S. Eliot's letters in the Rowse archive I am most grateful to his widow, Mrs Valerie Eliot. The letter from George Bernard Shaw on p. 98 is printed by permission of the Society of Authors on behalf of the Bernard Shaw estate.

Richard Ollard

I

Contradictions

Cornwall, the Little Land as A. L. Rowse, one of its most distinguished sons, thought of it, is like a tender towed in the wake of Britain. It is a tongue of land, seventy miles long and rarely more than twenty miles broad, buffeted to the north by the crashing seas of the Atlantic, indented to the south by the deep bays and estuaries of the Channel coast, sharing with Brittany a Celtic and a maritime inheritance that sets them apart from the great countries to which they have long been attached. Unlike the other large historic English counties it exudes no evidence of wealth. There are no smiling, fat, landscapes. Its beauties are either big, bare, dramatic, as most of its grand coastline or its central moors, or hidden, intimate valleys. It is not at all English. A fierce poverty, a fierce independence, are its human characteristics.

Alfred Leslie Rowse, born on 4 December 1903, in the hamlet of Tregonissey, on the hillside above St Austell in which it is now absorbed, proudly recalled that it 'like all the china-clay villages of the "Higher Quarter", escaped the stifling embrace of the squirearchy. And that fact, I realize now, though it was never thought of then, had a profound effect on our upbringing and social outlook. We were an independent folk; we never saw anybody in the village better than ourselves. I never remember seeing any sign of servility among any of its inhabitants. We were not in the habit of saying "sir" to anybody. I cannot recall my father saying "sir" to anyone; nor did the china-clay workers as a whole, any more than, I suppose, the free and independent tinners from whom they sprang had done in their day.'[1]

The tin mines to which he alludes, and in which his grandfather

1. *A Cornish Childhood* (1942), pp. 24–5.

had worked, had been for centuries, perhaps even from Phoenician times, the chief source of such natural wealth as the county could boast. The mining tradition it fostered enabled Cornishmen to seek their fortunes in the Gold Rushes in South Africa, Australia and California when the tin diminished. (It had finally given out a year or two after Rowse's death.) But it was succeeded in the nineteenth century by the china-clay industry, in which his father was employed, that still flourishes in the part of southern Cornwall in which he was born, lived and died.

Cornwall is now, to most English people except those who go there for seaside holidays (again like Brittany), as remote as Greenland. It is on the way to nowhere. It is an end in itself (as Rowse would passionately have wished it to be and as, for him, it always was). In 'The Seven Landscapes of Cornwall'[1] he describes the contrasts and particularities of its landscape, concluding with his own:

'What about the corrugated lunar landscape of the St Austell china-clay country – in the moonlight, under snow? I once saw an *aurora borealis* up there on a snowy day, over a thousand feet up.'

What indeed? But we must turn to the man himself. And there may be something to be said for introducing the reader to him by recalling how I was.

At my very first meeting with him, more than fifty years ago, I recall a snatch of talk arising from the fact that Harold Laski,[2] then the self-appointed *guru* of the triumphant Labour Party, had attacked Rowse as 'a traitor to his class'.

'What about HIM! Old Nathan Laski, respectable, prosperous pillar of Manchester capitalism . . .' The words are not exact: I did not take them down at the time and I certainly had no inkling that I should one day be Rowse's biographer. But the amused, high-spirited tone is as fresh in my mind as if it were yesterday.

It has often been observed that actors who have made their name in comedy will generally succeed in tragedy, whereas the converse is rarely true. Which was Rowse? He certainly saw himself, or liked to present himself, as a tragic character. But his humorous perception

1. *The Little Land of Cornwall* (1986), pp. 1–3.
2. For Rowse's considered view of Laski see below p. 85.

was acute. He was very entertaining company, his sense of comedy irrepressible if not often directed at himself. It was not that he was self-satisfied. He had a Pepysian power of turning a cold objective gaze on the nakedness of his jealousies, resentments, pettinesses, that most of us are happy to ignore in ourselves.

That he was unusually and variously gifted few of his detractors, no inconsiderable body, would deny. The positive and negative aspects of these qualities are related. Rowse was a brilliant historian, specializing in the Tudor period but by no means confining himself to it. He was a poet. He was an aesthete whose taste and knowledge in painting, architecture and music were not shallow. He was a notable biographer. He was an antiquary whose understanding of the Cornish past was profound and passionate. He campaigned as a Labour candidate in the 1930s when the tide was running strongly against his party. Forty and fifty years later he was to encourage a view of himself as the sworn enemy of the progressive intellectual. And yet he could – and did – argue that he had been consistent in his loyalties. To the end of his life he retained his admiration for Attlee and Bevin. It was the fashionable Left and its fashionable idols that he hated and despised, sentiments which were warmly reciprocated. Yet for all that he never retracted his early admiration for Karl Marx, finding in his historical analysis a powerful support for his own scepticism towards liberal principles and professions. It was from Marx that he learned, and continued to believe, that at the base of human history lay its economic facts.

Even those who did not find themselves berated as humbugs or derided as simpletons were disturbed by the diversity of his scholarly interests. Rowse never forgot that he was a poet, that he had won a scholarship to Christ Church in English, not History, that he had appeared in print with Graham Greene and others in an undergraduate volume *Oxford Poetry* for which some of his contemporaries, later to achieve fame as writers, had been rejected. Like it or not, Literature was as much his parish as History. The members of these two encrusted academic faculties, for the most part, did not like it at all. They liked it still less when he followed up a widely admired biography of Shakespeare with volumes on the sonnets and on the identity of the Dark Lady.

Whatever the merits of Rowse's arguments there can be no question that the tone in which he advanced them gave a huge advantage to his opponents. Rowse was quite clever enough to have seen this for himself. Why then did he adopt it? The answer that he gave was that a lifetime of rebuffs, of exclusion, of non-recognition, had exacerbated his proud and defiant nature. He knew and he did not care. He had nothing to lose. He might as well enjoy annoying people who had annoyed him. How well or ill founded this opinion was the reader should be better able to decide when he has finished this book. But there can be no doubt as to the fervour with which it was held.

Fervour, indeed, was the keynote of his personality. The mild distastes, the faint enjoyments, the neutralities that make up so much of everyday life were all but unknown to him. His response was always vigorous and vivid, though not necessarily lacking in subtlety or discrimination. None the less the speed and force of his perceptions, impressive, stimulating, provocative, denied him the insights incident to slow recognition except in those departments of exact historical scholarship where minuteness and particularity are both essence and entirety. The long, hard slog through documents difficult to interpret or even to make out, what researcher is not familiar with the sense of inching one's way towards what is very likely empty of meaning or value? The tedium, the sense of pointlessness, the guilty and resentful awareness of wasting time are intensified by physical trivialities. The room is too cold or too airless: one's wrist aches or one's back is stiff: half-heard chatter annoys. To the cool temper these are trying. To the ardent, still more to the consciously superior, they are exasperating.

Rowse was both. His ardour needs no demonstration. His consciousness of superiority took strong hold in childhood. Who can forget the little boy standing at the top of the stairs while his parents were still in bed and proclaiming at the top of his voice, 'Everyone's a fool in this house but me'? The successful struggles, against what in his day were enormous odds, to win a first-class education fortified this conviction. His election to a Fellowship of All Souls, a place where viceroys, archbishops and other figures in the front rank of public life as well as men of legendary learning mixed on equal terms with young men who only a year before had been undergraduates, concluded the matter. Indeed, All Souls came to take the place of religion, philosophy, ethics (a concept for which Rowse, in his journals, repeatedly expresses his scepticism).

Try as one will to avoid the word 'elitism', a nasty linguistic formation heavy with overtones of spite and envy, the cost to reader and author is too high. Rowse, at any rate, would have embraced, did embrace, the notion at its widest and most unqualified. In what became during the last half of his life a dark, despairing, but still defiant view of the human condition, there was on the one hand the vast mass of what he called the Idiot People, contemptuously ignorant and actively resentful of literature and the arts which constitute the light shining in darkness; on the other the handful of men and women who create, care for and seek to preserve them. Clearly discernible among this sacred band was, of course, himself.

So crude a summary may sound sneering. Certainly those who disliked him or were shocked by his intemperate and provocative assertions will so regard it. But, however clumsy the expression, that is far from the author's intention. It is impossible to understand or appreciate Rowse – or indeed any character worth exploration – without at times representing them in postures offensive to the *bien pensant*. Mr Podsnap would not have made much of a biographer. Rowse, had he been *per impossibile* his own biographer,[1] looking at himself from the outside with a sympathetic but observant eye, would at once have detected inconsistencies in a position which he liked to think of as intellectually impregnable. Solipsism, the view that oneself is the only reality, that other people and the world of ideas exist only as far as they impinge on one's consciousness, was his repeated profession. Nothing is either good or bad but thinking makes it so. He thought Shakespeare and Michelangelo good, the Idiot People preferred football and pop music. The simple fact of his preference was warrant enough for a superstructure of aesthetics and morals.

Morals? Here and there in the journals one can find hurried, almost furtive, but recognizable denials of the existence of right and wrong. Yet his history books and still more his journals, letters and private conversation show no such thing. On the contrary they ring with

1. He was, in several volumes, his own autobiographer; but that is not the same thing.

moral judgments, both approving (his temperament was warm and generous: when all is said and done he was an artist) and censorious. At times, particularly in his more popular history books, he likes to suggest that all such judgments are pragmatic and relative. We call an action good or bad according to whether it is in its context appropriate and rational. This gives us a comforting sense of being in touch with the great intellectual currents of our time.

But when it came to people he knew and had dealings with there were no hesitations. Take for instance his grateful and affectionate biography of Sir Arthur Quiller Couch (1988), 'a great gentleman, the greatest I have ever known'. Rowse was always quick to recognize baseness and generosity and to characterize them in unambiguously moral terms. Besides these simplicities, shared, one fears, with the Idiot People, there were moral obligations implicit in being one of the Elect. Talent, given the opportunity to develop it, imposed its own duty on its possessors. Gifted undergraduates who were his exact or near contemporaries, Graham Greene, W. H. Auden, Cyril Connolly, were never pardoned for their profligate neglect of their studies. Shirking hard work was a moral offence: and hard work, if one was clever (as they were) was all that was necessary to get a first in schools. *Ergo* not to have obtained a first showed that all is not sweet, all is not sound.

Rowse's claim to the reader's attention is not as a systematic thinker; and if it were the present author would be ill-equipped to write about him. He was an artist, a poet and a scholar. If he were to be compared with the Englishmen of the mid-seventeenth century Evelyn, Clarendon, Aubrey and Pepys would all be in point: Hobbes, Locke or Newton not at all. A sense of period, even a power of identifying oneself with a historical person as an actor identifies himself with a *dramatis persona*, a sense of place, of atmosphere, these were natural gifts which he diligently cultivated. The supreme master of them was his contemporary and friend John Betjeman. Indeed they once collaborated in an anthology of topographical photographs *Victorian and Edwardian Cornwall* (1974). The poetic, the intuitive, how these notes insist themselves in any contemplation of Rowse. In Betjeman's case these were combined with a good nature and a sufferance of fools that were apparently limitless. No one would think of saying any such thing of A.L.,[1] kind-hearted though he often showed himself to be. Impatience, anger, egocentricity, were simmering away even when they did not burst through the surface.

Betjeman leads – what better guide? – to Cornwall. Here, even deeper than love of Oxford and All Souls, than hatred for destructiveness and philistinism, lay the wellsprings. Partly it was simple patriotism, partly the strength of the first dawning perceptions of beauty. 'What my heart first awaking, Whispered the world was' but chiefly it was the sureness of independence, of knowing that one was different. A.L. for all his scorn for the Idiot People was fond of playing the proletarian card, of priding himself on working-class horse sense as opposed to the high-minded self-delusion of the bourgeois intellectuals. He and D. H. Lawrence, he repeatedly implies, shared a fierce realism denied to public school men, even to those who had, like R. H. Tawney or George Orwell, chosen to go slumming in maturity. But beyond the clarity born of the bareness of working-class life he prided himself on the perceptions derived from his Celtic antecedents. He was not an Englishman, but Cornish born and bred. This in his eyes explained or excused a certain deviousness not to say slipperiness of which he knew himself capable and which, if practised against him, he would have resented. Decency, gentlemanliness, qualities which in fact he admired, were not part of the Celtic inheritance. He explains the matter with his usual lucidity in the following passage (pp. 197–8) of his biography of Quiller Couch already mentioned.

Rowse relates how in 1940 the Cornish landed gentry, who had been appeasers almost to a man and thus his bitter opponents in the previous Parliamentary election,

... were willing to come round and be friends with me. They were too late. I had turned my back on the county. Q was saddened at the breach, but he had no idea how far it would go, how absolutely I would react. He wasn't a Celt; he had a nice English nature. He called me over to the Haven [Q's house at Fowey], the so familiar study, and told me a thing or two about the proprietor of the local newspaper that had attacked *A Cornish Childhood* (as if they could get away with it with impunity: I had too much

1. His preferred style of address among his intimates.

7

of that sort of thing throughout the thirties). He then said a wonderful thing: 'The best revenge is not to be like them'. That was Q: not me. I registered that he was right and at the same moment that I was not going to follow his gospel.

The concluding sentence exactly echoes a famous passage of Horace – except that the Latin poet advances no racial or cultural justification of his choice.

Perhaps a closer examination of this parallel may be enlightening. Horace wrote

> video meliora proboque
> Deteriora sequor.

'I see what is better and I approve of it; I practise what is worse.' The statement invites no sympathy, still less approval. If anything it is a recognition, so characteristic of the writer, of the truth about himself. It is certainly not a plea, direct or covert, for moral relativism or ethical pluralism. Anything but. It is a sharp assertion of black and white.

Rowse's remarks, looser and less succinct – after all he was not writing a poem but reminiscing about himself and an old friend – also present truths, not singular but plural, about himself. Their plurality is their most characteristic feature. He admires Q.'s clear application of his own creed as a gentleman and as a Christian. He even accepts its validity. 'I registered that he was right.' At the same time he rejects the general notion of a moral imperative which in common speech as well as in moral philosophy is implied by the word 'right'. 'That may be all very well, indeed admirable, for Q.,' he says, 'because Q. is an Englishman. I am not, and have never claimed to be. As a pure bred Celt I owe my moral allegiance to a starker, harsher code.'

It would be easy to demonstrate the inconsistency, the double standards, of such a position. But Rowse did not set up to be a moral philosopher, indeed often and emphatically expressed his scepticism towards the value of such an activity. What he is here stating and, unlike Horace, seemingly expecting approval for, is pluralism. To commit oneself to one standpoint is, in his eyes, to limit, not to intensify, perception and understanding of one's fellow men. Homosexuality, he asserts in his journals and sometimes suggests in print, equips a man with feminine as well as masculine insights into character, psychology, motive. Truth may be one but that does not preclude its having many aspects. The poet, the novelist, the historian who has grasped this will be the better for it. Rowse is explaining the secrets of his trade, showing the reader his tools and the use of them, not designing an unsinkable vessel to be launched on the strange seas of thought.

Yet the most striking quality of Rowse's pluralism is that it most certainly did not issue in a general indifferentism, an indulgent assent to the fashionable proposition that Anything Goes. No writer of the century was more censorious. Indeed the last decades of his life resound with denunciations of the world into which he had survived, with predictions of doom as dark as anything to be found in the Old Testament. This element had always been to some degree present in his work. It is not only his contemporaries but the historical personages of his studies that incur reproof. Dr Noel Malcolm in an eminently fair, indeed favourable, review of *Four Caroline Portraits* (1993) raises the objection 'that its whole method of tut-tutting and ticking off the past is somehow unhistorical'. The point is well taken: Rowse is both a professed sceptic and an inveterate moralist. It is yet another contradiction.

Dr Malcolm points us to one more. It is profoundly unhistorical, inexplicable in so sensitive, so learned and so imaginative a historian, to castigate the men and women of the Middle Ages or the sixteenth century for religious belief. Their historian is not obliged to share it but he must accept the fact of it. Even in the history of religious art and iconography the personal creed of scholars is beside the point. The work of Emile Mâle, an agnostic, is no less sympathetic to or perceptive of the ideas of the medieval glass-painters or stone carvers than that of M. R. James, a believer. One of the most powerful motives to become a historian is the desire to enter minds and worlds other than one's own. One could illustrate this, abundantly, from Rowse's own books. Yet, in the same volume in most cases, one finds him lecturing his subjects for the inadequate grounds of their beliefs.

The question of religion exemplifies his intellectual duality. Ready, indeed anxious, to demonstrate to Cranmer or Sir Thomas More the baselessness of their, or anyone else's, religious position he objected strongly to being described as an atheist. 'Agnostic' was the term he chose because it admitted a mystery at the heart of things while rejecting definitions and systems. But having disembarrassed himself of credal allegiance he enjoyed, vicariously, a partisanship in English Christianity. He liked the High – though not the extreme – Anglicans. He disliked Low Churchmen and detested Puritanism. He had never, unlike Gibbon and other historians later celebrated for their scepticism, been drawn to Roman Catholicism. Much might be pardoned for the patronage of the arts in which the Church of Rome had for centuries played the leading part. On the other hand the encouragement of superstition and downright silliness, typified for Rowse by Cardinal Newman's belief in the miraculous transport of the Virgin's house from Nazareth to the Italian town of Loreto, put it beyond the pale. But far, far worse were the Puritans who combined silliness with a deadly destructiveness, defacing carvings, smashing stained-glass windows, throwing paintings into the Thames.

Yet as he himself came ruefully to recognize Puritanism had got its own back on him for all his denunciations. What else but Puritanism animated his moral outrage at people like Cyril Connolly squandering time and talent on menus and wine lists that should have been devoted to the perusal of texts prescribed for the Final Honours Schools? Puritanism in its current secular sense stands for the triumph of the will, the imposition of self-discipline on the appetites of the natural man. Rowse had had to force this on himself to win his passport to the Republic of Letters. In an unpublished short story, of which the hero is a thinly disguised self-portrait, he wrote:

Was he himself a trifle inhuman? Certainly his iron control of himself was, and it took it out of him physically, in a chronic recurrence of gastric ulcer. Such discipline certainly was not natural to man.

The poverty and ignorance of the household into which he was born were unbearable to a vigorous, questioning intelligence. Questions demanded answers. Books, of which there were none in the house, were the obvious place in which to look for them. The educational ladder by which one climbed from a virtually illiterate home had in the years before the First World War few rungs. To contrast then and now is almost to contrast an escalator and a greasy pole. The struggle so vividly described in *A Cornish Childhood* developed characteristics in the author that were never to be effaced.

2

Origins

What is a historian? Nowadays, hoping to be taken for a scientist, he sometimes appears as a statistician or puts on the false beard of a sociologist. Opponents of this conception point out that in French and Italian the word for history and the word for a story are the same. Rowse's views, expressed in one of his earliest books and enlarged in *The Use of History* (1946) incline markedly to the second understanding of the function. But the Greek verb, from which French, Italian and English derive, means to inquire, to ask questions.

If ever a cap fitted, that does. In his first, most brilliant, autobiographical composition *A Cornish Childhood* (1942) Rowse achieved a self-description that triumphs by its unself-consciousness:

I admit that I was exceedingly inquisitive, devoured by an insatiable desire to know and in every direction; but I was never encouraged . . . There was a blank wall all round. The result was that I was very much thrown in upon myself, my head teeming with ideas and questions and comments of all sorts and kinds, which were, it seemed, never welcome and usually bitten off with: 'Little boys should be seen and not heard'. When I first heard this dreary, discouraging remark, I wondered quite what it meant: why should little boys be *seen*? Were they to be looked at as if on exhibition? And what was the point of that? And then the point that they were to be unheard – *seen* but not *heard* – sank in, and I realized that that was the point of the remark. How I resented it. I could feel a blush going down my neck, bristling the hairs on the way down. And always when cut off in the midst of some – to me – entrancing exordium, some trope of imagination, which I cannot but think intelligent grown-ups would have found fascinating from a small child of five and known how to deal with, but which the plain working-people in whose family I was born and brought up never showed the slightest interest in and cut short – always I remember the hot blush of shame and the confusion which overcame me when I heard: 'Little boys should be seen and not heard.'

I grant that I must have been an altogether too knowing little boy, or would have been if the questions had been answered – if they had been capable of answering them. But this process of stubbing every shoot of confidence on the part of a naturally sanguine and vivacious temperament had all sorts of unforeseen consequences, some of them detrimental to happiness. For one thing, this repressive, discouraged youth drove me in upon myself and made me excessively ambitious: not until I was thirty-five and nearly lost my life over a couple of duodenal operations did this pressure relax, and, with the possibility of enjoying life returning (for the first time since I was nineteen), there came a more natural attitude to life.

A Cornish Childhood is such a pellucid book, fresh, astringent, tender, that it seems irritating to gloss it. But it throws so much light on so much that is to follow that it can hardly be avoided. From the first the little boy, though mischievous and, as he says himself, vivacious, was fond of being on his own. And like another solitary boy of an inquisitive disposition, John Aubrey, he loved hearing about the past. Intellectually this can be explained as the necessary consequence of curiosity. The past is all there is to be curious about. The present, as soon as one's consciousness has apprehended it, is already past. And the future offers scope not so much for curiosity as for speculation. This argument was to be deployed in *The Use of History*. It can hardly have been present to the awareness of a small boy. What was undoubtedly present, and was to remain, indeed to strengthen with his strength, was a nostalgia, a topographical loyalty to the scenes of his early life. In time this assumed the forms of religion. In his nineties he sent me a copy of his poem; entitled 'Home':

> Christ keep the cliffs and coves
> The land that gave me birth.
> And let no harm come near to them
> When I am gone to earth.

Christ keep them as they were
When I was but a boy:
To walk the roads and come to them
Was all my summer's joy.

A sense of place implies a sense of its past. The combination of them is one of the springs of poetry. 'Home' to Rowse was the Cornwall to which his awakening perception thrilled, not the love and cherishing of the family into which he was born. It is a constant theme of his journals that love was a word to which he could attach no meaning so that the first conventional axiom of Christianity 'God is Love' conveyed nothing to him. But whether he knew what it meant or not he was certainly conscious of feeling affection and of needing it. His own self-analysis already quoted proves that.

Yet the portraits of his father and mother drawn in *A Cornish Childhood* are not without touches of tenderness in the depiction of his father, and of understanding, sometimes rising to an unwilling admiration, for his mother. They are at least presented as human beings, unlike the icy James Mill who stalks through the early passages of his brilliant son's autobiography with no word of encouragement or affection. This retrospect was written in 1941, some six or seven years after the death of his father, and before the obduracies of his mother, who kept house for him in Cornwall, had exasperated him to frenzy. The book had, he tells us, shaped itself in his mind in the intervals of recuperation while he was undergoing a series of operations that he and most of his friends thought quite likely to be fatal. The tone was therefore more subdued, the vision more elegiac, than was usual with him.

Neither parent showed the boy affection. The father, he suggests, rather through ineptitude, an inability to communicate born of his own bullied and joyless early life: the mother through a hard, cold, angry practicality that had no time for such things, a trait that, in his maturity, he was to remark in his own character. His elder brother George, from the start aggressively masculine and determinedly unimaginative, was naturally antipathetic. He is seen in the book simply as the product of a social environment itself distasteful, rather as Clarendon described the generality of victims in the Civil War 'dirty people of no name'. Only his sister Hilda, his elder by nearly ten years, broke this circle. She

had a growing girl's devotion to the baby of the family . . . It was 'Hoola' who made me say my prayers, dressed dolls for me, looked after the brown teddy-bear, and tended me in bed when I had the measles . . . One day I remember my mother stupidly posing the question before somebody else 'Oo do ee love best?' The answer was of course, firmly and uncompromisingly 'Hoola'. This was very ill received, with a frown and a scolding; but I was as obstinate as devoted, and wild horses would not have made me give the expected answer. It wasn't true and I wasn't going to say it: I think there was even thus early an instinctive resentment at the feeling of rejection, the importance of which in my make-up (or case history) I leave it to the Freudians to disentangle.

The obvious truthfulness of this account thaws the ice-bound vision of a childhood empty of affection. But it supports the author's contention of damage suffered and held as a grudge against his mother. Rowse from his earliest days seems to have had a keen sense of genealogy, like a horse-breeder, seeing people first as specimens of a collective heredity rather than noticing them as individuals. His description of his father and mother takes shape and life from his apprehension of their family characteristics: the Rowses fickle, combative, devil-may-care, reckless, improvident; the Vansons, his mother's family, clever, cooler, more controlled, physically more elegant and sexually attractive. Before composing the book he had enumerated and catalogued these strains in his own nature. Autobiography he tells us in his opening paragraph had long been among his favourite reading. The Rowses and the Vansons of whom we are given such vivid sketches set against a compellingly realistic background of Cornish village society at the opening of the twentieth century owe not a little of their vitality to the author's close observation of himself.

Autobiography can hardly be written without disclosing feelings about people who are still alive. This imposed a certain moderation on what Rowse then wrote about his mother. But it is permissible to wonder what she made of the paragraph following that in which the reader has been told that before her marriage she had been in domestic service at one of Cornwall's greatest houses, St Michael's Mount, whose history and situation are then romantically evoked.

Not much of all this, it may be supposed, entered the head of a very young, very lovely housemaid, with those wonderful dark eyes and perfect features, the exquisite line of mouth and nose, the small ears under wavy black hair, drawn straight back. A *bonne bouche*, a discerning eye would decide. Age: twenty. The reaction on her part, in terms of how many bedrooms (so much larger than Tregrehan) [the country house near St Austell where her father and mother were lodge-keepers] so many stairs and tunnels and passages in the rock; here you had to go downstairs to bed; you were for ever losing your way in such a large place. Here, too, the sacrosanct, mysterious routine of the gentry, on an even grander scale: at the apex of it the remote, the unseen figure of 'his lordship' [Lord St Levan]; the strangeness of a house upon an island in the sea, going to and fro to Marazion by boat, or, when the tide was low, over the causeway; the gale of wind blowing against those high, defensive walls. (And always against that background, the interminable passages, the Chevy Chase Room, the Chapel with its family memorials, the figure of the young Captain, invalided home from the East. Only a few years ago, with strange emotion, I saw his memorial, dead a year or two after that brief time, there along with the rest.)

The significance of this passage is thinly concealed in order to avoid embarrassment and preserve the decencies. His mother had had an affair with one of the sons of the house resulting in an illegitimate daughter. The St Aubyn family had evidently behaved well, had found another situation for the young mother and had made provision for the upbringing of the child. The father, a regular army officer, died while serving in Hong Kong two or three years later.

Why, it may be asked, did Rowse exhume, or if not exhume at least indicate the site of this long buried secret? His mother surely would have found it disturbing. The answer is that Rowse, at the time of writing, was convinced that Dick Rowse, the china-clay worker, was not his natural father. How could his own sensibilities, his innate fastidiousness, his distaste amounting in adolescence and young man-hood to active repulsion from working-class habits and pleasures, be accounted for except on the supposition that his true father was someone else? The young Captain had been dead some years before Rowse's birth, but the more he observed both the sexual promiscuity of Cornish villagers and the nature of his mother, the more probable it seemed that she had deceived the husband who was touchingly and simply devoted to her. The diaries often recur to the topic and settle ultimately on a lively but not noticeably aristocratic candidate. Not until 19 October 1964 was this issue apparently[1] decided by a visit to a town in Montana where emigrants from Tregonissey, the little village now swallowed in St Austell, had settled. Dick Rowse, he was now assured, was his true father.

Had not part of his mind accepted this all along? Why else go so thoroughly into the immediate Rowse antecedents and relate them to his own proud, intemperate nature? Why stress the historical continuity of the Rowses in Tregonissey? Why be overwhelmed with excitement at finding a document in the Public Record Office that showed a Gregory Rowse holding a substantial property in Tregonissey in 1602? Very probably like the D'Urbervilles in Hardy's novel, always one of Rowse's favourite writers, they had gradually come down in the world. Was not this a pedigree romantic enough to transcend the fighting, boozing, womanizing that absorbed the energies of Dick Rowse's brothers? Celtic ambivalence, on which A.L. plumed himself, disdains a clear answer.

The colours of family life in *A Cornish Childhood* are at first glance hard. But those of what is now called the extended family are soft and warm. The kindness of the Vanson grandparents, their lifelong devotion to each other, could not have been brought to life by an observer who was a stranger to affection. Uncles and aunts are recalled with gratitude rather than resentment. There is real sympathy for the harshness of their lot and appreciation of the marvellous generosity of the poor. Of his next-door neighbour Mrs Cornelius, a widow who had been deserted by her husband and left to bring up a family on what she could earn by charring, scrubbing and needlework, he writes:

Children, and this small child especially, were the soft spots in this poor lonely old woman's heart. But I am glad to say that, in return for Nelius's

1. Only apparently: it continued to disturb him. See below pp. 278–85.

Tregonissey, St. AUSTELL,

Dore by 191

ℳ _____ F 29 John Uince

𝕭𝖔𝖚𝖌𝖍𝖙 𝖔𝖋 **R. ROWSE,**

GROCER AND TEA DEALER.

Bill-head of Rowse's father's shop.

goodness to us, Mother and Father were good to her. She had a great relish for seed-buns – yeast buns flavoured with caraway-seeds, much appreciated in Cornwall, though not by me. Whenever there was a baking of seed-buns, infallibly once or twice in the week, there were a few sent up to Nelius. I think her great luxury was at our hands. The last thing on Saturday night, when the shop [kept by the Rowses] was shut up and Nelius had gone to bed tired with the week's work, father would carry a boiling hot cup of tea and a new seed-bun up to the old woman in bed . . . sometimes, if father was busy, I took it up to her . . .

Her last years were made easier for her by Lloyd George's Old Age Pension. If anybody ever deserved five shillings a week after a lifetime of honest hard work it was Nelius; and if there was anybody to whom it was an inestimable help it was she. The consequence was that she worshipped the name of Lloyd George – and quite rightly, too.

Passages such as this need to be remembered when the author is in full flood about the Idiot People and the iniquities of extortions made on their behalf from the hapless taxpayer.

To offer a substitute for *A Cornish Childhood* is no purpose of this book. The balance between the poet and the historian, between the adjective and the noun of the title, are both achieved there with a success that leaves little to be said beyond a commendation to read it. Of the themes that a biographer finds it necessary to extract poverty may perhaps bear a brief summary. That the Rowses were poor is obvious. But the village shop, whose servitude incessantly interrupted home study already difficult enough, did at least mean that they did not go hungry even if the diet was neither nutritious nor attractive. The poverty round them was keener. But there was no margin, no spending money. When the boy won a prize he was outraged that the money was appropriated by his mother to buy him a pair of boots. That however was the first reward of the career in which he was to make a name for himself.

3

Education

In the closing decade of the twentieth century there is far less agreement on what is meant by this word and what is to be hoped from it than in the first. Rowse was untroubled by any uncertainty on the matter. It was the development of the intellectual faculties, in especial the acquisition of the ability to distinguish and to demonstrate the difference between truth and falsehood. By this means knowledge was achieved and extended. The notion that education should be employed as a remedy for the ills of society or that it should be diverted from its essential purpose in order to promote this or that social ideal was, in his eyes, intellectual treachery.

Perhaps treachery is too dramatic. Rather it was the intellectual flabbiness induced by middle-class sentimentality and humbug, to which could be traced all the ills of the century from the appeasement of Hitler to the erosion of standards in education. His long life enabled him to chart in his own experience the rise and fall of hopes and expectations from the schools provided by the public authorities. In his young manhood he never ceased to be astonished, even shocked, at the complaints and recriminations of his privately educated contemporaries, anthologized by Graham Greene in *The Old School*. 'My schooldays were just happiness all the way along. It is a great tribute to day-schools' he wrote in *A Cornish Childhood*, admitting that public schools and even more preparatory schools of the late Victorian and early twentieth-century periods might have been pretty hellish for an unathletic boy who showed signs of developing into an intellectual or, worse still, an aesthete.

But what about the village schools? Wasn't there a good deal of bullying and rough stuff at break or on the way to and from school?

Rowse acknowledges that he was lucky but his reader may feel that he owed a good deal to his own pugnacity, a temperamental quality that can sometimes cow superior strength. Nelson's sister, asked to stop a fight between him and his bigger and stronger brother, replied 'Let them alone. Little Horace will beat him.' Rowse's two recollections (on page 179 of *A Cornish Childhood*) suggest a similar recognition.

He early realized that brains can offer advantages over brawn. The church choir at St Austell, along with the school the chief formative influence of his young mind, provides an instance of his success in eluding his fellow-choristers whom he knew to be lying in wait for him after choir practice. Perhaps even more than school the choir gave him scope for distinguishing himself. He sang solos. He organized mischief, even more seriously, a strike. Music remained his keenest artistic pleasure till in late age deafness deprived him of it.

A no less enriching by-product was the discovery of Cornwall's natural beauty:

It was not until the last year of the War, when I was between fourteen and fifteen, that I first went for a long tramp. One of the choir-men, an income-tax inspector of some education and reading, an Anglo-Catholic, took an interest in the intelligent lad with the fine voice and, after sending him a picture postcard when away on holiday . . . proposed to take me for a long walk. I had never been on one and never supposed that I could walk as much as ten miles. However, one afternoon we went to St Blazey and then up the valley through the woods of Prideaux to Luxulyan. It might have been the Tyrol; it was so strangely beautiful, and for all I knew that there was such country within half a dozen miles of the place where I was born, and had lived all my days. There's immobility and rootedness for you: absolutely characteristic of the people to whom I belonged. I could hardly keep up. I was so unaccustomed to walking. Breathless with nervousness, self-consciousness and exertion I laboured up the valley, among the oaks and ashes, the great granite boulders that strew the slopes, under the splendid aqueduct with the stream dashing noisily down among the withies, this while the shadows gathering fast, until we rounded the nip up into the village and caught sight of the church tower of Luxulyan with its little turret standing black and fortress-like among the trees before us, night fallen.

From that moment Luxulyan was engraved upon my heart. Again and again every year, in spring and summer, in autumn and winter, I have returned to it, often bringing my nearest and dearest friends along with me, still more often and no less enjoyably, alone. I do not attempt to explain the hold that place has over me, any more than Trollope could explain his passion for hunting. I only know that it is dearer to me than Tregonissey, though I wasn't born there, nor had my family any connections with it, and I had never set eyes on it until that evening. But I know I should be happy to end my days there – my chosen place.

The Church of England is, like the Cornish background, among the earliest and most enduring pieces of stage scenery in the theatre of Rowse's interior life. He sees himself against it even when he also feels it to be no more than canvas and plywood. It has not so serious, so deep a meaning as the moors and valleys of Cornwall. His earliest ambition, he has several times told me, was to be a bishop. In *A Cornish Childhood* he even elevates this to the metropolitan see of Canterbury. Could this perhaps be the colouring of an early memory by a later recollection of Archbishop Lang's kindness to him when as a shy newly elected Fellow of All Souls he found himself next to him at his first dinner in hall? But either way it was the position not the function that was the object of his ambition. Christianity as a system of belief by his own account never meant much to him. He was delighted by an American scholar who told him that he had seen Dean Swift's autograph marginal comment on the Nicene creed *Confessio fidei digna barbaris*. It was the Church as an institution, its buildings, its music, its art, its liturgy, its ceremonial, that engaged him. Yet his imagination could compass what his intellect could not accept. The bishop of the Cornish see of Truro appointed in 1923, W. H. Frere, is consistently admired, both in published writings and in the privacy of diaries and letters, as a saint and a scholar. The second term Rowse knew himself qualified to judge but the first must be supposed to have had some meaning for him.

Rowse was a man of gratitude as well as of grudges. The church had opened magic casements. But school opened more. He remembered it with a warmth of affection that home did not inspire. 'I loved it from the first moment [he started going to school before he was four] . . . so much more interesting than at home, where there was nobody to play with, nothing much to play with, for we had very little in the way of toys, and my mother had her hands full with the house and the shop.' The attachment grew ever stronger. The women who taught him were kind and encouraging: they were as delighted with him as he was with them. By the time he was eleven he was head of the school, taught now by a master, who arranged for him to compete for a minor scholarship to the secondary school at St Austell.

Here it was the same, only more so. His fellow minor scholars got on well with him and he responded. He remembers them kindly in his later years when he liked to pose as a Diogenes figure, hating the human race and asking nothing more of it than it should not stand in his light. In fact he was a courteous and encouraging correspondent to his old school-fellows as his files, deposited in Exeter University library, abundantly show. And his generosity extended beyond words and feelings. In 1925, just when he had won his Fellowship at All Souls, he sent a friend who was taking a language-teaching course in Paris £2, a large sum in those days and those circumstances for both donor and beneficiary. He kept the letters of his early friends, as he did those from his old teachers.

Mary Blank, so charmingly recalled in *A Cornish Childhood* as the form-mistress who had been the first to fire his life-long passion for English literature, was a fervent Wesleyan Methodist and, much to her pupil's sorrow, left to marry a missionary in India. Her last letter congratulating the boy on his success in matric. and commenting with professional care on his choice of examination questions is endorsed in his mature hand. 'Dear Mary Blank died in childbirth a missionary's wife in bloody India.' The feeling is evident: probably the final epithet applied equally to the propagation of the human race and of the gospel as much as it did to the sub-continent. Rowse's hatred of nonconformity and liberalism, that heady brew in the Cornwall of his youth, at first instinctive, was rationalized and strengthened by experience of its sour puritan philistinism and its power to obstruct, in effect to nullify, the efforts of the nascent Labour Party to overthrow the inert Conservatism under which he saw the country drifting to disaster. Methodist Mary Blank may have been, but her favourite author, who became one of the young Rowse's, was the highly unMethodistical Hazlitt. It was a marriage of true minds.

His egotism is a touchy and wayward feeling which takes the mask of misanthropy. He is always meditating upon his own qualities, but not in the spirit of the conceited man who plumes himself upon his virtues, nor of the ascetic who broods over his vices. He prefers the apparently self-contradicting attitude (but human nature is illogical) of meditating with remorse upon his own virtues. What in others is complacency becomes with him, ostensibly at least, self-reproach . . . He is angry with the world for preferring commonplace to genius, and rewarding stupidity by success; but in form, at least, he mocks at his own folly for expecting better things. If he is vain at bottom, his vanity shows itself directly by depreciating his neighbours. He is too proud to dwell upon his own virtues, but he has been convinced by impartial observation that the world at large is in a conspiracy against merit. Thus he manages to transform his self-consciousness into the semblance of proud humility, and extracts a bitter and rather morbid pleasure from dwelling upon his disappointments and failures.

Leslie Stephen's insight into Hazlitt supplies some suggestions about Leslie Rowse. Leslie: how warmly he professed his dislike of the name by which he was known to contemporaries, abbreviated by his family to Les. 'A.L.' was his preferred style to his intimates, though he, and they, often found themselves reverting to the rejected Christian name. But this does not apply to his boyhood, to which we must briefly return.

Briefly, because *A Cornish Childhood* is not only a classic. It rests on an exceptionally vivid and powerful memory and on such documentation as survives in his papers. Although too emancipated a spirit to assent to the proposition that one's schooldays are the best time of one's life, he was always ready to admit that they were happy, in contrast to the years of anxious ambition and losing struggle against ill-health that began at Oxford and ended with an alarming series of major operations in the late 1930s.

Early on his teachers spotted him as an intellectual Derby winner. His energy matched his abilities and perceptions so that he was not disturbed but rather stimulated by what was expected of him. At St Austell, unlike so many public schools of his time, school activity outside the classroom did not centre on the playing field, thus enabling a fat, unathletic boy to take a leading part. He edited the school newspaper. He played Malvolio in *Twelfth Night* to the Olivia of an attractive and intelligent schoolfellow Noreen Sweet. Shakespeare and sex, closely entwined in his later life, come up over the horizon together.

The impact of the playwright through the playing of a character so unmistakably fresh from his own hand Rowse has well described. Friendship and good taste (not a quality he was in principle disposed to overvalue) led him to say less about Noreen. She, it is clear, was attracted to him: and the lively if undetermined emotions of adolescence naturally responded. His joyous, vigorous, proud assertions of homosexuality so frequently repeated in the books, letters and talk of his manhood lay far in the future. If he is to be believed – and what superior authority can there be in the matter? – it was the medievalist Bruce McFarlane who convinced him of his sexual orientation – and that friendship, the longest of his Oxford life, did not develop until the early years at All Souls.

As a schoolboy and in the Oxford vacations he would go for a walk or a swim with her; they would picnic together; he would write a poem or two to her, but it would not be, it could not be, erotic. In the American usage of their day they were dating each other. She, in Rowse's view, came to want to marry him when age and circumstance made this feasible. When, ultimately, she married someone else Rowse as a wedding guest was divided between wondering whether after all he might not be better standing in the groom's shoes or whether he had not been too negligent of her happiness in keeping her so long in half-expectancy that he would come up to snuff.

Sex plays such a part in Rowse's analysis of himself and of other people that his biographer should perhaps put his cards on the table. Shameful though it may be thought I have no cards. I am entirely unqualified by reading or clinical experience to diagnose the condition of someone's sexuality just as I am incompetent to tell what is the state of their liver and how, if at all, it affects their state of mind. The medieval theory of the humours seems to me hardly less satisfactory as an explanation of human conduct and motive than the glib assumption that whatever cannot be traced to overt self-interest can be explained by sex. I hear the shade of my old friend hissing 'Second-rater: what's it matter what he thinks?' What indeed? None the less the reader is entitled to know about an author's opinions and prejudices where they bear on the matter of his book.

But leaving, as Rowse did at this stage of his life, sex aside, was his adolescence wholly happy and untroubled? By no means. Poverty and class were already an irritation and a constraint, as they would be for many years yet. Poverty, like other apparently unavoidable afflictions, can be accepted the more easily if the condition is generally shared and if it is in no obvious sense a matter of choice. Class is less straightforward. One of its most conspicuous manifestations is use of language and manner of speaking. From his earliest days at school Rowse aimed at correct diction and, easily achieving it, became more and more angry and resentful of his mother's obstinate slovenliness in the teeth of what we may be sure were constant attempts at reform. He could still remember, more than half a century later, the exact point in the road on his way home from school where he had decided henceforward to speak English properly. He was never ashamed, indeed was rather proud, of being poor. He cherished, no man more warmly, the old forms of Cornish dialect and vocabulary. But the slipshod and the vulgar were simply offensive.

No wonder that in antithesis to Shakespeare's vision he dragged his feet unwillingly from school. But his very success there generated its own anxieties. He threw himself, as he was always to do, so headlong into what he was doing that he was worried that he might lose his wakening instinct for writing poetry. An ardent adolescent could not foresee the toughness, the inexhaustible tenacity, which was to keep him writing till well into his nineties. He published a stout volume of collected poems entitled *A Life* in 1981, continuing to revise the text until the spring of 1995. An anxiety, especially when one is young, is not the less intense for proving unfounded.

More pressing was the question of securing admission to the University, without which the glory of the world's day would fade. Cornwall in good times had not much to offer in the way of a career, and the times were bleak and growing bleaker. The County scholarships that H. A. L. Fisher had introduced as Minister of Education in Lloyd George's coalition government had been cut. There was now only one for the whole of Cornwall. Rowse won it, thanks partly to the championship of Quiller Couch whom he had not then met. Much later on he heard from another source that while Q. was addressing the County Education Committee in his favour a note was passed to him: 'Do you know that this boy is a socialist?' Q. tore it up and took no notice.

Sixty pounds a year was a grand first step. But the minimum at which Oxford could be managed in the twenties was £200. And Oxford it had been from the moment that his university entrance had been mooted. His first, and most influential, headmaster had been an Oxford man. Exeter, the traditional Oxford college for West Country men, was the target. But Exeter was not offering a scholarship in English, Rowse's subject. The only immediate possibility was a history award in a group of colleges that included Balliol and St John's. Doubtfully Rowse went in for it and not surprisingly had no luck. However it appeared that Christ Church, the most magnificent of all Oxford colleges, was offering a scholarship in English. Instant decision was required. It was arranged that the boy should take the advice of Q., uniting the qualifications of a local eminence, Professor of English Literature at Cambridge and himself a devoted Oxford man. The account of all this, and its happy issue, crowned by an award from the Drapers Company that brought the total up to the required £200, is so vividly rendered in *A Cornish Childhood* that it would be a shame to spoil it for the reader. But not the least important point is that from this moment dates the friendship between the old man and the young, the courteous, tranquil, large-minded Tory and the brash, fierce, egocentric rebel, which was to set a pattern for so much of his future development. Bipolarity is the essence of his nature, perhaps the source of his seemingly inexhaustible energy.

> When the fight begins within himself
> A man's worth something.

In the case of A. L. Rowse it was a fight that lasted with scarcely so much as a truce from the dawn of consciousness to its extinction.

4

Christ Church

If Cornwall was the true love, Oxford was the grand passion of Rowse's life. It had a beginning and an end, it brought despair as well as rapture, it could never be remembered in tranquillity. The objects of such feelings 'by laws of time and space decay'. 'Decay' would certainly be the verb that best expresses his view of the changes that Oxford underwent in his lifetime. Perhaps few of his contemporaries, or near contemporaries, would have agreed with him. But the fact of change, almost it might be termed a remodelling, is obvious. The Oxford of the 1990s in ethos and atmosphere as well as in curriculum and balance of studies differs from that of the 1920s, when Rowse came up as an undergraduate, as widely as the 1920s did from the days of Mr Verdant Green.

It was, as it is today, in a state of flux. Evelyn Waugh's evocation of it in *Brideshead Revisited*, skilfully popularized in a television version, Anthony Powell's in *A Dance to the Music of Time*, above all John Betjeman's *Summoned by Bells*, vividly recreate the life of the rich and leisured undergraduate. Probably that had changed less in the previous sixty years than almost any other aspect of the place. But the institutional roots, deep and strong though they were, had begun to wither. Collegiate life was essentially clerical and celibate in tone and origin. There were still some very old men who had known the place when the taking of priest's orders was the necessary condition of holding all but a handful of college or university appointments and when marriage meant the immediate vacation of a Fellowship. One of Rowse's tutors, Keith Feiling, was one of the first Christ Church dons to profit from the relaxation of this rule. His wife, a spirited and witty lady, reacted to the mixture of condescension and disapproval with which she found herself treated.

'And what do you think of Oxford, Mrs Feiling?'

'It's like a muddy bank, with the stream of life flowing by.'

Hall and Chapel were still the formal outward expression of a common life. When taking the scholarship examination Rowse had stood about in Tom Quad watching the undergraduates going in to dine in hall, hoping to be one of them. At nine o'clock Tom's great bell sounded over Oxford and the colleges began to close their gates, securing them for the night at eleven or at latest twelve. In both symbol and reality the world was excluded. The echo of a religious foundation was clearly audible. The Ford Lectures, the great honour annually awarded by the Oxford History Faculty, were in Rowse's first year delivered by the then Dean of Wells on the Life and Times of St Dunstan. Technical and erudite to a degree that must have made them almost unintelligible to any but a specialist, their manner as well as their matter could hardly stand in sharper contrast to the performances of such recent honorands as A. J. P. Taylor or Sir Geoffrey Elton.

Oxford itself, the town as well as the University, was closer, much closer, to the Victorian age than to ours. So vast, so unexampled, is the havoc, moral, social, political, of the First World War that it requires an effort of mind to remember that Queen Victoria had only been dead for twenty years when Rowse came up. The town shops were those of saddlers, corn-chandlers, old-fashioned grocers, with bookshops and tailors for the university. Cars and buses had appeared: but boutiques, shopping malls, dry cleaners, supermarkets had not. The style of life of the undergraduates was that of Trollope's novels. No undergraduate rooms had direct access to bathrooms. A chilly walk in a dressing gown was part of that procedure. On the other hand a manservant, scouts as they were called, cleaned your rooms and your shoes, made your bed and would bring you a meal from the generally excellent college kitchens at a very modest price.

Academically the newly planted subjects were beginning to climb up the crumbling curtain walls. English, the faculty in which Rowse had won his award, had been granted *de facto* recognition. But Christ Church was still doubtful about *de jure*. The dons who had examined him were in no doubt about his ability and thought it a pity to risk it on an untried course of study, the more so as the College did not provide a tutor in the subject. An Arts man who had little Latin and less Greek had then only one respectable option: the Honour School of Modern History. Here Christ Church could field as strong a team as any. J. C. Masterman, later Provost of Worcester, and Keith Feiling, later Chichele Professor, were tutors of high quality.

Masterman, a bachelor who lived in College, perfectly fits the stereotype of Oxford Don to be found in the higher reaches of twentieth-century detective fiction. In fact he himself made a distinguished contribution to this branch of literature in *An Oxford Tragedy*. A notable athlete, he was President of Vincents Club, the Valhalla of the Blues. He refined and distilled his vision of Oxford in a book of discursive dialogue entitled *To Teach the Senators Wisdom*. Yet for all this he was not the type of hermit crab to which the crevices of an ancient university offered so congenial a habitat. He had joined the Navy as a cadet at Dartmouth and, finding it not the life for him, had deliberately run a launch aground in order to secure his dismissal. Caught in Germany by the outbreak of war in 1914 he had spent four years in internment at Ruhleben. After the Second World War he was to defy the veto of the Intelligence authorities by publishing an account of some of their secret activities based on sources in America over which Britain had no control. Although he had not been, as Feiling had, a Fellow of All Souls it was he, not Feiling, who suggested to Rowse and his exact contemporary Roger Makins, later Lord Sherfield, that they should stand and arranged special tuition for them. So far as can be seen his relationship with Rowse though never close was happy.

Such was not the case with Feiling, whose originality and distinction as a historian were of another order. As with his fiery Cornish pupil his subject engaged his passions as well as his intellect. His shyness and reserve, perhaps a certain well-bred coolness in personal relations, may have made for a lack of ease between them. Certainly in their later life they disliked each other. In the two John Aubrey-esque sketches of him that Rowse wrote in the 1960s he disparages him as a snob and social climber, unjustly in the opinion of the present writer who knew him quite well. Rowse noted, but strangely took little account of, his literary connexions. Feiling's mother was the sister of Anthony Hope the novelist and his first cousin was Kenneth Grahame, the author of *The Wind in the Willows*. Usually a close family link of this sort would stimulate Rowse's perception of the character in question. But in this case he draws no inference, apart from recording the gruesome circumstance of Feiling being called on to identify the body of Kenneth Grahame's only son who had committed suicide while an undergraduate at the House[1] only two years before Rowse himself came up.

Grudgingly, almost stealthily, he admits that as a historian Feiling was sensitive to character and imaginative in its depiction – usually a high recommendation in his eyes. He censures Namier,[2] whom he liked and admired, for his vindictiveness in blocking Feiling's election to the British Academy. *Odium academicum*, it is only too clear from these unpublished (and in his own time unpublishable) memoirs, took over where *odium theologicum* left off. The core of his judgment of his old tutor was that he was intellectually cowardly and in the phrase he ascribes to Lord David Cecil, also Feiling's pupil, 'lacked backbone'. But, as we shall see, there was to be a deeper reason for Rowse's resentment.

In his last term or two he had yet another history tutor, also like Feiling a Fellow of All Souls, the medievalist Ernest Jacob. Rowse fifty years later was to deliver in the Cathedral that is also the College Chapel of Christ Church a much admired and apparently affectionate *éloge*. His real view, stated at some length in his All Souls character sketches, was much less charitable. In the context of his time at Christ Church he still remembered with rage the hours he had spent at Jacob's insistence struggling through that historical slough of despond the fat volumes of T. F. Tout, only to find that in his Finals there were no questions that might have justified these efforts.

In the Oxford of that day dons often took an interest in junior members of their college whom they did not teach. For years to come R. H. Dundas, a Classics don with special responsibility for the Ancient History side of Greats, was to make a point of knowing every

1. The Oxford name for Christ Church.
2. Sir Lewis Namier (1888–1960), the formidable historian of Polish–Jewish extraction, who revolutionized the study of British politics in the late eighteenth century. A passionate Zionist and an expert on Eastern Europe, he is the subject of an affectionate sketch in Rowse's *Historians I Have Known* (1995).

undergraduate who came up to the House. Rowse and he never got on as is clear from an unusually candid correspondence between them of a much later date preserved in Rowse's papers. Yet in *A Cornishman at Oxford*, Rowse memorably recalls the tact and practical generosity Dundas shewed as Senior Censor, the don charged with day to day discipline and administration, when he needed money to support himself in the vacation and did not want to sponge on his parents. A. E. J. Rawlinson, then tutor in Divinity, and his warm-hearted wife Mildred both went out of their way to befriend this obviously talented young man. At the time Rowse was grateful. Later reflection however freed him from any feeling of obligation. It was, he came to believe, simply head-hunting on behalf of a creed that was losing its footing in its own intellectual citadel.

Of the other Christ Church dons who were not directly concerned with teaching him by far the most important, indeed in some ways a figure on whom he aspired to model himself, was Sir John Beazley, the great classical archaeologist. Rowse has described him in one of the most brilliant of his portrait sketches 'A Buried Love: Flecker and Beazley' printed in *Friends and Contemporaries* (1989). What gave him a special piquancy was that he had renounced a poetic gift of a power highly admired by the best judges to devote his talent and sensibility to create a new field of art history, that of Athenian vase-painting. For years Rowse was to feel himself torn between not two but three impulses: towards politics, towards literature and towards history. The last two he came to see were compatible: but the first, once given its head, would trample down the others. And Beazley had actually written, and subsequently destroyed, poems that had left their traces in the work of James Elroy Flecker. Flecker's early death had turned the current of Beazley's inspiration into original scholarship. Finally it was Beazley who had recognized and championed the quality of the St Austell Grammar School boy in the examination that had brought him to Christ Church.

All, or certainly most, of this must have been unknown to Rowse as an undergraduate. The kindness that Beazley and his wife, a formidable personality in her own right, showed to him then was continued by their hospitality to him throughout his Oxford career. Hospitality and kindness to the young were to lie at the heart of

Rowse's vision of Oxford: certainly as the present writer and many, many others could testify he practised it himself. No doubt it was easier in days of abundant and inexpensive domestic service: and with most of the dons living in college instead of driving in for the day's work it was a natural and agreeable part of the scheme of things. At any rate it was one of the ideas that shaped him and coloured his mind. The assertion of the independence and equality of the junior members of the University with their seniors, implicit in the substitution of 'student' for 'undergraduate', negates the avuncular relationship that the old ways had fostered.

What were the undergraduates like when Rowse came up and how easy did he find it to get on with them? 'Inter-war Oxford was overwhelmingly middle-class in its composition' writes Brian Harrison in the twentieth-century volume of *The History of the University of Oxford* which he edited.[1] As regards Christ Church he emphasizes its aristocratic quality, expressed in a snobbish *apartheid* of undergraduate accommodation: 'Tom, Canterbury and Peckwater quadrangles were respectable, but not the Meadow Buildings'. Naturally it was to Meadows that Rowse found himself consigned, but he seems not to have taken it as an aspersion on his humble origins but rather as a recognition of his status as a scholar, for whom there was a separate table in Hall. His delight at his new quarters, his spacious sitting room, the brightly burning coal fire, the noble view down the Broad Walk to the river, leaps off the page. And can Meadows really have been such a socially depressed area if Harold Acton was Rowse's neighbour on the next staircase? 'Almost every undergraduate generation has its bird of paradise, exerting a kind of fascinated ascendancy by its plumage, if not by real gifts ... But never can there have been *such* undergraduate *réclame*, such publicity, such a peculiar ascendancy as that exerted by Harold Acton in his day at Oxford. He was the recognized leader of the Aesthetes; everything that he did was news.'[2] The vivid sketch goes on for half a page. But it omits the most striking feature of so feline, so sophisticated a character, his unaffected and extraordinary good-nature.

1. Vol. viii, p. 94.
2. *A Cornishman at Oxford*, p. 23.

That Rowse must in fact have recognized this quality is suggested by a not wholly candid passage in *A Cornishman at Oxford*.[1] 'One night after seeing a big ramshackle American friend – who rather alarmed me by talking two and a half hours about sex and showing no disposition to go – off the premises, I called in on Harold on the way back. The poet was going to bed: he appeared at his bedroom door in a kimono of dark-grey silk. It seemed he had been spraying his face with Icilma or some such stuff. The fragrance that issued from the room was overpowering.' On reading the book Acton wrote a letter of pleasure and admiration, recollecting the occasion described in somewhat different terms. The unidentified American was Rowse's fellow-scholar, who features largely in the book and was later to appear prominently in the Alger Hiss case,[2] H. J. Wadleigh. He had made overt homosexual approaches that had thoroughly upset the young Rowse and Harold calmed him down. His generosity in writing as he did is the more notable as in a footnote on page 119 of the book Rowse delivers a gratuitous and resounding snub of the kind that he himself would never have forgiven. Such saintliness earned its reward. There is a justly admiring prose portrait of Acton in *Friends and Contemporaries* (1989) and a year later he received the dedication of a collection of Rowse's poems *Prompting the Age*.

The link – bond is too strong a word – between the two is that they were both poets. Acton's first collection of verse had been published while they were still undergraduates. Forty years later Rowse still recollected the thrill of envy and excitement on seeing it in Blackwell's window, remarking that the poems in it were no better than those he himself was writing at the time. It was the writing of poetry that brought him into contact with the clever and well-read public school boys, Acton, Peter Quennell, Richard Pares, whom he would otherwise have been too shy, too awkward, too poor, to get to know. They were full of schemes for forming clubs, issuing journals, publishing books in which their voices could make themselves heard.

1. ibid., p. 69.
2. The case, brilliantly described in Alastair Cooke's *A Generation on Trial*, turned on whether Hiss, a high official of the State Department, was a Soviet agent. Like the Dreyfus case it was widely seen as a confrontation between the forces of progress and of reaction, notably those unleashed by Senator McCarthy.

On all this, *A Cornishman at Oxford*, based as it is on the very full journals that Rowse managed to keep, needs no amplifying from a biographer.

What is already apparent is what one of his later friends was to describe as 'your intellectual energy, amounting to genius'.[1] Rowse was no recluse. He took the liveliest advantage of the long, uninterrupted evenings of intimate argument and discussion that the provision of one's own room invites. He wrote poems. He wrote long and affectionate letters to his parents. He was diligent in lecture-going and writing essays for his tutorials. And he was, almost from the start, a leading light in the University Labour Club.

The *History of the University of Oxford* already referred to acknowledges his impact.[2] Its reciprocal effect on him was no less rewarding. Suddenly, unexpectedly, he was meeting and talking to leading figures in the life of his time: Ramsay MacDonald, soon to be Prime Minister, E. D. Morel, H. W. Nevinson, publicists of real fire, Bertrand Russell, whom Rowse in his capacity as Secretary entertained to dinner at The Good Luck Tea Rooms.[3]

Bliss was it in that Dawn to be alive. But there were difficulties. The public school complexion of the University, the aristocratic aura of Christ Church, have been mentioned. Did they not cloud the enjoyment of this vivacious, outgoing, eager young man? The drunken antics of the rich and smart in which his contemporary Evelyn Waugh found so deep a spiritual consolation seem not to have impinged on him. What did was their less picturesque imitation by his fellow scholars on his own staircase who showed their oafish, intolerant disapproval and hostility, getting drunk and banging on his oak while he trembled inside not less, he tells us, from anger than from fear. This one can easily believe: courage in the face of bullies and brutes was never wanting to so passionate a nature. But this proved a diminishing nuisance. Christ Church was large-minded but it was not slack. Scholarships could be taken away and wasters sent down.

1. Richard Church in a letter written in 1946 or 1947.
2. op. cit., p. 398.
3. In *A Cornishman at Oxford* (1965) Rowse prints a mark of exclamation in parentheses after this detail.

Some of his fellow scholars, naturally enough, shared Rowse's aesthetic and intellectual zest. David Low, who was to remain a lifelong friend, became a distinguished rare book seller. Wadleigh, the half-American neighbour who took up so many evenings of their first year pouring out his opinions on Christianity and sex, faded as Rowse became more and more determined to reject the first and to shy away from the other. Wadleigh indeed was not the only offender. The one complaint constantly repeated about the otherwise enchanted world of Oxford was that there was far too much talk about sex. Rowse's subsequent obsession with the subject, lasting, even increasing, far into his eighties, suggests a theme for a Max Beerbohm cartoon of a dialogue between the Young Self and the Old Self.

The fellow scholar for whom Rowse felt the tenderest and most abiding affection, though he seems to have seen nothing of him in later life, was a Geordie mathematician called Tom Lawrenson. Hardly sketched though often mentioned in *A Cornishman at Oxford* he comes to mind again in the Journals whenever their author is in an elegiac mood of recollection. All that we know of him is that he was gentle, intelligent, pious and lovable. Both enjoyed long walks into the country to look at churches. Both liked doing their work companionably in each other's rooms: 'Tom Lawrenson and I enjoyed perfect domesticity.' On the same page Rowse writes: 'The real process of an undergraduate education at Oxford is that achieved by the undergraduates themselves, a process of dialectic . . . The arguments that went on till midnight and after were not loss of time: they formed our minds for us, they hammered out a position, or the foundations of a position, that would serve us through life.' After Oxford their ways parted. Lawrenson, always deeply religious, was ultimately received into the Roman Catholic Church. It is hardly too much to say that Rowse venerated his memory and was moved by the news of his death.

The last of Rowse's undergraduate friendships, formed only in his second year, was to have perhaps the greatest influence on his life and work. This was with Lord David Cecil, also a scholar of the House though two years senior and living out of college in the elegance of Beaumont Street. He suddenly appeared in Rowse's rooms, apparently as a result of J. C. Masterman suggesting that he would find their occupant worth talking to on the subject of literature. The torrential, elliptical, amusing flow of his visitor overcame any surprise or embarrassment that he may have felt. Like everyone else who had the pleasure of David Cecil's conversation, Sir Kingsley Amis only excepted, Rowse was soon captivated. As important as the exchange of ideas was the opening of yet another hitherto unknown world, that of the great houses and the great families. Hatfield and the Cecils, what could have been a more vivifying introduction for the future historian of the Elizabethan age, particularly for one whose perception of the past was intensely visual, artistic, personal? Neither knew anything about that at the time, just as neither of them knew that they were going to spend the great part of their lives in close propinquity as Oxford dons. But biography is born of hindsight.

Glimpses of the undergraduate Rowse through other eyes are uncommon. Nevill Coghill, an English literature don of rare distinction, wrote, nearly half a century later on the death of their common friend John Garrett, the brilliant headmaster of Raynes Park and then Bristol Grammar School,

'You may not remember, but it was in his rooms that I first met the sable-haired, flashing-eyed young Cornishman that even then was astonishing and disturbing Oxford! A happy moment for me it was.'[1]

This poetic vision seems truer to the real nature of the subject than the rather stolid well-built young man of contemporary photographs. Yet the stolidity was not altogether misleading. Rowse was determined to get a First in history: he had neither the money nor the tastes to distract him into the self-indulgence and conviviality of which he remained all his life a contemptuous censor. His pleasures, country walks and visits to churches, tea and talk in his rooms, political argument in the Labour Club, excursions into new literary territory with fellow poets in the making, could all contribute, if obliquely, to the equipment of a historian. The intellectual stolidity to persevere through the weary land of reading required for a First was there all right. Rowse never desired the palm without the dust: indeed he reserved a particular bitterness for those Etonians and Wykehamists

1. 10 January 1967.

who seemed to expect and, maddeningly, to receive it. 'I have always been a plodder' is the constant refrain of his private journals. For all the wit, the speed, the sheer fun of his mind there is a great deal of truth in it.

5

Success

Rowse's enjoyment of life, his appetite for it, his Pepysian power of recreating it in his well-lit theatre of memory, obscures the wretched condition of body with which he had to contend from young manhood to the threshold of middle age. His extraordinary energy, his effervescence of spirits were not, as one might imagine, the natural expression of physical well-being at a time of life that takes rude health for granted. Rather they were the fierce defiance, the impatient rejection, of yet another obstacle rolled into his path by a malign fortune. The duodenal ulcers which were not to be diagnosed and dealt with until, in his middle thirties, they had all but done for him troubled him from his undergraduate years. Pain and nausea, with consequent sleeplessness and depression, were always lying in wait. Ignorance of their cause gnawed and worried, inducing a sense of foreboding. Like the young Churchill who was convinced by the early death of his father that his own life expectancy was short, Rowse felt that what he had to do – and what an infinity glittered before him! – must be crammed into a brief space. No time must be wasted, no experience forgotten or left unexamined. The intensity of his nature was fortified, not weakened, by ill health.

People who have had to struggle for life against disease or wounds have, naturally enough, an aversion from the subject. Like fear or poverty the experience, if deep and of long duration, enters the soul: and the soul, if it seeks expression, finds prayer or poetry its proper medium. After boyhood Rowse had no belief in prayer but poetry was his true vocation. As an old man, contemplating death, he sent Raleigh Trevelyan a copy of his collected poems *A*

Life, amended and corrected for posthumous publication when his voice might be better heard. In the covering letter he first points to its value as contemporary evidence. 'I see as a historian what a true portrait of our appalling age – and even its events, the War and all – it is.' The sense of tragedy, of impending tragedy, is everywhere present. And this is complemented by his own awareness, in spite of driving himself to the utmost, of his own feebleness, his impotence. In the summer of 1944 'you were only a boy whose life might be sacrificed at any moment. I was useless . . . ! I was rejected from everything, even fire-watching at Oxford, gave me a dangerous duodenal haemorrhage . . . An appalling record – my one great triumph to have survived . . .

'So, reading through the poems as a whole makes an extraordinary impression. Not many poems describe physical pain, the processes of fear etc.'[1]

Serious, frightening illness silences babble. Overheard conversation in public places is, we all know, too often a recitation of symptoms unpleasant obviously but hardly life-threatening. It is a threat that has given some writers a sharpening of perception, a more intense awareness of the world around them. Among diarists Pepys and Kilvert come immediately to mind: among poets Keats.

That Rowse was another seems clear. The point has been laboured here because it is so easy to lose sight of it behind the ardour and high spirits, the passions, the enthusiasms, the rages, above all the seemingly limitless energy that he displayed throughout a long life.

We catch sight of it in his diary entries, begun in the period between the twin peaks of his happiness, the news that he had obtained one of the best Firsts[2] of his year in the Modern History School and his election four months later to a Prize Fellowship at All Souls. On the last day of October 1925 he opened a new volume of his diary: '. . . During the last few days, when I have been freed of both All Souls and illness, I have felt a real need to continue this diary – and I have said to myself "I must get a new book tomorrow." This evening,

---

1. Letter to Raleigh Trevelyan, 11 September 1991.
2. But see below p. 75.

now that I have the book and time to fill the gap, I am too tired to do it.'[1]

Those early years at All Souls are full of entries recording days lost through illness – and whatever else Rowse could or could not have been, a hypochondriac or a *malade imaginaire* was the last possibility. The symptoms of stomach ulcers are vile – vomiting, intense pain, exhaustion both mental and physical. The reader will gladly excuse their repetition but should bear them in mind. What is far more interesting and infinitely more attractive is the prospect that All Souls offered to a young man of talent, perhaps of genius, in the middle 1920s.

Rohan Butler, one of Rowse's steadiest friends who was elected some ten years later, recalls his scout welcoming him on his first afternoon: 'In this College, sir, if there's anything you want you have only to ask for it, however absurd.' The point of a Prize Fellowship was to throw the reins on the neck of the horse. He could make what he would of it. He could equip himself as a scholar, he could read for the Bar, he could enter the Diplomatic Service or train for Holy Orders, he could embark on a career in journalism or in publishing, in administration or in politics. Although several of the senior Fellows in 1925 held important positions in the city they had generally arrived there by virtue of having distinguished themselves in some other capacity – for example as having been members of that circle of able young men whom Milner had recruited to his staff in South Africa. To have won a Prize Fellowship and to have gone straight into merchant banking, as the high-flyers from the ancient universities were to do sixty or seventy years later, would then perhaps not have been thought a proper use of the highest distinction Oxford could confer.

Nonetheless the world was all before them. Better off than Adam

---

1. Rowse re-read his diaries several times in later years, notably when he used them as sources for his volumes of autobiography, but also when he had finally retired to Trenarren and was reading at large. On these occasions he often comments, amends and abbreviates, sometimes dating these scholia, which are easily identifiable by difference of handwriting and by the use of biro instead of the original pen. I have not felt bound to follow the earliest text, though I generally do. Where a variation seems significant, I draw attention to it.

and Eve, they had not been evicted from Paradise but emancipated from the constraints of prescribed reading and the tyranny of examinations. In Rowse's case he had, at a stroke, been set free from poverty. He could, within reason, buy what books tempted him in Blackwell's. He could even begin to think about buying pictures. Comfortable accommodation and excellent meals were provided without having to think about, let alone prepare or pay for them. A more complete antithesis to his experience of early life could hardly be imagined.

Now that he was as free as nature first made man what use was he going to make of his freedom? 'My head has been bothered lately by some of the old doubts as to whether this awful concentration on academic work which has been going on unrelieved for the last two years (and with especial emphasis for the last eight months) will not end in the atrophy of what is imaginative in me. So few have been the poetical ideas and images that I have had time for; and so much thought has been devoted to pure theory, on history and economics and art. I am reading Trotsky's *Literature and Revolution* for the moment, and with the ardour of a disciple . . .' Poetry was pushing its way up through his consciousness. It seems strange that with all his heroic work for the Labour Club politics, which had never like poetry been sacrificed to the intellectual extortion of final examinations, should not have been distinguished as a principal concern. Perhaps it had been subsumed under history: 'The materialist conception of history haunts me day in and day out, it is like an obsession. I can think of nothing but my historical theories come in and colour whatever I am thinking about.'

Of course his mind was in fact often disturbed by ideas that could take little of such colour, for example Love and Death, ideas only as yet, since he had no direct experience of either and even wondered whether he ever would of the first. His diary records briefly talking on these subjects to David Cecil 'the first time I have ever gone as far beneath the surface'. Re-reading and amending the passage in June 1994 he glosses it: 'O sancta simplicitas! How young we were – finding our feet.'

Intellectually he soon plotted his course. 'Next term I shall arrive at a way of life, which will achieve more in the way of work, while using the social amenities of the college to give savour (and no more) to the existence which I shall live to myself. I am going to read Marx's *Capital* during the vac . . . I intend to make myself a proficient Marxist, and a proficient historian. For the next five years I shall devote myself to laying in a stock of knowledge which will serve me for life. I am going to learn German and Italian: next long vac I shall therefore spend in Germany; it seems a grand prospect at present, but I have an eye open to the dangers of dawdling my life away in the comfortable society of dons, and their families. What a pleasant place this is!' Surely if the Old Rowse was to compassionate the simplicity of the Young One, this was the point to choose. He did in fact strike out 'and their families', an automatic reaction after years of self-congratulation on escaping the spread net of matrimony and domesticity. But 'the comfortable society of dons' records the illusion of youth. Fulminations against third-rate academics, their meanness, spitefulness, timidity – the seasoned reader of Rowse's published and unpublished opinions will be only too familiar with his mature judgment on the topic.

What, in fact, was All Souls like in 1925 and what did Rowse make of it? The late Lord Sherfield who, as Roger Makins, was Rowse's exact contemporary at Christ Church and was elected to an All Souls Fellowship on the same day, gave me an account[1] that tallies with Rowse's own. There were then very few Fellows in residence. The place filled up at week-ends with the grandees that gave it its public character. Makins himself made no use of its scholarly facilities, treating it in his own unserious expression as a hunting-box, dropping in for an occasional night during the week. There he would find two old boys, Major-General Sir Ernest Swinton, inventor of the tank and at that time Professor of Military History, and Sir Henry Sharp, an ex-Indian Civilian who had been commissioned to redraft the statutes of the University and made a member of Common Room, engaged in an unending but perfectly amicable argument with the young Rowse about the responsibility for the outbreak of war in 1914. Rowse, as an ardent Left Winger unspotted from the world, contended for an equal distribution of blame between the powers. 'Of course, Leslie made rings round them.' Not less remarkable than his stance, his

1. Interview, 9 February 1995.

later acquaintance may think, was the good temper, the intellectual courtesy, with which he conducted his side of the debate. No question he learned it from the much older, much more distinguished men, who treated him as their equal. Even these two old buffers, neither of whom owed their presence in the college to a Prize Fellowship, had made their mark in the world. And the Cabinet Ministers and Bishops, the Judges, Ambassadors and the rest who descended at week-ends were not less open and friendly. Narrowness, myopic specialism, which in our day have almost become the prized characteristics of scholarship were alien to the atmosphere of a university that was, if only gradually, accepting the idea of the country's imperial responsi-bilities and was, with its usual doggedness, still deeply attached to nineteenth- and even eighteenth-century conceptions of what a place of learning should be.

Both these tendencies, the old and the new, were represented by the two other Fellows who generally made up the company during the week. Edgeworth, born in 1845, belonged to a generation where the use of a Christian name was, in the professional and upper classes, confined to a minute circle of intimates. Rowse describes him with amused affection in *A Cornishman at Oxford*, pointing out that he distilled an aura of the eighteenth as much as the nineteenth century, since his father was the half-brother of the novelist Maria Edgeworth who had herself been born in 1767. What is clearer from the diary entries is the veneration felt by the young man for the utterances of this sage. From the instances Rowse records the decorous formality of language seems more conspicuous than the insight or originality. Yet original and distinguished Edgeworth must have been in a high degree as a pioneer of applying mathematics to the infant study of economics and what were then called the moral sciences. Death claimed him a year after Rowse's election.

The imperial interest so strongly represented in the All Souls of the nineteen twenties found its most attractive and influential exponent in Lionel Curtis, a man never spoken of except with Christian and surname inextricably joined. He occupies a unique position in Rowse's perspective of the college since he was there when Rowse arrived and was an important feature of the scene until the great romantic attachment to the college had dissolved into bitterness and reproach.

Through it all he seems to have impressed some of his own stead-fastness, his own complete rejection of self-interest and personal ambition, on the perception of his tumultuous, touchy, excitable young friend.

In old age Rowse wrote, and rewrote, a number of portrait sketches of those who had been Fellows in his time. His conscious model was John Aubrey but the choice was not truly congenial. Aubrey's extraordinary, inimitable, effects arise not only from subtle artistry but from his approachableness, his total freedom from dogmatism of any kind. He has not made up his mind on any question and, so far as one can see, has no intention of doing so and neither prides himself nor cries *mea culpa* because of it. No wonder the bigots of his day, like Anthony Wood, called him a maggoty-headed fellow.

Such an aspersion could never be cast on Rowse. The people of whom he writes are weighed and measured against the scale of his own opinions which he believed to be founded on rigorous intellectual analysis. In this he bears a closer resemblance to his Oxford prede-cessors Anthony Wood or Thomas Hearne. His account of Lionel Curtis is thus the more interesting because of an uncharacteristic reticence of judgment, an apparent readiness to admit that what he in principle despised might after all have something to be said for it. To begin with Lionel Curtis had not cleared the first fence in the Rowse handicap. He had certainly not been placed in the First Class in Schools. Rowse even believed – perhaps he found it too painful to verify – that he had got a Third, perhaps even two of them. His horrified surmise was in fact correct.

In this case Rowse's capacity for affection, a faculty sometimes in later life angrily disclaimed, provided him with insights for which he could find no satisfactory intellectual explanation. Curtis was a gran-dee without being grand. He had never been a Cabinet Minister or an Ambassador, not even a Professor or an MP, but his achievements were extraordinary. He had been Milner's right-hand man in South Africa, he had assisted Lloyd George in the successful negotiations that ended the civil war in Ireland, he was the founder of Chatham House, the Oxford Society and the Oxford Preservation Trust. And with all this he retained the humility and friendliness of a well brought-up young man. That he had a sense of humour is suggested by the ascription to him of the following limerick, surely inspired by the subject of this biography:

> There was a young man of Redruth
> Who set out on a search for the Truth,
> Which his elders, who knew
> That nothing was true,
> Remarked as a symptom of youth.[1]

The delicacy with which Rowse was made welcome in All Souls should not obscure the fact that the election of a working-class man of known Left Wing opinions was without precedent. Lord Sherfield who described himself to me as an establishment figure from his prep school days attributed his own simultaneous election to a desire to reinsure against this leap in the dark. For all that the college justly prided itself on its intellectual eminence, it was still, as we shall see, deeply conventional and conservative in tone. Had the brilliant young men killed in the war, such as Raymond Asquith and Patrick Shaw-Stewart, survived it might have been more sceptical, more worldly-wise. Rowse tells us that as a young Fellow he made quite a cult of them, studying their photographs in the Coffee Room and keeping them in memory. Perhaps their absence widened the gap in age and mentality, a gap that may have made it even harder for him to assimilate to social habits and codes very different from those to which he had been brought up. Christ Church had done a great deal to initiate him into these conventions; but even there he was excluded from convivialities and entertainments that required the wearing of a dinner-jacket. At All Souls they were worn every night for dinner in hall. Formality in such externals was in fact congenial to him. Anyhow he was quick to learn. Staying with David Cecil at Hatfield or with Roger Makins' parents in London helped.

If Oxford presented no difficulties that were not easily overcome, in Cornwall the shock of this social transition went deeper. More and more Rowse found the life style of his origins jarring. He could not

1. Quoted in the anonymously published *The Feet of the Young Men* (1928), p. 171. Its author may have been Lady Craik, sister of the 1st Lord Chandos.

invite the new friends he made to stay. There would have been nothing but embarrassment and humiliation. Increasingly indeed he came to feel these himself. The news of his success had created a stir. His parents were interviewed by a local journalist, the County authorities congratulated themselves. In *A Cornishman at Oxford*[1] Rowse recalls an unpleasant consequence, a venomous letter to his mother from a neighbour who had emigrated to Montana. 'It was more than the woman could bear, transported with jealousy . . . I read the letter to my mother, then tore it up and burnt it, so that no evidence of it should remain; but it added renewed strain and dubiety to my own make-up, increased the sense of insecurity, provided another trauma and was followed by another attack of ulcer.' Why? What was so special about this nastiness and why did it leave so deep a wound? It is clear from the diary that it was written by the wife of Fred May, with whom Rowse's mother had had a long and passionate affair, of which Rowse long believed himself to be the issue. In all probability this letter was the source of that disturbing suspicion. In any case it certainly intensified it.

1. p. 259.

6

1926

The year 1926 might have been expected to offer a period of tranquillity after the exhaustion and strain of two of the severest sets of competitive examination devised by the English system of higher education. In spite of the soothing friendliness of All Souls, where Rowse was repeatedly advised to take life easily and to look about before embarking on any serious work, advice which in his diary he too enjoined on himself, he found himself plunged into affairs which disturbed him and perhaps pre-empted the questions and decisions he had meant to take his time over.

He had been deeply upset by the sudden and brutal doubt cast on his paternity. Coming on top of the shock, delivered a year earlier, of finding out that he had an illegitimate half-sister, the suspicion was the more corrosive. If he was to set about constructing a career the last thing he wanted was to be unsettled about where he was starting from. He was anyhow, as his kindly seniors had noticed, exhausted by the long haul that had been crowned with success.

That it was success, that he was now a name beginning to be known outside his own circle, was brought home to him with gratifying rapidity. Before the end of January he had been invited by C. K. Ogden, later to win fame as the inventor of Basic English but then known as an editor of outstanding originality, to contribute a pamphlet on a subject of his own choice to a series charting the new intellectual horizons of the post-war world. Rowse was both flattered and, for once, diffident. Could he, in his present state of health both physical and nervous, do himself justice? The choice of subject presented no problem: it would be the ubiquitous, all-invading idea of historical materialism – the master key to the problems of humanity that Marx had fashioned. The invitation chimed so well with the course of reading Rowse had been sketching that he decided to accept. To get to grips with Marx meant reading him in German, even, perhaps, producing a translation of *Das Kapital* that would do for the twentieth century what Jowett's *Plato* had done for the nineteenth. This meant that Italy would have to give place to Germany as the first European country he would have to live in so as to master the language. Meanwhile his first expedition abroad to be undertaken in the Easter Vacation would be to Paris, partly to improve his French, partly to see what everyone with the faintest interest in European art and history must wish to see.

The income from a Prize Fellowship, £300 in Rowse's day, was not intended to finance travel and living abroad. Taking pupils from other colleges provided a useful supplement. One of the first to send pupils to him was A. B. Emden, the Principal of St Edmund Hall, who was later to give Rowse one of his greatest coups as a sixteenth-century historian, the discovery among the Chapter Archives at Canterbury of the hitherto unknown diary of Sir Walter Ralegh's brother-in-law. Emden, in the course of his researches for his Medieval Register of the University of Oxford, a work which he once described to me as a medieval *Crockford's Clerical Directory*, came across this extraordinarily interesting document and at once thought of the historian to whom he had sent his men thirty-five years earlier.

Rowse was a conscientious as well as a lively teacher. He got on well with run of the mill pupils, which is the true test. At the end of his first term he entertained them to lunch, an early manifestation of his natural kindness and hospitality. Settling down to life in college he even felt enough at home to be irritated. Young men who know themselves to be clever, and whose cleverness has been duly certificated and stamped by the competent authorities, are not likely to be patient listeners to the clichés of conventional wisdom. Among the duties of the Junior Fellow were the harmless superintendence of the dressing of the salad for dinner on Sunday nights and the more onerous nightly obligation of attending to the supply of port and claret at dessert until his seniors had had their fill. Enjoyment of good wine might palliate this obligation but Rowse was a passionate, contemptuous teetotaller. To have to listen to old General Swinton and Sir Henry Sharp droning on about how the world was going to the dogs was trying enough but what exasperated Rowse, and, it would seem, other members of his generation was the overbearing, dogmatic style of E. L. Woodward who had himself been elected as a Prize Fellow.[1] 'To have to sit in a state of repression and propriety after the glorious rudeness of my life at home and in the world in general,' he exploded in his diary.

Woodward soon became the focus of resentment among his more gifted juniors. Rowse's dislike, indeed contempt, for him did not soften with age. In the character of him which he drew half a century later he singles out his meanness, 'his pleasure at someone's downfall (his prominent yellow teeth grinning over loose wet lips)' as his leading characteristic and remarks on his pluralism of college offices that carried an additional salary and his endless examining, that first resource of the hard-pressed academic, a category to which Woodward did not belong. Earlier in life he had had thoughts of the priesthood and had briefly attended Pusey House, the academic centre of the High Churchmen. From this came his All Souls nickname, coined by two of Rowse's closest historical colleagues G. N. Clark and Richard Pares, 'the Abbé'. Was it Pares who composed the verses, pencilled on the outside of an envelope in which Rowse collected some of Woodward's letters?

> Plato was a Levantine
>   in the abbé's eyes
> So were Aristotle
>   Socrates likewise
> Sophocles or Sappho
>   The abbé would despise
>
> Xenophon and Homer
>   would barely recognize
> That they were not approved of
>   Among the really wise
> And they would hear that they were dagos
>   with extreme surprise.

1. In 1919, in preference to Aldous Huxley and other distinguished candidates.

The tone of mind, of personality, here depicted confirms Rowse's vivid account of a later evening at All Souls when he and Woodward were the only other Fellows dining besides Lionel Curtis, who had brought as a guest the owner of Wytham Woods, who in a fit of excessive Englishry had changed his name from Schumacher to ffennell. It soon became obvious that Curtis's object was to induce ffennell to bequeath to the University this beautiful stretch of untouched woodland only a mile west of Oxford. Woodward, perceiving this, went out of his way to talk sneeringly of benefactors to academic institutions who hoped to obtain in return honorary degrees or other marks of distinction. Curtis, Rowse noted with admiration, showed no sign of anger or disgust. Best of all, he in the end succeeded. Thanks to him Wytham now belongs to the University.

Making use of his position as Domestic Bursar, Woodward enjoyed chivvying the newly elected Fellows. Richard Pares, who had been elected the year before Rowse, became as Sir Isaiah Berlin made plain in his obituary of him, very much the leader of the Young Turks. Since he rapidly established himself as Rowse's closest friend and chief influence, coming later to share but not to relinquish the first character with two or three others, he must be introduced.

The best account of this brilliant, too short, life is that given by Rowse in his *éloge* in the *Proceedings of the British Academy*.[1] Pares started with every advantage that Rowse lacked. His father, Sir Bernard, was not only the leading scholar in his field, that of Russian studies, but a public personality whose lectures captivated his audience. The house was full of books. Learning was looked on as the chief business of life. In college at Winchester, a Brackenbury scholar of Balliol, he was taught and encouraged by men of great intellectual distinction. No prig, still more no Puritan, he threw himself into the pleasures of undergraduate life, consorting with the witty and talented and dissipated such as Cyril Connolly, Graham Greene and Peter Quennell. His love affair with Evelyn Waugh was no light flirtation.[2]

1. Vol. xlviii.
2. In an undated letter (*c.* 1963–4) Cyril Connolly, meditating a book of Oxford reminiscence, recalls Waugh's fury when he himself became the friend, perhaps the lover, of Pares at Balliol in 1923: 'E. W. was very jealous and never forgave me, he said, though I don't think I even knew E. W. at the time and he was not in the Sligger

He was a prominent speaker at the Union and a conspicuous member of the Labour Club where he first met Rowse. In his last year before schools he threw all this up, buckled down to his books, winning a First and an All Souls Fellowship.

In spite of, perhaps because of, his own sparkling gifts and his father's reputation he at first turned his back on what seemed an obvious invitation to an academic career. He opted for journalism and, declining an approach from Geoffrey Dawson, editor of *The Times* and a stalwart of All Souls, went off to join the *Liverpool Daily Post*. But it didn't answer and he returned to Oxford and All Souls. There his friendship with Rowse quickly ripened. The coincidence of their political opinions forged a strong link, beside their both being young, amusing, irreverent and, beneath apparent sharpness, of an affectionate disposition. Politics rather than history preoccupied Rowse in his first years at All Souls. The arguments that he was turning over in his mind for the pamphlet on historical materialism[1] might have led either way. But the current of events suddenly gained strength. Out of the blue came the General Strike in May.

He did not underestimate the determination of the Government or the problems of administration and technical control that would face his own side. Failure might do incalculable damage. 'Anything rather than a passive fight, digging our toes in while the spirit of the miners is worn away by a lower standard of living during the strike . . . I couldn't stand the talk in the common-room. There was Woodward – vulgar small bourgeois that he is, apeing the contemptuous attitude of the man of affairs, hoping that the General Strike just wouldn't come off through dry-rot in the trade unions. I went to see Ayerst to get him to move the Labour Club and keep me informed of what the Committee will do in raising money etc.: then I went down to [G.D.H.] Cole's house in Holywell but hadn't the brazenness to persist in ringing at nearly 11 p.m.

'Now I'd better write to my people and send them some money.'[2]

---

set (see below p. 91) like Richard and myself . . . Now we are both sixty and as Picasso said "At sixty we are young for the first time . . . and it is too late".'
1. Published as a neat little 16mo. in 1927, entitled *On History*.
2. Diary, Saturday 1 May. The strike was called for Monday.

Two characters of some importance in Rowse's life appear in this entry, David Ayerst and G. D. H. Cole. Cole was to be for many years Rowse's colleague and friend at All Souls. Fifteen years older than Rowse he had long been prominent as a theoretician of Socialism. He had only recently returned to Oxford as an Economics don. In 1944 he was elected to the Chair of Political and Social Theory at All Souls. Although their views of history and politics were later to diverge they always remained on excellent terms.

Such was far from being the case with David Ayerst, who appears in *A Cornishman at Oxford* under the *nom de guerre* of Otis.[1] He had been one of Rowse's intimate undergraduate circle at Christ Church, a keen member of the Labour Club, well-read, disputatious and ready to question accepted opinions. Even, it appears, those accepted by Rowse, to judge by the following passage, which cites the diary within quotation marks.

Young Otis I was carefully coaching along, for he was a promising historian, and I hoped he would win a Fellowship at All Souls. 'What is the matter with Otis? . . . He behaves in an extraordinary carping manner whenever a third person is present. When I get him alone he hardly dares to differ in matters of opinion; when there are others about he jumps at the chance to criticize. What is the explanation?' Nevertheless I did my best to get him elected next year at All Souls. When my early book *Politics and the Younger Generation* came out, he wrote a malicious review of it in the paper on which he was then a journalist. I thereupon dropped his acquaintance.

Two clouds no bigger than a man's hand appear at this point. We are given the first inkling of Rowse's ready resort to anathema. The denunciation of old and valued friends who found themselves unable to accept his explanation of Shakespeare's Sonnets or his identification of the Dark Lady are foreshadowed. And the re-writing of his own original material, painting out, touching up, is seen to be not only acceptable but a cause for self-approbation. Ayerst was indeed a promising historian: many years later he fulfilled it by writing a history of the *Manchester Guardian* as lively as it is scholarly.

1. op. cit., p. 280.

Rowse in his diary records that Ayerst's chances at All Souls – and he clearly was very much in the running – were fatally prejudiced by his active support of the General Strike. Rowse had himself urged Ayerst's election but was defeated by the forces of Old Bufferdom, as he was to be over his championship of Graham Wallas, the author of *Human Nature in Politics* and the most original political thinker of his time, for the chair of Political Theory. Sir Charles Grant Robertson and others could not contemplate the appointment of a man who could not accept revealed religion. But the real triumph of this tendency was the refusal of a Research Fellowship to T. S. Eliot, sponsored by his publisher Geoffrey Faber and supported by Rowse. In *All Souls in My Time* Rowse, half humorously, accepts partial responsibility for this fiasco:

As a Junior Fellow, known to write poetry and an admirer of Eliot, I was the only person to possess his Poems, and was asked to lend them around. Ingenuous as ever, it never occurred to me that others might hold them against him. However, when a couple of Scottish Presbyterian professors, MacGregor and Adams, encountered the amenities of 'Lune de Miel':

> A l'aise entre deux draps, chez deux centaines de punaises,
> La sueur aestivale, et une forte odeur de chienne . . .
> (What Eliot elsewhere calls 'the good old female stench'),

those sons of the manse were shocked and voted him down.'[1]

Elsewhere in his journals Rowse recalls that it was the word 'camisoles' that put the poet outside the pale. Perhaps it came up in discussion. But the diary entry written at the time, while mentioning MacGregor and Adams, places the prime responsibility elsewhere:

Colleges sometimes make mistakes. Here at All Souls at our last meeting we turned down T. S. Eliot for a Research Fellowship . . . The two bishops[2] only anxious to get their motion for a theological Fellow, and Headlam[3]

1. op. cit., p. 22.
2. Lang, an archbishop.
3. Bishop of Gloucester 1929–45. Rowse was always fond of him and at one time shared a set of rooms with him at All Souls.

obviously consumed with impatience, and gnawing not only his knuckles but his whole hand. Several sensible speeches from Grant Robertson, Malcolm and Brand.[1] And then a thunderbolt from the blue just when one might have thought Eliot had a chance in spite of his poetry. Doddering old Sir Charles Lucas[2] got up and said he'd never heard of Eliot before his name was brought before the college; that he'd read two poems the night before, and he thought them indecent, obscene and blasphemous; and why such a man should be regarded with approval, or rather singled out for high honour he didn't know, and he hoped he had not lived to see the college make such an election. This obviously shook the Archbishop. The fat was in the fire over this. There got up in a row those three high-minded and narrow-minded Scots, Lucas, Adams and Macgregor . . . After that, there could be no doubt. But on those grounds there is no literary man of any distinction who could achieve a two-thirds majority of the college.

The rose-tints of recollection soften the realities of All Souls in its grand days such as the young Rowse here experienced. Eliot was a candidate not for a chair of Poetry but for research into English literature of the late sixteenth and early seventeenth centuries. Yet the debate was such as might have taken place in any town hall of the time if the proposal had been to make him a Freeman of the Borough. Even the young Rowse's own views do not satisfy his mature inspection: for 'rather offensive poems' his later hand has substituted 'questionable'.

Another election whose impact Rowse initially over-dramatized (and for years could not quite summon up the sense to reduce to its proper proportion) was that to a history lectureship at his old college, Christ Church. Feiling and Masterman, his own tutors, had persuaded the college that the teaching load justified the appointment of another who would also in due course be elected to a Studentship (what in other colleges was known as a Fellowship). Early in 1926 Feiling asked Rowse if he would care to stand as a candidate, and Rowse, grateful

1. The two last, Sir Dougal Malcolm and Lord Brand, both Milner's Young Men and subsequently eminent in the City. Sir Charles Grant Robertson, academic historian, ultimately Grand Old Man of the College whom everyone loved and no one could listen to.
2. Civil servant and historian of the British Empire, born in 1853.

for all that Christ Church had done for him, accepted his invitation. His feeling that his election was pretty well assured was strengthened by Christ Church, which prided itself on teaching its own men within its own walls, sending him some of its history pupils. Hardly had the excitement over the General Strike subsided before Rowse was called to Christ Church to be interviewed for the post. A few days later he was informed that it would not be offered to him.

Humiliated, as he thought, by the institution to which he had given unquestioning loving loyalty, he surrendered to rage. He took his name off the books, refused all invitations to the college, even of a private nature, avoided as far as he could setting foot within its precincts.[1] It was the first of the Great Rejections by which he traced the course of his career, a theme about which he was ready to work himself up throughout the rest of his life. That it was at least in part pure theatre, that he enjoyed withdrawing into a corner of the auditorium to watch himself posturing on the stage, there can be no doubt. But in each instance there was a real hurt, a real sense of having been betrayed by those whom he had looked on as friends and supporters. Real, that is, to him. In fact, in this case, there were perfectly simple and in no way discreditable reasons for preferring another candidate who had not been known to be in the field when Feiling first sounded out Rowse as to whether he would be likely to take the job if he were offered it. Nearly fifty years later, J. C. Masterman, by then a past Provost of Worcester College and ex Vice-Chancellor of the university, and thinking of writing his own memoirs, took up *A Cornishman at Oxford* to refresh his memory. The account there given of the election to the History tutorship prompted him to write a long, calm circumstantial letter. The College had indeed first thought of Rowse: but quite unexpectedly an older, no less distinguished candidate had presented himself in the person of J. N. L. Myres, subsequently Bodley's Librarian and a scholar of unrivalled authority in the field of Anglo-Saxon studies. Myres was an academic through and through. A college teaching job with opportunities for research was what he wanted and was superbly qualified for. It was a perfect fit – and turned out a complete success. Whereas

1. But see below, p. 297.

Rowse was a man of many and powerful aspirations that would be likely to take him out of the purely academic world. He was passionately political. He was passionately literary. He might easily become a politician or a professional writer. Christ Church was right and Rowse was wrong.

From time to time in his journals he admits as much. He thanks his stars that Christ Church closed a half-tempting door and that when, a year or two later, Merton made polite overtures of the same kind he had the sense to reject them. Yet these private admissions never led to public acknowledgment. Some years later still, in his eighties, he reflects: 'I nursed the grievance, which I could perfectly well have got over if I wished. Why didn't I? Because I had that book to write, and with me literature takes precedence of life.' He explains that the book was *A Cornishman at Oxford* and he needed this personal drama to clinch the last chapter.

Literature did indeed take precedence of life. He had intended *A Cornishman at Oxford* to be the immediate sequel to *A Cornish Childhood*. But his priorities altered. A gap of twenty-three years separates the publication of the two books. In between came the great works on the Elizabethan age, the surveys of English history, the two volumes on the Churchill dynasty and heaven knows what. All this time the sacred flame of outrage had to be kept from guttering. It is perhaps equally characteristic that this absurd proceeding did not prevent him from real if stealthy generosity to his old college by subscribing to appeals for its library, its buildings and such like.

All these excitements took their toll. In July Rowse was rushed to the Acland Nursing Home, the victim of his as yet undiagnosed duodenal ulcer. So serious was his condition that his mother was sent for. Among his papers Rowse has kept the letter to her from Mary Coate, the history tutor at Lady Margaret Hall, offering to meet her at Oxford station and take her to the Nursing Home. He was always touched by such imaginative courtesy.

7

Germany

Rowse's response to what has been succinctly defined by a German historian as *Die Deutsche Katastrophe* was the pivot on which his life turned, politically, emotionally and intellectually. We have seen him already as a newly elected Fellow of All Souls, putting the old gentlemen to rights about the origins of the First World War and exonerating Germany from any special responsibility. Such was by no means his view as a boy of eleven. In an exercise book from Carclaze[1] elementary school is a clearly penned and vigorous letter (unsent) to His Imperial Majesty the Emperor of Germany dated 24 June 1915.

Your Majesty,

I am writing you, telling you of your wicked conduct. I have addressed you by your full coronation title, but I am sure you are not worthy of such an honour. Some time ago the *Lusitania* was sunk by a German submarine, if you had spoken the word, nearly two thousand harmless people would still have been living. That word was not spoken . . .

From 1866 onwards the Germans have been the bullies of Europe. While you have been pretending to be the friend of every nation, big or small, you have been behind the scene for fifty years, planning to be the master of the world . . . You declared war in 1914 because of these reasons; a huge war tax of five million pounds had been raised in Germany; the Kiel canal was just finished from its widening and deepening. On the other side the Russian railway people were all on strike; the French Government was at a crisis

1. The northern outskirts of St Austell where the children from Tregonissey went to school.

because they had just returned from a holiday in Italy, the British Government could not agree on the question of Home Rule and war was very near . . . It is rumoured that you look very old; just your own fault. 'It is the finger of God'! I hope you have not forgotten the last tyrant Napoleon: who died of a cansare through sorrow, without any one to love him, in the lonely isle of St Helena. Excuse me for telling you the truth, but you are war mad. Your latter days will be spent as a lunatic. Well however, you who impute all your victories to God, I suppose you go to church. Have your chaplain ever preached you a sermon on 'Repent, or ye shall all likewise perish'? You and your sect [Pan Germanism, adverted to in an omitted portion of this letter] have not repented therefore you will perish in the torments of Hell! Well, Goodbye, you monument of holiness!!!

    I am

      A true Briton, called

      Alfred Leslie Rowse

How cordially the mature, indeed the grey-headed, man would have endorsed these sentiments, bating only their theology. Jackie Fisher would have approved the point about the Kiel Canal, A. J. P. Taylor that about the importance of the railways. I have left the orthography and punctuation unaltered so that the reader can recognize the grasp, the wit and the itch to moralize so early and so clearly discernible.

Two principal causes of Rowse's reversion from the views of a clever young man who had swallowed, or was on the way to swallowing. Marxism whole to the justified outrage of early schooldays were his long visits to Germany in order to learn the language and his passionate friendship with Adam von Trott. Since they formed largely distinct episodes they will be considered separately.

Rowse's choice of season and milieu for his first visit to Germany reflects the high seriousness of his purpose. He left London in the middle of December 1926 and two or three days later had taken up his winter-quarters in the household of a Lutheran pastor at Hagen, an unattractive-sounding town in the Ruhr. The dourness, indeed the boredom, of this establishment is vividly evoked in *A Cornishman Abroad*, based firmly on the diary which solitude nourished. The pastor and his family were not a jolly lot. Rectitude, heaviness, self-satisfaction, obstinacy, arrogance, all the characteristics that the later Rowse was to regard as axiomatically German began to produce their natural reaction in a clever, critical young aesthete. He found himself taking against the language and the culture in which he had come to immerse himself. He turned with relief to French books. Only in music and in landscape, two deep instinctive loves, did he find Hagen rewarding. The town itself was ugly except when it was under snow, but the countryside in which it was set, hilly and well wooded, was empty and unspoilt. The lyricism and descriptive power that made him a poet responded to its beauty. As to music he was astonished by the quality and the adventurousness, so far superior to anything to be found in any English town of comparable size and wealth.

Two undated letters to Richard Pares, written from Hagen (both, at this stage of their friendship, begin 'Dear Pares'), emphasize both themes and convey his general feelings. 'There is no joy in life apart from the gospel of the young Generation, and I have enough German to make myself clear (though perhaps not convincing) to such students and hopeful young people as I meet. In Germany at least there is plenty of scope for such a movement as they don't know where they are or where they are going.' He descends from these higher considerations to complain of his dislike for the German language and especially of appearing the stupidest in any company, to whom every joke has to be explained. His second letter is a fine, high-coloured young man's invective, first against the brutishness of a nation that approved the murder of so civilized a man as Walther Rathenau and second against Lutheran vandalism, which takes no care of their lovely churches and even keeps them locked. In one of them Rowse induced the caretaker to lock him in for half an hour during which he sang such Latin motets as he could remember. In spite of the vigour of his reactions and the sharpness of his observation he is still plagued by ill-health and fearful that it may impede the intellectual and political activity he is itching to embark on.

The young Rowse carolling away to himself in a locked church – of whom does he remind us but the young Pepys? The same touch of theatricality, the same assertion of joie de vivre, the same endearing egocentricity – endearing, at least, in a very young man. Hagen was a period not just of solitude but of isolation, concentrating the mind in the same way that the monastic life or its briefer modern form of going into retreat is intended to do for the religious. Rowse, looking back on it all half a century later in *A Cornishman Abroad*, contrasts its loneliness and austerity rather sourly with the high old time that his contemporaries, especially the poets Spender, Auden, Isherwood, were having more or less simultaneously in Vienna and Berlin. Their approach to life was, to say the least, unbuttoned while his was still hair-shirted. The homosexuality they flaunted would, at this stage, have shocked him, did indeed shock him when Auden offered erotic advances in his rooms in Christ Church a few months later.

He left Hagen without regret at the beginning of spring for the rococo beauties of Munich and the congenial exuberance of a rich sensual Catholicism. On 27 March he wrote a letter of prodigious length to Keith Hancock, the first Australian to be elected to All Souls who had at the age of twenty-six obtained the Chair of History at Adelaide. Five years older than Rowse, a socialist and a Christian of austere habits, he was in many ways an obvious pattern, even in the political and intellectual objectives that were forming themselves in Rowse's mind a possible collaborator. In later years they drifted apart: Hancock did not conceal his distaste for Rowse's eager assertion of his own personality in his historical writings. In 1927 their relations were unreserved. Rowse summarizes the four months he has spent in Germany, revelling in the musical and artistic pleasures of Munich and ascribing all the defects of the national character to Protestantism. The Germans as a whole, he emphasizes, are good Europeans. He goes on to give a lively account of the Fellowship election six months earlier which Hancock in Australia had missed. He and the younger men had championed David Ayerst who had been defeated by the ancient historian A. H. M. Jones and the polymath G. F. Hudson. Rowse's enthusiasm for Ayerst's abilities was still generous and he attributes the final decision of the College to Ayerst's known support of the General Strike that was still fresh in everyone's memory.

Writing to Richard Pares or Keith Hancock was a savoured return to intellectual company – for already it is possible to discern the stirrings of Rowse's contempt for what Shakespeare courteously called 'the general'. It was not yet 'the Idiot People' at whom for the last four or five decades of his life he would tediously inveigh. Rather, as befitted a socialist, it was the middle-class and the well-to-do. All his life his charm and his engaging manners made it easy for him to get into conversation with strangers, whether on a train or in the pensions and lodgings suited to the modest means of his young manhood. Curiosity, that strongest motive of the historian, prompted him to listen to, indeed to provoke, recitals of opinions and personal circumstances that in print he would have tossed aside. Beside the historian there was also the writer. Was he going to be a novelist, a playwright, a master of the short story? He had already begun to try his hand at the last two. *A Cornishman Abroad* makes skilful use of his diaries, themselves stimulating his powers of all but total recall, to show him eyeing the monks with whom he shared a compartment on the express from Munich to Vienna or discussing German novelists with the lady clad in leopardskin who was reading Margaret Kennedy's *The Constant Nymph*. Arrived in Vienna he spent hours which should, he felt, have been devoted to the churches of Fischer von Erlach or the galleries of the Kunsthistorisches Museum listening to the life-story of a middle-aged Yorkshire heiress to an industrial fortune who was staying in the same pension.

He was in fact being true to his talent. It is the many-sidedness of Rowse's sensibility and imagination that gives his work its special quality. His love of the arts and his perception of the historical perspective of wherever he might find himself were too developed to be smothered by the pretentious superficialities of the leopardskin lady or the earthier recollections of the West Riding beldame. The contemporary context they supplied perhaps helped him to see that what he found so intoxicating about Munich was that it had the air of only just having been vacated by its owners, whose pictures were still on the walls of its palaces, whose gardens, theatres, churches, streets, markets were all as they had been. Visually, even atmospherically, continuity had not been broken. Whereas in Vienna, great had been the fall of it. The Empire of which it had been the centre had been broken into fragments, hostile to each other and eager to disclaim any Habsburg connexion. Munich gave a sense of roundedness, of the stability indispensable to civilized order, Vienna of the jagged, the neurotic, the unhappy.

Perhaps the weather intensified these perceptions. The glorious early spring in Munich captivated him coming after a winter in Hagen that might itself have been nailed to the church doors by Luther. It was April by the time he reached Vienna, already sated with sun and southern geniality. In both cities he had made the most of his musical opportunities: in Vienna he came in for the celebration of Beethoven's centenary. Beethoven was then and steadily remained his favourite composer, eagerly though he welcomed the masters of the late nineteenth and twentieth century some of whom he had heard for the first time at Hagen. He had already begun the habit which he maintained to old age of describing in his pocket books and journals the pictures he admired in the great collections which he visited assiduously. His taste was individual and unobvious without being eccentric. He looked at the pictures before he read about them and formed his own judgments. Above all he enjoyed them and, to an enviable extent, remembered them.

So far as his temperament and physique allowed he entered into the life of the city. He saw the great blocks of workers' flats going up, he visited Heiligenstadt where Beethoven had lived, he walked in the woods, he attended the ceremonies of Good Friday and Easter Day in St Stephen's cathedral and other churches, he took tea in the Café Hag. But the nightlife or even the drinking of the young wine in the taverns of Grinzing or the Kaysersberg were no more attractive than the dull and deep potations of his seniors at All Souls. He had in any case his reading to keep up if he was to produce a work that would demonstrate what was of real, permanent value and of immediate application in the teachings of Karl Marx. That, after all, was the reason he had turned his steps towards Northern and Central Europe instead of seeking the more congenial shores of the Mediterranean.

Returning to Oxford for the summer term he was quickly taken up with a host of interests, ideas and people that drove Germany out of the foreground of his mind. Apart from entertaining the wife of the Lutheran pastor from Hagen and showing her round Oxford he had nothing to remind him of his Wanderjahr. Marxism still dominated his attempts to formulate a satisfactory understanding of the world but he no longer thought of a translation that would reshape the intellectual landscape.[1] Rather it was from the emotions that Germany reasserted herself over his consciousness. He fell under the spell of Adam von Trott.

This phrase, though accurate enough, is not entirely fair. Von Trott was not a witch, consciously seeking to control the actions or thoughts of others. But the extensive literature devoted to him seems to be agreed that he was aware – how could he not be? – of his extraordinary powers of attraction. His physical beauty, delicacy of feature, vividness of colouring, his striking violet eyes, combined with great height to command astonishment. It was complemented by a force of spirit, a directness of response, that was irresistible. Such at any rate was the experience of a number of men and women who have left eloquent testimony. Often, though by no means always, there was a strong sexual element in the passion, not too wild a word, he aroused. Rowse, both in his diaries written at the time and in the recollections founded on them in his maturity (when he rarely missed an opportunity of writing about homosexuality) is explicit in denial of such feelings on either of their parts. He did indeed surrender to a rapturous longing such as he could never have imagined even hoping for in marriage. It was romantic love, not a friendship. But it was a love he was not ashamed to own as transcending sexuality.

Not every reader at this time of day will know anything about Adam von Trott zu Solz. Of those who do, many, like the present writer, will find themselves at a loss to explain him, to show what he wanted or why he left, as he undoubtedly did, so deep an impression

---

1. I have found no evidence of an exact date at which Rowse abandoned this project: but it seems probable that the publication in 1928 of a new translation, *Capital*, by Eden and Cedar Paul must have given it its quietus. The translators do not say how long their task took them, but such a labour is not a matter of weeks, and the knowledge that it was in hand would be likely to be common to every scholar interested in the subject.

Rowse's own copy of the book contains extensive (and for once not easily legible) pencil notes on loose sheets, together with a very few marginalia. I am grateful to my friend John Saumarez Smith of Messrs Heywood Hill for drawing it to my attention and allowing me to inspect it.

on so many highly intelligent and articulate people. Rowse devotes a chapter to him in *A Cornishman Abroad*. Diana Hopkinson, who knew him intimately a few years later, gave an account of him in *The Incense Tree* (1968) which Rowse much admired. Christopher Sykes, who never met him but sought out his widow and close friends in Germany as well as England, wrote a biography *Troubled Loyalty* (1968) which Shiela Grant Duff, another close friend of Adam's, in a letter to Rowse, considered a *tour de force* of sympathetic imagination. Rowse though describing it as 'admirable' in *A Cornishman Abroad* later revised his opinion, dismissing Sykes as 'a second rater', a term that usually indicated a refusal to accept as proven Rowse's conclusions about Shakespeare's Sonnets or the identity of the Dark Lady. Both books illuminate the tragic figure of the young German aristocrat who came to Oxford and, captivated himself, took England by storm. His value to Nazi diplomacy was exploited by his masters, unaware that he was secretly working against them until his exposure as a participant in the July plot of 1944 resulted in his execution by hanging from a meat-hook, gloatingly filmed for the delectation of Hitler.

The horror of the ending as much as the fog of confusion that enveloped this indisputably heroic life has a distinctly German character. And it was this Germanic quality that in the end quenched the longest and most intense love of Rowse's life. Quenched but not extinguished: under the ashes the fire smouldered as is plain from journals and memoirs of forty years later. To Rowse the very incompatibility of mind and outlook heightened the fever of desire. 'My emotional life was engulfed in Adam, quite anguished enough in itself' he wrote looking back in his diary for 1937. They had met in 1928 and corresponded for the next five or six years besides meeting each other in Oxford and Berlin.

It was, for all its probable brilliance, a dialogue of the deaf. Rowse set himself to dispel the cloud of German abstractions that encompassed that holy of holies, the philosophy of Hegel, with the sun of the French enlightenment and the searching winds of Marxist realism. He considered the letters that he wrote to Adam, subsequently destroyed in the War, the best he ever wrote. Adam's letters to him survive in the Rowse papers at Exeter University. A cursory inspection by the present writer suggests that the literary and intellectual quality was not evenly proportioned between the two. The opinion of Shiela Grant Duff in a letter written in November 1983 is very much to the point:

It is very sad that your letters have disappeared. I don't believe there has ever been in literature such an exchange of letters at such a moment in both their lives between two such people – a German and a Celt . . . It is strange, as you say, the contrast between Adam's second-class mind and his really extraordinary intuitiveness and his conceptions of what such a relationship of love and understanding could and should be.

It was not only Hegelianism, to Rowse the culmination of what he first identified as German Protestantism, that drove them apart. Von Trott though detesting the barbarities of Nazism wanted a revision of frontiers in Germany's favour. It was thus easy for him to appear, indeed he in fact was, an ultra-patriotic German about whom his official employers need have no reservations. In February 1934, after Hitler had been a year in power, he wrote a letter to the *Manchester Guardian* flatly denying anti-Semitism in Germany and praising the good-nature and good sense of the Storm Troopers with whom he had conversed. His Oxford friends, Rowse among them, were disconcerted. Even during the War when, at enormous risk, he came to see the British political intelligence agent in Switzerland, Elizabeth Wiskemann, he made it clear that if he and his friends succeeded in overthrowing Hitler they expected Germany to regain what they considered her historic frontiers.[1] The long, passionate confrontations (argument seems too rational a word) in Rowse's rooms in the Front Quad at All Souls in which one of his predecessors had hanged himself, how eloquent, how tragic in the retrospect of that tormented life. Yet even then though Rowse could recognize the confusion against which he was contending he still seems to have thought that he could remake one whom he loved in his own image:

When Hitler achieved power in 1933, I knew it was the end, and said to Adam, 'Roll up the map of Europe. There is no more to be done. Why don't

1. Personal information from the late Elizabeth Wiskemann.

you give yourself for the next ten years to a great work of scholarship? Burckhardt's *Civilisation of the Renaissance in Italy* needs its complement for Germany and Northern Europe. There's a magnificent subject waiting to be done.'

Adam said he couldn't do it, and went along his own path to his death – as Germany went along hers to her destruction.

Thus Rowse on page 286 of *A Cornishman Abroad*. Yet ten pages later, he roundly asserts 'he would never have made a writer'. The passage in his diary, on which and on Adam's letters he founds this judgment, records Adam's own profession of disbelief in Rowse's own *Weltanschauung*: 'He had never tried to write . . . he felt the mental picture melting away from him as he tried to put it into words, even to me at that moment. Standing up to go that night he said something that shocked me, with my conviction of the absolute value of art, that a poem after all was a dead thing: what was alive was the experience that moved in the mind.'

One may agree or disagree. One may find the statement transparent or opaque. But indisputably explicit as it is Rowse records it, draws conclusions from it, and yet, apparently, is incapable of accepting it. We shall see the same temperamental inability repeat itself in other relationships where his affections were deeply involved. It is not that he is imperceptive of ideas, standards, values, beliefs other than his own. As a historian and a historical topographer he always envisages the scenes he describes or the events he narrates peopled with real individuals. The desire to remodel a personality, to point people in the way they should go, was to him an inescapable part of caring for them. It was very often productive, particularly in suggesting subjects for writers or research students or in helping people to find an opening for their talents. Its dangers lay in its liability to egotism and wilfulness. With the past this did not arise, at least not in a direct personal relationship. 'Home art gone and ta'en thy wages.' Compassion and understanding could in that context more easily fulfil themselves.

Besides being unsuited both by gifts and inclination to become the Burckhardt of the northern Renaissance Adam like many others did not recognize as early and as fully as Rowse did the evil and the strength of the Nazis. On being told in the manner of the Younger

Pitt to roll up the map of Europe he may well have reflected that such a proceeding might not be altogether disastrous for his country. In a letter to Rowse as late as 1932 he had discounted Hitler's chances of coming to power. What he subsequently thought and felt has been disputed, as has the role he played as an intermediary in England on the eve of the War and in America after its outbreak. These matters lie outside the concern and the competence of the present writer and the reader interested in them should consult the already sizeable literature on the subject. Von Trott touched many lives and had the entrée to a distinguished circle. His importance to this study is that he came to personify for Rowse the idea of Germany, its inexplicable yearnings, its romantic impatience of a rational approach, its powerful appeal to the emotions. No doubt the letters destroyed in Adam's Berlin flat in an Allied air raid would give the fullest expression of this. But Rowse's surviving diaries and the distillation of them in both *A Cornishman Abroad* and *A Man of the Thirties* leave the reader in no doubt of the central place this relationship had in his perception of Germany. The sequel of Nazism deepened and darkened it, reversing the views that Roger Makins had heard him expounding to his seniors in his earliest days at All Souls. Both books describe his visits to Berlin, Hamburg and Dresden and other centres of German artistic and cultural life inspired or directly guided by Adam. It was all much grander and more spacious than the narrow household at Hagen. As he regretfully noted he came to know Germany much better than the Latin countries in which he would have been more at home.

During this time he had of course much else to occupy his energies and his affections. It is to these that we must now turn.

8

Friendships

The contradictions of Rowse's nature have an almost mechanical reciprocity. The need for solitude, the horror of commitment to another person (raised to its highest power in the institution of matrimony), the chuckling jollity of the Miller who lived on the river Dee, the vanity easily bruised by even the suggestion of adverse criticism, all these articulate themselves early. In maturity they are loud, in age strident. Yet all the time there is an unmistakable craving to give and receive affection, a true gift for friendship, even a readiness to lament mishandled opportunities of exercising it. It is not, fortunately, a biographer's task to explain this but he needs to be aware of it.

To say, as Rowse does, that in the late twenties and early thirties his emotional life was engulfed by Adam seems an oversimplification. It is difficult to see how the close friendships he formed, and which to a great extent formed him, can be relegated to the shallows. The three that affected him most strongly, re-echoing in his private journals and published memoirs, are those with Richard Pares, Charles Henderson and Bruce McFarlane.

Pares has already been briefly introduced: it will be remembered that Rowse writing from Hagen addressed him as 'Dear Pares'. Back at All Souls their friendship took wing. In the letters they were to exchange during Pares's year in America and the Caribbean 'Dear Richard' was soon to become 'Darling Richard'. Pares expressed himself less ardently. 'Dear Rowse' 'My dear Rowse' or, more often, 'My dear Professor' – the nickname he early gave him and never abandoned. There is a charming note of derision that doubtless helped to develop A.L.'s till then latent sense of humour. One of Pares's earliest letters, written during a college meeting, describes 'A curious instance of the incompetence of financial experts. Brand [Lord Brand, the banker] professed himself quite unable to understand the college accounts and it turned out that in the end the reason was he thought the accounts for 1926 and the estimates for 1927 were meant to be true statements of the same account, and was, not unnaturally, surprised at the discrepancy. The college mind is occupied entirely by the terribly important question of black waistcoats and white ties, of which a historical précis has been given by Woodward.'

Writing from Washington in November 1928 where he was watching the election results come in as Al Smith went down to defeat by 'that great stuffed pig Hoover' his imagination turns to the All Souls Day Feast: 'I kept thinking now they have got to the *foie gras* and Woodward is beginning to be genial with the young men . . . now that pallid, watery, middle-aged hack Feiling is asking perfunctorily "B-by the way has anybody heard anything of P-pares?"' Keith Feiling's diffident coolness of manner is caught as accurately as the stammer that expressed it. Pares could not resist making fun, sometimes cruel fun, of the people and places to which he was deeply attached. The moving dedication of his last book, written when he knew that he was dying, proves his love of All Souls. The brilliance and force of his mind could sometimes carry him too far in criticizing the work of his pupils. One of the gentlest and most distinguished of them wrote to congratulate Rowse on his obituary in the *Proceedings of the British Academy*: 'It was brave of you to seek to define him, though the wounds he inflicted and that were inflicted on him will take long to heal.'[1] With Rowse however he had, it seems, an infallibly happy touch. To have told him that he dressed as if he were a member of Ruskin College,[2] without giving offence, indeed only causing mild amusement, is a telling example.

Pares's self-confidence, his wit, his range, his precision flattered and delighted his much less sophisticated friend by the implication of equality. The world was all before them. Pares, fantasizing light-heartedly in a letter from Washington, sees himself as a future Prime

1. Professor John Bromley, 20 December 1963.
2. Founded for Trades Unionists who wished to attend the University as mature students.

Minister when he will make Rowse Regius Professor and take his advice about the preferment of high church clergymen to canonries in minor cathedrals. He had, in fact, for all the strength of his political opinions, come down firmly for historical scholarship. But he retained, rather like Raymond Asquith, a dandiacal self-admiring conviction of his own superiority in other fields should he choose to exert it: 'It annoys me to read of the boom of Christopher Hollis, Evelyn Waugh and Peter Quennell because I know I could do much better than they and I don't want the trouble of doing so; but I am not jealous of your successes.'

This undated letter, written aboard SS *Camito* off Venezuela, must refer to Rowse's early articles in the *New Statesman* and to his little book *On History* (1927) which had indeed been well received, even earning the favourable notice of André Maurois, then at the height of his reputation in both England and France. What had taken Pares to America and to the West Indies was a vast project of research. When he had returned to Oxford from his brief foray into journalism he speculated, in common room conversation at All Souls, as to what line of historical investigation he might pursue. Kenneth Bell, his former history tutor at Balliol who happened to be present, replied 'Sugar'. And without further ado Pares committed himself to a study of every aspect of the great trade of the later eighteenth century over which wars were fought and from which fortunes were made. The precipitate, almost frivolous, acceptance of a topic suggested out of the blue shocked Rowse, as he confided more than once to a close friend of a rather later period.[1] He himself was still weighing the claims of literature and politics and professional scholarship. When he did ultimately decide on the last he chose his special field, after further deliberation, for himself.

In spite of this one reservation Rowse's admiration for, and reliance on, Pares's judgment must command the enthusiastic assent of any reader of his letters. Watching the 1928 campaign in America he is struck by the belief of the electorate that by virtue of the Kellogg pact they have abolished war. 'They have a real mania for abolishing. I suppose they have got their eye in with slavery and liquor and they

1. Professor Jack Simmons: personal information.

can't stop.' His description of New York brilliantly catches its special quality. 'I suppose half the people come here to get away from Europe and the other half to get away from America and the result is something *sui generis*. Nobody seems to give a damn who you are and nobody stops you in the streets and tries to make you feel like a man and a brother . . . Everyone pretending to be in a hurry which is so much worse than being in a hurry.' The letter written aboard the *Camito* shows that he was well apprised of the baleful activities of the United Fruit Company in manipulating the politics of America's southern neighbours. Yet he is also aware of the hypocrisy inherent in the patronizing attitude of mind in which he has been brought up: 'When one makes fun of the Americans one should remember that they are what nine-tenths of the Europeans who make fun of them would sell their souls to be.'

Perhaps direct observation of America sharpened his perception of English politics. In 1931 Rowse saw the defection of MacDonald as bringing the chances of a Labour government 'with real power perceptibly nearer'. It cleared out the old gang and opened the way for younger men of whom he might reasonably have hoped to be one. Pares was less sanguine and more far-sighted in a long undated letter, evidently written very soon after the election. In particular he envisaged the move of industry to the south 'leading to the wrong kind of working-class growing up – I mean politically and as to its ideas – on the American *Saturday Evening Post* model.' Perhaps it was in answer to this – both disdained, as a rule, the dating of their letters – that Rowse acknowledged the superiority of his friend's analysis. 'It's so like you, Richard darling, to go and raise all the fundamental issues in about eight lines. It gives me no chance of answering even if I could.'

Politics rather than history was the subject of their more serious exchanges. As early as February 1929 Rowse had been offered the Labour candidacy for Westmorland, clearly unwinnable, and had declined. In the same letter, incidentally, he records a rather dismissive opinion of L. B. Namier's *The Structure of Politics at the Accession of George III* which Feiling had hailed as the most important work on the eighteenth century since Lecky 'and more important indeed'. A few months later he was adopted for his home constituency of Penryn and Falmouth, which he was to fight in the elections of 1931 and 1935, resigning only when his health made the prospect of a Parliamentary career unthinkable. What he was sacrificing in 1929 was not his commitment to history but to literature. He was working against time to finish his book on Swift for the closing date of the *Atlantic Monthly* competition '. . . the Swift correspondence: but there's six fat volumes of it. Never was there a life so documented: except Napoleon and John Wesley: Washington and Lincoln perhaps.'[1]

Political engagement, and the consequent missing of the *Atlantic Monthly* deadline, turned him from Swift (which was not to appear until 1975) to his first full-length book *Politics and the Younger Generation* (1931). This extremely well-written work – Rowse later bewailed the time and trouble he had lavished on it – was addressed as its title makes clear to a readership as instantaneous as its subject matter. What it had to say could convey its full meaning only to them. It seems therefore appropriate to cite the evaluation of it by David Ayerst in the *Manchester Guardian*,[2] which caused such mortal offence.

It would be foolish to question Mr Rowse's devotion to the Labour cause; it would be equally idle to deny that most people who vote Labour and many more intimately connected with the movement would find but few points of contact between his outlook and their own . . . Those to whom politics, and Labour politics in particular, are mainly a matter of social justice or business efficiency – gas and water Socialists – will be puzzled at the queerly abstract world in which Mr Rowse moves with so much assurance and charm. But it is not to them so much as to a severely academic or literary audience that Mr Rowse's book will appeal. The feuds of half-a-dozen common-rooms live again in the countless tart footnotes about this man's poor-spirited remark and that man's curious blunder. This provincialism is a blot on what is otherwise a notable book. The long discussion on the class basis of present-day society, the devastating attack on the non-productive interests (in which Mr Rowse would include all the Churches as well as the drink trade), and the stimulating analysis of the conflicting claims of liberty and security bring back a note of fundamental social criticism which has often been absent from recent Labour exposition . . . If Mr Rowse does not actually

1. His biographer might enter a claim for the present subject.
2. 19 November 1931, p. 5.

suggest, for instance, that, unless the atmosphere of secondary education is radically changed, an extension of it might be harmful, he is plainly very much out of sympathy with the outlook which such schools in general give . . .

Although the book lies so much out of the main track of Rowse's work that there seems little point in discussing it there are suggestive waymarks in its production and reception. Ayerst notes Rowse's conspicuous distancing of himself from the common herd both in its more, and less, elevated aspects. In the preface the author acknowledges his debt to his publishers at Faber and Faber: 'Mr T. S. Eliot and Mr Geoffrey Faber, for their criticism of parts of my manuscript, a debt all the greater since there is hardly a point at which their views agree with mine.' Since the failure to obtain a Research Fellowship for Eliot Rowse had contributed to Eliot's periodical *The Criterion* and had benefited from his unsparing editorial candour. There is no acknowledgment, perhaps surprisingly, to Richard Pares but among such major figures as R. H. Tawney and Graham Wallas appear the names of two friends of his own age, G. F. Hudson and Bruce McFarlane.

Whereas towards Pares there is always an unspoken deference with McFarlane it is otherwise. Sometimes there is an air of superiority, proved by Rowse's success and McFarlane's failure in winning a Fellowship at All Souls: sometimes an outraged competitiveness. And then there is the outspoken homosexuality, which McFarlane, according to Rowse, taught him to recognize in himself. All three of the great friendships, both these two and that with Charles Henderson, were by Rowse's account tinged with sex. The latter he records once made a pass (his own words) at him. 'Bruce was wholly, strongly, aggressively homo, and believed in it with absolution [sc. absolute] conviction.' So his old friend wrote in a sketch composed about twenty years after his death. Much of it indeed is taken up with accounts of McFarlane's affairs with pupils,[1] casual pick-ups, quasi-professional amorists. Let other pens than mine – Shakespeare's for instance –

---

1. This is emphatically denied by his later pupils. e.g. Bevis Hillier's review of his *Letters to Friends 1940–1966* in the *Spectator* (16 August 1997). Norman Scarfe confirms this and adds that he doubts if he had ever so behaved.

dwell on the raptures and frustrations of lust to which A. L. Rowse's, in later life, so eagerly turned. Cerebral voyeurism was evidently a taste they had in common (they were not lovers). But McFarlane's real gift to Rowse was not opening his eyes to his own sexual orientation (which it is hard to believe he had not already more than half discovered for himself) but opening them to the wonderful riches of the English countryside, its houses, its parish churches, its cathedral towns. The vacation jaunts to Lincoln, staying in the comfortable White Hart, the afternoon and week-end walks in the neighbourhood of Oxford: 'I first saw Stonor on a lovely walk with Bruce. Of course he had discovered it and we walked from Christmas Common down through the beech-woods, the house then shut up and emptied of its furniture. It was he who first took me to Hardwick . . . he introduced me to Derbyshire, took me to Tyldesley and Haddon; we both caught 'flu in the Peacock at Rowsley. He was always exploring England.' When one thinks of the enrichment of Rowse's work by the intimate, accurate recall of historical setting one recognizes that the debt was great indeed.

Rowse makes no bones about the question of status, particularly at the outset. It was McFarlane who solicited him, not he McFarlane. They had taken Schools the same year and McFarlane had got an undistinguished First whilst Rowse was the second best of the year, beaten only by Robert Birley, later Head Master of Eton.[1] In the All Souls examination where Rowse triumphed McFarlane came nowhere. He hung about Oxford on a Senior Scholarship hoping his luck would change. It was in his lodgings above Boffin's cake shop in the Cornmarket that Rowse, invited to call, found him eating liqueur chocolates. 'Politically obsessed and fanatical, I wasn't much interested, not in his *routinier* research into the finances of Cardinal Beaufort. He could never make them work out, so the thesis was never published.'

It did however win him a Prize Fellowship at Magdalen where, from the first a finished College politician, he cultivated his seniors so skilfully that they elected him to a permanent teaching Fellowship. 'It was his metier: he became the best history tutor in Oxford.'

---

1. Every now and again Birley is air-brushed out and Rowse's First is the best.

He also became, by common consent, the leading authority on England in the fifteenth century. A research addict, he would spend days, weeks, in the Public Record Office, the Bodleian, County Record Offices, pursuing with the remorselessness of a master detective the connexions and circumstances of some quite minor landed family. So vast was his accumulation of knowledge, so swift was he to mark what was done amiss, that other scholars in the field, anxious to publish and establish their reputations, held back, shifting from one foot to the other, unable to take the plunge. Meanwhile the great man himself remained obdurately silent, amassing material, training his horses for the academic Derby of the Final School, intriguing success-fully to get his own way in the affairs of the College. What on earth had he in common with Rowse, anxious above all to *far figura* whether it be in politics or literature and only too delighted to disembarrass himself of teaching?

The question was to make itself felt more and more insistently, despite the tastes they shared. Indeed these could themselves provoke discord. McFarlane was jealous of all Rowse's friendships, acutely so when their object was an attractive and intelligent young man. History too, when Rowse had settled for becoming a wholetime historian, divided as much, perhaps more, than it united them. Rowse's pro-ductivity was watched with suspicion, even disapproval, the tributes paid to his work coldly and silently condemned. The climax to this mounting cause of bitterness between them came with the publication of *The Expansion of Elizabethan England* (1955). Rowse described the scene several times in letters and journals with no substantial variations. The version here printed is transcribed from the sketch of McFarlane already mentioned:

I gave Bruce a copy, who returned it, saying that 'if he kept it, it might be taken to mean that he approved it. Better to return it.' I went straight down to Magdalen and said in front of Karl Leyser [ex-pupil of McFarlane's and himself a distinguished historian]:

'You regard Neale as the leading authority on the Elizabethan period?'
'Yes.'

'This is what he says about my book' I read him Neale's letter [quoted on p. 225] 'You have written, and must know that you have written, a great book.' 'If the book is good enough for Neale, it is certainly good enough for you.'

He turned absolutely white. And then

'I suppose you think we are all second-rate.'

There was the complex. Quite deliberately, I reflected, and said:

'Yes; that, I suppose, is what I must assume.'

But, of course, Bruce was not second-rate; it was just that his production was. He had produced only his *Wycliffe* [a short book in a series of which Rowse was editor] and two or three articles.

This passage is from Rowse in meditative, even elegiac, mood. His friend has been dead for twenty years or more and he still feels his loss. Yet the sharpness, the acidity of men to whom competitiveness was central has not mellowed. There was real affection, on Rowse's side real gratitude, between them. But McFarlane seems, by his account, only to have been capable of showing it when Rowse was ill or distressed. Rowse never forgot that it was McFarlane who had made him go to the specialist – a friend of his – who had diagnosed the ulcers that had all but killed him in 1938. He had been rescued only by surgery so drastic that his colleagues at All Souls had thought he would not survive it. As hopes of his recovery gained ground Isaiah Berlin would convulse the common room by his imitation of Warden Adams solemnly announcing:

'He has taken a little milk.'

It had been a close call. On his side too, Rowse, though he never says so, no doubt supplied the imaginative sympathy and simple kindness that his friends knew they could rely on in distress. That McFarlane's unproductiveness was a symptom of severe nervous disturbance seems obvious. Rowse recalls finding him in his rooms in Magdalen when he was composing his (almost) only published work, the chapter for the *Cambridge Medieval History* on 'The Lancastrian Kings': 'There spread out on his dining room table was the beginning of the chapter, written out ten or twelve times over with minute changes in the wording. After that he had his breakdown.'

The portrait of McFarlane is psychologically more intimate and more detailed in visual recall than either of the other two great friends of his young manhood. McFarlane's childhood and youth had been unhappy, even verging on the tragic. Rowse finds in the repression imposed on the homosexuals of his own early years a ready explanation of almost all the ills, psychosomatic and temperamental, from which his academic colleagues suffered. No doubt there is some truth in this. But the disentangling of cause and effect in the psychology of high-powered egotists is not to be enterprised or taken in hand lightly or wantonly.

One unlikely consequence of this friendship was the election to a History Fellowship at Magdalen of the man whom both were to come to deplore – A. J. P. Taylor. In his engrossing biography of Taylor, Adam Sisman passes lightly over this surely crucial turn in his hero's fortunes, ascribing it to the strong recommendation of Sir Llewellyn Woodward.[1] But Rowse's own *mea culpa*s over the matter have been loud and long in both private and public. Partly he had championed him out of admiration for his gifts, which Rowse continued to acknowledge in his furious denunciations of their misuse. But it was chiefly because he wished to strengthen the Left in the History Faculty at Oxford in the disastrous era of Baldwin and Chamberlain. 'I was largely responsible for his appointment at Magdalen, putting him across K. B. McFarlane. A great mistake' he scrawled at the foot of an unsent letter to the British Academy in 1966. Clear confirmation can be found in a pencilled letter of McFarlane's dated 1 August 1938 giving a brief account of final negotiations over his election.

'He has climbed down about hours and residence. I was rather sorry, as this trouble had made me feel that we should be well rid of him. However he is going to live in Holywell Ford for three years as soon as the present Groupists have been turned out. He was quite remarkably accommodating and asked if he might call me by my Christian name. I *don't* like him.'

This is followed by a long and brilliant analysis of late fourteenth-century English history and an outline for a book on the reign of Henry IV, studded with challenging aperçus and unfamiliar detail: 'Coulton and Trevelyan are so superficial'. Rowse's portrait of his friend was true to life. Six years later it was Taylor who found a

1. op. cit., p. 120.

candidate to defeat McFarlane for the Presidency of Magdalen – by one vote.

The last of the three great friendships, that with Charles Henderson, combined the two loves of Rowse's life – Cornwall and Oxford, in that order. As an authority on every aspect of Cornish history, landscape, place-names, churches, families, documents he was without a rival. From a boy he had seized on everything that might bear on the past of his county. By his teens he had made himself an expert on the abbreviations and contractions of court-hand that often take an eternity to puzzle out. Born into the landed gentry and inheriting a country house near Truro, he was welcomed by the aristocracy and old established families to sort through and calendar the papers that had piled up over the centuries. There was then no market for family archives as there is now and very few of the owners took much interest in them or even knew what they had got. Strictly speaking, as Rowse points out in a memorial address that he delivered fifty years after Henderson's death,[1] he was an antiquary rather than a historian. He is remembered now not for the books he wrote but for the wonderful collections of material which he bequeathed to the Royal Institution of Cornwall. None the less after a spell of external lecturing under the auspices of the infant University of Exeter (then the University College of the South West) he was elected to a tutorship at Corpus Christi College, Oxford.

It was there in 1928 that he and Rowse met and at once became friends. Henderson was a medievalist, like Bruce McFarlane, but with this narrower, deeper engagement with Cornwall. Their interests and expertise were thus complementary where they did not coincide. Rowse could point him in the direction of the books and articles that his pupils would need to know about and he could deepen and extend the foundations of local insight on which *Tudor Cornwall*, Rowse's first masterpiece, so firmly rests. Because they were near neighbours both at work and in vacation there is virtually no correspondence between them. The easiness of Henderson's temper, compared with the masterfulness of Pares and the prickliness of McFarlane, left behind the memory of a close, untroubled friendship. Those are the three

1. Printed in *The Little Land of Cornwall* (1986), pp. 291–6.

names that time and again recur to Rowse reflecting on his young manhood in his later age. They were the only three that he could bear to expose to his home life at 24 Robartes Place, the council house to which his parents had moved in 1927. It was under the wing of Henderson and his sister that Rowse was welcomed to the seats of all but the most philistine and stand-offish Cornish gentry. With them too he acquired an intimate knowledge of landscapes, churches, villages whose existence, though only thirty or forty miles from his home, he had never suspected. The Hendersons had a car and put it to good use. Rowse did not learn to drive until well after the Second World War. All this heated the passion for Cornish history that smouldered on, his first childhood delight, under the surface wrestlings with Marxian historical philosophy to burst into flame with *Tudor Cornwall*.

In all three of these friendships that shaped, or at the very least, influenced the course of Rowse's life there was, in his apprehension of them, an unspoken assumption of a common homosexuality. When this was shown by the marriage of two of them to have been a misreading Rowse was thunderstruck. The shock of Henderson's marriage in 1933 was hardly less devastating than the news that followed it almost at once of his death on his honeymoon. On the morning in 1937 that Pares told him that he was going to marry the daughter of Sir Maurice Powicke, the great medievalist, Rowse was going up to London to give a lecture. He was so overcome that he turned away from Oxford station to seek the solitude of the church of St Thomas which he had never previously entered. The sense of the ground giving way beneath him, of the walls of his world tottering on their foundations, is poignantly conveyed in the Diary. 'Put not your trust in princes, nor in any child of man.' How inevitably this despairing conclusion about one's fellow human beings forces itself on a solipsist. And how miserably it contributed to the growing sense of particular, Rowse-directed injustice of the whole scheme of things to which in his darker moods he grew more ready to surrender.

9

Home and Abroad

Home to Rowse meant, depending on his mood, either Cornwall or All Souls or both. There was never a day in his life in which they were not, however briefly, present to his consciousness, at least on the evidence of his almost quotidian chronicling of his own thoughts and feelings. Yet a lot of his life was lived away from them. After the War, or more exactly after his rejection (as he saw it) by All Souls, he spent half the year in America. In the decade before the War he spent a great deal of his time in London, living in a small flat in Brunswick Square, or rather camping out in it as he clearly never liked it or entertained his friends there.

What drew him to London was a complexity of attractions and repulsions. The undergraduate teaching by which he had financed himself in the first years of his Fellowship was becoming a weariness of the mind. Teaching is exhausting. To do it well, and Rowse could not be anything but a first-class teacher, draws on precisely those energies and responses that go into good writing. One's pupil is one's reader. Whatever Rowse was going to be, historian, politician, poet, man of letters, he was going to be a writer. In Oxford he could thank himself and his college that he was not as other dons were. His most valuable connexions lay outside the University, with John Buchan and his hospitable household at Elsfield, with Robert Bridges and Gilbert Murray on Boars Hill, with Sir John Beazley and his anything but suburban milieu in North Oxford, with the even wider circle of Lady Ottoline Morrell at Garsington to which David Cecil had introduced him. Complemented by the eclectic intellectual aristocracy of All Souls his horizon stretched far beyond a university that still thought of itself as standing apart from the busy hum of men.

The magnet that kept him in Brunswick Square was its proximity to the Public Record Office and the Reading Room of the British Museum, the first especially. For it was here that the archives of a government and of a system of justice, for centuries centralized as in no other great European country, were freely available for study. Research into the original materials for history easily developed into a passion akin to that for fox-hunting, incommunicable, even repulsive, to those who do not share it. Rowse himself has written an essay on the Public Record Office, amusing, evocative, passionate:

It takes time, it consumes time, it lives on time. It is the sort of place a young man goes into dark-haired, fanatical, full of hopes and desires, and emerges from grey-headed and old, rather gentle and courteous, old-fashioned and left behind by time, the dust having settled upon him, and all his ways. What has happened to him in the interval? – ah, that is the point, for he himself can hardly tell you . . .

It is a curious confraternity we form, and one of the strongest bonds we have in common is that we all know we are slightly mad. Not so mad perhaps as . . . that frightening old woman with the glittering eyes and the dangerous hat-pins, gaunt, *raide*, and six feet tall, who believed in the Evil Eye and worked ever at the same books for twenty years, standing up behind one's chair in a most advantageous position for cracking one's skull with a heavy paper-weight . . . I found that a terrifying experience and in that atmosphere: the silence, nothing but the rustling of paper, the turning over of leaves of age-old parchments and rolls, the slow raining down of smuts from the domed glass roof, covering oneself and one's work in a like oblivion.

Yet we are not without our excitements . . . we have before us, under our hands, the actual letters, State papers, secret instructions written by kings, queens, princes, cardinals, ministers of state, spies. Somebody over there is reading the very instructions written by the great Pitt with which he breathed his spirit into the conduct of the war over three continents (would there were a Pitt to inspire and lead us now);[1] somebody else has out charters signed by the greatest of our medieval kings, magnificent men of action though a trifle illiterate; I myself, cold with excitement, am turning over the very letters which Drake wrote from on board the *Revenge* to the Queen when the

1. Written in 1938 when Hitler was everywhere in the ascendant.

Spaniards were already in the Channel. It seems that the sand he sprinkled on the paper, having folded it up hastily for the messenger, still glitters . . .'[1]

The consciousness of being actually present in the past while being perfectly aware of living in one's own period with all its perils and disasters, its everyday oddities and pleasures, is the hallmark of Rowse's work. Dr Johnson defined happiness as the multiplicity of agreeable consciousness. Rowse's consciousness, multiplicitous to an extraordinary degree, rendered him both happy and unhappy at the same time. At a given moment one element would dominate, say the political. 'I have not known one moment's happiness for the last ten years', he would burst out in 1941, when the feebleness of pre-war political leadership and the terrible effectiveness of evil men had brought Western civilization within sight of its extinction. He was aware of this as a growing possibility in 1938. Yet also he was aware, as his friend John Betjeman would have been, both of the ethos and of the material embodiment of the Public Record Office: 'that sepulchral, prison-like building in Chancery Lane . . . the like of which exists nowhere else – the British Museum is light and gay, positively flippant compared with it – those long, stone corridors, one's footsteps falling dead as one goes, the excitement as soon as one enters and the doors shut behind one, the fascination of a world of its own.'[2]

The guiding spirit who had directed Rowse towards this scene was Richard Pares. Pares, like Bruce McFarlane, was a research addict, piling up mountains of transcripts and notes from which rescue teams of friends and pupils might pull out and bring to life the books that, left to themselves, they would have been incapable of writing. Looking back on it all nearly half a century later Rowse wrote: 'My youth was much more given to literature, and poetry in particular; the thought of writing history positively frightened me. It is true that in the Oxford of my younger days a great song-and-dance

1. *The English Spirit* (1944), pp. 41–2.
2. ibid. The bogus Tudor of the Chancery Lane building has obvious affinities with the castellated prisons of the same period. The modern PRO at Kew is an entirely different affair, slightly clinical in its overtones, suggestive rather of an up-to-date hospital or perhaps a health farm.

was made of historical research: the technicians made a cult of their expertise, rather frightening one off the premises than encouraging one to enter – and I developed an acute inferiority complex about the Public Record Office, the British Museum Research Room, the inner recesses of the Bodleian, Duke Humphrey and Selden End [the marvellously beautiful rooms above the even more beautiful Divinity School]; the demands of palaeography, diplomatic, state papers; patent rolls, close rolls, and the rest of it. In those days there were no seminars or classes for beginners – one was just thrown into the pool to sink or swim. I hesitated for long, shivering on the brink.'[1]

It was Pares who gave the decisive shove. But it was conversation in the All Souls Common Room that gave him his theme – the Reformation in Cornwall. The idea that great national and international convulsions, the Reformation, the French Revolution, could most profitably be studied by putting a particular area or a town, even a village, under the microscope is now a commonplace. Rowse's work was a pioneering venture in this field. Cornwall was an ideal unit for such an experiment, close-knit, conscious of its own identity, central to the author's consciousness of his own. Serendipity played a useful part. It was during the course of these researches that Rowse stumbled on a hitherto unknown account of an affray in which the young Sir Richard Grenville, later to be immortalized in Tennyson's ballad, had killed a man. His first scholarly work was thus *Sir Richard Grenville of the Revenge*, not the book that was, on Sir Charles Firth's suggestion, to appear as *Tudor Cornwall*.

But the first real book, reflecting the true priority of its author's concern, was *Politics and the Younger Generation* (1931). In later life, certainly in conversation with the present writer, Rowse was apt to bewail the pains he had taken over a work by its very nature so ephemeral. His intellectual energy was so inexhaustible that it is surprising that he should regret this youthful prodigality. For a writer it is never wasted effort to try to write as well as one can, no matter what one may later come to think of the opinions expressed or the positions espoused. The book shows Rowse's life tilting from Oxford

1. *Discoveries and Reviews* (1975), p. 1.

to London. This was the direct result of exchanging the Bodleian and All Souls for the PRO, the Institute of Historical Research and the London School of Economics. It was in this milieu that Tawney, J. E. Neale, Beveridge, Harold Laski, L. B. Namier and others were to be met. The obvious rationalization of such a *train de vie* was to obtain a post at LSE where Rowse almost at once began to do some part-time teaching. But it was a lean time for academic appointments. 'I am afraid', wrote Beveridge from the LSE on 8 June 1934, 'it is going to be difficult to give you as much connection with the School as you would like (we are being forced to contract in all directions) but I will certainly hope to keep some connection.' From the incisive pen portrait of Beveridge written some twenty years later it is clear that Rowse found him vain and cold, a monster of egotism. Fortunately Beveridge's formidable secretary and future wife, Mrs Mair, had a soft spot for the frail-looking young radical. R. H. Tawney after meeting him in the street wrote to him on 1 March 1936, 'I thought on seeing you, that, so far from going anywhere, you ought to be in bed. Are you sure that you have a sensible doctor and that you are obeying his orders? Forgive the fussiness of one who has suffered from a different sort of inside [Tawney had been severely wounded in the trenches] . . . It really does save time in the long run to make illness a full-time job.'

These names, even sixty years later, hardly need explicatory annotation, except perhaps for that of Harold Laski, whose best hopes of a niche in history rest on one of Clement Attlee's most famous put-downs: 'A period of silence from you would be welcome.' In the 1980s Rowse wrote a little sketch of him, unpublished but preserved in his papers, entitled 'Harold Laski's Little Ways'. It already asked: 'Who remembers him now? His books don't hold up, and never did, though he was a best-seller and pillar, if that is the word for it, of the Left Book Club . . . I have forgotten his *clichés* now, as I have forgotten the books. But not him. He had good qualities: spirit, courage, warmth of heart, generosity, loyalty. Pity they were spoiled by his sciolism and exhibitionism, the *itch* to be in the limelight.'

Besides slaving away in the PRO (from the transcripts in another hand it seems that he was already employing an amanuensis when he had identified a document he needed) he was living half-a-dozen lives at once. He was an active, indeed energetic, Labour candidate in Cornwall where he made and kept up a number of friendships with no trace of that intellectual contempt that vitiates so much of his later controversial writing. The name of Claude Berry[1] of the *West Briton* is not so well-known as most of those in this chapter but it was dearer to Rowse's heart than almost any. Loyalty and affection never failed of their response. Readers of his volumes of autobiography are sometimes repelled by the apparent lack of these very qualities in his dismissive remarks about his family. But the contemporary documentary evidence that was his lodestar as a historian points in a different direction. A letter written just after he had been adopted as candidate for Penryn while he was invigilating an examination at Oxford in 1929 to his brother George, who had emigrated to Australia, is one example from many:

I'm writing this from the Examination Schools, where I sit enthroned in a high chair, all dressed up as I used to try and dress myself up as a boy, in hood and cap and gown. Isn't it ridiculous: but there is one of my schemes that has come off, so why shouldn't others? And why don't yours? I daresay yours will in time – I'd love you to make a fortune after all.

To assist George he sketches a plan for buying a dairy farm of 140 acres near St Austell when he's earned enough money. He is evidently cock-a-hoop at his adoption:

As for the view that England is on the downgrade there is nothing in it: there is more that is really vital and hopeful coming off here than anywhere else. Germany also I have great belief in. I have been there again this summer . . . I have a great friend of mine whom I love very much living in Berlin, a young German called von Trott.

He wrote regularly to his parents, keeping them informed, as far as he could, of his activities and interests. His concern over his father's health and his readiness to help if he had to give up work has already been mentioned. His distress at his sudden death on 5 March 1934

1. Journalist and staunch Labour supporter.

after a short spell in hospital was intensified by not being there to show his affection and support. He kept the anniversary, noting forty-five years later, 'Poor father. He was proud of me and can never have thought that I might not be his son.' He still was, or at any rate on the evidence of his pocket books and diaries still believed himself to be, devoted to his mother. 'My mind is haunted tonight by the images of the two people I love in the world' (21 July 1930). They were his mother and Adam von Trott.

What about relations with the opposite sex? Horror of marriage, disgust at the thought of children, a growing belief in the superior intelligence and sensibility inherent in male homosexuality, combined to deaden the nerve of ordinary sexual desire. Yet there were vestiges of an *amitié amoureuse* in at least two of his longest and earliest friendships. Noreen Sweet, opposite whom he had acted as a school-boy, remained on affectionate terms with him till her death half a century later. He certainly admired her taste, her style and her intelligence. In 1965 he wrote to her 'You remember my early compliment "You dress like a lady with an independent income of £500 a year" when my great friend at All Souls Richard Pares was telling me that I dressed like a member of Ruskin College.' At her wedding in 1938 his thoughts as he waited in the church suggest that he had given her grounds for hoping that he might once again have been cast as her leading man and even prompt him to wonder whether he, at that final moment, regrets the role. The pocket books record fancies and impressions as they ripple the surface of his consciousness and should not be taken for more.

More serious, but still not altogether serious, consideration must be given to his assertion, often repeated both in speech and in writing during his later years, that he had come close to an engagement to Veronica Wedgwood. Veronica as an undergraduate at Lady Margaret Hall had been one of his earliest pupils and, as he often said until she committed the black sin of dissent from his Shakespearean arguments, the best. No one who knew her as the present writer did for many years could feel any doubts about her lovableness. A character of rare beauty, an intellect and a sensibility of pure quality, a gentle and affectionate disposition, she was for the greater part of his adult life his closest woman friend. No one, however, who knew them both in their maturity would have thought for a moment that they could ever have been man and wife. But what about their immaturity? Rowse was always emphatic on two points, first that the time was that of his earliest years at All Souls when she was his pupil: and second that the prime mover in the matter was Veronica's mother, Lady Wedgwood. Veronica, according to him, was not cutting the social swathe that her mother had hoped for. Not for her the deb dances and hunt balls. So why not outflank the conventional aristocracy by a brilliant marriage with a rising star in the intellectual firmament? This was Rowse's version in which, it will be observed, he was the pursued rather than the pursuer. Veronica never, to my knowledge, alluded to the affair. The only close friend of hers surviving from that period whom I have consulted knew of Rowse's account and assured me that it had no foundation. He was unashamedly vain of his looks and confident of his sexual attraction. His diaries name a number of ladies who had more or less explicitly indicated their readiness to grant him their favours. One who had, she considered, been encouraged only to be pushed aside took her revenge in a novel, published in 1938, of such stupefying incompetence that it would be gratuitous to identify it. But its portrayal of Rowse, disguised as an Eastern European intellectual, may be of some interest:

At most times his features expressed a dancing individuality, so animated that appearance changed with every thought or fancy. A feverish light shone through the pale skin, and seemed to erase the lines scored by his perturbed soul . . . His black hair scarcely curled, but each heavy lock, turned at the end, seemed to be a separate creature writhing from its fellows. No one who knew him could forget his eyes. They were blue but the pigmentation was so pale as to be startling . . . His body was never still, and he wore his clothes to bare patches at the knees and elbows. There are no words, no formal descriptions that can convey his strange magnetism. We only knew that beside him the rest of us waned in vitality, that he was dominant . . .

He had no lectures to attend, for he was a research student, and when the spirit moved him he would descend from the libraries, a hot jet of speech burning in him that would flare into a brilliant flame and set the whole company alight. He was older than the rest of us and he expressed for us our own conviction that the world was all wrong.

The identification of the hero is clinched by a passage in which he and the narrator heroine are sitting on a park bench and a giggling couple, the man's arm round the girl, pass by:

'Look at that! These are the fools we are trying to help, for whom we labour to build up a new system. They are not worth it. God! How I despise them – despise them . . . They only get what they deserve'.

Expressed in less ladylike language this refrain was to become only too familiar. The authoress, it appears, married happily and in her widowhood corresponded amiably, but without passion, with her old flame.

All through his time in London he saw a great deal of Veronica Wedgwood, dining together, going to the theatre and to Covent Garden. She supported her own historical researches by working on Lady Rhonddas's journal *Time and Tide* and as an editor for the brilliant, self-made publisher Jonathan Cape, whose history list in the 1930s was the most distinguished in London. Both these connexions bore fruit for her tutor.

Some of the scholars he met at the PRO and the Institute of Historical Research are well and sympathetically described in *Historians I Have Known*, notably Namier, J. E. Neale and R. H. Tawney. Some others such as Eileen Power the brilliant medievalist, whom he liked and admired, are not, though he set down in his journals a good deal of personal information about them. Eileen Power was, it seems, hag-ridden by the fear of scandals that might be caused by a drunken and disreputable father. Interestingly Rowse says that J. E. Neale used her as a lay-figure for his memorable portrait of Queen Elizabeth. Did Neale tell him? Very possibly, as they became professionally very close to each other.

The reader of Rowse's later fulminations cannot but smile at his delight in meeting the great Shakespearean Dr Hotson (whose amusing and brilliant research assistant, Nellie O'Farrell, was later to serve Rowse in the same capacity for many years. Her letters are as pithy and penetrating about her fellow-labourers in the PRO as about the documents she was inspecting or transcribing on his behalf). His Labour candidacy, reinforced by his Oxford friendships and connexions with such figures as G. D. H. Cole and Douglas Jay, brought him into the circle of contributors to the *New Statesman*, the *New Clarion* and the *Political Quarterly*. T. S. Eliot, as we shall see, regularly invited him to write articles and reviews for the *Criterion*. But deeper than all this, deeper than Labour activism or the serious journalism in which he was establishing a reputation, ran the current that was bearing him towards Tudor history. On 6 April 1935 he wrote in his diary: 'My interest in Tudor history goes back earlier than anything else in my mental life, far earlier than politics, before poetry, even earlier than my interest in the Church when, a boy of nine or ten, I used to call in at my great-aunt's on my way home from the elementary school at Carclaze, and she had an old book on English history there . . . I was fascinated by the middle chapters about "Bloody Mary" – Mary Tudor. Aunt Rowe was vexed at never being able "to get a word out of me". That book was so absorbing.' The child was father to the man.

10

Early Publications

Rowse's early books are of more interest for their connexions than for their content. *On History* (1927) with its admiring quotation of Froude and its lucid exposition of Marxian historical insights states positions to which, in spite of their unlikely conjunction, the author was to remain faithful. But its importance is not so much what it says as that it was both praised by André Maurois and approved by such *bien pensant* communist Fellows of Trinity College, Cambridge as Maurice Dobb and Piero Sraffa. Visits were exchanged, friendly correspondence was maintained and Rowse was invited by Dobb to join the editorial board of a projected Marxist academic journal, envisaged as an intellectual forerunner of the Popular Front movement of the late thirties, which in fact never reached the stage of publication. It is clear that Rowse was never regarded as a Fellow Traveller and certainly not as a potential recruit to the Party. His declared Labour affiliation was recognized as genuine. But his credentials as an informed Marxist were recognized too. His assistance was sought, somewhat testily, by the editor of a forty-volume edition of Marx's writings in obtaining a correspondence in the possession of 'Sligger' Urquhart, the Balliol don remembered (and sometimes caricatured in fiction) as the patron of the fashionable homosexual undergraduate literati of the twenties and thirties. Sligger's father, it appears, had been one of Marx's favourite correspondents. Rowse was never a member of Sligger's circle: indeed its conspicuously Public School composition would have raised his hackles. But Richard Pares was, and no doubt could have acted as go-between. I have found no evidence that Rowse responded to the request.

Politics and the Younger Generation (1931) marks a much more fruitful stage in its author's career. Fifty years later he remembered and valued it for the close involvement of T. S. Eliot in its gestation.[1]

The other day I came across the original manuscript of my early book, *Politics and the Younger Generation* which he nursed into print (along with the first volumes of my poetry). In the years between then and now Stephen Spender asked me if I wouldn't update the book in an article for *Encounter* . . . Truth to tell, after the appalling experiences that had intervened – the ruin of all our hopes with the rise of Nazism and Fascism, the deformation of Communism and the terrible example of Soviet Russia, the Second World War heralding a nuclear world – I could not bear to read that early book with its hopes betrayed, blown sky-high.

I still have not re-read it, and am not going to comment on it, merely use Eliot's comments on it all the way through as an intimate glimpse into *his* mind. Perhaps it will serve, too, as a unique example of that discriminating mind's reflections upon another man's work. Critical as he was, like all first-rate men he was fundamentally encouraging. He not only accepted for publication the idealistic young author's blue-print for the future, with all its illusions and imperfections, but constantly urged me to write about politics for *The Criterion*. This did not deflect me from history and historical research, but to some extent it postponed my writing history: perhaps not a bad thing, for history and politics go together and both are subjects for mature minds, not for the young, as I then was. After going through my manuscript carefully, Eliot came down to All Souls to discuss it: I can see him now, sitting on that capacious sofa in the Smoking-room, sharp pencil in hand, the precise voice, all as I have described him in a later poem:

> Look once more into your eye, limpid and sad,
> Note the old expression at once severe and gay,
> Diffidence and kindness in your anxious smile.

The article goes on to record editorial queries and criticisms and the arguments to which they gave rise. Eliot brought a more fastidious

1. 'T. S. Eliot Fifty Years After', *The Yale Literary Magazine*, vol. 149, no. 3, December 1981, pp. 67–73. The quotations in the text are from the holograph draft in the Rowse papers.

sense of language as well as a far more radical scepticism to the work in hand. His letters pull no punches. Thanking the author for sending him his *Tudor Cornwall* on 19 June 1942 he wrote:

I have been delaying my thanks and expression of appreciation until I could say that I know the whole book. What I can say at the moment is that I found it extremely interesting, it seems to me a good book and you do not seem to me to be taking that meticulous pains to write badly which is evident in some of your earlier work. If you are not careful you will end by writing very good English.

This might be taken as the licensed teasing of old friendship (Eliot's first letter to Rowse, accepting a letter for publication in *The Criterion*, is dated 30 September 1927). But not entirely. From the beginning Eliot gave his friend the benefit of the same searching criticism to which he subjected his own work. Rowse's review of Aldous Huxley's *Essays* on 14 November 1934 prompted this response:

I must really take you to task for the use of so many tired and worn out words and phrases, such as 'the nature of the beast' which only give the impression of your having written it in a great hurry. Must I be expected to re-write the works of the Left Wingers for them?

Earlier that year Rowse had sent him some of his poems. On 29 August Eliot replied 'I have made some comments on your poems . . . The matter of the poems seems to me to exist, but the poems don't seem to be written yet.'

A young writer might have found this rather Olympian. But Eliot, as Rowse recognized in the poem already quoted, never criticized *de haut en bas*. In a later letter (22 March 1941) he writes of his own methods of composing 'If I didn't kid myself into believing that I was only concerned with a technical problem I couldn't get on with it at all.'

If Rowse's appreciative 'Diffidence' is a happy application to Eliot, so is 'hurry' in Eliot's letters to him. He *was* in a hurry, a tearing hurry. He wanted to turn the country from the fatuities and injustices of a domestic policy which was set on preserving the value of the pound at no matter what cost in the social misery of unemployment, he burned to replace the vague benignity of the Labour leadership by the practicality of Bevin and Morrison, he saw from the first the hideous totality of evil personified in the Nazis, and when all this had been dealt with (no small order) he wanted to be a poet, a great (not a run of the mill) historian, a Cornishman who, assisted by his friends Charles Henderson and Sir Arthur Quiller Couch, would renew the ancient glories of that romantic land. And all this while fighting off the debilities and embarrassments of undiagnosed duodenal ulceration that came close to killing him.

Politics dominated the intellectual consciousness of the 1930s to an extent that a late Victorian or Edwardian would have found astonishing. Certainly the Oxford dons at the time of Rowse's birth would have. But politics took up a good deal of Eliot's correspondence with Rowse, whom he was anxious to consult and to employ as an exponent of Left Wing views. Eliot was emphatic that he wanted *young* comparatively unknown figures. 'I think I will try Ayerst . . . You're quite sure he has a mind of his own?' (10 February 1930). Ayerst's review of *Politics and the Younger Generation* was to give all too decisive an answer to that question. The comprehensiveness to which *The Criterion* aspired is well illustrated by Eliot's suggestion (27 August 1928) that Rowse should contribute to a symposium on Shaw's *Intelligent Woman's Guide* together with Laski, Belloc and Father D'Arcy. Did Rowse judge that this comprehensiveness verged on nihilism? On 2 March 1931, Eliot, informing him that he had put in a sympathetic note about Mosley in his next 'Commentary', wrote:

My own 'toryism' is only intelligible on the understanding that there are no Tories in politics at all, and that I don't much like any government since Charles I, and that Disraeli was a Jew film producer only commendable because so much less intolerable than Gladstone.[1]

Again and again the note sounded is that every case should be given a fair hearing. On 17 November 1928 Eliot urged Rowse to write an

1. In case this jape should be seized on by persons ambitious of founding a reputation on representing Eliot as anti-Semitic there is in the Rowse papers a letter of 8 January 1934 asking if he has any ideas about forming academic groups to help refugees, suggested by Eliot's friend, a New York Jew called Kallen.

article for *The Criterion* on Communism 'to succeed (and eclipse) mine on the Literature of Fascism'. In this letter he declines Rowse's proposal to put him up as a candidate for the Professorship of Poetry: 'I should have to take an M.A. and I have no time for such kickshaws unless they were pressed into my hand: and I am too disreputable a figure anyhow.' Fairness could not go farther than this (14 June 1929) 'I enclose a page proof of my notes on Barnes and yourself:[1] you will probably think it very silly and amateurish and if you care to show me up I will reserve three or four pages for you in the September number.' Rowse's retrospective annotation: 'What a gent!' was surely deserved.

The mellow recollection of Eliot's editorial criticism shows that it exposed not only slovenliness of language but also of thought. Many of his points went home, such as the insight that 'Communism flourished because it grew so easily on the Liberal root.' Rowse's own detestation of Liberalism was more political than Eliot's. In Cornwall it was the great lumbering Liberal Nonconformist consensus that obstructed everything fresh and original. It was the force that gave the Conservatives their easy supremacy over Labour. Eliot, knowing and caring nothing about politics, used the term, as Newman had done, to describe tendencies in philosophy and thought. Respecting each other's differing opinions the two often disagreed in their estimation of people. 'Some day I should like to get you and [Charles] Smyth[2] in the ring together' wrote Eliot in January 1929. He achieved this, to Rowse's fury, by sending him *Politics and the Younger Generation* for review. Eliot's reply on 13 January 1932 to what was evidently a very angry letter is a model of good sense and good nature. The happiest of relations were soon restored. 'I am convinced' wrote Eliot on 11 March 1932 'that you are the most lovable prig that I have ever known.' Rowse seems to have replied with a *tu quoque*, answered on 10 June 'Of course I know I have been called a prig, you goose: that's how I made my acquaintance with the word.'

1. Eliot's criticism of the two articles he had commissioned: from Rowse on Marxism and from J. S. Barnes, Secretary General of the International Centre of Fascist Studies on Fascism.
2. Fellow of Corpus Christi College, Cambridge, subsequently Rector of St Margaret's, Westminster and Canon of the Abbey. A preacher and controversialist of some reputation. Rowse regarded him as his intellectual inferior.

The publication of *Politics and the Younger Generation*, a book in every way so out of place on the Faber list, can only be interpreted as a declaration of intent to publish Rowse's future literary and historical works. 'We do not publish books; we publish authors' was the maxim of the best publishers of the day. Faber's were indeed to publish his poetry. But the historical books with which he made his name, *Sir Richard Grenville of the Revenge* (1937) and *Tudor Cornwall* (1941), and the first of the autobiographies that were to become bestsellers, *A Cornish Childhood* (1942), all came out under the imprint of Jonathan Cape. Eliot and Geoffrey Faber both had something to say about this as we shall see. But before rushing to moral judgments it may be helpful to chart the course of Rowse's literary activity. This was, in the thirties, largely political, though by no means exclusively so. He tried his hand at short stories, a medium he continued to toy with for the rest of his life. He reviewed books on Tudor history. He published one or two learned articles in the approved Ph.D. manner such as 'The Dispute concerning the Plymouth pilchard fishery 1584–1591' in the *Journal of Economic History* for January 1932. He began his successful career as a broadcaster with a series of talks presenting the Elizabethan Age through the personalities of some of its outstanding figures. At Veronica Wedgwood's suggestion he embarked on a play about the Queen, of which we shall hear more. And of course he wrote poetry. But politics, both theoretical and immediate, dominated his output.

Sometimes his articles could be expanded, or simply reprinted, as separate publications, such as *The Question of the House of Lords*, originally an article in the *Political Quarterly* but subsequently published by Leonard and Virginia Woolf as a pamphlet. This form achieved its most interesting effect in the publication – in hard covers – of *Mr Keynes and the Labour Movement*. Briefly its argument was that the *political* consequences of Keynes's *economic* doctrine contained in his *General Theory of Employment, Interest and Money* logically ranged its author on the side of the Labour Party. Rowse sent it to him before publication and Keynes's reply, dated 12 May 1936, was extremely encouraging. He agreed that there was 'little divergence between the political implications of my ideas and the policy of the Labour Party . . . I should officially join that party if it did not seem to be divided between enthusiasts who turn against a thing if there seems a chance that it could possibly happen, and leaders so conservative that there is more to hope from Mr Baldwin'. He added that he was sending a copy of his letter to Harold Macmillan as an encouragement to publication. Macmillan did indeed publish, in an orange-tomato jacket appropriate to the colour of the contents. Keynes wrote another appreciative letter on 6 October. 'Some of it makes me blush a little . . . It is a problem how best to bring ideas into relation with politics. I am of course in favour of a popular front' in favour, that is, of 'groups seeking affiliation with the Labour Party'. To effect a junction of official Liberal and Labour was, in his view, altogether too difficult.

Unlike his fellow luminary in the constellation of Cambridge Apostles, Bertrand Russell, whom Rowse had never thought much of and came to think less and less, Keynes always shone brightly above the darkness. Four years earlier Rowse had circulated an article sketching the argument developed in his book, which had elicited a letter of qualified approval from Roy Harrod, but unqualified praise for its subject: 'I do think there is probably more wisdom and truth in him than in any living Englishman' – curiously Victorian phraseology for a letter written in July 1932. The relationship was never close but continued, unlike so many, unclouded. 'A very excellent letter in to-day's *Manchester Guardian*' wrote Keynes on 24 October 1938 a propos of Rowse's denunciation of 'the Inner Cabinet that has led us to this pass [the loss of all that had been achieved at the cost of a million lives in the war of 1914–18] – Mr Chamberlain, Sir John Simon, Sir Samuel Hoare' and his call for a reconstruction of the Government on national, non-party lines. Labour must come to an understanding with 'the Liberals under Sir Archibald Sinclair, who has been right all along on these issues' to support such an administration, which would contain such prominent conservatives then out of office as Churchill, Cranborne, Duff Cooper, Amery, and Ormsby-Gore. 'I conceive that it would be led by such a person as Mr Eden.' This long letter was reinforced by editorial support.

From his correspondence with Veronica Wedgwood it appears that she suggested the idea of his writing a play about Queen Elizabeth in 1933. The first draft was sent to Bernard Shaw, not, so far as I can discover, even an acquaintance of the author. The courtesy, thoroughness and point of the reply, written in pencil in his own hand, demands printing in its entirety.

Ayot St Lawrence, Welwyn, Herts.

5th Nov 1933

Dear Rowse,

This play is too long: it would take more than four hours to perform even if, like St Joan, it were all done in one stage set.

The first scene is a false start. It prepares the audience for a play of which Raleigh is the hero. As he peters out completely afterwards it is a mistake to introduce him under so famous a name. In a play a nobody must be an unknown: if you call him Alexander or Hercules the audience will expect great things from him and want its money back if they are not forthcoming. The part is really only that of a gentleman-usher. Call him Smith and cut him down to his bare function of introducing the situation. You can then let your fancy loose on him by making him amusing.

As the rest is pure chronicle there is no arguing with it. Elizabeth and Essex, Cecil and Bacon are well drawn and have effective parts within chronicle limits; but Shakespear would have put in a strong scene of Essex astounded by Bacon's ingratitude and reproaching him in a big tirade.

I think you carry the dramatic parsimony of the conscientious chronicler too far in Elizabeth's death scene. A great actress would ask you for a little more stuff. The recollection of how Mary was deserted on her deathbed, the feeling that Nelson must have had in the cockpit when he realized that nobody would attend to his orders now that his number was up, the suspicion that they were all communicating with James (why not let her hear the horse gallop away, and overwhelm Cecil in a last transport of fury as she guessed the errand and the sender, the order to send him to the Tower being cut short by the death rattle in her throat?): surely there are lots of chances for the actress if only you would offer them to her.

The trial scene is very literal; but here I think you are right not to interfere with it, though the Essex–Bacon motive should be exploited as aforesaid.

Elizabeth's heartbreak about Essex is a bit conventional. Why not make more of her contempt for his political incompetence finally getting the better of his worn-out sexual attraction? I cannot believe that she was not glad to be rid of him.

I think this is all I can usefully say. The historian has the upper hand of the dramatist in this play; but that will wear off with experience.

In great haste,
   busy rehearsing
     G. Bernard Shaw

It is sad that this brilliant criticism, so generous and so encouraging, did not stimulate Rowse to a creation worthy of it. There is evidence of some reworking but the typescript of the final text entitled 'Essex and Elizabeth' would give Shaw little ground for altering his judgment of the original, that the historian has the upper hand of the dramatist. He sent it to John Gielgud and to Edith Evans, who found it 'insufficiently theatrical, by that I mean lines to be spoken upon a stage'.

He also sent it to Eliot who wrote on 21 March 1938 a sympathetic and encouraging letter, promising to send it to Ashley Dukes, at that time manager of the Mercury theatre where he had achieved an immense success with Eliot's *Murder in the Cathedral*. As usual Eliot put a suggestion of criticism as though it were directed at himself: 'One of the great difficulties, I find, in dramatic writing is that of remembering all the characters at every moment. You simply cannot leave people doing nothing . . .' He had consulted Rowse about the historical reading he had undertaken. He was pleased by Rowse's appreciation of the play and made gentle fun of the inference of Right Wing opinions:

I observe that my friends who have leanings towards the Left are inclined to suspect me of being a fascist, and if I knew any fascists, which I don't, I should expect them to accuse me of flirting with communism. It is, I think, almost essential to the position of any heretic to suspect anyone who does not share his particular heresy, of being committed to the opposite complementary heresy . . . The Right is just as alien to me as the Left.

Earlier, in 1934, there had been talk of their sharing a flat. In a letter of 12 October Eliot had set out the difficulties presented by his marital and legal status and the idea lapsed. In view of Rowse's strong and ever stronger preference for solitude and his quickness to take, and give, offence this was surely fortunate. Only six months before the friendly letter about his political opinions just quoted Eliot had written, on 18 January 1935, 'Dear Rowse, In reply to your peremptory and supercilious card I don't either truthfully or mendaciously mean to say anything at all.' That had been in reply to a demand that a book Rowse thought important should be reviewed in *The Criterion*. Domestic peace could hardly have been maintained when it became plain that Rowse was going to publish his first historical biography elsewhere.

The reason for this, as distinct from its justification, is fairly clear. Jonathan Cape, an entirely self-made publisher of no formal education, was the most remarkable of a generation of publishers that included Victor Gollancz, Stanley Unwin and Billy Collins. His success rested on his having come up the hard way into the book trade, errand boy, bookpacker, travelling salesman and then manager, combined with that quality, eluding definition, which shelters behind the name of flair. Jonathan's flair was in picking literary advisers and backing their judgment. In the middle thirties his adviser on the choice of history books was J. E. Neale, of whose seminar in Tudor History at the Institute of Historical Research Rowse was a member. 'When I had finished, as I thought, my biography of Sir Richard Grenville, I deliberately opted for Cape as publisher, because I wanted it to be vetted by our leading Elizabethan scholar, who was reader for that firm'[1] wrote Rowse candidly more than half a century later. In an unpublished sketch of Geoffrey Faber, among those portraits of his All Souls colleagues already mentioned, a rather different explanation is advanced. He admits that he wanted the book vetted by Neale. But he prefaces this by the statement that Fabers did not lose money on *Politics and the Younger Generation* and that they had refused a collection of broadcasts and articles written in collaboration with G. B. Harrison, submitted under the title *Elizabethan Essays*, which Fabers had promptly stolen for T. S. Eliot's next book of criticism. The collaboration with Harrison was, he adds, published by Allen and Unwin.

Well, well. One can understand the feelings of Faber and of Eliot, expressed with admirable irony by Eliot in a letter of 25 March 1943 after Rowse had published not only his *Tudor Cornwall* (1941) but

1. *Historians I Have Known*, p. 85.

also his best-selling *A Cornish Childhood* (1942) with Cape. 'I can understand your honourable motives for offering your autobiography to Cape as an inducement to publish *Tudor Cornwall*. The arrangement does credit equally to your own modesty and to his acumen and I am sure that neither of you has cause to regret the bargain, but you know you did promise Geoffrey the autobiography at the time when we took the poems: he seems to have chosen to overlook this but I had not forgotten his mentioning it with quite definite assurance at the time. That really is the justification for my having exhumed the question later.' Rowse seems to have defended himself by bluster about Fabers refusing to publish the text of 'Essex and Elizabeth' to which Eliot replied on 10 April in a letter of exemplary urbanity: '[To publish] any play, however good, is a hopeless undertaking unless it has already been performed with a success of esteem at least. Plays are meant to be PERFORMED. A musician can judge of the merit of a composition by reading the score; but Nobody knows about a play before it is realized on the stage; . . . though I don't say an unproduced play by Bernard Shaw wouldn't sell; and I might get a modest sale myself (1500) because some people would want to know whether there was any poetry in it . . .' The letter opens with thanks for '. . . an undeserved compliment . . . I shall cherish yours second to that of Bernard Berenson who opined that I was wasting my talents over literature and ought to be writing political leaders.'

To judge from the rest of the letter the compliment appears to have been paid on Eliot's professional and commercial astuteness, a tribute more appropriate to Cape who by the sheer saleability of his list forced the book trade to reduce their customary discount. Not less professional was the editorial rigour of J. E. Neale. The reader will perhaps recall Rowse's phrase quoted a page or two ago 'when I had finished, as I thought, my biography of Sir Richard Grenville'. What lay behind it was Neale's powerful letter (undated) of criticism after reading the two volumes of typescript:

I liked the Virginia chapter (far more readable than the Last Fight chapter), the Armada chapter and the closing few pages. But even in these best parts there is often a diffuseness. There are other parts . . . that need criticising as drastically as the first volume.

You obviously *can* write to interest the general reader when the material readily lends itself to this. What you have to do is to impose this interest on the story when the material is hostile . . . I should not be honest if I did not say that drastic work is needed on it and not a mere touching up . . . And I am too much concerned about your reputation to be polite.

Good luck to you, Rowse, and pardon my momentary role as a brute.

In spite of ill-health, a host of other commitments both political and literary and that combination of relief and fatigue that follows the end of sustained literary effort, Rowse set to. The fundamental difficulty of writing the biography in the first place had been the wholesale destruction of documentary evidence. Two Grenville family houses had been pulled down and at the second of these catastrophes all the papers had been thrown away. The archives of Bideford, the port from which Grenville had conducted his privateering operations and had set sail on his own colonizing voyages, had scarcely a scrap of paper surviving from the period. The life had therefore to be built up from what could be found in the Public Records, always fragmentary and in this case made more opaque by the misdating of key documents in Grenville's career. Rowse's discovery of a contemporary account in the Spanish archives of the last fight of the *Revenge* transformed the image so powerfully projected in Tennyson's poem.

The absence of personal papers had led Rowse to open the biography with an account of Grenville's family connexions and social setting, matters on which long hours in the PRO had provided an abundance of material. This Neale forbade, making him cut ten thousand words and bring the subject of the biography on stage in the first chapter. His stern directive cost the author three months' work: but he never ceased to be grateful for it. The publication of the book in 1937 rescued a vivid and important Elizabethan figure from an obscurity that had been overlaid by literary legend and established the reputation of its author as a scholar equipped by temperament as much as by learning to make his mark in the study of that age.

II

A Man of the Thirties

The title of this chapter is borrowed from the continuation of the autobiography begun with *A Cornish Childhood*. The volume, published in 1979, is not true to its description since it ends with the year 1931 which Rowse had come to identify as the turning point to disaster. Yet as a description of its author it is agonizingly true. We all know the classic situation of nightmare in which, mysteriously rooted to the spot, we await the closer approach of some terrifyingly malignant, if impersonal, force whose only known quality is that we cannot escape it. That was how Rowse saw the world, after Hitler had come to power at the beginning of 1933.

At the time, of course, he had not accepted the inevitability of disaster. Alive, much more alive than most of his contemporaries, to the danger he was active, urgent, in trying to rally his party to such leading figures as Dalton and Bevin who saw the folly of pacifism and disarmament and the self-deceiving feebleness of appeasement. Contemptuous of the lazy indifference of Baldwin and the National Government he was enraged by the idiocy of the Left Wing intellectuals such as G. D. H. Cole or R. H. S. Crossman,[1] whose gifts made idiocy a sin. At my first meeting with Rowse in 1946 I remember his giving an account of walking round and round Radcliffe Square with Crossman one night in the mid-thirties, Rowse growing more and more frenzied as Crossman denied the menace of Nazism on the grounds that the name of the party, National Socialist, showed that its heart was in the right place. It may sound laughable

1. Roger Fulford in a letter to Rowse remarks 'there is something undeniably sinister about three initials in full use – the mind leaps to A.J.P.'

now, but Rowse's anger and despair are easily understandable.

By the time he came to write *A Man of the Thirties* Rowse had come to think of himself as rejected and rejecting. Although he quotes from his diaries and pocket books they have become documents like those he was accustomed to interpreting in libraries and record offices. He readily breaks off to give an acrid summary of what happened after they were written, to draw a general and generally disillusioning inference about the subsequent course of events, or to denounce some individual of the late 1970s whose attitude he dislikes. The essays, articles and reviews that he collected and published in *The End of an Epoch: Reflections on Contemporary History* (1947) give a far better panorama of what he thought and wrote in the thirties. A shorter summary of his unchanging, indeed unchangeable, view of that dreadful decade, focused on the personalities of his senior colleagues at All Souls, is presented in *All Souls and Appeasement: A Contribution to Contemporary History* (1961). With the single exception of its misrepresentation of Sir Hubert Henderson[1] as an appeaser it gives a brilliant and incisive account of the mismanagement and plain refusal to face facts of the half-dozen men principally responsible for the conduct of affairs, three of whom were Fellows of All Souls and personally on friendly terms with their vehement young critic.

The indictment carries the more conviction because the author liked the men he was attacking, Geoffrey Dawson, the editor of *The Times* throughout the whole disastrous period, and Simon and Halifax, both Foreign Secretaries and when not at the Foreign Office supporters of the Appeasement Policy in Cabinet. He liked them and he nowhere imputes base or unpatriotic motives to them, in contrast to *Guilty Men* (1940), the effusion of three Beaverbrook journalists who concealed both their authorship and the fact that their employer had

---

1. Henderson's widow wrote strong letters of protest, both to Rowse and to Warden Sparrow, who promised that a correction and apology would be printed in any future edition. He also instructed the Librarian to insert Lady Henderson's letter in the prelims of the copy presented to the Codrington. Rowse admits (p. 111) that Henderson was one of the only two Fellows of that time whom he did not like. Sir Isaiah Berlin confirmed to the author that Henderson was a consistent opponent of appeasement.

himself been an Appeaser of the first water. An even rarer evidence of authorial candour is the fact that Rowse admits himself guilty of misjudgment in a letter to *The Times*, printed in the prime position on the morrow of the Norway Debate which finally brought Chamberlain down, urging that Halifax should be invited to form a Coalition Government.[1]

Thucydides is perhaps the last historian with whom Rowse invites comparison, yet *All Souls and Appeasement* is the most Thucydidean of his books. Both writers were passionate, but both had their passion under control: both had played, or done their best to play, some part in the public affairs of which they wrote and both had, in practical terms, failed and were conscious of their failure: both thought that avoidable disaster had overtaken the great civilization each loved with the special intensity of adoption, Thucydides a Thracian who saw Athens as the Hellas of Hellas, Rowse a Cornishman forever distinguishing his Celtic temperament from the Englishness of England. The book evoked a wide response, nearly all enthusiastic. The Dutch historian Pieter Geyl admired and approved though dissenting from Rowse's conclusion that the condition of Western Europe was terminal. Erich Eyck, the German historian, congratulated him both on the book and on his rejection of A. J. P. Taylor's arguments. Sir Anthony Eden and Noel Coward approved, Coward[2] enthusiastically so. But perhaps the most interesting letter of all was from Willy Bretscher, editor-in-chief of the *Neue Zurcher Zeitung*, the great Swiss newspaper whose tradition of well-informed, objective reporting is second to none. Bretscher had joined the paper in 1917, served as Berlin correspondent from 1925 to 1929 and had become editor-in-chief in 1933. 'I have rarely been so fascinated by a book dealing with the pre-war period ... I am deeply impressed by your insight into the particular psychology of the prominent British personalities who were responsible for most of the decisions.'

The most perceptive of all his insights is into the mentality of

1. See below, p. 139.
2. Coward had spent some of his childhood at Charlestown, the little port of St Austell where Rowse's parents had been married and now lie in the churchyard. Rowse obtained a generous cheque from Coward towards the restoration of the bell tower.

Geoffrey Dawson. The case against him verges on the criminal. He deliberately suppressed, altered, or toned down the despatches of *The Times* Berlin correspondent, Ebbutt, a first-class reporter with a penetrating understanding of the country, and eventually recalled him. He consistently intrigued, with ultimate success, for the replacement of our outstanding ambassador, Sir Eric Phipps, by a self-satisfied nonentity, Sir Nevile Henderson. Was this a faithful discharge of his duty to his readers, let alone to his country? Rowse, alive to the wickedness and folly of actions which went against all that he was fighting for, yet acquits him of any dishonourable intention. What Dawson and his circle were intent on was the preservation of our overseas Empire. Hitler's determination to undo the Treaty of Versailles presented, in their eyes, no direct threat, whereas the possible hostility of Fascist Italy might. At all costs Italy must not be antagonized and what went on in Eastern and Central Europe was no concern of ours unless it led to the extension of the power of Soviet Russia, the one overt declared enemy of all Empires except its own. Dawson and his friends had never read *Mein Kampf*. Rowse had and never for a moment, waking or sleeping (his mental life was extended and stimulated by his dreams) forgot its terribleness.

As we have seen, to be a man of the thirties in an active sense of the term was to be, like it or not, preoccupied with politics. Having to take to the boats because the ship one is aboard is sinking does not predicate an initial interest in navigation or seamanship. It is not choice but a stark question of survival. Rowse was, as it happens, actively interested in politics but it was only one of the irons in the fire. Music, painting, architecture, poetry, history, literature in general, all of these interested him even more.

A conversation with David Cecil on a summer night in Wadham garden in 1929, both young men intoxicated by the charm and beauty of Oxford, is in point. 'He went on about politics, wondering why it was I was attracted by it: he thought I should so dislike the life of practical compromise. Not for the first time I saw that David doesn't think me suited for politics.[1] He sees so much the literary and the

---

1. Annotated by Rowse half a century later: 'He was right – so much more adult and sophisticated, and with all that Cecil experience.'

hermit intellectual side of my life (like my diary). The other side he doesn't see much of.

'I'm elated tonight, for I have been hammering at a poem the last few days, this moment finished.'

The last paragraph confirms, artlessly, David Cecil's insight. Rowse rarely writes about politics in his diary, except to record. They do not fire his imagination, as books, places, atmosphere, talk, do. Even the politicians he admires, such as Herbert Morrison, whom he wished to see Leader of the Labour Party and whom he entertained at All Souls, are not described and realized as literary figures are. Take for instance his call on AE[1] while visiting Dublin at Easter 1929. 'I lumbered up many stairs of a Georgian mansion, not prepared for the mountain of flesh which filled the chair at the untidy desk. He started to talk immediately and went on and on. I thought I should never get a word in. He had got on to a story of how James Joyce first came to see him and was difficult to get going, arrogant and silent; and how himself blathered away until Joyce was ready to say something – was he playing the same game with me?'

Rowse's portraiture like John Betjeman's sets his subject in its proper milieu, to the extent that the milieu itself can often suggest the subject. Roaming through the ex-Kaiser's rooms in the Schloss in Berlin with Adam von Trott whose uncle had a flat there, or through Frederick the Great's *Sans Souci*, the long-departed occupants come alive for him. To engage with the living meant yielding too much of one's own privacy. The dead could be loved or hated without fear of reciprocity. Quick sketches of contemporaries, sometimes as quick as the flash of a speed-camera, are as a rule all that he permits himself. Thus on Baldwin:

It was in the Codrington Library at All Souls, one day early on in my days there; I was seated at one of the long tables in the bay working, when Warden Pember in full silvery handsomeness came with his old Harrow friend the Prime Minister, walking in a leisurely way down the length of that noble room. When they came abreast they looked in my direction, Warden Pember

1. The pseudonym of G. W. Russell (1867–1935), Yeats's friend and fellow poet, co-founder of the Abbey Theatre.

with his usual nervous self-consciousness, Baldwin alert, powerfully-built, countrified. There were the so familiar, so often caricatured features, the sparse, rust-coloured hair parted in the middle: the iron-master, leader of the Tory Party, master of Britain.'[1]

That is a glimpse from the days of comparative innocence before Hitler had come to power and Baldwin, for all his high-minded love of his country, was steering it for the rocks. But with the best will in the world was it possible to expect much more effective opposition to Hitler from Léon Blum, the French Socialist leader soon to head a Popular Front government, whom Rowse met tête à tête on 10 January 1934?

I liked him at once, and instinctively: one could sense his was a nice nature and a sincere one. He had the professional bonhomie of the politician, took me by the shoulders and beamed altogether more amicably than the chore of my visit warranted. But I had the feeling that, beneath it, he was not displeased by the presence of a young man: as if he genuinely *liked* it.

He received me in a curious garb which I couldn't make out, I didn't like to look too closely, for it was open at the neck and his feet were bare. I thought of those dreadful Fabian women going about barefoot in honour of the prophets,[2] later I realized he was in pyjamas and dressing-gown, in fact was not dressed at noon!

I couldn't help thinking what with this and the exquisite surroundings he lives in, an apartment in a beautiful seventeenth-century house, with the best French furniture, a piano, charming statuettes and his hall stacked with books that anything in the nature of a revolution, or even vigorous socialist action could not come out of such a milieu.

Would Rowse have wanted it to? More than a year earlier, on 4 November 1932, he had written

Tonight, for the first time, it struck me with force how paradoxical my way of life, or rather the sources from which I draw my subsistence, and the

1. *All Souls and Appeasement*, p. 54.
2. Presumably Hubert Bland et al.

world I am always arguing for and to which I am pledged, are. Going down the miserable side-street in the rain to the post-box, I thought, here I am, bent upon rooting out all these interests living upon the rent that others produce – and my living is provided out of the unearned increment of north London at All Souls; and out of donations from capitalists whom I want to make an end of, at the School of Economics. Not only that, but, save for a small group of realist, hard-minded people – Morrison and Ernest Bevin above all; Dalton it is impossible to like and Cole ridiculous to think of following – I cannot collaborate with the people I most agree with.

A rigorous intellectualism flinches from recognizing that not all good ends are compatible with each other. If they are good, they must be; or else the term is meaningless. For some minds relief can be found in the tenebrosities of mysticism or the easy chair of pluralism. But not for the feverishly energetic, fiercely defining, Rowse. 'I look into my heart and what do I see? A socialist. I look into my head and what do I see? A fascist.' This undated outburst in a pocket-book of this period politicizes what were, and always had been, the contradictions inherent in his temperament and in the multiplicity of his responses. Never was there a more complete antithesis to Bagehot's telling judgment of Macaulay 'an inexperiencing nature'. The day before calling on Léon Blum Rowse had attended Vespers and Rosary at the church of St Roch, conscious of his own unbelief, reflecting that if one was a Frenchman one would have to be brought up a Catholic if one was to enter both into the historical essence of one's country and into the sceptical rejection so characteristic of the French mind. Moved, he yet records his preference for the liturgy and the music of the Church of England that had always meant much more to him than the Christianity that was its raison d'être.

All this on top of the strenuous political activity to which he had committed himself was edging him towards the sourness and sterility of a solipsism that did not sort with the warmth and generosity of his nature:

The people suffer: but it is largely their own fault, especially in so far as they have never wholeheartedly supported their own cause. Poor fools: half of them voted for the National Government. I have never forgiven them that . . .

You cannot trust the people; you cannot trust anybody, only one or two rare individuals: in the end, there is oneself alone. There is hardly a soul that I can really consult – in the sense of opening to him my own troubles of mind.[1]

He had tried it with von Trott, or would have done if he had not found himself after his first anxious steps sinking into the fogbound ooze of Hegelian verbiage. He had tried it with Claude Berry, his staunch Labour supporter in Penryn and Falmouth, to be met with perplexity and disapproval. Manysidedness has its penalties even if they are not so obvious as its advantages.

Rowse, at all stages of his long life, combined it with what Richard Church in a letter to him well described as 'energy, amounting to genius'. Even in middle life he thought nothing of a ten or eleven hour day of writing and research, kept up over weeks at a stretch. As a young man, and, let us remember, not at all a fit young man, here he is on 22 July 1933.

However, I've done a fair day's work. Two articles, one for the *Cornish Labour News*; a really good one on the World Economic Conference for the *Clarion*. Letters and correcting the proof of a review. The past week I have worked like hell, written two reviews, two articles, addressed a Sunday Conference at Maidstone, 3 p.m. to 8 p.m. pretty solid; spoke to a school discussion club at Croydon, dined with Veronica Wedgwood, worked very hard at my Cornish research, having made detailed notes of the Douai Diaries[2] and potted laboriously the whole of Savine's book on the Dissolution of the Monasteries. Also three longish, unhappy, incomplete poems of the sort I write now, while walking in the evenings; besides a score of letters or more.

The focusing of his Tudor studies on the little land to which he felt such passionate loyalty brought an immediacy which extended itself to his later work on the age as a whole. He sought out the places and,

---

1. Diary, 4 November 1932.
2. An important source for the history of the Cornish recusants, drawn on in chapter XIV of *Tudor Cornwall*.

where he could, the descendants of the people who occupied his mind and his imagination. The greatest of all the Cornish families of the sixteenth century, the Arundells of Lanherne, had been among the staunchest of adherents to the old faith. The old house had been turned into a convent: the family had long left Cornwall and the last survivor of its Wardour branch with whom Rowse formed a rewarding friendship was to be killed in the war. On 5 September 1931 Rowse, accompanied by the architect of Blackfriars at Oxford, paid the ladies a visit:

Doran Webb and I were shown up to a shabby room (the whole house was down-at-heel) with two chairs set for us before an iron grille with a black muslin drawn across.

Doran Webb, completely at ease (he had been there often), said 'I've brought Mr Rowse to see you, who's a Fellow of All Souls College, Oxford.' 'We're pleased to see him.' 'We're very glad' said the voices from behind the veil. 'He's interested in the Arundells' he explained. 'Oh' said they, their voices in a little flutter of interest; 'then he's interested in Lanherne. It's a wonderful old place with a most interesting history. Have you see the chapel yet?' No, I hadn't; I should be glad to, if I might. 'Oh certainly.' It had been the ballroom, the sacristy a banqueting room (more likely the chapel was the hall, the sacristy a dining parlour at the dais end). The latter had a low plaster ceiling, with a room above; when altered, they had to re-roof it. But perhaps it was a providence, for they found the roof badly needed repair and in twenty years or so it might have fallen in.

All this with a sort of eagerness; half the nervousness of meeting a stranger.

I went on this tack for a bit and asked if the house had had a chapel.

Yes, said they together. Then one 'we call it now the Chapel Cells. We had it made into cells for the sisters, but you can see the roof decoration and the plasterwork still.'

Rowse still felt tense while Doran Webb led them on to small talk and then to their co-religionists.

'Mr Rowse knows Father D'Arcy at Oxford.'
'Oh!' again the eager interest.
I told them I knew Martindale a little and what clever men they both are.

This pleased them and they launched forth about D'Arcy's new book *The Nature of Faith*. I teased them a bit by telling them how much it was praised by the Dean of St Paul's.

'Are you a Catholic?'

'No, but I've a great many Catholic friends in Oxford.'

They went on to discuss Newman and Manning and so back to the Elizabethan persecution and the sufferings of the Arundells. When Rowse touched on the martyrdom of Cuthbert Mayne, a missionary priest who was seized at the Arundell castle of Chideock in West Dorset

. . . I drew near the centre of their life's interest. They were quite excited, you could almost hear them lean forward on the other side. One said it was their greatest hope to find some clue to the whereabouts of his body. It was quartered, you know . . . Dorothy Arundell, who was a great relic-hunter, secured his skull . . . If ever I came on any clue, would I let them know?

'I would willingly, but it is so unlikely,' I said.

'Oh, but it's the unexpected that happens so often.'

What a world they lived in: of providences, of the unexpected happening, of compensation for their life-long devotion in the forlorn hope of a victory here and there . . . They were so sweet and charming, and, in spite of being so enclosed in their own little world, so lively and intelligent.

This much abridged but still long and affectionate account shows how much more Rowse was capable of entering into religious attitudes he did not himself share than we would guess from the sneers and finger-wagging that have irritated, if not disgusted, so many readers of his published work. And what worlds away from the angry Labour candidate, the prophet of Marxian enlightenment, the Platonic lover of Adam von Trott and half a dozen other roles in which he had cast himself. This strong nerve of his consciousness is allied, strongly allied, to the poet, the researcher into the Tudor period and the Cornishman. It was agitated by two deaths: that of his father in March 1934, preceded by that of Charles Henderson the previous autumn.

Rowse had long looked on the empty beautiful house at Trenarren, three miles out of St Austell towards Black Head, its camellia and rhododendron circled garden sweeping down to a view of the sea, as the haven where he would be. On 12 June 1934 he wrote in his diary:

> Trenarren House.
>
> I have broken off in the middle of writing at my book, because there came into my mind too powerfully, the haunting image of how the road looks at Trenarren just where it turns into the house, that narrow neck where the trees open and you come suddenly into full view of the bay.
>
> Thinking of it so much – is it that I shall never live there after all? So much of my effort nowadays, working hard to make money and saving, is directed towards someday going there to live. I used to entice father with the idea, so that sometimes he may have half-thought we should go there; in the end he knew, and one day on his last drive there, looking over the gate he said to mother that someday when they were in the grave I might live there, but that he never should: it was too late for him . . .
>
> I see it so frequently when I am away from home: the bend of the road and the wall starred with primroses in spring, the fringe of beeches, leaning away from the south-west: the granite pillars on each side of the shut gate with a 'gentility ball' on each; inside, the desertedness of the house, always empty, except occasionally for a thin straggle of smoke ascending among the trees, always waiting . . .

It was a true vision. He was to spend the last forty-five years of his life there.

12

Arts and Letters

Dividing and categorizing seems almost the literary equivalent of vivisection. Maintaining a sequence of time in any work of history or biography obscures the wholeness of its subject. Narrative and analysis, both of which are needed if one is to understand anyone or anything outside one's direct experience, even, perhaps, within it, are *mauvais coucheurs*. Rowse's long life, his continuity of intellectual and aesthetic concern, reduce any attempt to isolate a stage or even to describe a period to a still photograph outside a cinema. A biographer cannot explain the cause of life and motion with the excluding singleness that a pathologist can establish the cause of death.

Not to write about Rowse's recognitions and excitements in arts and letters because his principal preoccupation was political and his professional ambition was to establish himself as a Tudor historian would be even more unsatisfactory than to compartmentalize them. Besides, it would be false to his own lifelong conviction that history not only was itself a form of literature but demanded from its student a knowledge of and sensibility to the arts and letters of his period. Certainly he set out to educate himself in the painting, the music, the architecture as well as the poetry and prose of the Tudor age. Not that he confined himself, by any means, to the sixteenth century. Like Pepys he stood in a strange slavery to beauty and like Pepys he found music the most enslaving of its forms until the deafness of extreme old age robbed him of its power. He had spent his first tutorial earnings on buying a Christopher Wood, that leader of the St Ives school, whom he would have loved to meet. In the Lutheran starkness of Hagen music was his illumination. Of English twentieth-century composers he was from the first a whole-hearted admirer of Vaughan

Williams, resenting the disparagement of the highbrow critics, of Britten (on 26 June 1945, he wrote to Norman Scarfe that he thought *Peter Grimes* 'the most indubitable work of genius in English music since *Belshazzar's Feast*') and of Michael Tippett, who proposed a collaboration on some Cornish theme. 'I've long been meditating [this] . . . I've always felt you know more about the background to the Fitzwilliam Book[1] than anyone else because of the particular melange of your musical sensibilities and local traditions and top-ranking scholarship.'[2] On 3 May 1950 he asked Rowse to suggest a Cornish monosyllabic name for the hero of *A Midsummer Marriage*. Rowse came up with Mark.

Among the painters and sculptors from whom he preserved letters are Augustus John, John Piper, Henry Lamb, Peter Lanyon, Barbara Hepworth, Patrick Heron, John Ward, Sean O'Sullivan and Sir William Coldstream. The two last both painted portraits of him, Coldstream's unhappily destroyed by enemy action. Coldstream's letters include one written in April 1941 urging him to write something about the exhibition of the Euston Road School held at the Ashmolean in that year. After the war Rowse was painted by Bratby and a portrait drawing was executed by Andrew Freeth RA in 1972. Throughout his life he bought pictures from living artists: Minton, Nash, Piper prominent among them. But it was with writers and scholars that the business and pleasure of his life chiefly lay. In *Historians I have known*, published only two years before his death, Rowse shows how vividly he apprehended the personal element in history and in those who wrote it in his own time. All the great names are there and nearly all of them are treated with appreciative understanding. The exceptions are those who had publicly criticized his work or privately dissented from his conclusions about Shakespeare's sonnets and his imperiously asserted identification of the Dark Lady. It is a remarkable book, astonishing for a man of ninety. But its judgments would not have been the same if he had written it in his thirties. A few of the writers

1. The Fitzwilliam Book was a large manuscript of keyboard music copied by the Cornishman Francis Tregian while in the Fleet prison between 1609 and 1619. It is now in the Fitzwilliam Museum at Cambridge.
2. This letter is dated 26 October but no year: probably c.1952.

he had not yet met or hardly knew. And in one case at least the estimate of the young Rowse would have been less favourable. The essay on G. M. Trevelyan ends with the ringing assertion 'I never had any doubt of his greatness as a man or his genius as a historian.' 'Never?' 'Well, hardly ever' as the libretto of *HMS Pinafore* has it.

While on holiday in Italy in 1937 (he had been given an introduction to Mussolini's Jewish mistress, Signora Sarfatti, whose offer to arrange an interview with the Duce was politely declined) he jotted down reflections on the intellectual and artistic life of England. Trevelyan does not come off well. He is allowed the merit of clear, good writing. But he plays up to mild liberal prejudices, seasoning his work with banalities about the beauty of the English countryside and the virtues of the English constitution. Balfour's criticism of his work on Italy, that the characters are all flat and there is no sharp appreciation of motive, is cited with approval. In his trilogy on Queen Anne the historical research is condemned as 'inadequate', altered in a much later hand to 'not up to date'. To sum up, his view of history lacks depth. 'But this is the way to the great heart of the public. This is the way to become in politics, Prime Minister, and in Literature an O.M., the similarity of character, intellectual indefiniteness, vague aroma of Englishness, utter out-of-date unrealism [later corrected to "complacency"] etc in the two characters of Mr Baldwin and Professor Trevelyan gives them much in common. No wonder they have a high [?regard] for each other.'

Away from his research material, away from his journalistic commitments, away from the gossip of All Souls and the Institute of Historical Research, away from his obligations as a Labour candidate (though it was probably these that led him to refuse Signora Sarfatti's invitation), Rowse has a rare moment to pause, to take stock, to evaluate and to compare. What a justification for the appointment of young men is that of Kenneth Clark to the National Gallery. The pathetic young Conservatives are all in their fifties, the young Liberals in their sixties. Clear out the old men. Herbert Morrison for Prime Minister. Who are the most brilliant men in England? Six. J. M. Keynes, Lancelot Hogben,[1] Auden, Russell, Shaw, Yeats.

1. Author of *Mathematics for the Million* and *Science for the Citizen*, two immensely successful works of popularization.

The absence of Cambridge mathematicians and physicists from a list which includes Hogben is strange. So is the inclusion of Russell, usually written down by Rowse. That Auden should be preferred to Eliot is even odder. Italian charm and sunshine must have encouraged him to kick up his heels. 'The English are a *great* people. Cornish, I see them from the outside . . . We have been absorbed, thank God, ever since the sixteenth century into a larger, richer life. Why does nobody say these things? History is so full of moans and complaints of dreary, moping Celts (ever since Gildas,[1] moping seems to have been their favourite occupation . . .)' Such sentiments sound more characteristic of Hugh Trevor-Roper, at that time a brilliant under-graduate whose career Rowse was concerned to foster, not the unfor-given author of a mocking review of *All Souls and Appeasement*.

Italy delighted him. He admired Viareggio railway station 'what I like modern architecture to be like' as well as famous buildings and paintings and the landscape, relating them to each other as an artist does. 'A forest of stone-pines. Not very largely grown but with bushy green tops and straight trunks so that you can see clear into the wood.' He is reminded of 'Uccello's painting of a forest scene by night in just such a wood – one of the loveliest pictures in the Ashmolean.' He recalls the Ashmolean collection 'mainly seventeenth and eighteenth centuries, and that appeals to my unprofessional, uneducated, rather freely arrived at, taste.' There ought to be many more local galleries where paintings now only to be seen in inaccessible, occasionally opened, country houses could be seen. England ought to take more care of its inheritance. 'I don't mind MSS so much going to America, but works of art, No!' Taking a wider view of the state of the world he deplores 'the ingenuity of clever men going into either direct obstruction of progress and good causes or (b) defeatism. Cf. Eliot, Wyndham Lewis & Co. If one tithe of this energy went into helping our human struggle what a difference! The diabolical effectiveness of the criminals of the modern world, Mussolini and Hitler and Ludendorff, directed to encouraging men to make war on each other, to regard peace as an illusion.' Beyond this confrontation of good and evil there were 'more difficult struggles to be won . . . disease, adverse

---

1. Sixth-century British historian.

external conditions of life, minor controls of mind making for happiness (in which we make some progress as we become older).'

From all this we see that Rowse in his middle thirties was not so alienated from the ideas of his generation as he sometimes liked to make out. Like all clever men he was often irritated by stupidity and intellectual laziness. In a notebook, undated but belonging to the same period, he sums up his view of Left and Right: 'On the Right you have sense and wickedness, on the Left idiocy and goodness. And I'd much rather have wickedness and sense any day than goodness and idiocy. It's the *idiocy* of people that lies at the root of all our troubles rather than wickedness.' Rowse was a historian, not a moral philosopher, still less a theologian.

Reading for the book that was eventually published as *Tudor Cornwall* but was at this stage still intended as a study of the Reformation led to a friendship with an ex-Oxford don whose learning, as well as his personal history, made him especially interesting to Rowse. Geoffrey Baskerville, a promising historian, had been a Fellow of Keble before the First World War when to everyone's astonishment and consternation he was convicted of homosexual offences and sent to prison. The heir to a beautiful house and estate near Henley he resumed his researches and published in 1937 his *English Monks and the Suppression of the Monasteries*, a racy account of a social upheaval far more readable than Savine's volume on the subject which Rowse records labouring over in the quoted extract from his diary in 1933. A long friendship and correspondence ensued. Both men loved gossip and enjoyed tittering over the sexual irregularities of long-dead divines. Baskerville was a friend of my father's (neither of them ever mentioned the catastrophe of his career. *Autre temps, autres moeurs*) and he and Rowse were amused by my father's refusal to include in the *Fasti Wyndesorienses* which he was then editing an anecdote about an Elizabethan canon of Windsor who kept a familiar spirit that slapped people's bottoms. Baskerville's setting, that of a country gentleman of independent means who was very much a serious scholar, refreshed and stimulated Rowse. The tradition of the eighteenth- and nineteenth-century country clergymen who produced the unsurpassed county histories and printed invaluable collections of historical documents still had some life in it. As David

Cecil's guest at Hatfield he had already experienced the thrill of studying historical sources in the actual surroundings in which they had originated. It is like seeing a picture in its contemporary frame. The friendship of Charles Henderson had made the same thing possible in Cornwall. 'You know more about local archives than anyone else in this country' wrote W. G. Hoskins, himself generally regarded as the leader in this field. The compliment, paid in an undated letter written about 1960, may have been an exaggeration. But the point that it makes, that Rowse's view of the past rested on and was informed by a thorough acquaintance with local actualities and the families and individuals to whom they had once been the facts of life, is an important one.

Staying in great houses such as Hardwick or Felbrigg was later to become as much part of his life style as his sojourns in the great libraries of America. For the raven-haired young radical who had only recently published *Politics and the Younger Generation* it was hardly appropriate. In spite of the suggestion that he should share a flat with Eliot, Rowse was decidedly not a metropolitan figure, as were his Oxford contemporaries, such as Quennell, Connolly and Graham Greene. Like them he contributed reviews and articles to the weekly journals, in his case mostly to the *Spectator* and the *Listener* rather than the *New Statesman*, then the liveliest as well as the most Left Wing of them. He also wrote for Leonard Woolf's *Political Quarterly*: indeed in 1941 Woolf invited him to join the editorial board. But though the two men evidently respected each other they were never friends. Perhaps Rowse found his forthright editorial criticism and his decisive excisions less acceptable than Eliot's constructive emendations. It is clear that he enjoyed writing for *The Criterion* though he steadily declined Eliot's invitations to attend *The Criterion* dinners. Partly this was a consequence of the miserable state of his digestion but mainly it was a social aloofness deriving from the circumstances of his young manhood. Except for All Souls where from the first he entered enthusiastically into the common life of the College he was not a clubbable man, indeed disdained the concept. The University Labour Club he accepted from necessity, not from choice, as he did the social duties of a Parliamentary candidate. The Rowse that charmed his fabulously wealthy American hosts, who was acclaimed by a succession of American Universities as the most enlivening Visiting Professor they had ever known, who was a welcome guest at Blenheim Palace and a marvellous host at innumerable grand luncheon parties at All Souls or dinner parties at the Athenaeum was a much later development. Health certainly came into it. After the fearsome surgery he underwent in 1938 he at least knew what to look out for and understood the extreme care he needed to take if life was to be tolerable. He could claim with St Paul that he kept under his body lest he himself might become a castaway, though his motives were very differently inspired.

His cultivation though wide in range was thus unusually solitary and perhaps for this reason narrow in its intensity. The arts, generally, make for conviviality. Musicians, painters, writers like to argue and compare, to talk and to listen. The most obvious and easy way to do this is over a drink or a meal. Yet except when travelling round Cornwall with Charles Henderson and his sister or exploring cathedral towns and country churches with Bruce McFarlane the young Rowse preferred his own company. This was conspicuously true of his early expeditions abroad. He actually ran away from a companion on his first visit to Paris. The desire for solitude and the yearning for friendship remained constant, often in later life provoking him to reflect on the contradictions of his nature.

Among the friends he had made as an undergraduate at Christ Church was the classical scholar A. R. Burn. After a brief period teaching at Berkhamsted Burn became in 1927 the Senior Classical Master at his old school Uppingham. For someone of a literary and scholarly turn it was an enviable position. The sixth form of a good public school was sure to provide a stream of lively and intelligent pupils with whom the reading and re-reading of the masterpieces of ancient literature would be stimulating. How different from the lot of the historian who, as John Evelyn eloquently pointed out, 'must read all, bad and good . . .'tis not easily to be imagined the sea and ocean of papers, treaties, declarations, relations, letters and other pieces, that I have been faine to saile through, read over, note and digest, before I set pen to paper: I confess to you the fatigue was unsufferable, and for the more part did rather oppress and confound me than inlighten, so much trash there was to sieft and lay by.' Yet

Rowse, for all his long hours in the Public Record Office and longer struggles with the ponderous verbosities of learned writers who had thought it beneath the dignity of scholarship to make their works readable, repeatedly urged his friend to abandon schoolteaching and become a don. Burn, whose study of ancient history later bore fruit in a number of books including one in Rowse's Teach Yourself History series, resisted. He was better off where he was. School holidays gave him plenty of time to travel in Greece. He was not to be the last of Rowse's friends who had to show that they preferred to plough their own furrow. Independence was instinctive to Rowse, but it did not prevent him from trying to remake the careers of people he cared for in the image of his own.

Sometimes this led to fierce exchanges or even estrangement but not in this case. In 1934 Winston Churchill's cousin, Esmond Romilly, ran away from Wellington and attempted to raise the flag of revolution in the public schools. A graphic account of this bizarre endeavour is to be found in Philip Toynbee's *Friends Apart* (1954). Romilly was known to Burn who evidently thought highly of him. Far from pursing his lips or averting his gaze Burn wrote to Rowse, urging him to invite Romilly and another rebellious and talented boy, Roger Roughton, to meet him and help him make something of their lives. The letter is evidence of the generosity that Rowse's friends expected of him.

It was a quality that he never failed to recognize in others. Q., whose initial kindness he always cherished, was at this time Professor of English Literature at Cambridge. Staying with him there Rowse queried his choice of Swinburne's poetry for the *Oxford Book of English Verse*. It was, it appeared, the poet himself who insisted on the inclusion, in its entirety, of his long and vigorously anti-Christian poem 'Hertha'. Otherwise all permissions to his copyright would be refused. The compositor at the University Press who had been charged with setting the volume up in type wrote to Q. asking to be excused from handling this blasphemous item. His scruples were respected.

All his life Rowse kept abreast of the new writers who were coming to the fore in England and America. On the whole the readiness of his sympathy, even enthusiasm, is striking. But there were blind spots. He prided himself on never having read a thriller or a detective story. To have missed Raymond Chandler and Simenon seems a conspicuous loss. And the skills proper to the novelist that so many writers of detective stories brought to their art surely make that form a considerable expression of the period. Do not the thrillers of Eric Ambler or the entertainments of Graham Greene hold a mirror up to the world in which they were written? It is perhaps in point to mention that Rowse also prided himself on never having been into a pub. Abroad he would never have hesitated to sit down at a café. Is there not here a suggestion of priggishness, perhaps sharpened by a conscious rejection of working-class pleasures, at any rate English working-class pleasures? Above all he could not bear middle-class *schwärmerei* over the social and moral nobility of working-class life. He had seen too much of the evils caused by poverty and ignorance to have any patience with people from easier circumstances who allowed their admiration for the stoicism and generosity of the poor to be touched by sentimentality.

This, surely, must be the explanation of the low opinion he constantly repeats in his journals of the work of George Orwell. Like Rowse himself, Orwell expressed so many opinions on so many topics that instances of shrewdness and silliness, of profundity and petulance can be found without much difficulty. What would be much harder would be to find an ill-written paragraph or a passage that left the reader uncertain of its meaning. The free-running clarity of his prose, the bold absence of ideological clutter, should in the end preserve him from the epigoni who have tried to take him over. It should certainly have commended him to a reader whose first literary love was Hazlitt.

A writer who has not yet achieved the success or the recognition which he feels he ought to have is naturally jealous of those to whom these things seem to have come easily. If, like Rowse, he is an egotist he will feel this more intensely. The thirties was a period in which poets could hardly complain of neglect. Both by the critics and by his fellows Eliot was accorded a place to himself. But Auden, MacNeice, Spender, Day Lewis, Betjeman were all names well known as rising poets, and all had been more or less Rowse's contemporaries at Oxford. In his *Auden: A Personal Memoir* (1987) Rowse does not conceal a certain envy at their ascent of Parnassus, as if by ski-lift. He forgets that he was devoting a great deal of his energies to politics and to equipping himself as a professional historian. And though poetry was in theory, and perhaps in practice, his first concern he had serious thoughts of trying his hand at other kinds of writing. His little pocket-books are full of transcriptions of overheard conversations, much of it recording Cornish idioms and terms of speech. He had always admired Q.'s novels and short stories, many of which were based on close observation of their fellow Cornishmen. He saw his own Cornishness as the source of his strength and never tires of warning his fellow writers not to pull up their roots. Yet at the same time he can never rid himself of the suspicion that it is his Cornishness that gives the fashionable metropolitan critics, Harold Nicolson, V. S. Pritchett, Raymond Mortimer, their grounds for keeping him out in the cold. Did they in fact keep him out in the cold? The friendly and encouraging letters from them preserved in his papers hardly support his suggestion. But the notion was always lurking in the dark corners of his mind, ready to flare out if his sense of what was due to him were provoked or irritated.

13

Return to Oxford

The termination of the temporary lectureship at LSE in 1935 removed the last reason for maintaining the flat in Brunswick Square. Rowse's research at the Public Record Office had reached a point at which writing was demanded. Thankfully he resumed wholetime occupation of his rooms at All Souls to devote himself to it.

The rhythm and companionship of Oxford life suited him much better. It was also a superior vantage point from which to observe the political scene and extend his political contacts. As we know from *All Souls and Appeasement* discussion and argument over foreign policy was vehement and outspoken. The grandees, Halifax, Simon, Geoffrey Dawson, were active promoters of appeasement. The great exception was Leo Amery, a past and future Cabinet Minister then on the back benches. Rowse indiscreetly quoted him in 1938 on the Government's concealment of German rearmament at the time of the General Election of 1935 and received a sharp letter of reproof. Some of his contemporaries were even firmer than Rowse himself. Douglas Jay, as early as March 1933, agreed with Layton, the owner of the *News Chronicle*, and Norman Angell that the country must prepare for war in defence of the Locarno Pact and described Geoffrey Dawson as 'a mixture of low cunning and complacency'. Richard Pares and Geoffrey Hudson, Rowse's two closest friends in the College were vigorous anti-appeasers.

G. F. Hudson, who had been elected the year after Rowse and who died in 1974, was a lifelong friend whose brilliant gifts and tireless energies excited both admiration and perplexity. How could so clever and so industrious a man achieve so little? And how could someone so apparently balanced, even wise, make such a mess of his life? Early in his career he had, according to Rowse, fathered an illegitimate child in Istanbul, skilfully concealing the reason for his annual revisiting of the city from his colleagues. His two experiments in matrimony were sudden, short and disastrous. But the learning and perspective that he brought to his study of foreign politics prompted Rowse to collect a volume of his Essays, which had to be withdrawn from publication because of a libel on an American Communist. Even in his expertise there sometimes appears a want of practical sense that might in someone else have provoked Rowse's scorn. In September 1939, considering how to reverse or mitigate the effects of the Nazi–Soviet pact Hudson suggested sending Lloyd George to Moscow, 'the only one Englishman who could cope with Stalin . . . What perhaps we might do is to bid for Russian oil, manganese and copper at such fantastically high prices that Germany could not possibly compete and the Socialist Fatherland might be drawn by sheer force of lucre into the path of anti-fascism.'

An important ally much better acquainted with the conduct of affairs was Sir Arthur (later Lord) Salter who became a Professorial Fellow of All Souls in 1934 on his appointment to the Gladstone Chair of Political Theory and Institutions. Salter had been one of the most brilliant young civil servants in the First World War when he had been charged with the allocation of merchant shipping and had subsequently served for many years in the League of Nations secretariat at Geneva. Rowse and he struck up an immediate friendship which lasted until a sad falling out over the Wardenship election in 1952. In 1945 Rowse inherited his beautiful set of rooms in the Hawksmoor building. A much older man he was reckoned a confirmed bachelor. On his sudden marriage in June 1940 to the American widow of a League of Nations colleague his scout at All Souls voiced the general opinion of the College. 'Whatever next? First the fall of France and now – This!'

Salter brought together a number of public figures in an attempt to concert pressure on the Government. On 26 February 1938 Rowse recorded in his diary a seminar on foreign policy held in Salter's rooms attended by Harold Nicolson, Clifford Allen, Gilbert Murray, Walter Layton and Liddell Hart. Two of these were well known to Rowse. Harold Nicolson, generally the easiest and most agreeable of men, contrived to raise Rowse's hackles. At their first meeting when

Nicolson was a guest at All Souls he offended the then rather puritanical young man by making (or so Rowse thought) a pass at him. He
aggravated the offence by gently critical and slightly patronizing
reviews, for which he was not forgiven: though his wife, Vita, won
Rowse's heart by her enthusiasm for his poetry as well as his historical
writing. Gilbert Murray was on the other hand friendly and encouraging from the start. Rowse's letters to *The Times* in August and
September 1937 opposing its support of appeasement won his especial
congratulation. 'I am particularly glad that *The Times* (23 August)
gave you so much room. They could hardly have given you more had
you been an Old Etonian discussing what clothes they wore when
beagling in the '70s.'

Although Bevin and Dalton were the Labour leaders in closest
sympathy with his views on the all-important issue of foreign policy
Herbert Morrison was, as we have seen, the man whom he would
have chosen to lead the party. His success in capturing control of the
London County Council and the flair he had shewn in running it
shone the brighter in Labour's days of national defeat. Rowse had
Morrison down to stay at All Souls but he evidently liked and respected
Attlee who had held on to the leadership in the face of Morrison's
challenge. Bevin's great rival as the statesman of the Trades Unions,
Walter Citrine, forfeited Rowse's good opinion by accepting a knight-
hood from the National Government. A (wisely) unposted letter in
Rowse's papers begins:

5 June [1935]

My dear Citrine,
     Fancy your letting them make a fool of you by becoming a knight! . . . it
is extremely disappointing to people like myself who have always thought
very highly of you and who follow your lead as against the fools on the
left-wing and the young Communists – for it exactly corroborates what they
say of you . . .

As Rowse later came to recognize he was not cut out to be a politician.
He never had, or claimed to have, any use for modesty. But stronger
even than vanity is the tone of exasperation. He was far from well.
He knew that the country was being swept by powerful currents to

the horror of another European war. He knew, too, that his own party had no stomach for the rearmament that, logically, offered the only hope of avoiding catastrophe. Had he, in his heart of hearts, the stomach for it himself? If only people would be reasonable and see where their true interest lay there would be no need to waste money on guns and bombs instead of spending it on hospitals and schools and the general amelioration of the life of the poor.

In his diary for 1935 Rowse recapitulates the position he took in an argument over dinner at All Souls:

It is not that people prefer the bad things: armaments, lowering standards of living, economic and political conflicts, war . . . It is simply, I said, that in order to safeguard their own position, to keep themselves on a standard of living above that of their neighbours, to keep the working-class down, they put all their energy into supporting a system which leads to these consequences. They don't see it. All my poor fools of the League of Nations Union at home who want peace and international agreement, and yet go on voting Conservative, are destroying with one hand what they are trying to build with the other. Or take the case of pure Conservatives who don't even bother about the League of Nations. They want peace. But they put all their energies behind the Conservative Party, supporting the existing system – and to keep it going, encouraging the appeal of nationalism, obedience to superiors, monarchy, the armed services, Empire, all the things that lead to conflicts with other peoples and to war. I.e. for the sake of keeping themselves above their neighbours in the social scale, they send their sons to the slaughter house. They don't see it. There are some people to whom the whole thing is clear enough; – and they are more in favour of sending other people's sons to the slaughter. The German upper and middle-classes support the Nazi régime because it has destroyed socialism, and smashed the power of the working-class. In order to achieve this they embark on re-armament, and maniac nationalism, in the end it will involve a European War.

When millions of lives have been sacrificed, a beautiful patriotic legend will be woven about their sacrifice – *They fought for freedom* (in every country imagine the War Memorials: the Chairman of the Rural District Council in an English village, the maire of the commune in a French, the bürgermeister of the German town etc. – all fools, all reasonable people, – they are the normal ones, (not I – I feel these things too deeply – abnormal).

Re-reading this passage many years later Rowse reflected 'I was, as usual, thinking my way clear in the Diary, thinking my way out of Marxism for myself – though in revolt against *la condition humaine* – arriving at my permanent Swiftian position: no inherent reason why humans should be such idiots. I see now that there was no point in revolting against it: this is what they *are*. Accepting that, I wouldn't raise a finger for them to-day. January 1979. Early morning – a splendid Tiepolo cloud sails over Trenarren.'

Both passages bear the obvious marks of truthfulness. There can, surely, be no doubt that that is what the author thought when he wrote them. And in both cases the swift running clarity of the prose distracts the eye from any shallowness that closer inspection may detect, a shallowness that certainly is not to be found in the feeling with which they were written. Rowse felt intensely that European civilization was rushing to its destruction. Forty years later he felt, with equal intensity, that emotion felt at such a prospect was emotion thrown away. Common to both perceptions is an Olympian conscious-ness of personal superiority.

Variety, we are told, is the spice of life and it is certainly the solace of Rowse's biographer. Although his dominating recollection of the thirties was of despair and of Cassandra-like foreseeing of disaster, this, though true enough as his diary bears witness, was true only of one side of a many-sided consciousness. Take for instance his delight in Oxford:

Today [Sunday 24 March 1935] in pursuit of health and to steady my nerves, I went for a day-walk with Geoffrey from which just returned sunned and refreshed. Oxford's quadrangles and gardens are full of bells (it being Sunday) and birds singing. The place is a paradise to come back to. David Cecil used to say that Oxford, like Venice, was a place to be always coming back to; if you lived there all the time you became dulled to the enchantment.

I remember the first excitement on coming back to Christ Church as an undergraduate, entering Tom Gate from the noise of St Aldate's; the stillness of the quad, the splashing of Mercury, the rippling of the bells around the walls, through the cloisters and echoing about the Hall staircase. Oxford has never lost this magic for me. Tonight after a dozen years it is still as magical. The light is going from the garden; blue dusk has descended upon the long line of Queen's beyond. Every moment the trees grow darker; the bells are far away, ringing somewhere for evensong; a boy in the kitchen is whistling happily.

I feel the need to catch every detail, for time is flying, as if this moment were my last.

It was not only the poetic vision of Oxford, so often and so rewardingly captured by other pens, that held him. The intemperate denunciations of the whole academic profession with which his name has come to be associated belong to a later period. Inevitably, and not unjustly, these sentiments have been reciprocated. Historians who have come to maturity during this later period have not bothered to take him seriously. One occupant of a chair at his own university even proclaimed that he had never read any of his books. But as a young man he was appreciated, even admired. The Regius Professor, Powicke, congratulating him on an article on the work of his friend and fellow historian G. N. Clark, wrote 'You have the gift of making people think.' Cruttwell, the Principal of Hertford and himself a Fellow of All Souls, had so high an opinion of his qualities, not least the courage with which he faced chronic ill-health, that he left him £500 in his will. Rowse was deeply touched as well as astonished. Cruttwell is now remembered, if at all, as the object of Evelyn Waugh's undying malice, caused, according to Rowse, by his replies to the inquiries of Waugh's future mother-in-law, Lady Burghclere, as to his character. Cruttwell's authorship of the best single-volume history of the Great War of 1914–18 and his unsuccessful Tory candidacy for a University seat in Parliament offer no obvious affinity with Rowse's activities and interests. But it was this very diversity that Rowse valued in Oxford as a whole and in his own college in particular.

Labour politics brought him into contact with other dons who shared these sympathies but were otherwise very different in outlook and taste. Literature brought more friendships, such as that with Nevill Coghill. The life of the mind, the disinterested curiosity that leads men to wonder why, that has traditionally distinguished the idea of a university from that of an applied study of any individual subject of the many that go to the making of such an institution, had a strong appeal for him. The households he most enjoyed visiting were those of Sir John Beazley, a scholar of the widest artistic cultivation whose daughter married the poet Louis MacNeice, and that of John Buchan out at Elsfield. Buchan, ennobled in 1935 as Lord Tweedsmuir on his appointment as Governor-General of Canada, was a conspicuous example of the large-minded, generous, encouraging spirit that to Rowse was the elixir of Oxford. A life-long Tory he sympathized with Rowse on his defeat in the General Election of 1935 and congratulated him on increasing his party's vote when the tide was running against it. As Governor-General he wrote a long letter in his own hand praising *Sir Richard Grenville of the Revenge*.

It is a fine piece of historical scholarship . . . and it is a fine piece of literature, admirably written, with no false rhetoric and therefore all the more moving. Your last pages are wonderful: also it is written with that good breeding which is so rare to-day and which is most needful in the case of a man like Grenville.

The work on that book prescribed by Neale's well-judged criticism had taken its toll. Rowse realized, sometimes despairingly, that he could never count on the good health he needed if even half of what he aimed at was to be achieved:

August 17, 1937. Half-past ten, and I have the greatest difficulty in making myself get down to write. I am so tired – staying on in Oxford into the depths of vacation when the college is officially closed: so disturbed – the papers are full of world order breaking down, this hideous Japanese action in Shanghai, the incompetent Chinese bombing their own civilians to death in reply, Franco continuing his advance into Basque territory, a Spanish Government steamer torpedoed in the Eastern Mediterranean obviously by an Italian submarine; meanwhile the Spanish Government forces paralysed, the incompetence and hopelessness of the Left everywhere. The breakdown of the European order is largely due to the sabotage of the British governing classes . . . If the disintegration goes much further there will be a shocking price to pay: perhaps the eventual break-up of our position as a first-class power . . .

One can only sit here and observe. I have an alternative line for myself:

writing patriotic[1] history. And my head is bursting with subjects for books, plays, poems, articles, essays, reviews; ideas for campaigns, political propaganda, issues to be fought and how they should be put; schemes to advance, the right people to run them; projects I want to see taken up and advanced; means to power. My mind is undefeated. These things merely accumulate and threaten to burst the bounds while waiting. Perhaps there is something pathological about it; the natural way for an active, energetic being is to get on with each job as it comes. One cannot do that; one can only sit and do one's best not to be submerged. Perhaps a day will come.

The inner sympathy with which Rowse wrote of the Elizabethans surely drew much of its strength from this sense of the shortness of time, the limitation of means, in which to find expression for talents and energy enough for ten. Their short expectation of life was the simple fact of common experience. His intuition of it, intensified by his clear perception of the course and speed of international events, probably arose from serious undiagnosed illness. Evidently he thought so. In the spring of 1938 Bruce McFarlane insisted on his seeing his friend the surgeon Peter Wright. The result was a series of operations, long and serious, that began towards the end of May in University College Hospital London. One of them, occasioned by a relapse, was thought likely to be fatal both by the surgeon and the nurses. As soon as he was strong enough to hold a pen and put on his clothes at the beginning of July he recorded

. . . the simplest, but the most exquisite pleasure. I suppose it is the sense of life returning . . . Perhaps it is the very strength of that, one may call it alternatively will-power, will to live or instinct of self-preservation, which has pulled me through.

He went up to the roof of the hospital to enjoy the fresh air.

I felt like a boy out of school, or rather like myself when as a youth I used to work so hard, all day at school and all evening at home; then late I would go up to Carn Grey or Look Out for a walk in the fresh night air before going

1. Rowse later – ?how much later – deleted this adjective.

to bed. Today there was London spread before me: the red, lobster-coloured Hospital buildings on one side, and the dome of University College immediately behind. It is odd what effects of perspective this height gives: for St Pancras Church-tower looked next door to University College dome, and in a line with Woburn Square, though far off on the horizon it seemed, was that fine church tower I took to be St Saviour's, Holborn.

How deep in his consciousness were the poetical and aesthetic roots. The faint echo of Wordsworth's sonnet on Westminster Bridge, the recollection of Canaletto, inform the early, still feeble, return of powers that for all these accretions were still unmistakably his own. Soon he was back at Oxford for a few days before going down to Cornwall to recuperate.

Every visit to Cornwall awakened the old excitements which still, for all his recording, all his scrutinizing, remained mysterious:

The images swam in and out of my mind, glimpses of places, a turn in the road, a hedge in spring, a ploughed field with the gulls upon it, or idly read the names of the generations who once lived at Trenarren or Penrice. The Hexts at Trenarren seem . . . to have been prolific. I looked up their pedigree, following it back from the old Colonel who was born in 1847 and survived to be a name in my youth up to the War: last of the Hexts to live at Trenarren . . . the Colonel was one of a band of six brothers and five sisters: they must have been a full house at Trenarren in those days. I fancy the voices of children in that valley where everything echoes. It gives me pleasure to read all the names, the dates of their births, baptisms, marriage and burial. I cannot say in what the fascination consists: if only I could, that would be to yield up the secret of history. It has some relation to life itself: as if Time is standing still for a bit, and I am watching life pass by as in a mirror.

It is not, at its most intense, the people themselves that I visualize: this other pleasure does not take place at that level of experience, but at a deeper one: where things are less differentiated. It approaches more the pure aesthetic experience of music and poetry: the real (and partly secret) values of my life . . .

No crowded family of Hexts at Trenarren now. For years the house stood empty . . . Now new people from South Africa are living there: the windows are opened once more to the sea-air and the scents of the shrubs and trees (there is a eucalyptus-tree in the garden, feather-plumed, for ever moving to and fro with the least movement of the wind). But in one sense, the place is mine: it is identified with my dreams, the sense of my own life. It is the house of my imagination: the chimneys, the gate – I have never been inside – where my father stopped the last time he was there and said that though I might live there someday he should never live to see it – the spring flowers, ferns and mosses in the crannies of the hedges, the sea-clouds sailing over the tops of the trees, and everywhere the sense of the sea.

That passage was written eighteen months earlier in his rooms at All Souls, recovering from influenza, guiltily turning the pages of Vivian's *Visitations of Cornwall* when he felt that he ought to be at work on his book. The nostalgia for a Cornwall he had never known, entwined with desire for Trenarren ('my Naboth's vineyard') and resonant with self-reproach at absence from his father's deathbed, and still keener grief at the loss of Charles Henderson deepened each time he returned.

On the day before his operation Charles's widow, Isobel, had written him in his own words 'a brilliant letter, describing the pre-Waterloo atmosphere' of the Encaenia celebrations at All Souls. The epithet is well deserved:

This is a maddening enough planet when one's guts are sound and really one can't face it with a tummy gone Bolshevik. I only hope that an efficient digestive system won't turn you Conservative.

The All Souls party was extremely beautiful, the men outshining the women. The Codrington full of Doctors' robes looked like some Handel opera. It was the day of the Czech frontier incident: first Halifax was called away and then about 9.30 a Messenger (à la Sophocles) came and pulled Sir John Simon by his D.C.L. gown and he vanished like the Snark, leaving chilly puffs of rumour curling round the room. It was all very Waterloo Night, and gave one the nastiest feeling one has had for a long time.

However, Waterloo hasn't followed yet. Lindemann seemed to have enjoyed himself at Churchill's party, where he was the only one who could talk German to Henlein[1] . . . Meanwhile the Cabinet is probably practising saying 'Herr Hitler's move was inevitable', for some future occasion.

1. The leader of the pro-Nazi Sudeten German party in Czechoslovakia.

Her intuitions were all too sound. Rowse himself, reading in the Radcliffe Camera one afternoon shortly before he went into hospital, observing a group of pleasant-looking young men at a neighbouring reading desk, suddenly saw them as cannon fodder and felt cold with horror. Yet on his return to Oxford early in November, only a couple of months after Chamberlain's flight to Berchtesgaden and its consequences in the agreements at Godesberg and Munich, his first diary entry, for 3 November, makes no mention of all this. The muffled peal rung from Magdalen tower occasioned by the death of some unknown Fellow puts him in mind again of Charles Henderson '. . . hardly a glimpse, muffled like the bells, and yet I feel the tears starting in my eyes. So much in vain to think of him! Early this term I went for the first time, since his death, to see his rooms.' Everything had been changed. 'Oh, all again as it never can be, that life gone.'

14

Battles Lost and Won

By the time Rowse took up his Oxford life again he knew the result of the two issues that had overshadowed his life. There was now barely a hope of avoiding a major disaster in world affairs. On the other hand the fearful prospect of disabling ill-health, even perhaps of early death, threatened no longer. It had been a near-run thing. He retained, and often expressed, profound gratitude to his surgeons. He was still far from the robust young man that his build and his liveliness at first suggested, but he knew that if he took care of his diet and stayed alert for the recurrence of symptoms he could now identify he had as good an expectation of active life as the next man. In fact, as we know and he didn't, a better. As the years went by he came to recognize the value of precarious health. The cracked pitcher and the creaking gate of the popular proverbs were very much in point. Besides, as he had already recognized, a doubtful tenure of life puts a high premium on the use of it.

To what extent did the defeat in public affairs and the victory in personal ones impinge on each other? Politically he must have realized – and if he hadn't, his doctors would have told him – that if a General Election were called, as was constitutionally due by 1940 at the latest, he was in no condition to fight it. The Declaration of War on 3 September 1939 resolved that question. It was not until June 1943 that Rowse formally and finally resigned his candidacy for the Penryn and Falmouth constituency, recommending in the strongest terms as his successor the name of Michael Foot. The reader may rub his eyes. The whole Foot tribe are so often exhibited as prime examples of canting, nonconformist Liberal humbugs that the sharp exchanges of more recent years between the two men seem truer to life. But the

Foots did at least read: Rowse thought that Michael's father, Isaac, had the only private library in Cornwall larger than his own. And when it came to electioneering in the pre-television era there was no doubting Michael Foot's verve and charm and talent as a public speaker. Rowse was still a member of the Labour Party even when he had found in Churchill the real focus of his political loyalty. He had put a lot of work into trying to win the seat and did not then regard it as work thrown away.

If he would not have been fit to fight a Parliamentary election still less would he have been fit for military service. Had he been, no doubt he would have enlisted straightaway like his colleague John Sparrow. He tells us repeatedly that in his early days as a Fellow he made a personal cult of his young predecessors who had given their lives in the First War. It is only in his later books that one comes across the refrain, 'And so the fighting fools fought' and suchlike expressions, suggesting that for persons of superior intelligence, such as himself or Erasmus or Montaigne, there was a happy isle from which sounds of armed conflict were banished. What he means is that had he been present with an apparatus of knowledge and ideas accumulated in the twentieth century he would not have felt disposed to risk his own life or take somebody else's for the ideas and beliefs of the sixteenth or the seventeenth. To censure our ancestors for doing so, is, as Noel Malcolm pointed out in a review quoted earlier (p. 9), simply unhistorical. Rowse was never a pacifist and he certainly never doubted for an instant that the Second War was, in Charles I's words from the scaffold, 'a righteous cause'.

What he would or could do he had, not surprisingly, no clear ideas: but when war came he put his services at the government's disposal. Why they were not used is obscure. Perhaps – this is pure speculation – it was felt that his personality was too rebarbative, his capacities too decided and too idiosyncratic for him to fit into a team which the collective effort of running a war so relentlessly demanded. Perhaps, anyhow, it was just as well. No one could say that Rowse sat on his hands during the War years and in fact much of what he produced made a more inspiring statement of the country's aims and character than the forc'd hallelujahs of the Ministry of Information.

But we must return to what remained of peace. Fearful as he was of impending disaster, bitterly resentful of the now unquestionable necessity of pouring money into engines of destruction, moved by compassion for the cheerful young men with whom he got into conversation on trains, he yet savoured to the full all Oxford had to offer to a man with a book, in fact two books, bursting to be written. *Tudor Cornwall* and *A Cornish Childhood*, which will be considered in a following chapter, were both simmering away. Rejecting the pleasures of the flesh with a puritanical rigour Rowse was intoxicated, seduced, by the beauty of an Oxford that had changed little in the seventeen years since he had come up to Christ Church. As an undergraduate he remembered the thrill of coming through Tom Gate, leaving the world outside, conscious only of the faint splash of the fountain in the silence and space of the squad. The same relief at excluding ugliness and disorder filled him as the iron gate at All Souls clanged behind him after letting out a guest late at night into Radcliffe Square. It combined a delighted sensibility with a consciousness of exaltation such as, in some religious natures, accompanies the knowledge that one is saved. The keenness of his perceptions was even sharper than the scepticism of his intelligence.

Oxford before the War preserved an uncrowded detachment, almost the unselfconscious provincialism of a market town or an old-fashioned cathedral city (both of which it in fact was), that is irrecoverable today.

> Fair city! Still a Jewel, though worn how foully
> On the sprawled hand of factory-fingered Cowley

Rowse's friend, the poet Martyn Skinner, catches the last, already doubtful, sense of this, elaborated in brilliant detail by so much of John Betjeman's poetry and prose. Colleges were open, doors were left unlocked, as indeed they continued to be for a few years after the War. But the bombing of London, the relocation of so many people who worked there, altered the character of the place. It became an annexe to the metropolis.

In that summer of 1939

I turned in at Magdalen and looked for a moment at the porch of the chapel, which has been cleaned and restored: the little statues have all of the fifteenth century in them, the quaint gestures and poses of body: St John the Baptist with hand raised in blessing and the Lamb of God in the crook of his arm: a medieval worthy, King or something, next to Mary Magdalen in the centre, with her vase of ointment; a bishop with crozier next her, and another fat, stocky, little bishop without crozier at the end. This was Waynflete [Founder of the College]; who was the other I wondered. I must ask Bruce . . .

The bells are faint and far away now: the wind must have changed. I am distracted with the beauty of the world and of life, this dream I live . . .

It was, for England, still a time of sleep-walking. To be fully awake was frightening. Even Rowse took an enjoyable holiday in the south of France, recollecting which he used to quote, admiring the imaginative use of language, the phrase of a guide: 'La Garance est une rivière assez capricieuse.' The initial impact of the War on life in All Souls was scarcely perceptible. The young men began to vanish – but they would have vanished anyway. John Sparrow joined up as a private in the Oxford and Bucks Light Infantry, living in a barrack room but coming in to dine on off-duty nights. Air raid alerts, as that dispiriting wail was called, were rarely heard and then usually turned out to be false alarms. There seemed no reason not to go on with the two books that were clamouring to be written. Travel was still easy. Rowse went back and forth to Cornwall, spending a couple of nights in Plymouth (not yet pulverized by German bombs) and finding the conversation of the young sailors he approached moving in its apparent innocence of what lay in store for them.

The spring and summer of 1940 changed all that. No one could be in any doubt that the country faced extreme and immediate danger. The fall of the Chamberlain government, so long the objective of Rowse's political efforts, opened new vistas not only in his politics. Two of his All Souls colleagues had been instrumental, Leo Amery in the most powerful denunciation from the benches behind the government and Quintin Hogg (the future Lord Hailsham) who was one of the few Tory members to go into the opposition lobby, an act the more courageous as he had been elected only two years earlier in the Oxford by-election fought largely on the policy of appeasement. Rowse wrote a letter to *The Times*, which was given pride of place, calling for the formation of a coalition government headed by Halifax, then Foreign Secretary. In *All Souls and Appeasement*, written twenty years later, he makes his own apologia. 'Instinct told me that Churchill was the man, but I did not dare go so far. Chamberlain was still in command of the majority in the House, the Tory party was behind him ... It has only lately been revealed that the King preferred Halifax, and so apparently did Attlee. So I was in good company, but nevertheless wrong.' No one who remembers that unrecapturable moment can doubt the truth of this handsome admission. But a good deal more might be said in self-justification. Not only Attlee and the King, but Hugh Dalton, the doughtiest Labour opponent of appeasement, favoured Halifax,[1] who had himself, as Andrew Roberts has demonstrated in his brilliant book *The Holy Fox,* changed his mind on the question. That Rowse indeed had perceived this is proved by an earlier letter to *The Times* printed on 27 January.

I should like, as a Labour candidate and a supporter of the Opposition to pay tribute to the magnificent and unanswerable statement of the Allies' cause and their aims in the speech of Lord Halifax at Leeds. No Foreign Secretary of late years has so penetrated to the heart of historic British policy, or from the historian's point of view put it more soundly, or stated the justice of the case more judicially ...

The fall of France brought over a number of Frenchmen who nonetheless felt that duty required their return to their own country. Among them was Léon Blum. On 27 June G. F. Hudson wrote to Rowse urging him to come to London to see Blum who was said to be in a state of nervous collapse. Hudson wanted Rowse to encourage him to stay in England and rally the French working-class by means of pamphlets dropped by the Royal Air Force. Such a policy, Hudson feared, would be opposed by the forces of Right Wing defeatism in the Foreign Office. I have found no evidence that Rowse took any notice of this suggestion or would have thought it worth noticing.

A recollection of that numbing period of defeat is to be found in his reply to a letter of inquiry from Richard Cobb in November 1981

1. Dalton, *The Fateful Years.*

about some French naval officers who were briefly quartered in All Souls: 'Yes, I remember those three Anglophobes distinctly and their disdainful hauteur as they passed through All Souls on their way to repatriation. We did not give them dining rights but, so far as I remember, a meal – lunch – a day. They were visibly hostile and sullen and spoke not a word, but *looked* what they thought.'

The formation of the new government evidently moved him to offer his services. On 9 July G. F. Hudson wrote 'I certainly think Bevin has behaved badly in referring you to the Ministry of Information instead of giving you a job himself.' Bevin's letter, dated 22 June 1940, survives. He can see no opening for his personal services but is sending on his letter to Mr Harold Nicholson (*sic*) at the Ministry of Information. Fortunately, the reader may feel, nothing came of this.

Rowse could then, with a clear conscience, devote himself to getting on with writing his books. This did not preclude him from his journalism or from his poetry. When in 1981 he collected his poems he entitled the book *A Life*. He always insisted that his poetry gave the truest picture of what he was and what he thought: further, that his best claim to literary survival rested on it. An author's judgment of his own work is no more infallible than anybody else's but it tells us a great deal about the man himself. It is not practicable in this biography to do more than glance at the corpus of Rowse's poetry. But the reader should bear in mind that its composition was seen by its author as the real achievement of his life and the fullest expression of it.

Similarly the vast output of journalism, broadcasts, radio and – later – television interviews all offer material for understanding and for criticizing the mind that produced them. In those early years of the war the sheer volume and range for a man who was at the same time hard at work on a major book is astonishing. In three consecutive numbers of the weekly *Spectator* he reviewed – and he was a conscientious reviewer – books on the sixteenth century, the late seventeenth and the middle ages. Some of his articles and reviews were by-products of *Tudor Cornwall*, such as the lively account of *The Mirror for Magistrates* critically edited for the Cambridge University Press or the evocation of a remote Manor House near Newquay which had once been the comfortable country retreat of the Prior of Bodmin.

He was characteristically generous towards the first works of colleagues or future colleagues as is evident in his notice of Isaiah Berlin's *Karl Marx* in the *Political Quarterly*.[1] His review of Hugh Trevor-Roper's *Archbishop Laud* in the *New Statesman*[2] was enthusiastic in its recognition of both literary and historical quality. 'With this life of Laud a new star, of great promise, appears on the horizon.' Rowse emphasized the challenging character of the introduction '. . . it reads almost like a manifesto. The joke is that though it comes to very much what we Marxists think, it is in fact written by a young Conservative. The explanation is just that this young Conservative is very intelligent.' In the same journal a year later[3] he was no less emphatic in his praise of Rohan Butler's *The Roots of National Socialism* 'a very remarkable book, very well documented and well written . . . the first book of an author who will be heard of: one of the two or three most promising of our young historians.' The review gave Rowse the cue for a brilliant summary à la Santayana of the whole course of German political thought.[4] So telling was it that Kingsley Martin, the editor, thought it necessary to deplore it in his leading article. Rowse had supported the candidacy of each of these three authors, in two cases successfully, in the Fellowship Elections at All Souls.

In one important respect his circumstances improved out of all recognition. He bought a house on the southern outskirts of St Austell, moving in during August 1940 with his mother acting as cook and housekeeper. The cramped bedroom in the council house, 24 Robartes Place, with not so much as an easy chair, which was all that he had had in which to write his books and entertain his friends, gave way to a pleasant, modest 1920-ish roughcast house (now much extended) standing in its own small grounds with an uninterrupted view across Carlyon Bay to the Gribbin. To enjoy it to the full Rowse took the first floor room looking out over the bay for his study, placing his desk against the window. 101 Porthpean Road was the address which, anxious to preserve the link with its now vanished past, he changed to Polmear Mine.

1. XI, pp. 127–30.
2. 9 March 1940.
3. 2 August 1941.
4. Santayana's *Egotism in German Philosophy* (1916, republished 1939) was repeatedly praised by Rowse.

At the same time his Cornish life was enriched by the arrival of King's School, Canterbury, evacuated for safety from its home to what with the fall of France became the scarcely less vulnerable coast opposite the Breton ports. The headmaster, Canon F. J. J. Shirley, was quartered in Trenarren, itself vacated for fear of invasion, who immediately struck up a friendship with his distinguished neighbour. After the War, Rowse succeeded him in the longed-for tenancy. Perhaps as a form of War work Rowse befriended the school, delivering within a month of their arrival what Norman Scarfe, then in the sixth form, remembers as 'a wonderful lecture on Cornish history, covering for us in clear outlines the main themes of Cornwall's history, and then describing how we could set about discovering it for ourselves in walks and bike-rides to Lanteglos-by-Fowey, Restormel and so on'. One of the secrets of his lecturing, as of his writing, was that he never grew tired of his subject. The desire to dominate, which was certainly one of the strands in his nature, never converted itself into a readiness to bore reader or listener into subjection. What was not lively was deadly. Generous as always in his friendships he brought Q., Lord David Cecil, Maurice Bowra, Sir Charles Grant Robertson and Arthur Bryant to talk to the boys.

Virtue was, for once, rewarded. Norman Scarfe, winning a prize offered by Rowse for an essay on a local subject, was enchanted to find his work returned with marginal comments in that elegant hand (still elegant in his nineties) and to be invited to lunch at Polmear Mine. It was the beginning of the deepest, most durable, most enriching of Rowse's many friendships, closing only with his life. Scarfe came up to Oxford in the Michaelmas Term of 1941 on a year's course that combined the usual academic life with two days a week of military training. Thus the darkest days of the War unexpectedly offered Rowse the most sunlit passage of his life. The two imponderable threats of the thirties, his health and his fear for his country, had been resolved by surgery and war. He had written a magnificent book on Tudor history and was in the full, confident flow of a masterpiece in a totally different medium, his *Cornish Childhood*. In a couple of years he had passed from being a notably clever and articulate young man to the front rank of contemporary literature. And in spite of himself, in defiance of his fierce determination not to allow his affectionate nature to give hostages to fortune (marriage and fatherhood were nothing more than a trap) he was to his intense happiness suffused by an emotion which had the character of both.

To crown the supreme ambition of his life 1941 saw the publication of his first volume of poetry *Poems of a Decade* with a blurb written by T. S. Eliot himself. (In a letter of 10 November 1943: 'writing blurbs always throws me into a fever of scrupulosity and I am never satisfied with any that I write. It is a form of composition that seems to me to require more labour and offer less reward than any other and I am all the more gratified by your approbation'.) This literary *annus mirabilis* demands a chapter to itself. But, as always, Rowse found time for much activity on other people's behalf. At the end of 1940 he wrote to Herbert Morrison pressing the employment of the brilliant Spanish refugee surgeon Dr Joseph Trueta, the pioneer of a technique which saved the lives of many who had been hideously wounded. On 3 January 1941 Morrison's private secretary wrote back to say that 'arrangements have now been made by which his services can be used in an advisory capacity at Oxford and for him to be remunerated'.

On Monday 23 March 1941 Rowse was called up for an Army Medical Examination. He must have known that he was unfit. But he confesses to some trepidation – 'is this a turning point in my life?' – as he waits and waits in the dreary squalid ante-room of the little Wesleyan chapel in New Inn Hall Street. 'I move over to the light to go on correcting the proofs of my autobiography.' Danger he might have enjoyed: but could he have endured the boredom, the compulsory vacancy, of military life? Fortunately it was not to be put to the test.

In the autumn he pleased Attlee by an inspired recommendation: 'Your admirable suggestion of the O.M. for Beatrice Webb. My general rule is not to recommend for any honours except those which, like Privy Counsellorships, are part of our Parliamentary tradition but this is certainly a justifiable exception. I am therefore mentioning the matter to the P.M.' It will be remembered that that great man had once declared that 'he would not be shut up in a soup kitchen with Mrs Sidney Webb.'[1] Was the recollection decisive? At any rate she

---

1. Quoted by Lady Violet Bonham Carter in her *Winston Churchill as I Knew Him* (1965), p. 154.

didn't get it, and died two years later. Perhaps as an *amende* her husband was awarded the honour in October 1944. It surely marked a missed opportunity.

15

Tudor Cornwall and
A Cornish Childhood

To have produced two prose classics and to have published a first book of poems in less than a year is no mean literary feat. *Tudor Cornwall: Portrait of a Society* and *Poems of a Decade 1931–1941* were both published in September 1941, *A Cornish Childhood* in June 1942. It adds to amazement that the two prose works were executed in two utterly different forms, the one a formidable piece of original scholarship based on extensive research which was yet a delight to read, by turns amusing, evocative and moving; the other an autobiography of Pepysian candour, which for all its subtlety and truth in its portrayal of Cornish working-class life in the early twentieth century constantly reminded the reader of what it was like to be a child and never allowed a doubt of the genuineness of childish recollection.

It may be argued with some justice that the appearance of these works hard on each other's heels is not necessarily evidence of the fertility of genius. All three of them, the *Poems* professedly in its title, had been maturing and forming in the author's mind over a considerable period. But is this not, or may it not, be true of other astonishing instances of literary productivity? When Dr Johnson wrote *Rasselas* in a week to pay for the expenses of his mother's funeral we know that it was not the first time that he had turned over in his mind the themes with which it deals. The apparent facility, well attested, with which Dickens and Trollope composed works of extraordinary imaginative power surely points to the same conclusion. And when Tennyson, whose own supreme poetic art might be held some qualification, told Jowett that there was one intellectual process of which he entertained not even an apprehension, namely Shakespeare's powers of composition, he was surely enunciating a principle that puts criticism in its place. Rowse himself in some moods would have endorsed it. He was insistent on the mystery of things, finding fault with the criticism of John Sparrow, whose acuteness and force he admired, for its too exclusive intellectuality. 'The lawyer in literature' he called him when he wanted to bare his teeth. But at other times, for example, in his *Shakespeare's Sonnets* (1964), he charts Shakespeare's course of composition with a confidence to which Tennyson did not feel himself equal.

Putting aside for the moment *Poems of a Decade*, the two prose works, so different in form and conception, have Cornwall in common in their titles. And both titles were suggested by other people – *Tudor Cornwall* by Sir Charles Firth in conversation at All Souls and *A Cornish Childhood* by Jonathan Cape, the publisher, in a brilliant critique of Rowse's original draft. It is a mark of Rowse's outstanding gifts as a publishing consultant that he who so often found the right title or the right subject for somebody else should have unhesitatingly accepted guidance for his own most intimate and ambitious work.

Tudor Cornwall is the inner bailey of Rowse's historical achievement. Curtain walls of so vast and sprawling a fortification may from time to time be overrun by fierce and well-equipped marauders, bastions may be undermined by the skill and science of specialists in demolition, but over *Tudor Cornwall* the flag still floats bravely in the breeze. Indeed its very strength was turned by hostile critics against the weakness of some, perhaps by implication all, of his later works. *Tudor Cornwall*! Ah, that was a real book, written by a real scholar, long ago. Such has been the drift of fashionable opinion in academic circles, reflected in the bibliographies of many subsequent books on the period.

Rowse's own conception of the book is explained with exemplary clarity in his Preface.

My intention was originally to call it *The Reformation in Cornwall*; for it came into being as an attempt to answer the insistent questions that arose from my study of the sixteenth century: what *was* the Reformation when you come to study it under the microscope? What did it mean? What did it do and how did it work? What were its effects upon the development of our society?

These questions led me far afield into the social history of that period in all its aspects, economic, political, military, religious, cultural. It is to that attempt to give a complete picture, a rounded whole, and the consequent necessity of mastering so many and varied sources of materials, not only in different places but of different kinds and categories, that the long delay in this book's appearance is in part due.

It may be readily appreciated that a study on such a scale – a one-inch ordnance map of this particular tract of history – can only be done for a small area. Fortunately that lay ready to hand in my own county, which provides a fascinating example of a small homogeneous society, up to that period a remote Celtic-speaking province, which in the course of the sixteenth century became absorbed into the main stream of English life, at that time of greatest tension in our history. From being a far-away insignificant corner of the land, sunk in its dream of the Celtic past, with its own inner life of legends and superstitions and fears, its memories of Arthur and Mark and Tristan, lapped in religion and the cult of the saints, it was forced in the course of the Elizabethan age into the front-line of the great sea-struggle with Spain . . .

But in the end the county was absorbed. That process is the subject, the story, of this book, which has developed from its original conception into something much larger, namely a portrait of Tudor society as you see it in all its elaboration and richness and individual detail reflected in the small mirror of Cornwall . . .

If ever a subject entwined itself with the roots of its author's being it was this. The life of the working-class provincial from an illiterate home who found himself hobnobbing with leading thinkers, statesmen, archbishops and plunged into a political struggle on which the life of the country and the hopes of civilization depended was foreshadowed in the story he had to tell. No wonder *A Cornish Childhood* was pressing on its heels. No book of his exhibits in a higher degree that combination of scholarship and imagination that distinguishes a fine historian from Dryasdust with the grime of his researches carefully preserved from soap and water. The opening chapter 'Evidences and Survivals' alerts the reader to the humanity, the curiosity, of its author's approach, exciting expectations that are not disappointed. The past is livingly and lovingly handled, not hauled out of the deep freeze. Take, for instance, this examination of the Cornish miracle-plays:

. . . The Cornish plays omit the whole of the Nativity from the subjects of which they treat; rather strangely, one cannot help thinking, for this part of the biblical narrative had an obvious popular appeal. But its place is taken by an elaborate treatment of the exquisite and moving legend of the Holy Rood: how Adam, weary of his life and sorrows, sends Seth to the gate of Paradise for the oil of mercy:

> ADAM   O dear God, I am weary,
>   Gladly I would see now
>   The time to depart.
>   Strong are the roots of the briars
>   That my arms are broken
>   Tearing them up without number . . .
> (to Seth)   Follow the prints of my feet, burnt;
>   No grass or flower in the world grows
>   In that same road where I went
>   And we coming from that place . . .

Seth goes to the gate of Paradise and, looking within, sees the tree of knowledge all dry and made bare by his parents' sin. He is bidden by the angel to look again and sees the roots of the tree descending into hell. A third time he is bidden and sees a new-born child high up in the branches: He is the oil of mercy. Seth is given three seeds of an apple from the tree, which he is to place in Adam's nostrils and beneath his tongue when he dies and is buried. From these spring the three rods of Moses, the tree under which David repents of his sin with Bathsheba and commences the psalter (*Et tunc sub arborem sedens incipit psalterium: viz. Beatus Vir*, reads the stage direction); and in the end, in the *Passio Christi*, it is from this tree that a portion is taken for the Cross.

The minute accuracy of the scholarship is illuminated, dazzlingly, by the profound imaginative sympathy. Rowse has forgotten that he is an agnostic, a Marxist, a brilliant young Fellow of All Souls whose literary and intellectual powers have been unfairly neglected in comparison with the high-fed, highly trained racehorses from the stables of Eton and Winchester. He has forgotten himself because selfhood has been subsumed in the matter of his art. Selfhood, not personality, Rowse's personality leaps out of the passage. He was surely right in insisting that what gives distinctive, memorable, quality to all writing, history, poetry, novels, plays, is awareness of personality, an individual creative intelligence which has shaped and ordered whatever it is that moves or delights us. The Ph.D. thesis in which the passive voice is always to be preferred to the active in case some aspect of the writer's personality might be indecently exposed was not for him. Its advantages might, to borrow Dean Gaisford's reported phrase in his Good Friday sermon, enable us to look down with contempt on those who have not shared them and fit us for places of academic emolument, but they would not encourage the talents that came to fruition in *Tudor Cornwall.*

The notes of pathos, of loss, almost of bereavement, harmonize with the central melody of life and continuity. Commenting on the half-English, half-Cornish names of long extinct tin works above his native St Austell he writes: 'You may still see some of these workings out on the moor, some of the names remain the same: all that survives of these dead tinners, except their blood that runs in our veins.' It is this combination of down-to-earthness with an ear for echo and an eye for the significant, a combination common to his friend John Betjeman, that gives Rowse's best work its special quality. Down-to-earth *Tudor Cornwall* certainly was. How people wrested a living from an ungenerous environment, how some of them enriched themselves at the expense of others, how some were moved by compassion for the misery of which there is always plenty in a primitive economy, all of these are both vigorously realized and thoroughly documented. Rowse could not help enjoying, even to a degree admiring, successful roguery. A paragraph on page 179 swiftly and brilliantly expounds the tricks and dodges by which crooked lawyers cashed in on the Dissolution of the Monasteries. It concludes with two sharp, telling sentences: 'In the event they mostly got away with their loot. Upon them rests the greatness of modern England.'

Here again the resolved antitheses of Rowse's nature stimulate and excite where the smooth periods of a considered verdict might at best command a somnolent assent. He is equally vehement, equally impassioned, as Counsel for the Prosecution as he is as Counsel for the Defence. The issues, at least in his historical and biographical works, are tried by jury not by a judge sitting alone. Thus on page 191, summing up for the defence of the Dissolution, he is quite clear that not only was it inevitable because of the general decay of discipline and of any sense of purpose, but that it did not come a moment too soon. Yet it would not be hard to find elsewhere in the book denunciations of the vandalism that destroyed so much of the rich artistic heritage of the medieval church, the silencing of its music, the dissipation of the great monastic manuscript collections.

The two chapters entitled 'The Elizabethan Church' and 'The Cornish Catholics' touch greatness. The honesty and courage of the persecuted recusants are justly admired. The oppressive, cruel, greedy unscrupulousness of the Protestant *apparatchiks* is fully and fairly delineated. The tragedy is finely achieved. But even here Rowse's impatience breaks in. 'The ordinary fool – so characteristic of life'.[1] 'Any sort of change alarmed the idiot people'.[2] These petulances are already audible. In his later books they were to become strident.

One admirable characteristic of the book that fades in his last writings is the proper acknowledgment of debts to other scholars. His prefaces and dedications always reflect the generosity and appreciativeness of his nature. But, most notably in his Shakespearean studies, the work of other men from which he freely borrows is unacknowledged or, much worse, dismissed in vulgar and insulting terms. His admirers can only be saddened by the resentment and vindictiveness that caused this but it would be both idle and dishonest to deny it. And to whatever faults Rowse was ready to plead guilty (his diaries and letters show a high degree of self-awareness, even sometimes of penitence) these two were not among them. *Tudor Cornwall* is gratefully supported by a wealth of citations of original scholarship as well as original authorities.

Both J. E. Neale, the greatest living authority on the Elizabethan period, and G. M. Trevelyan, generally regarded as the head of the

1. p. 378.
2. p. 232.

profession, praised the book in the highest terms. Perhaps more unexpected was the enthusiasm of Dom David Knowles, the historian of English monasticism. On 9 November 1941 he wrote to the author:

The primary interest for me lay in your treatment of the Cornish religious houses, as I have been making something of a study of medieval monasticism for some years, and at present in what time can be found am investigating the period just before the Dissolution. Your chapters give an admirable picture which shows exactly, in a kind of photographic enlargement, what I had come to feel was the general condition of things over the greater part of England south of the Humber . . .

Two points, in particular, emerged for me with a new clarity from your pages – the very successful endeavours of the religious when they felt the wind blowing to make friends of the mammon of iniquity – and the very substantial bits of salvage that they managed to clear out of the wreckage. Two problems, also, put themselves . . . the first is one (put implicitly by yourself) that your figures suggest: why did Henry and Cromwell give such unnecessarily high pensions to superiors? It was certainly not kindness, nor, on the other hand, was it good business. The second is – why did the Crown allow so much property to leak away before it got to the Augmentations Office?[1] Was it a conscious realization that the support of a vested interest was more valuable than an increased financial yield, or was it that a whole hierarchy of avid and unscrupulous agents could not keep their fingers out of the pie? Modern secularizations have, I think, been more successful. In Italy in the 70s and in France in 1903, the governments concerned rounded up most of the spoil.

I found the book full of fascination . . . [especially] your exquisite vignettes – alas, too few.

With one bound Rowse had won a place in the front rank of English historians. And not only of historians. There was not much prose better than his being written in England in 1941.

All this must have lent wings to the writing of the book that he had been meditating ever since his brush with death in 1938. It was a

---

1. The court set up by Henry VIII to administer the business arising from the suppression of the monasteries.

different kind of book entirely. The style it required was looser, swifter, more daring. It shared with its predecessor the *nourriture terrestre* of Cornwall, that passionate plea for its eternity that lies at the root of all his most deeply felt work. Its direct inspiration was the pent-up consciousness of powers not brought to fruition. What if he had, as so many of his friends expected, died in 1938? What would there have been to show for all that aesthetic and literary experience, that unsleeping observation and curiosity, that heroic wading through the swamps of unreadable academic boredom without which he could never have reached the firm ground of All Souls? Towards the end of the book[1] he recounts how his father, ignorant of and uninterested in his son's intellectual promise, tried to get him an office job in the china clay business, the economic mainstay of St Austell now that tinning was finished, and failed through not having the right contacts.

I think my father understood the position very well, and resented it; and it may have been partly due to that he raised no more opposition to my going on at school . . . But it had been a narrow shave. I have sometimes wondered what would have happened if father had succeeded in getting me a job 'in an office' – height of an elementary schoolboy's ambition – and taken me away from school. I know what I should have done: I thought of it at the time. Consumed with resentment, I should have concentrated on making myself independent and left home. I'd have gone into lodgings and spent all my spare time writing: they'd have got no more out of me. It was very lucky for them that they didn't take me away from school; for later on I was able to take care of them, and in a sense I never left home.

But some years later at Oxford, when my research work was held up by continual illness and I had not the strength to finish the books I planned, I played with the thought sometimes whether it would not have been better if I had *not* gone to the University and my whole development not have been turned into academic and intellectual channels . . . If Thomas Hardy's fate had been mine, and I had not succeeded in getting through those portals, no doubt – I used to think – I should by this time have half-a-dozen books – stories, poems, novels – to show for myself. The way of historical research and political thought was stonier, and for years I suffered from a real feeling

1. pp. 191–2.

of diffidence in writing about either. That very much cramped my natural fertility of mind – that, plus illness and too much teaching in my early years as a don; so the books didn't get written.

This book was written to redress the balance, to exhibit the powers of a writer, not a historian but a writer *tout court*, hitherto thwarted by his circumstances. Besides that it was, of course, a straight auto-biography of unusual interest and unembarrassed candour. And beyond that it was in the full sense of Newman's work an *Apologia pro vita sua*. In reprinting that work Newman changed the title to *History of my Religious Opinions*, and that too, *mutatis mutandis*, might have served. In his exaltation at finding himself restored to the full enjoyment of his powers had not Rowse crammed too much into one book?

Such was emphatically the opinion of Jonathan Cape, who amongst his other shrewd perceptions had taken Rowse's measure. They were never exactly friends. But there is an amused, ironic intimacy in their exchanges, neatly expressed in Cape's habit of addressing Rowse as 'My dear Nephew'. On 10 January 1942 he wrote him a long and cool letter of constructive criticism:

I have now read your *Autobiography of a Cornishman* ... not one of those hurried or perfunctory publisher's glances but really the result of careful reading and serious reflection.

The book is good: rich in texture. That is my real quarrel with it, it is too rich in texture. I could imagine Edward Garnett [long Cape's principal reader] ... writing 'He has material here for two books, and is squandering it on one' ... Your book is called *The Autobiography of a Cornishman* but by the time you finish off 400 pages you have not yet reached the age of manhood. The book as it stands is really A Cornish Boyhood. Such a book can be excellent, but it needs to be shorn of most of your literary opinions concerning Shakespeare, Proust, Virginia Woolf [There follow some detailed criticisms of various quirks and tantrums].

Now as to publication. If you go off the handle as a result of this forthright criticism, I would say, Very well, let the MS stand and let it be published. But the result would not come up to your expectation and hopes, that is my firm opinion.

If I can only make you see *why* it has to be cut, and not merely that it is expedient to cut it, we shall have gone a long way. There is a risk if this book goes through, particularly if it achieves some measure of success – at present you have the press with you – of your becoming a prolix, unself-critical writer. In course of time this will make itself evident in your historical writing also. You have a splendid chance to make this autobiography a first-class book. You have the material and the ability.

Few publishers could have matched this combination of penetration and firmness. Cape followed it up by another on 22 January outlining his general principles of publishing and asking Rowse if he would like to act as historical scout for the firm. The pains he had taken were rewarded. On 16 February he wrote that he was 'very glad that you have felt able to get right down to the question of revising the Cornish Childhood. The typescript has rolled up safe and sound.'

The book was well but not rapturously received. The devaluation of critical language still lay several decades in the future. 'Stunning', 'Brilliant' – terms now habitually applied to very ordinary perform-ances – were not then the loose change of the reviewers' vocabulary. Yet its real success was very soon evident. In the half century since its publication it has sold, worldwide, half a million copies. It is the best known of his books and the most personal, both consciously and unselfconsciously revealing. The reader who has reached this point in the present work will have perceived how much it is coloured and informed by it: indeed its influence will be present up to the last page. If this whole biography may be read as an extended commentary on that text it would be out of place to embark on a critical survey. So much has already been said, so much more will show through. It is not, however, superfluous to consider some of the immediate reactions to it. Rowse himself was most pleased by the remark of an academic colleague, not belonging to the faculties of History or English Litera-ture, that no other autobiography recaptured so authentically the feeling of what it was like to be a child. In an earlier chapter of this book the question was raised of what his mother, still and for many years very much alive, might have felt at the recitation of circum-stances, probably not immediately intelligible to strangers but easily recognizable to her own acquaintance. A recent fortunate conversation with an old Cornish friend of the family, only three years Rowse's junior, has convinced me that she never read the book, or indeed anything else her son had written. Her illiteracy was invincible as was, by his account, her complete indifference to her son's world and to the successes he had won there.[1]

But so candid a self-exposition could not be achieved without provoking some distaste. Raymond Mortimer, who reviewed the book in the *New Statesman*, wrote from its offices on 17 June 1942:

'I've read your book with fervent interest and have written about it. I hope my frankness will not seem to you offensive, for I have joined issue with you on several points, particularly about the thorny question of class. It seems to me that you entertain illusions about the aristocracy for you talk as if they were all like Gerald Berners and David Cecil. I believe "inanity" – as you call it – exists about equally in all classes.'

Even more daringly the letter goes on to censure him for 'blowing your own trumpet . . . The charm of eighteenth-century France was partly dependent on the suppression of "le moi" . . . In an autobiography "le moi" must be prominent, but it need not be praised.'

Finally Mortimer returns – and granted the book and the author in question who can blame him? – to the question of class. 'I can't see why you insist that you are *still* "proletarian" – you are not. You are a Highbrow. I come from the comfortably off professional middle class – my relations are doctors, lawyers, stockbrokers, soldiers, sailors, members of Lloyds etc. But I feel no gulf when I talk to Gerald Berners or to you or to David Cecil. I do feel a gulf when I talk to my own relations. [It's] the class one is in, not the class one was born into that matters.'

It is surprising that Rowse, so refreshingly ready to prefer common sense to ingenuity, did not recognize this manifestation of it. But class remained all his life something that he meant to have both ways, professing exasperation at the idiocy of 'the people' at the same time as he was congratulating himself on the working-class 'horse sense' (a favourite phrase) that preserved him from the sentimental follies

1. My informant was Mr John Pethybridge, a lifelong friend and for many years his solicitor.

of the middle class. H. G. Wells to whom a complimentary copy had been sent wrote on 18 June a quick note of reproof: 'Don't specialize in early disadvantages. I spent most of my childhood in an underground kitchen under my father's bankrupt shop because we couldn't afford two fires. You had a great advantage over me so far as food and air went.' The same note was struck nearly fifty years later by Margaret Forster in a spirited correspondence arising out of her biography of Daphne du Maurier, Rowse's neighbour and friend in Cornwall.

But these are small points to set beside the Pepysian vividness of perception, the zest for life, that lights up the book. John Bromley, future Professor of History at Southampton, then working as a wartime civil servant, wrote a year later to express 'the debt I feel to you for it. It seems to me a deeply moving fragment, unique of its kind, the nearest thing we've had in English to Gide's journal in daring, intimate, magnificently honest self-knowledge – the revelation of a temperament, no posing, immediate (as you intended it should be) in impact.'

16

Poetry and the Poet

Two literary forms were instinctive to Rowse: poetry and autobiography. History and biography, criticism and controversy make up the great proportion of his published work. There are periods in his life when one or other of them seems to absorb his energy. But there is no period at which part of his consciousness was not engaged in forming, shaping, ordering the multiplicity of impressions of which he was so keenly aware into a composition either poetic or autobiographical. The relation of the two was, in his mind, very close. When, at the suggestion of his friend John Betjeman, he collected his poems into a single volume he entitled it *A Life*. To quote the second paragraph of his Preface

Looking through it all now, I see that it is an authentic record of my inner life – rather than of the external public life, given to history and (for a time) politics, though it also offers a true commentary on the history of our ruinous, tragic age. Poets are prophets – those savage poems of the thirties offered more truthful witness than the complacent humbug of politicians or the optimistic illusions of the liberal-minded.[1]

To anyone who is not a mystic the inner life will be influenced, even dominated, by the outer. Grief, anxiety, happiness arising from external events or pressures colour our consciousness. Poets at their most exalted or their most profound may indeed be prophets: even seers, uttering truths about the human condition whose full implications they could not themselves explain. But no one can sustain such

1. This is further discussed below on pp. 302–3.

a degree of tension for any length of time. Poets are also human beings. When you prick them do they not bleed? A great deal of Rowse's poetry is, so to speak, distilled autobiography: firewater from emotional reaction to direct experience.

Firewater, not a smooth, mellow potation. For that one must go to the topographical and historical evocations of people and landscapes so much praised by Betjeman. Anger, resentment, self-pity, even hatred of the human race are the emotions that power the poetry of personal feeling. His lyric gift, supported by the musicality of his language, seems more likely to preserve his poems. And it was as a poet that he wished to be remembered:

> All my life I have been keeping
> Poetry at bay, like madness.
> Work, work, work put in the way
> All day and every day.

So begins one of the last poems in *A Life*. There is no doubting the truth or the strength of this. His first published work was his contribution to *Public School Verse* (1921) and his early journals constantly record the fulfilment or the frustration of some impulse to poetry. Discussion of verse with which the reader is not familiar is irritating as well as pointless. An example, admired by Betjeman, may be cited from *Poems of a Decade*.

> How many miles to Mylor
>   By frost and candle-light:
> How long before I arrive there,
>   This mild December night?
>
> As I mounted the hill to Mylor
>   Through the dark[1] woods of Carclew,
> A clock struck the three-quarters,
>   And suddenly a cock crew.

1. So amended by the author for future republication. *Poems of a Decade* has 'thick'.

At the cross-roads on the hilltop
   The snow lay on the ground,
In the quick air and the stillness,
   No movement and no sound.

'How is it' said a voice from the bushes
   Beneath the rowan-tree,
'Who is it?' my mouth re-echoed,
   My heart went out of me.

I cannot tell what strangeness
   There lay around Carclew:
Nor whatever stirred in the hedges
   When an owl replied 'Who-whoo?'

A lamp in a lone cottage,
   A face in a window-frame,
Above the snow a wicket:
   A house without a name.

How many miles to Mylor
   This dark December night:
And shall I ever arrive there
   By frost or candle-light?

The craftsmanship is accomplished. Pope's requirement 'The sound must be an echo to the sense' is perfectly satisfied. The use of alliteration, the delicate varying of metre and rhythm, the colouring of the lines by situating Cornish place-names where the emphasis naturally falls, display a technique characteristic of his verse.

A year or two earlier he had shewn one of his poems to John Sparrow, rather surprisingly in view of his repeated estimates of his limitations as a critic. Sparrow's letter written on Christmas Eve 1940 certainly does not deserve Rowse's characterization 'the lawyer in literature'.

I will tell you what I thought of it, mingling praise and blame – indeed the two are inextricable because what I thought was this: it is, or seemed to me to convey, an impression (which remains with me) of a countryside and a mood – both of which are doubtless just what you meant to convey. It also left me in no doubt as to the depth of your feeling for the places and the person commemorated.

And I think the poem is, in a sense, faultless in taste: everything, every image, every word, is very 'choice'. Why am I dissatisfied, then? Why can't I be enthusiastic about it as I should like to be? For two reasons I think. First, the whole seems to me like a perfect imitation of a poem, rather than an actual poem – something written by someone familiar with poetry and anxious to write a poem. Perhaps that is what is meant by critics who use the word 'literary' in a derogatory sense.

I do not mean that it is imitative in the sense of being an imitation of this or that other writer (though I do detect traces of T. S. Eliot) but rather that it seems like an exercise, a 'version', a 'copy of verses'. This does not in the least contradict (as you will understand if I have made my meaning plain) what I said about the sincerity of it, nor does it mean that the poem fails to convey a sense of the depth of your emotion.

The second reason why I am not enthusiastic is that there are no passages, lines, phrases, that dwell in my memory. The feeling or matter does not seem at any point to determine the form so that one is conscious of something *unique* and *permanent* (I mean a passage, line or phrase). This seems to me a characteristic of much great poetry, and it is something like this (I don't express it well) that accounts for the pleasure that I, at any rate, get from much poetry. It is an obvious characteristic of (to take an extreme case) Gray's Elegy – but it is also true of Tennyson (a less extreme case) – Yeats, T. S. Eliot and (as I write I begin to think I must add) surely of *all* poetry?

But – to return to where I started – the poem as a whole does by its form and by its choice of language convey the impression you intend to convey – both the internal and the external picture. And you will probably say that in doing that you have done what you set out to do.

So you see what I meant by saying that the praise and the blame are inextricable.

On the publication of *A Life* Veronica Wedgwood congratulated its author on its unmistakably personal perspective 'but for the most part seen with a clear, almost dispassionate objectivity' observing the development of 'the adventurous mind, the developing sensibilities, the ultimate objectivity'. Perhaps objectivity was what John Sparrow found both the virtue and the inadequacy. It is certainly a quality rarely singled out for the highest praise in the criticism of poetry.

On Christmas Day 1958 John Betjeman wrote an enthusiastic letter on the appearance of *Poems Partly American*. 'I think the best poem of all is the one on the death of your mother . . . What is so wonderful about your Cornish poems is that they are all *South* Cornwall. The last stanza of Cornish Spell made me almost cry with admiration and memory.'

> What is this sweet and summer smell
> That hangs in hedge and field as well
> And speaks of what I cannot tell
> But what is dead – a honeyed spell.

The poem that Betjeman most admired is the most intensely autobiographical:

> Late September sun fills the room with light
> Where my mother is lying,
> Ribbons in her hair, hands shrunken on the white
> Counterpane: she has gone back to childhood:
> She is dying.
>
> Through the open window in this strange house
> In the afternoon haze see St Stephen's church-tower,
> Where as a boy I sang and returning late
> My mother came down from the village to wait
> For me in the summer night.
>
> She is beyond remembering, she is already elsewhere,
> The liquid eyes clouded, the speech thickening,
> She has been waiting for me to come:
> It is the hour of Evening Prayer.

'Lighten our darkness we beseech Thee, O Lord,
And by thy great mercy defend us
From all perils and dangers of this night,
For the love of Thy only Son,
Our Saviour, Jesus Christ. Amen.'
She does not speak again.

It seems that this was what she was waiting for
To die in peace. Too delicate,
Too proud, to ask. All too late
We come together after years estranged,
And still we do not meet.

It is too late. If only one might recall
The angry words, the anguished years:
I bury my head on her breast.
Too late, now gentle as a child at rest,
She is no longer here.

Quietly I withdraw from the light-filled room,
Taking my last look at the familiar face,
Already so strange, head fallen to one side:
I leave her in this stranger's house, I
Leave her there to die.[1]

The authenticity of the scene and of the emotions evoked is documented in the journal. Rowse did read to her, at her request, the third
collect from the order of Evening Prayer. He did feel the acute remorse
of the poem. On the day of her funeral, Michaelmas Day 1953, he
tore out two pages of an entry made seven months earlier: but those
that remain are bitter enough.

The whole time I have been in the new house – since 1940 – with housekeeper
after housekeeper, none of whom would stay with her for her tongue,

1. I have incorporated the two minor emendations and one typographical correction
made by the author in the copy prepared for possible republication.

her bullying, the tigerish personality, her nastiness, caring for nobody. Hilda [Rowse's elder sister] came home from Canada – they were barely on speaking terms before very long. I had hoped she would stay and look after the house. Not a bit of it. The old woman was too much for her, as she is for everyone.

At last, after I came back, she was moved to Truro, where she was comfortable. No doubt she made other people very uncomfortable – that is her genius in life: getting her own back for what life did to her earlier on. There is nothing more ghastly than such a woman with no interest of any kind, except sex and food, when deprived of sex and incapable of looking after herself, no extrovert interest of any kind, nothing but this savage concentration, eating up, destroying anything that comes near her. (She had told – and disgusted – Hilda, at eighty, of the men she had had. On leaving the house – one cannot call it home – her daughter said, 'I hope I shall never see you again.' That did not distress the mother.)

This is an abbreviation of a passage which Rowse himself had already toned down and sanitized. Readers who are shocked that a son could so write of his mother should remember the valiant efforts he had made – the more valiant in that he had in his own opinion inherited her unforgiving nature – to feel affection for her. 'My mind is to-night haunted by the images of the two people I love best in the world – Adam von Trott and my mother' he had written in July 1930. Noreen Sweet who had known him intimately from schooldays bears independent and emphatic witness to the kindness he shewed to both parents. From his first days at All Souls he had done what he could to ease their hardships. In the unhappy experiment just described he had paid for Hilda's travelling expenses as well as providing a wage during the time she acted as companion to her mother.

This intrusion into family affairs has been made to illustrate both the intertwining of his poetic and autobiographical writing and to confirm Veronica Wedgwood's judgment of their objectivity. Betjeman, who knew him less intimately than Veronica, recognized with the sure instinct of a poet the expression of truth from the heart. Not all Rowse's deepest emotions and responses were called out by people. Landscape, houses, churches, the evidences of a past, not a present, humanity as a rule moved him more powerfully. 'Memory and desire' he wrote in his journal 'are the twin pillars of existence'. They are, beyond doubt, the twin pillars of his poetry. Memory with Rowse was the keenest faculty of apprehension. His powers of observation crowded his mind, like a postal sorting office at Christmas. It was memory that did the sorting. And the order it imposed was not only intellectual but in a sense moral, restraining the fierce emotional reactions that were the promptings of his nature. He early recognized its importance to him as can be seen from this extract from his diary written on 31 December 1929:

I always write a little in this diary on the last day of the old year and now something would be lacking if I missed it this year.

Perhaps it would be a good omen if I did . . . four years at All Souls and nothing achieved: it's hard to defend myself and harder to know how the time has gone. I hate myself for being so old:[1] there's no such consolation as Richard [Pares] finds in the thought of Julius Caesar at twenty-six crying because Alexander the Great at that age had conquered the world.

There are only the bells for consolation: I am happy to be in sound of them. Yet they tell me how the years go on; and I remember other New Year's Eves. Always first I think of that one some time just after the war – 1919 or 1920, when I sat up alone with the lamp in the old kitchen at Tregonissey, reading the first war memoirs[2] – Col. Repington's and Margot Asquith's. And in Germany too – already three years ago, when I heard the chorales being played in the square outside the Pastor's house at Hagen. Was it then, too, that I saw the shadows of the ringers leaping up and down fantastically on an upper window of a church tower, and the people, dark figures, hurrying along the street to church?

If I remain faithful to memories like that – and to the greater memory (if it is to be no more) that has made this year memorable[3] – I shall not have to fear as sometimes in the middle of all the public salutes and buffetings I do fear, the drying up at the springs of my most real, because inner, life.

1. Twenty-six!
2. Rowse re-read his diaries and sub-edited them: but perhaps here he is using 'first' in the sense of earliest.
3. Presumably the Labour victory in the General Election.

His memory in fact never deserted him. In his nineties it was as rare for him to search for a name or a reference as it is for most people to have them at command. This exceptional power of recall must have been a boon in the examinations that had got him off to a flying start, the Christ Church scholarship, his First in history, his election to All Souls. But might it not at least partly account for the derivative note that John Sparrow detected in his poetry? Sparrow mentions T. S. Eliot. But, as we have seen, among other poets living close to Oxford whom Rowse used to visit and whom he admired were Robert Bridges and John Masefield. Is not Masefield's influence perceptible in 'How many miles to Mylor'? In mood and outlook he was perhaps nearest to Hardy. He was fond of remembering that his friend David Cecil had years ago said that he and Rowse were the only two people who fully understood him. Understanding, sympathy, is distinct from identification. David Cecil's serene Christianity preserved him from the cosmic pessimism that Rowse, after a brief honeymoon of political hope, came to share with Hardy. A passionate love of the past, deep roots in the south-west, a clear consciousness that they did not belong to the upper class made the identification closer.

Identification with an admired figure came to have an attraction surprising in a man who prided himself on his independence. Partly it strengthened the heartening conviction that he stood apart from the unthinking mass of humanity with its gross tastes and second-hand opinions. A few, a very few, select spirits stood with him on the Lucretian shore calmly observing the turbulence out to sea. Dean Swift had early established his position as one of these. To write his biography had been one of Rowse's first literary ambitions, realized at last nearly fifty years later. During that time he had convinced himself that Swift was a major poet, in spite of Dryden's reported advice to his kinsman 'Cousin Swift, you will never make a poet': in spite, too, of the failure of his admired friend Q. to include a single poem of Swift's in his *Oxford Book of English Verse*. Swift's social brilliance, his intellectual high spirits, counterpoised by his horrified contempt for the human race as a whole echoed Rowse's view of himself. Swift wrote poetry to which the world had paid little attention. So had Rowse.

. . . those two, equall'd with me in Fate
So were I equall'd with them in Renown.

The transition of thought is easy. But if Swift's poetry influenced Rowse's it was in sentiment, not in form.

Much later in life A. E. Housman came to be numbered in that sacred band. Rowse did not, so far as I can discover, know him though he certainly was a guest at Trinity during Housman's time. If he had, it would seem impossible that he would not have mentioned the fact in his journals and any scrap of correspondence, however curt, would have been reverently preserved. The combination of homosexuality with finely tuned poetry that rejected fashion, and scholarship that found its most glittering expression in contempt for fellow academics was irresistible. It was tempting, too, to see Housman's deliberate offensiveness as the mark of transcendent scholarship and to identify this with his own behaviour in Shakespearean controversy. Probably his allure was strengthened by the close friendship that developed between Rowse and Professor E. B. Ford, who had known the Housman family intimately from boyhood. Ford, a geneticist and already a Fellow of the Royal Society, had been elected to a Fellowship at All Souls in 1958. Described, by one who knew him well, in the *Dictionary of National Biography* as a homosexual and misogynist he found himself in natural sympathy with one of the roles in which Rowse was fond of casting himself.

Was Housman in fact a direct poetic influence? Perhaps in aspiration. But the strict metrical form, the extreme economy of language, which Housman so much admired in the odes of Horace were neither of them congenial to Rowse. His poetic gift was romantic, not classic. It is in his best prose, not in his verse, that the classical virtues are seen to advantage.

17

The Riches of Friendship

The middle years of the War, from the autumn of 1940 with the victory in the Battle of Britain to the D-day landings in the summer of 1944, were probably the happiest in Rowse's life. Success, unmistakable success, had come to him both as a historian and as a writer. He had, what he had always longed for, a house of his own in a beautiful situation in his own part of Cornwall. Whatever the fortunes of war – and in the summer of 1940 they had looked dark – at least the nightmare of appeasement was over. And his health, if not rude, was no longer an obstacle to achievement. He had much to be thankful for.

Best of all he found himself capable, after all, of love, that concept he had long believed to have no meaning. Or so he had often and emphatically asserted in his journals, rejecting Christianity on the grounds that its fundamental axiom 'God is Love' was so much gibberish, not because the first term was meaningless but because the second was. If the immediate, complete, profound sympathy that developed between him and Norman Scarfe does not deserve this designation it is difficult to see what could. Commercialization of the term has confused it by an implication of sexual desire. What Rowse meant when he said that his childhood knew nothing of love was certainly not that: rather it was the deeper perception of St John that 'Perfect love casteth out fear'. To feel towards another person that one will never be misunderstood, that one will not be required to justify oneself, that there need be no thought of keeping one's guard up, and that this relation is wholly reciprocal, comes much closer.

Half a century later Norman Scarfe's recollection of it is still fresh. Of his first visit to Polmear Mine he remembers

. . . a delightfully designed small house with a sensational view over the bay from the upstairs study. The walls were bulging with irresistible books, leaving just room in the front hall for some strikingly attractive modern oil paintings. I still remember a William Coldstream, the Cornish painter Christopher Wood, and the fisherman 'primitive' Alfred Wallis. He [A.L.] was thirty-eight when I first knew him, and always extraordinarily good company, perceptive about people to a degree well beyond anything his advantage in years explained, imaginative about everything, but everything, in ways I hadn't known among friends at school (the brightest of our young masters were already 'joined up'). A.L. in that summer of '41 was writing, with pen and ink and in that unchanging hand across sheets of white paper, unlined, but the lines of his writing were evenly spaced, and written with such obvious confidence. He wrote at a steady speed, and with a kind of excitement . . . He would read me bits of *A Cornish Childhood*, or of a *New Statesman* review or article, with a wholly infectious delight.[1]

Part, a large part, of the charm each found in the relationship was that both were natural writers, a talented apprentice and a master who had improved his gift by close attention to his craft. Part that they were both natural connoisseurs, looking at buildings, paintings, nature with an observing eye. But entire sympathy, love, call it what you will, is a miracle which those who have been fortunate enough to experience know that they cannot analyse. Was there, in this case, a hidden release of paternal instincts and affections that Rowse loudly and thankfully disclaimed in repeated tirades against marriage and family life? Did he protest too much? His delight, his surprised delight, was unclouded by the irritability and impatience which characterized his other friendships, however close.

When Norman Scarfe went up to Magdalen at the end of the Michaelmas term in 1941 he found himself invited to dine at All Souls. It was the night of Sunday 7 December, the day of the Japanese attack on Pearl Harbor. The news came through in the middle of dinner: one of the scouts had been listening to the wireless. Hitler's immediate declaration of war on the United States in support of his ally confirmed every one from the Prime Minister downwards in the opinion that

1. Private communication from Norman Scarfe.

victory, hard though the winning of it would be, was now simply a matter of time. Undergraduates at that stage of the War divided their life more or less evenly between military training and academic study. It was in any case, except for one or two rare categories, only a year's course. At the end one went straight into the forces; in Scarfe's case, he was soon posted as a subaltern to a Gunner Regiment already training with the Infantry Brigade that led the assault on the beach in front of Caen. By the beginning of 1943, the war in North Africa was visibly drawing to its close and the assault on Europe had become the urgent objective.

It is difficult to recapture the prospect of a historical event. Incidents are more easily remembered than our imagination of them. For that we turn to poetry or fiction, supported perhaps by autobiography or letters. D-day is a great historical event, the longest day in the title of a famous book covering the whole gigantic operation. But was it longer to the men who experienced it than the days that had preceded it, tossing in filthy weather aboard the lubberly landing craft that made the worst of it? Norman Scarfe, who went in on the first wave and subsequently wrote a notable account *Assault Division*, had been told by his Brigadier that they were to expect eighty per cent casualties – in plain English the virtual certainty of death or hideous wounds. First-class training and brilliant operational planning, by his account, reduced casualties to less than a quarter of the Brigadier's estimate.

Rowse's anxieties, denied the anodyne of action and immediate responsibility, were more acute. During the eighteen months between leaving Oxford and landing in Normandy Scarfe and he had seen a great deal of each other. Without family ties Rowse was free to travel to wherever Scarfe might be quartered and the hospitality of All Souls was always open when he was on leave. In the days following D-day Rowse recorded in a special journal the intensity of his emotion. 'One knows in one's bones that if things could go wrong, they would: the deepest conviction I have. What makes me always so apprehensive. And yet – no, the more so – because with N. and me things have always gone so absurdly well. It is that that makes my intuitive reaction so strong. "Too good to be true. Too good to last." . . . This experience of complete happiness which has come to me late, and so strangely . . . the perfection of sympathy.'

A week later he wrote. 'I cannot bear it. I cannot bear it. This is what it is to have imagination, the apprehensive sensibility of the poet, too great a capacity for suffering.' Two days after D-day he had written 'Perhaps I am at heart religious and what I want is a faith to believe in. I have sometimes thought that all this would drive me to it.' Ten days later he reverted to the desire for belief and the loneliness of agnosticism. The page is much corrected. Palestrina and Byrd prompted the reflection 'perhaps the human mind is such that there is as much to be said for belief as for reason.' The strain was mounting. On 24 June he had a haemorrhage, leading to three weeks' illness which led him to read Barbey d'Aurevilly's *Le Chevalier des Touches* (much recommended by Cruttwell) '. . . it is to me, as it was to Barbey, a *soulagement* to write.' Nonetheless he was still evidently much disturbed. Back in Cornwall in early July he recorded a vivid dream of his brother George attempting to murder him.

This anxiety for the lives of the young men fighting the war was not confined to Norman Scarfe. He felt it for the sons of his colleagues at All Souls and for his many friends from Cornwall. Reviewing his life in a letter to Raleigh Trevelyan already quoted he recalled 'the young men like you, my pupils at Oxford, on whom it fell to pay the price [of appeasement] were heroes to me. It was only natural to be emotionally involved for them and with them, worried to death about them (it gave me a slight nervous breakdown in the summer of 1944, something different) . . . you were only a boy whose life might be sacrificed at any moment, I was useless (I wasn't a reserved occupation, I was rejected from everything, even fire-watching at Oxford gave me a dangerous duodenal haemorrhage and another month in the Acland).[1] An appalling record – my one great triumph to have survived.' It is characteristic of the writer's unresolved contradictions that after this eloquent and obviously truthful confession of concern for others he should sign himself 'the really solitary solipsistic Leslie'.

Concentration came so naturally to him that he easily convinces himself (and thus his reader) that whatever topic or person fills his mind's eye at the moment of writing monopolized his consciousness. Happily for his sanity this was not the case. He was writing books.

1. The University Nursing Home.

He was reacting fiercely to any breath of criticism. He was conducting – always – an enormous correspondence, literary, historical, controversial, public and private, all of it in his own hand. He was making new friends. He was attending to old ones.

Among the new friends was one of the best of his many brilliant correspondents, Violet Holdsworth. (It may be observed in passing that in the whole of his archive it is the women who shine the brightest, Veronica Wedgwood, Elizabeth Jenkins, Rebecca West.) Mrs Holdsworth was not, like them, a professional writer though she had written some distinguished books, mostly dealing with Quakerism in its literary and historical connexions. Some thirty years older than Rowse she was the eldest daughter, and had been the amanuensis, of one of the most remarkable private scholars of the late nineteenth century, Thomas Hodgkin, author of the seven-volume history *Italy and her Invaders*. A Londoner, who made his fortune as a banker in Newcastle-on-Tyne where he was the inspiration of local historical studies and rescued Bamburgh Castle from decay, he married another Quaker of the famous Cornish family of Fox. Caroline Fox's journal was the starting point of Rowse's acquaintance and it remained one of his favourite works. She had been as a young girl on intimate terms with Carlyle and with Sterling, who had wanted to marry her. Violet Holdsworth was a living link. She had been a great friend of Mary Coleridge, herself the pupil of William Johnson Cory, the most stimulating teacher in the history of Eton, and, in her youth, the friend of Caroline. Marrying late in life and soon widowed Mrs Holdsworth had long been established in Cornwall first at Glendurgan and subsequently at Bareppa, near Falmouth, two beautiful houses with even more beautiful gardens largely formed by her. Her own literary and scholarly friendships, her range of cousinhoods and family alliances both on the Hodgkin and the Fox sides made her a wonderful, as well as a highly articulate, source on the innumerable questions of interest to a scholar who interpreted the past through individuals and their relationships.

Their earliest letters date from 1943. Both sides of the correspondence are in the Rowse papers and her hand is not less elegant and legible than his. The fact of her Quakerdom added to his interest. 'What do you *do* at your Meetings?' he asked the first time he met her. 'It was rather like being asked what do you do when you breathe' she later wrote, having parried the question at the time. But she took trouble to explain and he was obviously interested, regretting that he had made no mention of the Quakers in *The Spirit of English History* (1943) and meditating an insertion in future editions. For his part he sent her proofs of his forthcoming *Poems Chiefly Cornish* (1944). Her comments were enthusiastic. Where she did not like something she felt no need to say so, except where she felt that some expression of bad temper or spite spoiled a thing of beauty. 'Hate creates hate – doesn't it? My father used to say "Write it all down and get it out of your system, but be sure to burn it next morning." Forgive my candour. But isn't magnanimity the master-word for us all?' Even more boldly when he sent her the draft of his piece on Caroline Fox and her Circle she took issue with his abuse, notably the word 'fool', directed at those who did not think as he did: '. . . not the facts so much as the tone of voice: "Never sneer," my Father once said to me, so incisively he never needed to say it again. "A Victorian taboo" you will say, perhaps? Well we are, he and I, both Victorians.' She was not the only one of his friends to regret these lapses of taste and manners, so ugly in a man who took pains to cultivate both these qualities.

The same affectionate warning counsel had been given, at least by implication, by his oldest literary friend and mentor, Q.

25 June 1942

I have just finished a second reading of *A Cornish Childhood*. Fascinating, for me, all the way through. But it and the *Poems* together have set me worrying about you: and as a friend I wish we could 'have it out' in a good talk. (Letters are no use in this kind of trouble.) Briefly, I want you to be happier in mind – for your own sake, of course, but also because you can do more good so in the future in which in the course of nature I must leave you before very long . . . Of course you are vastly too kind to me in the book. But how should I wish it otherwise?

Six months later he wrote again, even more emphatically:

22 December 1942

I love you too much not to hate your cultivating cynicism. You won't do any good that way, and all the excuses you can put up won't excuse your giving way to *that* drug. It's like philandering in one of its effects – it 'petrifies the feelings' . . . [In 1981 Rowse, re-reading this passage, wrote in the margin 'True – and it happened'.] And the one text (it seems to me) in these days to preach upon, is my favourite from Marcus Aurelius (VI.5) as translated by Meric Casaubon, sometime of Christ Church, Oxon 'The best kind of revenge is not to become like unto them.'

The impact of this advice was such that Rowse remembered it and quoted it almost perfectly in his biography of Q. (1988), even though he had forgotten its source and ascribed it to his old friend. In spite of resentments for past injuries or anxieties for the present and future of his young friends, 1943 saw the publication of the most optimistic of all his historical works. *The Spirit of English History* is a brief and brilliantly achieved epitome. If it does not quite glow with the Christmas Card cheerfulness of his friend Sir Arthur Bryant it is strikingly free from the dire assertions of a doom, not to come but already coming up the stairs like the statue in *Don Giovanni*, which darken the tone of his later books. The poverty and bareness of the life of the medieval peasantry are uncompromisingly stated as against the merrymakings round the maypole that colour other accounts. The force, the daring, the sudden soaring of the Elizabethan age give the reader a foretaste of the richness of the wonderful post-War trilogy. But the harshness, the cruelty, the greed, instrumental to the Tudor achievement is not disguised. Time and again the emphasis falls on the positive, the fortunate, elements in the historical situation. The swiftness and dexterity with which the arts and sciences, developments in overseas trade or domestic agriculture, are interwoven into a straight, simplified, political narrative may look easy. It is in fact the product of extraordinarily wide reading combined with a sense of perspective and proportion that conceals the art with which it is presented.

History in Pieter Geyl's happy definition is a debate without end. New knowledge or, more commonly, old evidence examined from a new angle would make this book unsuitable for use as a textbook. Of course there are minor errors and, as Rowse himself evidently realized, considerable omissions. For instance the Jacobean bishops are generously praised for the translation of the Authorized Version of the Bible without so much as a mention of their unblushing plagiarism of Tyndale, who is not even indexed. Pedantries of this kind could be multiplied. But for an account of English history written at the height of its greatest struggle it would be hard to imagine anything more concise, more vigorous or more heartening. No wonder the book was everywhere praised, not least in America by such distinguished scholars as Henry Steele Commager and Wallace Notestein. No wonder that in addition to the ordinary trade edition published by Jonathan Cape the British Council also published it in both paperback and hardback for distribution overseas.

Its success prompted Rowse, always swift to mark what he thought had been done amiss, to accuse Jonathan Cape of failure to exploit it and to threaten to move elsewhere. Veronica Wedgwood, who herself had given the book an enthusiastic review and was in regular touch with her old tutor in her combined capacities of editorial assistant both at Cape and on Lady Rhondda's journal *Time and Tide*, implored him to stay.

My dear, I *know* it's maddening about the *Spirit of English History* but I do *most* strongly recommend you to avoid the snare of a publisher like Collins[1] or Macmillan as a general thing. It is a short-sighted policy to leave a good firm and get on to an inferior list with a lot of second-rate novelists etc. merely for the quick sales of the present moment . . . Will they treat you as well as Cape? I wonder . . .

What a tribute it is to the old man and his advisers that in only a little under 20 years he should have brought out so many books of permanent value needing to be kept as far as possible in print – yours, Neale's, mine, T. E. Lawrence, Silone, Day Lewis etc. It's a bit hard to penalize the better publishers by leaving them, just because they *are* better publishers: and I really wouldn't for your serious historical work, contemplate any one else. I don't myself, whatever the results in William's[2] *immediate* sales.

1. She herself took this primrose path a decade later, probably attracted by the editorial skills of the late Milton Waldman. The present writer succeeded to his responsibilities at that establishment.
2. This undated letter must from internal evidence have been written about January 1944. Her *William the Silent* was published that April.

The Spirit of English History, though not in itself as remarkable a book as its two predecessors, consolidated Rowse's position as the heir to the laurels of G. M. Trevelyan and Macaulay. Its dedication to Churchill 'Historian, Statesman, Saviour of his Country' asserts its author's standing as a public figure. One does not play such tunes on a pennywhistle. And the acknowledgments in the Preface – admirably brief as always with him – certify the book's authority. G. M. Trevelyan's own *History of England* is gracefully saluted: Bruce McFarlane, Oxford's most learned medievalist and Dr Charles Singer, the renowned historian of science, are thanked for their assistance in their respective domains. But the greatest obligation expressed is to Jack Simmons, a friend whose wide learning, fastidious taste and invincible good temper illuminate a correspondence that lasted over half a century.

Now Professor Emeritus at Leicester where he held the chair of history for nearly thirty years Jack Simmons has long been recognized as the leading authority on railway history in Britain and among the most productive scholars in the general field of the history of transport. As a local and topographical historian he is hardly less eminent. But in 1943 all this lay in the future. Ten years younger than Rowse he had, like him, been a scholar of Christ Church where he had read History.[1] Unfit for War service he had helped Margery Perham to produce an anthology of African exploration and had been in 1943 appointed to the Beit Lectureship in Imperial History. Rowse, who was introduced to him as someone who could both type the manuscript and make the index of *Tudor Cornwall*, recognized both his quality and the unusual combination of historical, literary and topographical interests which they had in common. Rowse would have liked to have him appointed to a post at All Souls but his election to the Professorship at Leicester in 1946 not only gave him far wider scope but undoubtedly helped to preserve the longest untroubled friendship of Rowse's life. He was among the first and most constant guests at Polmear Mine, continuing as such after the move to Trenarren in 1953. The housekeeper there told Rowse, and we can well believe her, that he was a

---

1. Although he had wanted to read English Literature the College still, as in Rowse's day, disapproved of the school and kept no tutor in it.

different person when Professor Simmons was staying. Like Bruce McFarlane (but never with him) he was a frequent companion on those enriching tours that took in cathedrals, churches, great houses and small towns. He was the reader whose advice, encouragement and criticism were most profitable. In all this the fact of physical separation played no small part. Rowse was like most egotists extremely irritable. He was fortunate to have so good-natured a friend: but as we shall see even the best of natures could not escape the resentments of unchecked egocentricity.

18

Becoming an Institution

To become an institution necessarily involves a restriction of one's perceived personality. The person in question is not in fact spiritually or mentally arrested. C. S. Lewis, Mother Teresa, Sir John Betjeman, Bertrand Russell, to name but a few of Rowse's near contemporaries, went on thinking, feeling, developing as we say when talking of adolescents: but their image cast them in a particular public role. It is rather as if they were bound to go on wearing clothes of the same size and cut regardless of changes in age or situation.

As a rule people of an active, inquiring turn of mind find this irksome. In Rowse's case this seems doubtful. Indeed he once confided to a friend, who had remonstrated with him about one of his too often repeated *boutades*, in this case against the Idiot People, that he did it in order to build up a public persona, in a word to institutionalize himself. Tracing origins is always to some degree speculative. But the closing years of the War and the coming of peace seem an obvious place to look. *Tudor Cornwall* had established him as a historian: *A Cornish Childhood* as a writer with a voice not afraid to make itself heard. *The Spirit of English History* by its title stakes a claim to speak from the heart of the nation, a claim rapidly reinforced by the publication a year later of *The English Spirit*.

This, one of the most engaging of all Rowse's many collections of essays and reviews, allows an expansiveness that the tight, taut energy of its predecessor had forbidden. In *The Spirit of English History* he had rounded up modern English literature in one short paragraph, sending a copy to T. S. Eliot. In his letter of acknowledgment Eliot wrote:

I have looked at page 136 and am flattered, though the construction of the sentence is faulty. You mean simply that there have been new schools of music and painting as well as a new school of poetry. People tell me that Hardy was a great poet.

Affectionately T.S.E.

The passage so magisterially considered is indeed hurried:

Hardy, after a full-length career as a novelist, proved himself a great poet in his old age. Yeats, like Wilde and Shaw and George Moore the novelist, was a recruit to our literature from Ireland: the most lofty and admired poet of his time. His successor in this eminence is a recruit from New England: T. S. Eliot. The creator of a small body of poetry himself, he has had an influence comparable to that of Coleridge in its effect upon the poets coming after him: the new school of poets, like those in music and painting which have emerged since the last war.

The English Spirit, by contrast, shows Rowse's range, his curiosity, his sensibility, at its most charming. The piece on the Public Record Office discussed on p. 82 is here. The sketch of Queen Elizabeth at Rycote, evoked by a visit in the company of Bruce McFarlane, exemplifies his visual and poetic quality, its haunting overtones reminiscent of Kipling. 'The Spanish College at Bologna,' like all the best topographical writing, lets the place observed make the reader aware of the person observing it. The portrait of Sarah Churchill in Old Age, brilliant, sympathetic, witty, has more than a look of its author at any age. Yet for all its marked and agreeable idiosyncrasies the book is free from egotistic rant. A review of his clerical colleague at All Souls, F. E. Hutchinson's[1] edition of George Herbert is notable in its perceptions and mercifully free from cheap gibes about the irrationality of religious belief. High spirits, vivacity and love of life are not vitiated, as in some later works, by vulgarity and spleen. In a word the book is generous, not least to Leslie Hotson 'and his faithful accomplice, Miss O'Farrell' who was later to devil indefatigably for

---

1. Hutchinson's charm of character and distinction of mind, much valued by Rowse, are admirably sketched by John Sparrow in the *Dictionary of National Biography*.

Rowse in the British Museum and at the Public Record Office.

That the book, for all its rewarding by-ways, marked a stage on the main road is made clear by its dedication to G. M. Trevelyan, by giving pride of place to an understandably adulatory essay on Churchill and by the tone and content of the preface. Like the dedication it may call to mind Rowse's remarks on the kind of history one should write if one wishes to be honoured by the Order of Merit. Perhaps the irreverence of youth is giving way to the sober judgment of maturity. Perhaps, like the elder Pitt, Rowse knew that he could save the country and that no one else could. He had seen the country led by false political doctrine from the apparent strength of a world power to within a hairsbreadth of ruin. To be heard at last, to be respected at last, after a decade of Cassandra-dom, must stimulate any but the most inert, and Rowse was never that. He had resigned his Parliamentary candidacy in 1943 so that route was closed. But he might still influence events if he could establish himself as a public figure.

Such considerations probably played a part in his decision, against Veronica Wedgwood's advice, to move to a larger publisher. He had flirted briefly with Collins but Macmillan won the day. On 5 January 1944 Rache[1] Lovat Dickson, the Canadian-born chief executive of the firm wrote to say how much he was enjoying *A Cornish Childhood* and it was from Macmillan that *The English Spirit* was launched the following December in a generous edition of 10,000 copies. For wartime, and for the years of paper-rationing that lasted until the early fifties, this was big stuff. Rowse, never a tranquil and rarely a grateful author, had been constantly complaining to Cape that they were letting his books go out of print. 'My dear Nephew' wrote Jonathan on 5 October 1945 'What a peevish and disgruntled fellow you are.' Ten years later (for Cape still controlled the rights to *Tudor Cornwall* and *A Cornish Childhood*) nothing had changed. 'My dear Nephew, I sometimes think it would be a pleasure to get from you a letter which hadn't a grievance.' The main paperback houses had declined to offer for *A Cornish Childhood*. 'Well, we can't help that. They declined it in 1953. We have only a small stock remaining . . . and then the question will be as to whether we are to reprint it.'

1. Abbreviation of 'Horatio'.

Re-reading the correspondence many years later Rowse's resentment was unappeased. 'He was *mean*' he wrote on the first of these two letters.

Nineteen forty-four had also seen the publication of *Poems Chiefly Cornish*. If Rowse wanted to move from Cape, Geoffrey Faber and T. S. Eliot may justifiably have felt that Faber and Faber had first claim. He was, as he himself was beginning to realize, a valuable property and to realize also in the words of an earlier poet 'How pleasant it is to have money, heigh ho. How pleasant it is to have money.' As he wrote in his notebook on 27 October 1948 while staying with the Alingtons at the Deanery of Durham, surely one of the houses least suggestive of such ideas:

'There's nothing like money I'm beginning to find – belatedly: I should have thought of it before. All through the thirties I was too high-minded and fanatical, and ignorant, to bother; though I saved a little and helped to keep my parents. I didn't begin to make money from my books until the forties; when there was the War and double taxation which I willingly accepted to fight the War. All the same high-mindedness is ignorance.'

He had always been quick, his friends thought too quick, to resent a slight and to get his own back, if possible with interest. Humility was in any case a virtue to which he did not pretend. Self-importance grows naturally from solipsism. Veronica Wedgwood in her capacity as assistant editor of *Time and Tide* more than earned the title to sanctity conferred on her by her colleague John Betjeman: 'the saintly backbone of all our lives' in her tactful restraint of her old tutor. 'Dearest. Our lawyer has been on to me about libel. He thinks you're very near the wind with "illiterate schoolgirls", "Bottom the Weaver" and "the obituary columns of the local press."' It will be seen that the literary weapons employed were not always of the subtlest. Sometimes she managed to forestall trouble by a skilful appeal to vanity. 'Dearest Trelawny [her affectionate nickname for this embattled Cornishman], No, don't go for Grigson. He's not worth your powder and shot, or your steel, or whatever metaphor you like.'

A particular source of irritation was the neglect of his poetry by the fashionmakers in criticism and the attention paid to that of contemporaries whom he thought his inferiors, notably Stephen

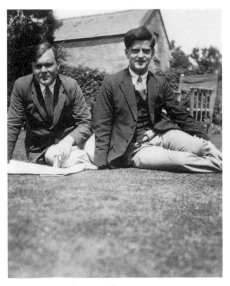

Bruce McFarlane and ALR at
Chipping Campden, 1926.

Outside 24 Robartes Place.

With his Vanson grandparents, *c.*1912.
'Neddy was a spirited and well-fed donkey who went like a pony.'

Two of his seniors whose good
opinion Rowse set most store by:
G. M. Trevelyan (right) and Sir
Arthur Quiller-Couch (*Picture Post*,
24 December 1943).

The young officer: Norman
Scarfe, newly commissioned
in 1943. (Photograph by
Dorothy Wilding)

The young Fellow of
All Souls: ALR, *c.*1930.

Trenarren: the library.

ALR's bedroom, where he read and wrote in his eighties and early nineties.

Trenarren in sullen mood, spring 1970.

'My cat and I grow old together.'

At Lynchburg, Virginia, April 1982.

With Fleet Admiral Nimitz at Drake's Bay, northern California, pointing out the anchorage in which Drake is supposed to have careened his ship in 1578 during his voyage round the world.

William Golding receiving instruction from the Master at a National Trust gathering at Trelissick in 1988. Golding's right-hand neighbour is David Treffry.

Roger Grose and ALR at the china-clay pit where his father worked.

In the window of his beautiful set of rooms at All Souls, the Radcliffe Camera in the background. (Photograph by Douglas Glass).

Windy Encaenia: M. R. D. Foot, partially obscurred by mortarboard. Michael Dummett and Isaiah Berlin in conversation. Herbert Hart behind.

Spender.[1] Spender had compounded his offence by disparaging Rowse's work and, in his capacity as assistant to Cyril Connolly at *Horizon*, waving away suggested contributions. That Spender was also prominent on the Faber poetry list may have weighed with Rowse in choosing to go to Macmillan but this cannot have been more than a minor consideration. He was after big game.

And yet, as so often with him, the minute one thinks a statement about him incontrovertible, contradictions manifest themselves. He *was* after big game: but that did not stop him from pursuing a host of unrelated objectives or entertaining projects that were plainly incompatible with establishing himself on a plinth in the national pantheon. In publishing alone not content with launching himself on the Macmillan list, badgering Cape to put on yet another reprint and making sure that Fabers continued to publish his poetry without his having to throw them a bone from his prose sideboard, he was active in two other important fields. He had agreed to act as historical adviser and scout for Odhams, a firm that had plenty of money and a paper allocation beyond the requirements of a very modest list. Even more substantial was his commitment to Hodder and Stoughton (strictly to their subsidiary imprint English Universities Press) as General Editor of the Teach Yourself History series. The idea of the series was his and he undertook to write the introductory volume, the key to the whole project, entitled *The Use of History* (1946). He wrote in his General Introduction:

I am convinced that the most congenial, as well as the most concrete and practical, approach to history is the biographical, through the lives of the great men whose actions have been so much part of history, and whose careers in turn have been so moulded and formed by events.

The key idea of this series, and what distinguishes it from any other that has appeared, is the intention by way of a biography of a great man to open up a significant historical theme: for example, Cromwell and the Puritan Revolution, or Lenin and the Russian Revolution.

1. The object of the attack in *Time and Tide* which Veronica Wedgwood and the lawyer were trying to abort.

The book is short, about 45,000 words, but one of his best and liveliest. Perhaps it might be regarded as one of the last works of the proto-Rowse period, full of good humour, generosity to other writers, a sense of fun and of the enjoyment of the breadth of reading everywhere evident. Above all it is unembittered. The jealousies, the resentments aroused by becoming a public figure have not clouded the sky. It was written at a time of relief, almost exhilaration. The anxieties of D-day and the weeks of fierce fighting that followed were over. The War was palpably won. From internal evidence the book was begun in the autumn of 1944.[1] The imagery is vigorous, the ideas fresh. Some of the bad habits criticized much earlier by T. S. Eliot occasionally re-assert themselves; cliché adjectives such as 'vital' are allowed to shoulder weight that ought to be borne by the construction of a sentence. But re-reading the book fifty years after I heard it, in substance, delivered as a course of lectures in the Old Library at All Souls when I was an undergraduate I was gratefully reminded of how stimulating it was.

Like so much of his best work it belongs at least in part to the category of autobiography. He brings in his friends, his colleagues and his pupils. He traces the germination and growth of his own understanding of history and his attempts to find in its study a satisfying explanation of the human condition such as was supplied, in earlier ages, by religious belief. We see that Jacob wrestling with the angel was a foreshadowing of the author's struggle with the historical materialism sketched but not fully worked out by Karl Marx.

> With thee all night I mean to stay
> And wrestle till the break of day.

Moral sternness, a sense of the duty the intellect owes to itself, is the backbone of the book. It was, he tells us, to Oxford, to the friends he made there, to the arguments he had with them, that he owes this. Before that everything was emotion, rapidly solidifying into prejudice. Not, he hastens to add, that this has made him a Puritan or a kill-joy. The book is dedicated to Bruce McFarlane and some of its most

1. op. cit., pp. 27 and 188.

charming passages are drawn from the walks they took together in the neighbourhood of Oxford or from voyages of exploration made into parts of England or Scotland they did not know. The same quality, compounded of poetic sensibility and topographical observation, is generously praised in the work of Sir Maurice Powicke and Sir John Betjeman. Not that undue prominence is given to the famous. The unnamed history masters at Rotherham Grammar School[1] are enthusiastically praised for producing a local source-book to encourage their pupils to look for their history in what they see around them.

Praise indeed is handsomely distributed. Books like Duff Cooper's *Talleyrand* and Philip Guedalla's *Palmerston* are not dismissed with the usual academic sniff. J. A. Williamson's excellent introductory expositions of English history and of the overseas expansion that played such a part in it are worthily commended. Belloc and Chesterton, condemned as propagandists making nonsense of our history, are justly, even generously, admired as writers of genius. There is very little sitting in the seat of the scornful. Enjoyment and encouragement are the keynotes: 'It is endlessly interesting and fascinating to have a mental life.'

In view of his later dismissive attitude towards Braudel[2] it is worth remarking that on pages 127–8 he states, and tentatively claims originality for, an interpretation of history that seems to come close to his:

The point is whether we mean by history the surface story, which is capable of infinite variation, or the underlying story which is profoundly conditioned.

I do not know whether this distinction has been made before by any writer; and yet it is for lack of it that there has been endless discussion, largely due to this confusion.

The book was well received. Trevelyan's praise, measured yet substantial, was probably the most gratifying. What was to follow? For years Rowse had had a long list of subjects he meant to tackle. Swift, the

1. ibid., p. 170.
2. His *The Mediterranean and the Mediterranean World in the Age of Philip II* (trans. Siân Reynolds. 2 vols. 1972–3. Original French edition 1949) won world fame for the *Annales* school of historiography over which he presided for some thirty years.

Godolphin family, an extension of the themes of *Tudor Cornwall* to the broader canvas of the nation. Or should he rather narrow and deepen them? With the historical world all before him he thought seriously of throwing it all up and devoting the rest of his life to a History of Cornwall on the heroic scale that would be worthy of Charles Henderson. In one of his Notebooks begun in November 1946 he wrote, perhaps in reaction, 'I am haunted by Cornwall, the obsession that awaits me around the corner when I am away from my friends, nearly all of them *English* ... they exorcise for me those bitter memories, the endless disappointment, the nausea, the impertinences ... the familiarities ... the treacheries and worse, the letting down by friends.' He did collect and publish two volumes of essays, short stories and broadcast talks *West Country Stories* (1945) and *The West in English History* (1949) but these were retrospective not new minted. The same is true of the more important *The End of an Epoch*, already discussed. This reminded the reading public that its author was as much concerned with the contemporary scene as with the Tudor age. At Leonard Woolf's invitation he had joined the Editorial Board of the *Political Quarterly* in 1942. In October 1946 Michael Sadleir, one of the directors of Constable, was discussing the possibility of commissioning him to write a book on Graham Wallas.[1] But in the end the England of Elizabeth won the day. His knowledge of the background, his love for its literature and its music, were powerful inducements. And the central theme of David and Goliath, a small country pitted against the overwhelming resources of the European superpower, reflected not only the reading of our history defined in the titles of his two recent surveys but his own most passionate political commitment.

An additional attraction, incidental rather than causal, was the opportunity of staying in the great houses of England while they were still lived in by the descendants of the men and women with whom so much of his imaginative life was spent. Hatfield and Hardwick still had papers, pictures, furniture, tapestries, perhaps even clothes and domestic utensils, to distil an atmosphere to those capable of perceiving it. Visiting houses open to the public can give even the least knowledge-

1. Author of the classic *Human Nature in Politics* (1908).

able a powerful impression of an age very different from his own. For a learned man living and working in such surroundings the rewards are proportionately richer. Besides Rowse was unashamedly excited by the company of the eminent, the rich and the aristocratic. Does that mean that he was a snob? An unhesitating affirmative may be expected from the *bien pensants* who dislike him or deplore his opinions. Against such a judgment he was never subservient to his betters or negligent of people on the grounds of their social origins. He enjoyed, savoured, the gradations of society and, even more, distinction of achievement or intellectual quality. It made life more fun.

A letter written to Norman Scarfe in the station-master's office at Taplow after his first visit to Cliveden in June 1945 – how many guests at that supremely grand establishment would have arrived or departed by local train? – is full of excitement not in the least abated by the fact that his hostess had been the high priestess of appeasement. They got on like a house on fire: two uninhibited, richly gifted egocentrics whose spheres of interest and activity were complementary rather than competitive, both of them, though capable of brutality, essentially kind-hearted and both with vitality enough for ten. When Nancy Astor died her niece Nancy Lancaster wrote to Rowse to say that of all the notices of her life and character his was the best and truest.

A visit to Althorp at about the same time was no less successful. A cultivated nobleman[1] who took care of his possessions, knew about them and was ready to share his knowledge with anyone who was informed and interested would find Rowse the most appreciative of guests. To rehearse these pleasant interludes of country-house life would distort the perspective of an intensely busy, active life which still had its rubs. Called to the telephone one day at Polmear Mine when he was expecting a call from both the BBC and the *Sunday Times* 'Is that Mr A. L. Rowse's house? Look, what I want to know is – is there a Mr John Rowse in St Austell? He do maake baskets.' One fears the caller's curiosity remained unsatisfied.

---

1. Grandfather of the present Earl Spencer.

19

War in Heaven

The loose-knit chronology so far followed must now give way to a more thematic treatment. All Souls, which had for twenty years been the haven in which Rowse could shelter from the big seas running outside, was itself to be exposed to the full force of the ocean. The metaphor conflates events which were separate in themselves and took place over some seven years, but it will be less confusing for the reader to abstract them from the general course of Rowse's life with which they interacted.

In January 1945 Warden Adams retired. His kindness and common-sense, his almost stolidity in that airy, sometimes self-etherealizing society, are consistently recognized in all Rowse's published and unpublished writings on the College. He had, it seems, attained the post by virtue of his inconspicuousness. When in 1932 Lord Chelmsford, an All Souls grandee of the classic type, ex-Viceroy of India, Cabinet Minister and whatnot, had succeeded Warden Pember more or less by divine right, a long and prosperous reign was expected. His sudden death after only a few months caught the College unprepared. Adams, the sensible, conventional Presbyterian Scot who had voted down T. S. Eliot for a Research Fellowship, was Sub-Warden. In the absence of any immediately obvious candidate, here was a safe man. It turned out an excellent choice.

At the Common Room meeting on 14 January to consider possible successors seven names were put forward. Rowse, who was unable to be present, proposed by letter the name of Sir Arthur Salter.[1] Rowse, who was enthusiastic for maintaining the special position of the

1. For Salter's career see above, p. 125.

College as a bridge between the world of learning and the world of affairs, had welcomed his appointment as Professor of Political Theory and Institutions and quickly became a friend. But the pure intellectuals, of whom Richard Pares was the leader and Isaiah Berlin the rising star, looked down on him. He was swiftly rejected, as were four other candidates, among them Rowse's old tutor Ernest Jacob and the future Warden Sparrow. In a straight fight between Rowse's early friend the Australian Hancock and the Balliol history tutor Sumner whose ex-pupils formed a distinguished proportion of the electorate Sumner narrowly carried the day.

Sumner and Rowse were the antitheses of each other, except in the accidental respect that both suffered severely from duodenal ulcers. Sumner was upright, puritanical, desperately serious, descended from a long line of office-holders in church and state, a Wykehamist of the Wykehamists. In Rowse's view he was a repressed homosexual, a characterization that gained on his interpretation of mentality and temperament, especially those of his fellow dons, as the years went by. Their relations were correct: Rowse respected his conscientiousness, his self-discipline, his dedication – if the word is not beyond rescue. He did not think much of his judgment or of the natural authority of his personality, those essential qualities in the Head of a House. The England of the forties and fifties was less deferential than that of the twenties and thirties, less ready to accept without fuss conventions of dress and behaviour which contribute to the establishment of an esprit de corps. Again in Rowse's view the young Fellows elected after the War included a number of potential Thersites figures who needed firm handling. There were scenes at College Meetings – unthinkable in Rowse's years as a young Fellow – of the Warden and one of his more aggressive juniors trying to shout each other down. Rowse, by seniority Sub-Warden, found himself having to deal with the consequences of all this when Sumner was incapacitated by illness. As Sub-Warden he had advised against the appointment, bizarre by any standards, of Goronwy Rees, soon to win notoriety in the Burgess-Maclean scandal, as Estates Bursar.[1] Sumner shared, by

1. Sir Raymond Carr, who kindly read this chapter in typescript, gave me a very different account of this extraordinary appointment. By his recollection, Sumner surprised a Stated General Meeting (the full meeting of College Fellows held once a

Rowse's account, his opinion but felt that he ought not to exert his power of veto. 'It's your own funeral' said Rowse. But it wasn't. It was his. Sumner died almost immediately after a sudden operation, leaving Rowse responsible for the fortunes of the College.

Rowse was away in America on the first of many fruitful visits of research and of lecturing when he heard of Sumner's death. He cut short his programme as much as he decently could but even so did not arrive in Oxford until after the first exploratory meeting of the College to choose a successor. Sir Edmund Craster, senior Fellow in residence and previously Bodley's Librarian, reported the proceedings to him. Various names had been put forward, Isaiah Berlin, Rowse himself, John Sparrow and Ernest Jacob (Rowse's old tutor who had defeated him for the Chichele Professorship in spite of G. M. Trevelyan's decided preference) but it seemed quite clear that the College as a whole was united in wanting to elect Sir Edward Bridges, son of the poet, Secretary to the Cabinet and Head of the Civil Service, who was within months of retirement. He was, in fact, the obvious choice and had indicated his willingness to accept. All therefore should have been plain sailing. Four days before the meeting at which the College was to make its offer in due form, Bridges withdrew. Attlee, the Prime Minister, had appealed to him to stay on: his services were indispensable.

Here was a pretty kettle of fish. A number of the senior Fellows at once pressed Rowse himself to stand. Unhesitatingly he refused to do so. Sumner's ill health had given him more than a fair sample of what the Wardenship involved. He had only recently, with relief, obtained leave from his Sub-Wardenship to spend some months on his *magnum opus* on the Elizabethan Age and to attend to the publication of the first volume in America. Writing was his life, even more than the scholarship that went into it.

But if he was not prepared to offer himself as a candidate, who could be found to take Bridges's place? After much thought Rowse

---

term at which decisions were taken) by announcing that, since the College needed a new Estates Bursar, he had the week before given lunch at his club to Goronwy Rees and had found him ready to accept the post. Goronwy Rees was thereupon elected by the margin of a single vote. Even as a junior Fellow Sir Raymond was astonished at a decision of such importance being taken so off-handedly.

plumped for another distinguished public servant, Sir Eric Beckett, head of the Legal Department of the Foreign Office. Rowse did not know him at all well but liked him and especially approved the opposition he had shewn to the policy of appeasement. This, however, was hardly a recommendation to a number of his senior colleagues, as Rowse himself was to show in a book he published ten years later.[1]

It was not from his seniors but his juniors that a vigorous, indeed by his account[2] a virulent, opposition manifested itself. Goronwy Rees had been informed of Rowse's opposition, as a member of the Estates Committee, to his appointment as Bursar. He and J. P. Cooper, an ex-pupil whose election to a Fellowship Rowse had supported, put it about that Rowse was imposing his own candidate on a college that hardly knew him. In Isaiah Berlin, whose name had been among those considered at the first exploratory meeting, they had a candidate whose personal charm and intellectual distinction was familiar to every member of the Common Room. Why, one wonders with the hindsight of nearly half a century during which Berlin was to be the founding Head of a new college (Wolfson), President of the British Academy, the secular Pope of the Sacred College of the Great and the Good, was he not elected with instant acclamation? The answer seems to be that in the eyes of his seniors with whom Rowse was in general agreement he lacked both *gravitas* and substantial achievement. In 1951 he was a teaching Fellow of New College and his only published work, apart from some brilliant articles in the philosophical journals, was a little book on Karl Marx in the Home University Library. His wartime despatches as a supernumerary attaché to our embassy in Washington had excited the admiration of a necessarily small but eminent circle of readers. His lectures, his broadcasts, his emergence no longer as a philosopher but as the historian and expositor of a vast untravelled country of thought and sensibility all lay in the future. Even so it is not surprising that the younger Fellows, many of whom had found Rowse arrogant and domineering, welcomed the possibility of electing a Warden so easy, so approachable and so amusing. Rowse,

---

1. *All Souls and Appeasement* (1961).
2. Taken from his diary which is the source of what follows where no other source is cited.

it must be again emphasized, was not himself a candidate, had indeed declined in the clearest terms. But his own candidate, little known in the College, was easily recognized as the standard-bearer of Rowsism and the culture of the seniors. Isaiah (no one would have thought of referring to his rival as 'Eric') was no less clearly the promise of the *nouvelle vague*.

What did Rowse think of the new challenger? Oddly enough in all his copious estimates and sketches of his colleagues and contemporaries most of which contain some adverse criticism I have found no hostile remarks about Isaiah. Quite the reverse, I may add, of what that usually genial man said to me about Rowse when I went to see him in the course of writing this biography. On Rowse's part there is sometimes a remorseful jealousy both of the public recognition and the private affection so freely extended to Isaiah while denied to himself. But this is the merest, mildest outgrowth of the egotism that, as the years went by, gained so strongly on him. 'He is such a dear' is Rowse's usual verdict. And strangely for so feverishly sensitive a man he seems to have had no notion of Isaiah's real hostility.

What explains this bitterness underlying so smooth a surface? Only a year or two before their deaths Isaiah wrote to thank Rowse for sending him an article on Mozart and Joseph II. And at the time of this election Rowse went round for a long and very friendly discussion with Berlin in his room in New College, recording in his diary their agreed conclusion that whatever the upshot might be nothing should disturb their friendship. This is confirmed in identical terms in a letter from Isaiah in the Rowse papers. Isaiah's own account, given to me more than forty years after the events, differed substantially. He claimed that he was in America during the whole time and that he never had the least desire to stand, indeed so informed his supporters at the earliest possible moment. In both these particulars it seems that his recollection was at fault. But of the strength of his dislike and contempt for Rowse I was left in no doubt.

My friendly acquaintance with Isaiah extending desultorily over some forty years gives me no right whatever to interpret his personality. The only explanations I can suggest are therefore circumstantial. As an undergraduate at Corpus Isaiah was the especial protégé of Rowse's great friend, Charles Henderson, in whose rooms they often met. The personal importance of this connexion is notable because Isaiah was then a classicist, reading Greats, followed by so-called 'Modern Greats',[1] while Henderson was a history tutor. It can hardly be doubted that it was Henderson, seconded by Rowse, who urged this brilliant young man to go in for the All Souls Fellowship, on which occasion Rowse both spoke and voted in his favour. Just as Rowse had been the first working-class man to be elected, so Isaiah was the first Jew.[2] The sleepy, residual anti-Semitism of even highly educated Englishmen in the 1930s before the horrors of Hitlerism had forced people to examine their prejudices – an operation comparable to unblocking drains – takes an effort to recall. But high as All Souls flew, pure as was its air, we have only to think of the absurd reactions to the proposed election of T. S. Eliot a decade earlier to realize how far the forces of sweetness and light still had to go. Within a year of his election his and Rowse's great friend Charles Henderson died. It was Rowse to whom his widow and his family turned to commemorate this much loved and valued figure.

Similarly when Richard Pares, the most brilliant, most irreverent, of all the brilliant and irreverent young Fellows elected between the Wars, died prematurely in 1958 it was Rowse who was chosen by his family to speak at his memorial service and invited by the British Academy to write his obituary in its Proceedings. Isaiah's memoir of him appeared in the Record of Pares's old college, Balliol. It had been Rowse, not Berlin, who had been the driving force in having Pares, by then confined to a wheel-chair, re-elected at All Souls and Rowse who had regularly wheeled him about. That Berlin thought Rowse a third-rate mind admits of no doubt. He had ample experience of his conversation and intellectual equipment of his own more than

---

1. 'Greats' is Oxford terminology for *Literae Humaniores*, a syllabus of Greek and Roman history, combined with Philosophy from Plato and Aristotle to the present day. 'Modern Greats' is also known as PPE – Philosophy, Politics and Economics.
2. John Foster, the clever and popular womanizer elected a year before Rowse may, if the gossip Rowse reports in his unpublished *Lives of the Fellows of All Souls* be true, claim this distinction. He was never able to produce a birth certificate and David Cecil, who was at Eton with him, told Rowse that Foster was at least a year older than he claimed. Rowse's information was that he was born in New York, the illegitimate son of his father by a Jewish mistress.

sufficient to form and to defend such an opinion. But in the course of his condemnation he was no less sweeping in judgments where his qualifications were less obvious. Rowse had no quality as a historian. He had never done any serious research. Assertions such as these at once suggest a presumption of resentment or of jealousy. If jealousy were the cause it certainly could not derive from their respective standing in the academic world, still less in the great world outside. It could, perhaps, arise from the consciousness of talents one had considered inferior to one's own being preferred by the people one most admired.

Or, more obviously, it might be the knowledge that an old friend and colleague had prevented his election. 'You have done the College a great service' said Salter to Rowse after one of the long and contentious meetings at which it had finally become clear that a majority could not be mustered for Berlin. It was not that Rowse had personalized the issue. He had put forward a candidate, no particular friend of his but in his eyes suited to the position, and having put him forward was bound to stick to him. The personalizing was, according to Rowse's clear and circumstantial record, the initiative of Goronwy Rees and J. P. Cooper, the leaders of the younger men whom Isaiah himself had been used to describe as the *Sans Culottes*. They were against Rowse's candidate because he was Rowse's candidate.

The emergence of this party feeling was made evident in a subsidiary issue that came before the college at the same time, the election, or re-election, of two of the Senior Fellows, Coupland and Feiling, into the category of Distinguished Fellow or continuation in that of the £50 a year Fellowship. These petty squabbles and manoeuvres need not weary the reader, but they did exacerbate the never tranquil sensibilities of the Sub-Warden. Party spirit is out of place in a college: and even in politics, where it belongs, Rowse was never a sound party man.

The impasse was ultimately circumvented by the election of a compromise candidate, Sir Hubert Henderson. It was only after Isaiah withdrew his own candidacy that a majority could be found. Rowse was unenthusiastic, indeed dissatisfied. He did not like Henderson (whom he seriously misrepresented in *All Souls and Appeasement*). He thought him insufficiently distinguished. And he knew, and pointed out to his fellow-electors, that his health gave grounds for anxiety. Only too soon he was proved right. In spite of his generous initiative in inducing the College to spend a great deal of money on the lodgings, to pay for their lighting and heating and for the cost of the first two servants, Henderson never lived there. For some months he was not thought well enough to manage the stairs and at his first attempt he had a mild heart-attack and had to retreat to his house in North Oxford. At Encaenia in the summer when the French President was among the honorands Henderson had a more serious attack in the Sheldonian Theatre. Rowse had to take his place at a moment's notice and Henderson never entered the College again. He did not, however, immediately resign. The winds that were blowing up on the academic ocean of the 1950s made it especially dangerous for so richly laden a vessel as All Souls to drift rudderless for long. The Senior Fellows urged the need for action. Some of them, Lord Brand and Lord Simon, most senior of all, had on Sumner's death called on Rowse to stand. The idea was now mooted by a number of others. But first Henderson must be persuaded to resign. According to Sir Isaiah Berlin, Rowse himself went up to the South Parks Road and bullied the ill and unhappy Warden into signing the document. Rowse's journal gives a different account. Simon came down one week-end, insisted that any further delay would be prejudicial to the interests of the College and himself went up to the Warden's house the following afternoon returning with his resignation in his pocket.[1] Once again the College had to choose a new head. Once again Rowse was the Sub-Warden in charge of these proceedings. The difference was that this time he had agreed to let his name go forward as a candidate. Why?

The motives of so complicated a character are hardly susceptible of a simple explanation. Their springs, though contradictory, can however be identified, at least in part. Did he want the job? More exactly, would he have been pleased if he had found himself Warden? A pretty confident 'No'. He had, through the ill-health of both predecessors had an exceptional opportunity of finding out just what it entailed. For nine months, he tells us, he had not written a line of any book. To so furiously driven an author this was, in Pepys's famous

1. This account appears in *All Souls in My Time*, p. 162.

phrase, 'as much as to see myself go into my grave'. Furthermore his closest, most trusted friends Jack Simmons and Norman Scarfe had from the start been categorical in advising him against even thinking of it. He knew too that even if he won a majority there would still be a body of Fellows implacably hostile towards him. In the rough seas ahead a mutinous crew might prove hardly less dangerous than the want of a rudder.

Reason, on these considerations, counselled refusal. But what of Emotion? All Souls had been his real home, where from the start he had been welcomed, encouraged, put at ease by men of the highest talent and achievement, in contrast to his nominal home at St Austell where he was in essential respects a stranger, always on guard, a fish out of water. All Souls stood for everything he most valued, the recognition of the supremacy of the life of the mind, the acceptance of public duty and of pride in one's country, the cultivation of good manners and of domestic elegance. Was not all this under threat from the *Sans Culottes*, to whom Warden Sumner had through high-minded ineffectiveness given so much ground? Was it not the best of the older men, the heart of the College to which he had been elected a quarter of a century earlier, Sir Edmund Craster, Lionel Curtis, all the office-holders of the College with the grotesque exception of the Estates Bursar, who now pressed him to stand up for what they believed to be the true character of a unique and uniquely precious institution? Rowse was a man of passionate loyalties.

He was also, as has been the consistent argument of this book, a complex of contradictions. He liked – who doesn't? – to have things both ways, priding himself indeed on what he claims to be a Celtic inwardness, impenetrable to the crude Anglo-Saxon. (One had almost added – he certainly would have in his later years – the word 'heterosexual'). He wanted both to avoid the Wardenship and to have been elected to it. One is reminded of the backing and filling of A. C. Benson, the favourite candidate to succeed Dr Warre as Head Master of Eton in 1904. At the final interview the Provost was driven to ask him whether he would accept the post if offered, explaining that the Governing Body would not wish to be put in the position of having its offer refused. 'In that case I feel the offer should *not* be made' replied Benson. Even then he did not rule himself out for another three days, writing at last to say that he definitely would refuse. Yet, after all this elaborate minuet, he still contrived to feel that he had been rejected.[1]

Rejection was central to Rowse's vision of himself. Whatever his accolades, however brilliant his successes, his string of scholarships, his First in Schools, his election to All Souls, the praise and the popularity won by his books, he was always, somehow, rejected. His friends and admirers constantly pointed out to him how little this view squared with the facts. Indeed at moments he himself would triumphantly assert that he had lived just the life he would have chosen to live, that he had beaten his rivals and detractors at their own game. But his restless superabundance of nervous energy, which he would have preferred to describe as his Celtic temperament, made impossible the calm recognition of Gibbon that he had drawn a high prize in the lottery of life. Rejection played the part that in some theatrical interpretations of Christianity is played by a sense of sin, with the comforting difference that sin is one's own fault while rejection is someone else's. Rejection, if it did not exist, had to be invented. At several points, even in his published writings, he admits that he kept alive the flame of resentment against Christ Church not because he was convinced that the College had rejected him for the tutorship but because he needed the idea as a culmination for a future volume of autobiography. 'With me writing always comes first.' It was the same story again with the two elections to the Chichele Professorship, first when Oman retired and Feiling succeeded and secondly when Ernest Jacob followed Feiling. On neither occasion did Rowse in fact covet the chair. He was fond of telling people (including the present writer) how G. M. Trevelyan had come over from Cambridge to call him to his duty only to be astonished by Rowse's insistence that his view of his duty was to write his books, a commitment that Trevelyan had found easily compatible with his tenure of the Regius chair. Yet both occasions featured prominently in the litany of rejection. What more dramatic, more conclusive evidence, than to be rejected by the college to which he had offered his heart and hand? Even as he experienced emotion Rowse was thinking about how to render it in literary form.

1. See on all this David Newsome, *On the Edge of Paradise* (1980), *passim*.

Did Rowse think that he would have been a good Warden? I have found no evidence that he did, beyond the negative conviction that he would not have been a bad one. He had already discharged the routine duties and knew that he was well up to them. He knew that he was not weak, lazy or self-indulgent. He had no conviction of special gifts or talents such as he certainly had when it came to writing. Indeed what were his general convictions at a period of nervous strain such as prompts a man to reckon up? A page or two of his diary, written at the time, may shed some light. His point of departure is a comparison of himself with Grant Robertson, the unsuccessful though far more distinguished candidate in 1914 when Warden Pember was elected:

Now I am in the same situation, with some of his defects, and without much of his strength. He had the strength of his Scottish moralist foundation; of his middle-class, Anglo-Indian[1] family and environment, of his conventional upbringing and training by his remarkable mother. I have none of these; I have always been alone, everything to do for myself. And the crumbling times we live in have affected me far more deeply than most: I have ended with no belief. No belief in people – they are *all* fools, even (often particularly) the clever ones; no belief in the future – the world I care for is crumbling, without my ever having had a share in it; I loathe and detest – when I do not fear – the present. It is not so much its dangers that appal me as its squalor, its meanness, its envy of all distinction and achievement, its lack of any sense of quality. I feel that everything is going down the drain; I do not wish to be involved in going along with it.

Yet now I may be involved. That is the awkward position. Since I was finally *made* by illness to let go any hope of a political career, my leading idea has been – not to be caught. Not to be caught by any of the usual entanglements of life – marriage, family, but above all by a job, by commitments, obligations.

Now I may be caught. I may catch myself.

The obvious candour of this passage makes it harder to see any reasonable ground for his taking it so hard when the College elected John Sparrow. Indeed part of him recognized at once that he had had

1. i.e. Indian Civil Service, not Eurasian.

a narrow escape, a recognition that gained ground as the years of literary production and controversial fame lengthened his shadow. In the windings and turnings that preceded the election it soon became clear to Rowse that he was not going to win. He did not keep a day to day journal during that time, finding it altogether too tense. He records that at the first preliminary vote with thirty-five Fellows present there were '18 votes for Sparrow, 10 for me, 7 blank . . . I regard the game as already lost'.

A few days later King George VI died. Rowse and others in full academic fig crowded into the Sheldonian to hear Bowra, the Vice-Chancellor, proclaim the new Queen. Rowse pushed Richard Pares in his wheel-chair and they gossiped about Sparrow and other colleagues as they waited for the Vice-Chancellor to make his entrance 'fat and short, a ridiculous figure who yet contrives to maintain his dignity by sheer force of character'. That afternoon, walking through the Codrington Library

I caught sight of John Sparrow working at his briefs, alone at the table reserved for Fellows. Should I go up and speak to him about the election? Or would that be a mistake? It might be a mistake to 'concede' the election in so many words, though I regard it as lost. We had a very agreeable conversation. John was in a happy, purring mood; never have I seen him so much at ease with me. As well he might be – for 18 votes to 10 is not likely to be reversed. Would *he* have been so agreeable as I was, had the vote been the other way round? I am sure he would not. And yet these younger Fellows who don't know me think of me as an ogre.

I told John that 'if and when' he was elected, he knew that I would be a loyal supporter. But that I had a request to make. Sumner had protected me in accomplishing my work. To write these books – though people who did not do it themselves thought that it came easily – in fact it took everything I had to write them. I wanted to bury myself now for another three years to write the second volume of my Elizabethan Age. Humphrey [Sumner] had not minded my not coming to his parties, nor my shutting myself up to write. And I hoped John wouldn't. After all I was in a sense the College *goose* who laid the golden eggs; our best argument as an institution was the work we put forth. I quite realised whose work and whose books the College was identified with in the country . . .

John was most amicable in return. From which I learned the real reason why he wants so much to be Warden. It completely agrees with what Richard Pares said to me. I had thought that John would be making a sacrifice of a career in London. Richard, who had known him since he was a boy,[1] said that John has not been much of a success at anything, it wasn't quite obvious what he is for. If he becomes Warden of All Souls it will be evident to the world what he is for.

John bore this out, to an unexpected degree. I said – 'you are being such a success at the bar now, I realise it is a sacrifice for you.' He said 'Well no, I get along, I bluff my way. I don't really know the law. To know the law you have to have your heart in it – like Wilfrid Greene or Simon. I haven't. I get pleasure from doing a case well and pleasing my clients; but I have to mug it up all the time. I don't really know it.'[2]

So far, so admirably rational. But the tides of emotion soon swept over the sea wall. Loyalties, jealousies, resentments, an egocentricity that saw an adverse vote, whatever its real grounds, as a betrayal of friendship submerged the civilized objectivity on which Rowse prided himself. He forgave, at least in theory, those who wrote to him before the actual election explaining that they were going to vote against him because they thought that the Wardenship would be a waste of his gifts and that it was not a question of merit or personal esteem.

The antipathy towards the group of younger Fellows whom Rowse had identified with the party management of Goronwy Rees in the earlier election lost none of its sharpness.[3] Towards the older men such as Simon who had originally encouraged him to stand and had then, as he believed, abandoned what they considered a sinking ship

1. Fellow Wykehamists.
2. Re-reading this passage twenty years later Rowse commented in the margin: 'Wasn't that extraordinarily candid? So revealing. Later, when he applied, he was refused silk.'
3. Raymond Carr's speech at the crucial College meeting was reported to Rowse as having been fatal to his chances. For a year or two thereafter Rowse refused to speak to him, pointedly moving away from him in the Buttery if they happened to come in for lunch at the same time. Suddenly, one day Rowse came up to Lady Carr in the street and inquired 'Are you and Raymond still breeding like rabbits?' Ordinary relations were resumed.

his coldness is easily understood. But the poison that festered was the anger towards old friends, pre-eminently Salter, who had voted against him on the same grounds as those he had forgiven but had not, as they had, explained themselves beforehand.

Besides and beyond individuals there was an inescapable collective personality, the College, that abstraction so indefinable yet so real, so present to its members, especially to the romantics among them of whom Rowse was decidedly one. All Souls had been his home since young manhood. And now, he convinced himself, it was rejecting him.

This severe disturbance, originally at least partly self-induced and subsequently embittered by self-regarding reflection, coloured the rest of his life. To support so large an assertion two documents are printed as appendices. To abridge them so as to fit into a narrative framework would rob their evidence of its accumulated force. The first is an extract from Rowse's diary, written soon after the election in the comfortable seclusion of the beautiful country house of his friend Wyndham Ketton-Cremer. The second, dating from several years later, is his terrible reply to kind Arthur Salter, who hoped to revive their old friendship. In his last years, another couple of decades on, Rowse records his remorse at having written it.

By contrast the closing scenes at All Souls were marked by a dignified restraint:

March 15 1952

I left All Souls this morning under a cloud – in my own mind: left the College meeting early to catch the train, and also to avoid the strain of having questions put to me about the College business which I have been having to conduct for the past two years more or less. Also the strain of having to put up with the affectionate approaches from people who voted against me: no strain in watching my successful rival conduct the business I have been used to doing. I heard the Warden's business through, seated with my back turned to the Hall in a patch of spring sunlight blistering Wren on the wall. (Let the portrait blister – it has nothing to do with me: I've done enough being public-spirited, going round turning off lights other people have left on late at night, taking care of this or that.) . . .

Last night I presided at dinner in Hall for the last time as Sub-Warden.

As I looked down the table I couldn't help thinking of them almost affectionately – as for so long I have – as a party of friends. There was dear Lionel
Curtis, now eighty, though looking hardly any older than I have always
known him, who came home all the way from Cyprus to vote for me and
protested to the last that I ought to be Warden. Opposite me was G. M.
Young, who was chiefly responsible for preventing me getting the Chichele
chair, but who on this occasion was divided in mind, did not favour his
friend Sparrow, inclined to me but in the end went with the majority. Next
him Dougie Malcolm, who described himself as 'torn in twain' between the
two of us – but in the end did not fail to vote for Sparrow. So too Amery,
who had more reason to support me and was fairly equally balanced between
us. Beside me sat Salter, who had been my close friend hitherto. Next him
Geoffrey Faber was wanting to sit next me to describe his own emotions
about the difficulty of the choice – he has been writing me long letters about
it all – and his own autobiography. Then Cyril Falls, who has been a faithful
supporter all through and a most sensitive friend. Then Ernest Jacob – one
of my oldest and most intimate friends – who has behaved neither like a
friend or even a good acquaintance.

On the opposite side Goronwy Rees, all smiles and giggles and Welsh
good looks – an open and unresting enemy throughout. Then dear Geoffrey
Hudson, gentle and absent-minded as ever, – whom I had to propel into the
Sub-Warden's chair this morning. I wished him 'Goodbye and Good Luck'.
Craster too – with his shrewdness and judgment – who kept his counsel all
through and at the end told me to my great surprise that he had supported
me throughout the election . . . At the bottom of the table the unbroken
ranks of the Junior Fellows, not one of whom voted for me . . .

Eighty pages of typescript later the diary completes the account:

I dutifully gave John Sparrow a good send-off in proposing his health in
Common Room the night of the election – so 'warmly' that he leaped to his
feet to thank me. Ken Wheare, a supporter,[1] said 'After all, a great man';
but he, no more than Rohan Butler, could have foreseen that it was just duty
and a piece of acting – it was a farewell: I was turning my back.

1. Of Rowse's, for whom the high compliment presumably was intended.

20

The New World Redresses
the Balance

If it is more than doubtful that Rowse would have made a good Warden of All Souls it is certain that both the pleasures and the duties of the office would have denied him his second flowering in America. He had been paying his first visit there when the sudden death of Warden Sumner called him back to Oxford. His subsequent resolve to turn his back on All Souls pointed him all the more urgently in the direction of the United States. The wonderful libraries, wonderful not only in their holdings but in the facilities offered to scholars, the generous research grants and visiting Professorships provided seven-league boots for a historian with as much ground to cover as Rowse had. And the welcome everywhere extended, the honour everywhere paid, was all the more enchanting after the bruising of the Wardenship elections.

Rowse's zest for life, his adventurousness, his readiness to enjoy new landscapes and climates, new writers, are often obscured in his journals by jeremiads of one sort and another. But the man one met, even in the closing stages of his long life, still gave abundant evidence of these qualities: in his late forties they captivated his hosts. 'We have never had a visitor in the twenty years that I have been a member of this Department who has been as stimulating and as good company as you' wrote W. L. Sachse of the University of Wisconsin. At the Huntington Library in California where from the late fifties Rowse was for many years a Senior Research Fellow, John M. Steadman was one of the highly distinguished group of scholars who found the place a shadow of itself when Rowse was away. Rowse prided himself, not unjustly, on his knowledge of, and feeling for, America. He had been in many more states of the Union than most Americans. He had all the eagerness of a born and observant sightseer to visit famous towns, houses, museums and galleries, to notice colour and light. Beyond this he had a number of axes to grind. He had long had in mind a book on the Cornish emigration to America, stimulated in the nineteenth century by the demand for skilled miners and especially by the temptations of the Gold Rush. He was to deliver in 1958 the first series of Trevelyan Lectures at Cambridge, published a year later under the title *The Elizabethans and America*. His passionate admiration for Churchill and his own engagement in the history of his own time naturally led him to seek out the statesmen and the great commanders such as Fleet Admiral Nimitz who had played no small part in great events.

He was, in any case, increasingly and unashamedly, drawn to the excitement of eminent acquaintance. He was not a snob in the sense that he would have thought less of a man for being the son of a coal-heaver. On the contrary, he would probably have thought more of him, sympathizing from his own experience with the difficulties of overcoming the social and educational obstacles of such origins. But he certainly liked in England to hobnob with Duchesses, Cabinet Ministers, eminent persons in any profession, provided that they were neither dull nor ill-mannered. Similarly in France he would put up with being kept waiting for hours, nearly missing his train, in order to lunch with Princess Bibesco. No doubt she was worth it, given the extraordinary record of her life and loves.[1] But one has only to imagine what a torrent of abuse would have surged through his diary had he been so treated by a Professor at a provincial university. In America it was the same, except that on the whole it was enormous wealth rather than aristocratic lineage that was the cynosure.

His friendship with Caspar Weinberger, who had reviewed a number of his books, opened many doors (in England it had even opened that of No. 10 Downing Street during Mrs Thatcher's tenancy). Nixon gave a small dinner for him at his house in New York, Jacqueline Onassis an even more intimate lunch to which only two other guests were invited. He kept up with the Aldriches, the Bruces and the

---

1. Brilliantly epitomized in Sir Steven Runciman's review of *Enchantress: Marthe Bibesco and Her World* by Christine Sutherland (*The Spectator*, 12 April 1997).

Annenbergs whom he had known in their days at the London Embassy. Before deafness increased an already strong proclivity to monologue he was excellent company. But he did not let his social opportunities override his proper concerns. Wealth and fashion were well enough: but he preferred them to be combined with a love of books and scholarship as for instance in the case of Boies Penrose.

First, last, and all the time Rowse was a writer, generous and open in his appreciation of the work of other writers. He had long admired such novelists of an older generation as Edith Wharton and Willa Cather, whose formative environment in Nebraska he was anxious to see for himself. Similarly with two Southern writers of his own generation and younger, William Faulkner and Flannery O'Connor, he wanted, like his friend Betjeman, to envisage not only the physical but the psychological, intellectual and religious influences that had given their work its particular quality. Of course too he wanted to see – though he didn't much like – such icons of literary criticism as Edmund Wilson. He was agog to excavate the literary site of D. H. Lawrence's years in New Mexico. He wanted to – but any attempt to catalogue his intellectual, literary and artistic appetites and ambitions in the New World is fatiguing even to contemplate and would be false to the facts by wearying the reader instead of exhilarating him as it certainly did Rowse.

Professionally and financially the annual transhumance to the United States was of the first importance. In Cass Canfield at Harpers Rowse was to have an enthusiastic publisher and in Perry Knowlton at Curtis Brown a no less effective agent. When he first went to New York in 1951 his US rights were handled by Macmillan, New York, then still part of the London firm. But before the conglomerates had laid their deadening hand on the lively and highly professional publishing houses that were in spirited competition with each other and before the great anarch, television, let the curtain fall, the potentialities of the American market in the 1950s were too considerable to be regarded as merely subsidiary. Rowse had still no literary agent in London, a surprising omission in so contentious, not to say suspicious, an author but he wisely decided to employ one in New York.

The terms of his Visiting Professorships, too, were liberal as was the scale of fees he earned from lectures and articles. Like Pepys he derived both pleasure and a sense of achievement in totting up his earnings from year to year. Figures in an age of inflation require so much qualification, that they lack that rocklike solidity which is their especial charm. An Appendix gives some of the details that a practised eye can interpret without well-meant but probably inept authorial assistance. The point to be made here is that his earnings were substantial and soon, with bonuses such as Book of the Month Club Choices, became very large. He was rich: not in the sense that he could have bought Petworth or even Boconnoc or Lanhydrock had they come on the market. But rich enough to know, in spite of repeated wails about the licensed robbery of taxation, that he could live as he wished to live and could afford to buy pictures and books except for those whose prices had shot up with the sudden fever of fashion. Financial security was his main object. Its successful attainment opened the way for others.

High among them was intercourse with American historians and literary scholars such as Steadman, Alfred Harbage and Lefty Lewis, the editor of Horace Walpole. With the historians he was on much easier terms than with their English counterparts. None of them had written hostile or even cool reviews of his books or cast doubts on his scholarship. (This was before he had embarked on his Shakespearean explorations which will be dealt with in a later chapter.) The tone of American manners, so courteous and so hospitable, called out a similar response in so warmly responsive a nature. American historians could be presumed well disposed until there was evidence to the contrary, an assumption certainly not extended to their English confreres. There were already some whom he had long admired, notably Samuel Eliot Morison whom in the work of his late age *Historians I Have Known* (1995) Rowse classes with, or even above, G. M. Trevelyan. It is pleasant to record that this admiration was cordially reciprocated. In an undated letter in his own hand Morison wrote 'Your writing is so superior in style as well as content that one becomes spoiled – for anything less good is just distressing.' Like Rowse, Morison was a stylist and a man of letters – a kinsman, it appears, of T. S. Eliot who drew on this great maritime historian's knowledge of New England waters for his poem 'The Dry Salvages'. J. H. Hexter and Wallace Notestein, scholars of great distinction who both specialized in seventeenth-century English history, were on good, but never close, terms with Rowse. In June 1940 when things were at their blackest Notestein had written to him:

You cannot teach English history all your life and work in English archives and watch English methods without coming to have a feeling that is deeper than anything else in you . . . God prosper old England and Scotland. I think we shall soon be in the war. But our young people, in the twenties, are so everlastingly pacifist, as yours were a few years ago . . .

The historian whose period was all but the same as Rowse's was Garrett Mattingly. When his fine book *The Defeat of the Spanish Armada* was published in 1959 he wrote to Rowse:

I was overwhelmed by your review in the *New York Times*. I feel as if I had been knighted by my general on the field of battle and in view of all my comrades in arms. There is no hand in the world from which I would rather receive the accolade.

'Unlike most American academics' wrote Rowse in *Historians I Have Known*

Mattingly was a good linguist . . . Also we were at one about American academic writing (so too the Master, Sam Morison). Standards had been deeply damaged by the cult of the German Ph.D., dominant in the later nineteenth century. Germans were thorough researchers, but in writing up the results they had little sense of proportion or relevance and piled everything in.

I had already had experience of making three or four such books publishable. It was necessary to cut them down by a third, they were so repetitive . . . Early on at the Huntington Library I had a telling experience with a young woman's thesis on Graham Wallas. It needed severe pruning. She was an intelligent student. At the end she said, 'I know that you are right, but if I followed your advice I should not get my Ph.D.'

Hence their inspissated unreadability.

Had he been writing about English academic life where nowadays a Ph.D. is a *sine qua non*, he would have said much the same. It was the nature of the examination, not the intellectual quality of American academics, that he was criticizing. On the face of it anyway. But as so often with Rowse the minute one has said anything about him instances to the contrary crowd to the mind. He could be coldly cutting and superior. 'Armed with a dagger in one hand and a rapier in the other' as one of his Huntington colleagues humorously characterized him to me. Yet the vast weight of the evidence shows him as encouraging, constructive, stimulating to his American colleagues. The gentleness and tact with which he shows how an overloaded portentous passage can be turned into clear and easy exposition without loss of scholarship makes it hard to believe that the same man could be rude and crushing. Again the real sympathy and generosity of feeling he shewed in grief or personal difficulty remain in the affectionate memory of his American friends.

To follow him round the campuses of America would require a book in itself. What is obvious is that he everywhere responded to the appreciation and admiration so enthusiastically accorded him. He held Visiting Professorships or was Special Lecturer at a great number of the large State Universities and enjoyed them, but as he wrote to one of his friends at the Huntington, Professor Andrew Rolle, in November 1986 'You know that in the US I like the smaller liberal arts colleges best.' Of these Lynchburg, Virginia seems to have been a particular favourite. The freedom of his conversation and his readiness to range over topics outside his accredited expertise appear to have been the qualities especially enjoyed by his hosts.

It is on the Huntington Library at Pasadena and the circle of friends there that this account must centre. He first went there in the late spring of 1951, returning each year from 1961 to 1966 as Senior Research Fellow, arriving in the autumn and coming back to Cornwall with the swallows. Like the great country houses at which he was so fond of staying the Huntington combines grandeur and informality, beauty and businesslike efficiency. Its splendid library and its superb picture gallery are surrounded by gardens full of rarities, especially cacti and flowering trees. Below in the distance one sees the tall buildings of Los Angeles, but mechanization and the roar of traffic belong to another world from the Tennysonian Avilion in which the Huntington is set. The climate of Southern California at the turn of the year when Rowse was in residence there is perfection. Long sunny days undisturbed by wind or rain, cool, clear starlit nights. The Athenaeum, the University Club in Pasadena, at which he stayed, comfortable, welcoming, well-run, is about half an hour's walk through rich, exquisitely maintained residential avenues where the only human beings one meets are the occasional jogger or Mexican workmen digging up the electricity cables or repairing the water supply. No one is walking to the banks or the shops because there are none nearby, and all such necessities are attended to by car since there is no public transport. The backdrop to this shining Mediterranean villadom is provided by a formidable range of mountains.

Rowse was at once captivated. After his first visit he wrote to the seventeenth-century historian Godfrey Davies, who had originally invited him. 'I simply and absolutely loved my time with you ... You've no idea what an impression it all made on my heart.'[1] The combination of such dazzling physical beauty with an Aladdin's cave of books and manuscripts specially collected for the study of English history and literature, the whole enhanced by the company of an intimate circle of witty and learned men reawakened the wonder and excitement that he had felt in his early days at Oxford. Wonder and excitement are the strengths of Rowse's best historical writings. The Huntington blew them into flame when they might have smouldered.

The circle who stimulated him there consisted principally of Allan Nevins, Ray Billington, Jack Pomfret, John M. Steadman and Andrew Rolle, of whom the two last, surviving, have kindly allowed me the run of their memories. Allan Nevins was the dominant personality, in many ways an American version of Rowse, copious of information, instant in opinion, intolerant of argument. Rowse's sketch of him in *Historians I Have Known* is unflattering, even grudging, despite the admission that Nevins was his oldest American friend, to whom 'I owed my introduction into the intimacy of American family life, where for long I felt an outsider.' Perhaps he was irritated that, industrious and productive as he himself was, Nevins excelled him in both respects. Certainly he was irritated by Nevins's progressive liberal

1. Huntington Library, DG 47(46), 4 July 1951.

certainties, the fugleman of political correctitude. Yet it was Nevins who nearly persuaded him to apply for American citizenship and to settle at the Huntington where he was confident of securing him a permanent appointment. And it was Nevins for whom Rowse obtained an honorary doctorate at Oxford. Oddly, because he goes out of his way both in *Historians I Have Known* and in private correspondence to make it clear that he thought him merely useful and worthy without distinction of mind or grace of style.

All of them, except for Steadman who had taken the world of literary history for his parish, were famous for their work in the field of American history. Jack Pomfret, the Director in the early sixties when Rowse was a regular visitor, features as Mr Kindheart in Rowse's little *jeu d'esprit* about the Huntington *Brown Buck* (1976). It is not the happiest of his productions (though he had a defensive conceit of it and his publishers did him proud, with illustrations that achieve an easy charm towards which the text labours). It is dedicated in most affectionate terms to the Pomfrets: perhaps at last he had forgiven Mrs Pomfret, a doctrinaire feminist, for her insistence that he must have owed his remarkable success to the support and encouragement of his mother. White with rage, Rowse contained himself in silence. But his letters and journals explode in vituperation, not least at the impertinence of presuming to tell him about the intimacies of his family life.

It is the kindness, the good-nature, the contentment of Rowse's friends at the Huntington that contrasts so strongly with his own jealous, competitive watchfulness. 'I still find the Huntington the academic paradise that I have always viewed it, and bless the fates that brought me here' wrote Ray Billington to him in 1972. Could Rowse ever have said the same? He was sincerely grateful to the place, sincerely fond of it. But an agitating sense of his own superiority kept impelling him to snarl and to wound. One day at lunch in 1966 the talk turned on Kenneth Clark. A very senior figure opined that Clark's reputation rested on his popular success and that he lacked real quality. 'What do YOU know about quality?'

Silence descended.

Rowse never again applied for a Fellowship at the Huntington.[1]

1. This scene was described to me more than thirty years later by one who had been present.

How much he was missed is evident from the affectionate correspondence of those kind, forgiving men. His visits to other American centres of learning continued for another fifteen or twenty years and still met with warm appreciation, so well expressed by the literary scholar, Fredson Bowers:

I shall never cease to be interested in the magnificent range of your reading and thought and the way in which this total experience of living informs not alone your writing of history – and especially of poetry – but also the most casual form of your conversation.

This gets to the heart of Rowse's peculiar quality, a quality that offended so many other scholars, such as Keith Hancock and Hugh Trevor-Roper, the intrusion, as they saw it, of the personality of the writer on the matter in hand. How much America stimulated him, in a way restored him to himself by liberating him from bitterness at not being elected Warden of All Souls, not being given the OM or made a peer or even a knight, may be seen from a passage in his diary for the fall of 1960:

In the afternoon I took the Greyhound bus and had an enjoyable ride through fine country to the Massachusetts border and into Connecticut. Big hilly country with forest, rocks and valleys, the road going on interminably as is the way in this immense country.

At Hartford – with Providence, R.I., one of the country's Insurance capitals – I was met by Lefty Lewis's man-servant and luxurious car, and driven out to Farmington. As distinguished as ever, even more rewarding, more pictures, more treasures – but this time Lefty alone, without wife, more cosy on a bachelor basis.

Every comfort on every side, waited on hand and foot by domestics, women and men; house, my room, bed, all delicious; everywhere books, and outside the additions containing thousands of manuscripts, books, prints, drawings, most of Horace Walpole's library and many of his possessions. Outside my windows the garden, beyond, the orchard, in which at times expensive dogs wandered, not allowed in, nor the poor little white cat.

Lefty is going to leave the whole place, as yet another foundation, to Yale, with half-a-dozen Fellows to research and be also at ease in Zion. Already he must employ a dozen staff at Farmington and at Yale, keeping the MSS and editing the Letters. It must all cost an enormous sum. Once more, brought home to me how agreeable to be rich; and how disagreeable not to be.

October 26. Lefty drove me on a honeyed morning, the trees full of light, into New Haven, where I spent the morning happily in the University Library copying out Froude's letters to George Eliot, with eyes as usual on a far future book. I hadn't finished – and Lefty generously promised to give me a photostat of the remaining letters – when he carried me off to Wallace Notestein's favourite table in the Club, carved with names of students a hundred years ago. A group of historians to meet me, but conversation with Wallace was best. He was pleased at my return to local history with the St Austell book[1] and wanted a copy. We agreed about Robert Cecil being a much bigger man than he is usually considered – Wouldn't he be the best person to take, instead of Leicester, for my 'Eminent Elizabethans'? Who were they to be? Bess of Hardwick, Leicester or Robert Cecil, Lord Henry Howard, but who was the fourth for my converse to Strachey? I have him in my notes. To be followed by 'Lesser Elizabethans'; Sir Richard Hawkins, Topcliffe, Henry Cuffe etc. Life isn't long enough. [Annotated by Rowse 'Most of this was accomplished years later.']

Notestein said that he and Neale agreed that we want more biographies – very different from the discouraging attitude I met with over my *Grenville*. Dear Richard Pares could never bring himself to say a word in its favour, or in favour of historical biography at all. Discouraging, but wrong.

What zest for life, enthusiasm for his subject, energy and imagination in planning future work, in collecting material and holding it in suspension while he was writing other books, lecturing, travelling, observing, recording – what a many-sided man, and, transparently, what a happy one, this passage displays. The motto that his cranky old friend at All Souls, the geneticist E. B. Ford proposed him for 'Labor fons laetitiae' was apt indeed.

Not that work was the only source of his pleasure in America. He enjoyed, marvelled at, its enormous wealth and approved the pliancy that created it. He applauded the readiness of the rich to spend their money on the support of literature and the arts. He even won praise

1. *St Austell: Church. Town. Parish* (1960).

from Edmund Wilson, hardly to be reckoned an Anglophile, for his appreciation of the American landscape.

> You are good on the American landscape for which many Europeans have little real feeling . . . The difference in this relationship from the European one lies in one's feeling that in order to function – to think, to realize oneself, to do solid work, etc. – one has to *pit oneself against* the country, which at the same time, however, will give one support.[1]

This remark may well have been prompted by *The Elizabethans and America* (1959) one of the most successful of his works in spite of comparatively modest sales. Combining his many-sided historical knowledge with literary sensibility and an awareness of how the one fertilizes the other it is notably generous in its acknowledgment to other scholars, particularly in the geographical and textual fields. Delivered as the first of the series of lectures founded in honour of G. M. Trevelyan it owes its composition as much to Rowse's recent visits to America as to his long-standing friendship and admiration for the honorand. In quality and tone it may stand as the last product of proto-Rowse, before the balance of his mind has been disturbed by the self-preoccupation that fed on his feelings of rejection.

To a nature so inveterately self-contradictory even the comfort and charm of America had its obverse:

> Akron-Canton Airport, 19 October 66, delayed by fog. I have tried to squeeze into a corner to get as far away from filthy T.V. as possible, loud, brash, intolerable, the Idiot People guffawing away at its inanities. I had an impulse to kick the thing as I passed by . . .
>
> I had an unforgettable experience at Detroit at the week-end. Peter,[2] in the goodness of his heart, had laid it on for me to stay the week-end with 'extremely nice' people, living on a fine estate with three lakes and sixty acres of orchards. I went into it with my eyes open, ready for an experience. They were represented as fans of mine, who had wanted to meet me for years. (They will not meet me again.) The husband had been twice married before,

1. In a letter dated 17 February 1959.
2. Unidentified.

a retired General Motors executive, or economic/statistical adviser, above average intelligence, had started with nothing, now worth several millions. The wife, also twice married before – leaving her well off. Herself of New England stock, a poor Baptist minister's daughter, Irish on her mother's side, with a Cornish strain. During her last widowhood she had spent some time in Cornwall . . .

She was all over me at first – had for years wanted to meet me, knew so many of the people I knew in Cornwall, why hadn't she met me when she was there (she was so bitterly disappointed with her English experience), 'Aren't you nice?', 'Can I come and see you in Cornwall?' (Not on your life) . . .

She would come into my bedroom in her scarlet dressing-gown, lace nightdress showing underneath, and languish on my bed while she exposed her nasty nature; or she would skip gallumphing up the drive to show how young and happy she was. 'Aren't you wonderful' she would say the first day. Or 'You're the most perfect guest' as I helped to clear the table. Then 'Isn't it wonderful that Steve and I are so happy?', suggesting that I find someone to be happy with too. 'Of course, Steve is very bright – brighter even than you' . . .

I made a mistake in making up to her at all. I tried to make myself amusing, by saying what a tease her good looks must have been to those old girls of the Girls Friendly Society in Cornwall. 'You mean they're all lesbians?' she put it crudely. 'How *a'ful*! I'm entirely man-oriented . . .'

I was a fool to try and amuse her, for of course not a grain of humour.

This is a much-abbreviated extract: but it is long enough to remind one what an eternity a week-end can be.

A year earlier (26 September 1965) he had set out the pros and cons of the New World in outspoken terms:

Oh God! here I am in London Airport once more, on the conveyor-belt to America, which I won't be off again until back here at the end of March. What a fool I feel, uprooting myself from Oxford, where I like being best, from my rooms, august and lovable; and from Trenarren, where I have never felt happier or more fulfilled than this summer.

And what for?

The squalor of the down-at-heel Hotel [in New York], noisy, dusty, run-down from what it was when I first went there. For an exhausting lecture-tour, scrambling aboard planes, worrying about engagements, meeting boring people, public exhibitions of myself – O do you Fortune chide . . . that did not better for my life provide than public means which public manners breeds. Then my annual penance of shutting myself up in a bed-sitter in Pasadena . . .[1]

No Earl Grey tea laid on, afternoons, in the smoking room; no excellent dinners to go down to in candle-lit common room or hall; no short walks round Magdalen or Meadows; the dear old Humber waiting for me in the chestnutty, leaf-strewn drive, for expeditions out in the Oxford countryside, to medieval Weston-on-the-Green to dinner, to Brackley to meet Jack, or traipsing off across midland counties to meet Robin at Lincoln, or explore the depths of Lincolnshire, lunch at Grimsthorpe, talking to the cheerful women among the lit rhododendrons of Woodhall Spa.

Then what *am* I uprooting myself for?

Primarily dollars; a literary career, to make hay over there while the sun shines; because the Americans seem to want me more than the English do, treat me better, far more generously, with more good will. Negatively, because my idea is to *s'évader*, to run out, to turn my back where I am not well treated, to make myself scarce.

I *have* built up an alternative to this deplorable country. Because I hate modern society, the welfare state, pop culture and mob-civilization I am going to the home of it all, the pattern modern state. But over there I have no obligations and no responsibility, only to do my best for what I am paid for.

Then there are compensations. I have friends. Apart from the people here I am most fond of, I like people better over there. More good will, more generous. One can breathe.

1. i.e. Staying at the very comfortable Athenaeum whilst working at the Huntington.

21

Some Softening Gleam

In the passage quoted at the end of the preceding chapter Rowse divides the nostalgia already setting in at London Airport between 'Oxford, where I like being best' and 'Trenarren, where I have never felt happier or more fulfilled than this summer'. Oxford, All Souls indeed, has made quite a come-back. This was written in 1965, thirteen years after the Great Rejection. His relations with Sparrow are wholly agreeable. Sparrow writes to him gossiping about Isaiah Berlin's supposed matrimonial intentions or thunderstruck by a proposed emendation to the statutes which would open the Fellowship Election to women.

Oh, how I envy you being away from here ... I was on Saturday 14th October presented (without any previous warning from the signatories) with a Notice of Motion signed by 10 Fellows to amend the Statutes so as to admit women as Fellows. A day or two later one of the Fellows told the Press, and of course it is in the headlines. Signatures: Monteith, Zaehner, Millar, Caute, Dummett, Abraham, Lyttelton, Neill, Tyson, Fawcett. I like the last four: they ought to have known better.

Rowse gives friendly advice and, more percipiently than Sparrow, seizes on the project of offering Visiting Fellowships as the only means of preserving the ethos of the College and the endowments that underpin it against the root-and-branch reformers at the gates. Among Sir Penderel Moon's papers at the India Office Library is a letter from Rowse amounting to a three-line whip for the College meeting at which this issue was to be decided.[1]

1. I owe this information to the kindness of Professor Roger Louis of the University of Texas at Austin.

So far from shaking the dust of the College off his feet it remained the centre of many untroubled friendships, such as that with Lord Hailsham who once felicitously said of him that he was the only man he has known 'in whom a degree of vanity was an ornament and not a defect of character'.[1] Among his seniors one who did not easily lower his barrier of reserve, Lord Radcliffe,[2] wrote to him with remarkable openness. His praise of *The Expansion of Elizabethan England* (1955) 'I thought it so exceptionally good – most moving to read, real mastery of the huge range of material – and about life itself. I am glad that history has proved a vehicle for your natural poetry' prompted Rowse to encourage him to write an account of himself and his opinions. Radcliffe's reply reveals a pessimism deeper than Rowse's: 'I think some of us had much *better* keep quiet. It is the best we can do for the brave, uncomplaining, not very imaginative race of people who *are* the world. If the human condition is tragic, as I think, they gain nothing from being reminded or persuaded of it; and the weaker brethren – who must not be caused to stumble – may lose much.' A few months later, in July 1975, hearing that *A Cornishman Abroad* (1976) was shortly to appear he wrote that he looked forward 'not only to learning something about yourself in the early years but also something about Oxford, which I have never understood – or if one is to tell the truth – much liked or been happy to dwell in.' Radcliffe, like Cruttwell and G. N. Clark, two other seniors with whom Rowse always got on well, had, he thought, never fully recovered from the horrors of the trenches to which they had been exposed at a tender age.

Rohan Butler, whose book on *The Roots of National Socialism* Rowse had reviewed so enthusiastically, remained a steady friend and a steady supporter of the old ethos of the College. In a way, Rowse came to think, almost too much so. His scholarly perfectionism prevented his biography of Choiseul from appearing for some thirty-five years: and when it did it only took its subject, in a thousand

1. Taken down by Alan Bell, then Librarian of Rhodes House, at a seminar concerned with the College history of All Souls and kindly communicated by him.
2. One of the outstanding intellects among the lawyers of his day and in great demand as Chairman of important Royal Commissions, among them that which settled the boundaries of India and Pakistan in 1947.

pages, to the threshold of his ministerial career. An even more fervent opponent of change, especially of the admission of women, was the geneticist E. B. Ford. 'All Souls is finished as a College' he wrote to Rowse on 15 February 1979, informing him that the decision to admit women had gone through on one vote. His own scientific paper 'The Abilities of Men and Women' might have warned his colleagues of the mistake they were making. But was he an altogether disinterested witness to truth? The article on him in the *Dictionary of National Biography* (1996), referred to on p. 166 suggests a doubt. His letters show an affection and a veneration for Rowse, to whom he offered the dedication of his *Taking Genetics into the Countryside*, not a field of inquiry one would have thought congenial to the honorand. Ford's passionate and scholarly interest in the treasures of the churches in the diocese of Oxford offered common ground, as did his intimate acquaintance with the Housman family, of which he gives a fascinating account in a letter of 28 October 1978, a xerox of which is preserved in the Rowse papers. A. E. Housman, the solitary poet and scholar of genius, became in Rowse's later life an icon with whom he chose to identify himself. How much that cold, fierce, contemptuous spirit would have relished this homage one may wonder.

Other old friendships formed in the College happily persisted, G. F. Hudson, G. D. H. Cole, Douglas Jay, a constant correspondent over many years. Some new ones were formed or renewed after a long interval such as that with Penderel Moon, who became Domestic Bursar. His view of the degeneration of the place, quoted with emphatic approval by Rowse, is summed up in his final instruction to his successor: 'Remember, they're all scroungers.'

Rowse's strictures were not unreciprocated. His colleagues had much to put up with. Sir Michael Howard remembers Rowse at breakfast in College, bursting into the room already in full flood of monologue as though he had been wound up and not pausing until its occupants had escaped. Solipsism does not make one an easy messmate.

He exploited the facilities for entertaining offered by the College to the full. At Encaenia, the grand summer beanfeast when the University confers Honorary Degrees on statesmen, captains of industry, writers and artists, luncheon (nothing but the full substantive will do) is laid on by All Souls in the splendour of the Codrington Library. Fellows have the right to invite guests, a right usually exercised with caution. Not so Rowse. Bevies of his American hosts and hostesses turned up, drowning the low cathedralesque murmur of the great and the good with the cheerful noisiness of holidaymakers out on the spree. A statutory restriction of number was introduced forthwith. Apart from that Rowse often gave large luncheon parties, which college kitchens are well equipped to provide.[1] He was a generous host and he liked to encourage writers who were just taking their first tentative steps by inviting them to dine and stay a night.

The last of his great Oxford friendships, that with Bruce McFarlane, was ended by death in July 1966. It had suffered from the ugly scene, described in chapter VIII, that followed the publication of *The Expansion of Elizabethan England* in 1955. Richard Pares, increasingly enfeebled by creeping paralysis, had died in 1958. Rowse's memoir of him in the Proceedings of the British Academy won a letter of unstinted praise from John Sparrow. One friendship that belongs entirely to post-war Oxford was that with John Buxton, Fellow and tutor in English Literature at New College. Their correspondence, indeed their intercourse in general, was much more professional than with most of Rowse's fellow academics. Buxton was a very learned man, widely and deeply read in the poetry and prose of the sixteenth and early seventeenth centuries, an independent scholar, who, like Rowse, wrote books rather than specialist articles in the journals. Like Rowse too, he was openly sceptical of fashionable opinion and deplored what he saw as the tendency of academicism to retreat into debate about minutiae. There the similarities ended. Buxton's career owed nothing to Rowse's fostering. Indeed he was a refreshingly improbable academic, a country gentleman, a fine naturalist (as a prisoner of war in a cattle truck he had been able to tell his companions where they were heading by his observation of the birdlife) he had none of Rowse's interest in cultivating the acquaintance of the great. What he had was originality of mind. It was this that Rowse recognized and valued. It is the more regrettable that Buxton's careful and reasoned refusal to accept the certainty – though he allowed some

1. See Appendix H.

probability – of Rowse's identification of the Dark Lady led to his relegation to outer darkness.

The great friendships, with Jack Simmons and Norman Scarfe, were in the 1950s centred on Leicester where Simmons was Professor and Scarfe a Lecturer. Both men experienced Rowse's extraordinary talent for friendship and his no less remarkable fondness for subjecting it to intolerable strains. Kenneth Rose, another old friend to whom Rowse dedicated *Friends and Contemporaries* (1989) allows me to quote an entry from his diary for 2 May 1968. Rose was, as Rowse well knew, a close friend of Harold Nicolson:

> Telephone ALR to tell him I cannot lunch with him today – a tentative plan we had. He doesn't mind that: his thoughts are occupied in rejoicing at Harold Nicolson's death, and such is his insensitivity that he says: 'The best news I have seen in the newspapers for a long time.' I merely reply 'You must not say things like that to me' and put the telephone down.
>
> Poor ALR, he enjoys breaking friendships more than the friendships themselves.

And yet, as in the case of Kenneth Rose, the friendship survived: perhaps Rowse had an instinct for hearts that were larger than his own.

Jack Simmons is frequently, and deservedly, acknowledged in Rowse's publications as his first reader and most valuable critic. Their correspondence shows that this was no empty compliment. Until Rowse set himself up as the sole and unquestionable authority on Shakespeare he listened to and profited from private criticism which he had himself solicited. Instances have already been given, such as Sir John Neale on his *Sir Richard Grenville* or, no less tellingly, Jonathan Cape on *A Cornish Childhood*. Kenneth Rose was sometimes invited to say what he thought and, with some inner trepidation, did so boldly. But Jack Simmons discharged his office faithfully for all Rowse's major books from *Tudor Cornwall* on.

It was not this that strained their relationship but Rowse's no doubt well meant but none the less irksome assumption of proprietorship over the lives of his friends. As we have seen in the case of his Christ Church contemporary, A. R. Burn, he was sure that he knew better than they did the way that they should go. On at least one occasion Simmons, exasperated, told Rowse that he had long ago given up trying to explain what the direction of his own literary and scholarly effort was as he knew that no attention would be paid and that he was not prepared to put up with intellectual dictatorship. In relation to Norman Scarfe Rowse cast himself in the role of Pygmalion. He saw that his young friend had powers and perceptions of the kind he most admired and he was, he thought, in a position to shape a career that might reflect his own. In 1949 Scarfe took his Final Schools and instead of the First that to Rowse was the gilt-edged guarantee of intellectual quality was placed in the Fourth class, an interesting survival, since abolished, of the nineteenth-century Honours system. The shock was terrible (to Rowse, not to Scarfe or to his tutor Bruce McFarlane, the expert trainer for this academic sprint). Neither wisdom nor self-restraint qualified his reactions. It was after all, to his way of thinking, the crack of doom, the collapse of his dearest hopes. In his own life the obtaining of a First had been the ticket of admission to the Garden of Eden, the foundation on which his whole life had been built, the object of years of concentrated and unwearying effort. That his case and Scarfe's were by no means the same he could not, or would not, recognize. Scarfe had served with distinction in war and had published, already as an undergraduate, an admired book. His circumstances and outlook were not interchangeable with, or even similar to, Rowse's. No doubt it would be very nice to have a First, but the lack of it could be contemplated with equanimity. A shocked intake of intellectual breath could be Rowse's only reaction to such blasphemy.

Regret and rage, rage at what he obscurely took as a personal betrayal, eventually began to simmer down. 'This particular test was the worst that could be applied to the closest and dearest relation of my life.' He recalled David Cecil telling him á propos of Margot, Lady Oxford and Asquith 'that when Puffin [her son, Anthony, subsequently famous as a film director] got a Second you'd have thought he'd committed some frightful crime and was going to prison.' Rowse admitted to Asquithian standards in these matters. By the end of the year, however, matters had much improved. Rowse even apologized (a rare concession) for having been 'too dogmatic' and went so far as to admit that his friend was 'α with a flaw, like the rest of us'. They went, enjoyably, abroad together, though Rowse's puritanism recoiled from his companion's habit of drinking wine with meals. He did not mind spending money on good, even very good, food or on comfortable hotels. But wine easily offended him. It smacked of Cyril Connolly or of the self-indulgence of John Bowle, a clever man who had trodden a similar primrose path without the wit and the ear for English prose that enabled Connolly to make a precarious but successful literary career. Bowle was not really a friend: in fact Rowse disapproved of him. It is one of the puzzles of so busy and censorious a life why he should have taken as much trouble – as he undoubtedly did – to find visiting professorships in America or Europe for Bowle, who often rewarded his efforts either by turning up his nose at what was offered or by offending the patrons who had been found for him.

Norman Scarfe in fact joined Jack Simmons' Department at Leicester and rapidly established a name in the field of topographical history of which Leicester was the unrivalled centre. Even more than with Jack Simmons, Rowse wanted to shape his career and to sketch out a programme for his literary productions. As with Jack Simmons it came to grief. When, after fourteen years, Scarfe decided to abandon university life and settle in Suffolk, his native county that was to him all that Cornwall was to Rowse, there were reproving letters. In 1963 Rowse hoped to reclaim him for academe by securing a tempting offer from Birmingham, Alabama. The courteous, hesitant letter Scarfe wrote back is covered with furious, hurt, annotations. The hidden, unacknowledged paternalism intensified the possessiveness of Rowse's deep affection.

Although Rowse would have dismissed with a snort the concept of original sin he came to formulate a somewhat similar notion to explain the faults he found in himself. It was his mother from whom he inherited his evil, destructive egocentricity. No one knew, or could guess, what struggles he had had with himself to win even a degree of humanity against the cold, savage, malicious selfishness that he recognized as his genetic inheritance from her. The violence of his revulsion sometimes made him fear for his sanity. What made him despair was his clear identification in himself of the horrible things he saw in her. Vain he might be, but he was not self-satisfied. He knew that he was obsessively egocentric and, not to put too fine a point upon it, selfish. Sometimes he defiantly erected intellectual barricades, such as the often repeated contention that he was not interested in ethics and that they had no meaning for him. Sometimes he loftily claimed a sort of moral tax-exemption to which genius, in his view, was entitled. But the real misery of some of his intimate letters and notebooks was not to be kept at bay by such flimsy defences. That his mother was not a good or kind or happy woman seems evident. That her difficulties of temperament were exacerbated by senility is only too probable. For her son this was what awaited him when he returned from the nervous exhaustion of the All Souls election or a long stint of intensive work on a book or several months travelling, lecturing, and living out of a suitcase in the United States. No wonder he was vulnerable and unbalanced.

Mercifully, as we have seen, he was reconciled to his mother as she lay dying in the spring of 1953. So, too, he could after years of self-inflicted wounds recover a friendship, even a love. As long ago as Good Friday 1949, under the stress of his mother's behaviour, he had written to Norman Scarfe

Ethics, that have always bored me so much, are at last catching up with me; for it is driven home to me here daily that the root of all trouble in personal relations is egotism and jealousy. It is a wonderful lesson for me, for I know well enough that they are two of my chief vices.

There are always two sides to Rowse.

His principle of conduct 'With me, writing always comes first' may be applied to his friendships. With the exception of Jack Simmons and Norman Scarfe they seem to have thrived best on paper rather than in companionship. In his correspondence with Violet Holdsworth or Elizabeth Jenkins he achieves an intimacy and a balance that often eluded him in personal contact. Not, of course, that he didn't meet them and that when they did they found each other rewarding. But like the characters of history and literature they existed in a world of their own, not his; he could meet them, understand them, compare ideas with them without being forced into the reconciliations of divergent personalities that made marriage and family life so repulsive.

The friction of human contact was eliminated as it was in his affection for animals. As a child at Tregonissey he had loved their donkey: *Peter, the white cat of Trenarren* is commemorated in a book of his own. Rowse used to ring up from America in order to hear him purr. Whatever he might say about establishing an emotional redoubt of solipsism he needed to give and to receive affection.

Oxford still retained its power to bruise and bless. Among the champions of Rowse's Shakespearean contentions, perhaps unexpectedly, was Maurice Bowra. There are letters expressing admiration and enthusiasm. But Rowse must have known of Bowra's ribald verses about his Oxford contemporaries and perhaps had his suspicions of Greeks bearing gifts.

In the early seventies All Souls amended its statutes to enforce a retirement age of sixty-seven on all but those elected to a Distinguished Fellowship. In Rowse's case a special dispensation extended his tenure to the age of seventy, a mitigation that he expressly attributed to John Sparrow.[1] The hurt and resentment that he felt was not voiced so loudly as might have been expected. Beside the excitement of reading Simon Forman's casebooks in the Bodleian and of the deductions he was drawing from them everything else paled.[2]

1. *All Souls in My Time*, 193.
2. See below chapter 24.

22

Always Scribble, Scribble,
Scribble
The Elizabethan Age

Whatever criticism may be made of Rowse's work, the verb 'scribble' bears no relation to the firm, elegant hand in which all his books were written. The word-processor, even the typewriter, played no part in their composition.

Something has already been said of his poetry and of his prose works up to the publication of *The Use of History* (1946). His writings on the plays and poems of Shakespeare and the controversies which he fanned into flame demand a chapter to themselves. But it is high time to consider the astonishing productivity that continued with hardly a pause over the last four decades of his life.

No bibliography of Rowse has yet been published[1] and this chapter makes no pretension to offer one. Even to draw a bird's-eye perspective of so extensive a landscape is ambitious enough. Perspective perhaps ought to be in the plural: avenues radiating out from a central point. But even so qualified the metaphor falls short of the diversity of Rowse's imagination, sensibility and scholarship, to say nothing of the violent prejudices, the outraged loyalties, the intellectual impatience that keep breaking in, sometimes to delight, sometimes to infuriate.

The first place in any such survey must be given to the great series of books on the Elizabethan age, after which it will be convenient to consider the rich crop of Elizabethan biographies, before going on to consider the field of general history, biography, literature

1. This is shortly to be remedied by the Scarecrow Press (USA) with the publication of that compiled by his friend, Sydney Cauveren, the work of many years. I am indebted to it for much that I would otherwise have missed.

and miscellaneous works from which both Cornwall and the continuation of the autobiographical series demand a place to themselves.

To begin, then, with that astonishing age with which Rowse's name
is specially associated. The first volume to appear was *The England
of Elizabeth* (1950). From the opening chapter its vitality and range
are such that it is easy to forget that the work rests on long years of
labour in the Public Record Office and indefatigable reading in the
printed sources. What the reader is at once aware of is that the author
goes and looks at things and remembers, and reflects upon, what he
sees. There is nothing static about his engagement with his subject.
As in a naval battle the vessel herself is under helm as she fires at a
moving target. The tone of the book is cheerful: the English people
to whom it is addressed are not seen as backsliding, unworthy heirs
of a noble past but as fresh from their triumph in the great trial of
the war with Hitler. The note of proto-Rowse is still dominant though
the scorn for those who held views other than his own is audible, if
not so strident as it was to become.

Best of all Rowse makes no bones about the difficulties, indeed the
inadequacies, of which a historian must be conscious:

It is difficult to render the sense of movement in what is essentially a
portrait. But in the case of the towns, especially of London, it is easier to
grasp with the eye of the imagination the pulsating rhythms of the life that
passed in and out of them, the ups of some places, the downs of others,
the emptying by plague and epidemics and the rapid filling up from the
countryside, the movements like cloud or sun passing over the landscape
which bring some areas into light where others are left in shadow. We can
thus visualize pictorially something of the effect of the radiation of a money
economy more widely over the country. Like water finding its own level, the
balance of wealth becomes a little more equalized over the regions. In
medieval England some regions were rich and others were poor: we have
ocular demonstration of this in the splendid churches and finer domestic
architecture of the eastern countries and the clothing districts of the West,
compared with the remoter West, Wales and the North. Now with the
extension of a money economy and greatly increasing wealth, things were
beginning to even out a little: one has the clear impression that the West is

coming up, towns in the North are beginning to go ahead. The landscape is changing under our eyes.[1]

Love of Elizabethan music, architecture, literature and feeling for even such minor arts as woodwork and tapestry enrich the presentation. As in all his work, people are characterized, not just left as names or holders of official posts. The biographer, perhaps even the autobiographer, has insights to offer. The old Oxford school of Modern History that made its pupils start with the Romans and the Saxons and persevere until they reached King Edward VII and Lloyd George contributed to the sense of continuity, of reading history both backwards and forwards, that it is now fashionable to sacrifice to minute analysis. 'If Burghley had lived in the reign of Charles I he would have been a Parliamentarian – as his descendants were.' How aghast at such boldness, such pithiness, a Ph.D. examiner would be. Yet how much that tells the reader about the man who is really the hero of Rowse's story.

The Queen, though viewed from an infinity of different angles, in different contexts, at different ages, in different moods, is of course the heroine. Neither she nor Burghley sat to Rowse for a full-length portrait. Each had recently been the subject of a major biography; that of the Queen by J. E. Neale, a book that Rowse particularly admired. No praise that he himself received was more valued than Neale's letter on the appearance of the next volume in the series, *The Expansion of England* (1955):

6.12.55

My Dear Rowse,

. . . I thought you would not mind if I delayed this letter until I had an opportunity of reading [the book] and could register my pleasure.

You have (as you must know you have) written a fine book. I admire its conception. The approach through the Celtic lands was an inspiration. It is fresh; it is absolutely right; and artistically it unifies the whole story. It gives one a grasp of the age. The Irish 'bog' and the confusion of Wales become full of meaning. I admired your insistence on bringing individuals to life and showing their significance as groups.

1. op. cit., p. 158.

As for the story itself, it is told with tremendous vitality – I read it with gusto. It really is Elizabethan England and sparkles with ideas and suggestions. When this whole work is complete it will be a remarkable picture of an age.

I offer my congratulations and my homage. How you must have worked! And yet you keep a sense of excitement throughout. Of course you write with your whole personality as well as your head. That is the secret of a live work. And yours is alive.

One hardly knows which to admire the more, the percipience of the appreciation or the felicity of its expression. After such a letter from the recognized head of the profession – as far as Elizabethan studies were concerned – one wonders why its addressee bothered about public honours such as the OM. The explanation must surely lie in the radical, fundamental lack of self-confidence that many detected beneath the boasting.

Perhaps no other work of his exhibits so clearly the qualities I have loosely identified as proto-Rowse and those that came to dominate, sometimes to deface, his later productions. The opening chapter on the Borderlands, the Scottish Borders and Cornwall is animated by that vivid visual suggestiveness that sometimes puts one in mind of Macaulay, sometimes of John Betjeman, and yet is unmistakably itself. Our realization of the administrative and institutional structures that upheld a fragile government in remote and violent places is awoken by little-known facts such as Henry VIII's original intention to found a Cornish Bishopric at either Bodmin or St Germans.

The Reformation that divided so much of northern Europe and lay at the heart of the foreign and domestic menace to the Queen is too often treated by the later Rowse with cheap dismissive contempt. 'Silly fools, why didn't they conform?' is a comment that hardly suggests a profound understanding of recusancy or indeed of the sixteenth century itself. Yet the opening chapter concludes with a passage not less eloquent, not less imaginative, than the opening chapter of *Tudor Cornwall*:

Of the defeated side curious bits of flotsam and jetsam fetch up in odd places. Sir John Arundell's[1] son retained Winslade's grandson, Tristram, as his servant at Lanherne. At the time of the trouble over Cuthbert Mayne – the first martyr of the seminarists, caught and hounded to death by Grenville – Winslade and his father disappeared from Cornwall, no-one knew whither. Carew says that 'Winslade's son led a walking life with his harp to gentlemen's houses, wherethrough, and by his other qualities, he was entitled Sir Tristram: neither wanted he (as some say) a "belle Isoult", the more aptly to resemble his pattern.' When Drake captured Don Pedro de Valdes' great ship *Nuestra Señora del Rosario* from the Armada, Tristram Winslade was aboard. From his examination we learn what had happened to him and his father: the father had fled to Brittany, thence to Spain and Portugal, where he died at Lisbon. The son had gone to Ireland, thence through France and Germany to Italy. A few weeks later Topcliffe had permission to rack him in the Tower. But he survived to die in sanctity at Douai where he was buried in the chapel 24 November 1605.

Back on the Scottish Border, another of the circle – Nicholas Roscarrock – had come safe into harbour at last with Lord William Howard and his blind harper at Naworth. He had been much in prison, had taken many risks and had some narrow escapes. In the Tower he had managed to smuggle out letters for Father Crichton. In the Fleet with the Tregians, he was watched and reported on by a Catholic spy. Now with James on the throne, with Lord William for company and his books around him, he could give himself up in peace to his antiquarian studies. Far away in his Border fastness, it was Cornwall that held his mind, a Cornwall he could never go home to: bit by bit, patiently, lovingly, he was piecing it together in his mind writing down endlessly in his great folio all that he could remember, all that he could find, of the lives of the Cornish saints, of their legends, their parishes and holy wells, of the observance and rites in their honour in the days that had vanished for ever.

This is Rowse the poet, the Celt, perhaps almost himself the blind harper. But Rowse the rationalist comes bustling in: 'People think what suits them: one never has to have any respect for the intellectual

---

1. The Arundells of Lanherne were the leading recusant family in Cornwall: indeed their influence and possessions extended beyond their native county.

positions human beings take up.'[1] What is this but a bastard Marxism? These are matters of tone, which seems itself to derive rather from the mood the author was in when he took pen in hand than from any discernible principle. Pragmatism is generally applauded, as on page 397 when Henri IV changes his religious profession and the Queen is grudgingly and disapprovingly allowed to have been sincere in being shocked. But moral principles are asserted, or appealed to, too often to require citation. There is no hypocrisy in this: it is the unresolved conflict in Rowse's nature of which he himself was well aware.

The passages that treat maritime expansion have all the Rowsian virtues of vividness and telling detail that is never allowed to impede the development of a central theme. The conclusion admirably draws together all the issues of the long war and valuably emphasizes how much better England had become in every aspect of military technique by the last decade of the reign. Here, perhaps, was an echo of what men of his own generation felt when the Churchill administration took charge of the conduct of the War in 1940.

Arising out of the themes of the book was that of Rowse's Trevelyan Lectures already mentioned – *The Elizabethans and America* (1959). The formality of the occasion perhaps imposed a useful discipline on the author's exuberance. Is there indeed a degree of self-recognition in his fascinating portrait of Dr John Dee?

'Dee was a Welshman: no-one ever possessed more recognizably Celtic characteristics, the touchiness and suspicion, the acuteness and imagination, the originality along with a certain haphazardness, the tendency to go over the borderline.'[2]

Altogether the book has a wisdom, a restraint, a fairness that are not always the leading virtues of his work. The account of early voyages of exploration in which particular attention is drawn to the contribution of the French puts one in mind of Pepys's succinct judgment: 'Of the four great discoverers we the last and least.'[3] Relating this to its largely Huguenot inspiration, throttled by the horrors of the St Bartholomew's Day massacre, Rowse does not, as he well might,

1. op. cit., p. 173.
2. op. cit., p. 17.
3. *Samuel Pepys's Naval Minutes*, ed. J. R. Tanner (1926), p. 223.

allow himself a diatribe against the absurdity of religious belief but appraises very fairly the Puritan virtues that played so essential a part in the early settlements.

The third panel of the Elizabethan triptych, *The Elizabethan Renaissance*, had in the end to be split in two. The first, and briefer, half, subtitled *The Life of the Society*, appeared in 1971. Granted Rowse's view that the true interest of history consisted in the life of the mind and that creative achievement alone redeemed the crimes and follies of mankind, we might expect to be offered a skeleton, with the flesh and blood to follow. Such is far from the case. The book is lively, even racy, displaying the author's sense of amusement as well as distilling his mature thought. Above all it is down to earth. There are chapters (out of a total of nine) on Food and Sanitation, on Sex, on Parish and Sport. Probably the author of *Politics and the Younger Generation* who wished to divert the money spent on hunting to more productive social investment had not lost his private distaste but at least he communicates something of the enjoyment and enthusiasm the chase inspired in even such serious figures as the Queen and Robert Cecil.

The chapter on Class and Social Life opens with a recognition of the advantages conferred on a historian by his own particular location in the historical landscape and, on the other hand, of the impossibility of saying the last word:

... Until the earthquake of the First World War of 1914–18, society remained recognizable as continuous, at least in rural England, from Elizabethan days. It exemplified an organic structure, which recognized a principle: it was based on hierarchical order, in which social class expressed social functions. People knew their place in it, where they stood and how they were expected to behave – always with a margin of exceptions, the inassimilable, the misfit, the criminal ... Here is a principle on which to thread the immense tapestry of social life, which this book is to portray. Here we can only illustrate how it was organized. Completeness is impossible; even the plays of Shakespeare, the most complete portrait of Elizabethan life, omit one of the most important areas of society – the religious.

The book is shot through with reflections on the writing of history. 'One is *not* studying the unobservable, the dead and vanished: they are all around one. The subtlety lies in catching the differences of inflexion; the art of the historian – how few achieve it! – in rendering them like an artist.'[1]

An example – increasingly uncommon – of Rowse as a vigorous but not vituperative controversialist may be found in the arguments he deploys against Professor Trevor-Roper's recently published essay 'The European Witch-Craze in the 16th and 17th Centuries'.[2] He handles a lance so well that one regrets the resort to the bludgeon. The whole book, after an unpromising opening chapter full of personal and credal cross-references, sparkles. Take, as a concluding instance, his comparison between Elizabeth and Henry VIII:

> The contrast is visible between her Court and her father's, between the power, the hardness and latent cruelty in the portraits of Henry VIII's circle, and the refinement and sensibility of those of his daughter's. The reserve in the faces painted by Holbein is reserve in the face of omnipresent danger, the reserve of fear. This is not present in Elizabethan court-portraits: there was no fear for life, but an open-eyed civilized wariness. Behind Henry's one sees the law of the jungle; behind Elizabeth's, the slippery ladder of favour, the competitiveness, the exhibitionism encouraged at the top, a world of flattery, attentive to the ladies – in a Court ruled by a lady.[3]

The concluding volume *The Cultural Achievement* (1972) is written with as much verve as its predecessors, but the mass of material to be disposed of can hardly be managed even by so finished an artist. This forces itself on the reader's consciousness in the second chapter on Language, Literature and Society, which nevertheless contains brilliant insights and stimulating judgments such as that on Sir Philip Sidney, interestingly compared for his influence on his age with T. S. Eliot for his on ours. The chapter on Words and Music – how many other scholars would have been equipped to tackle so elusive a subject? – presupposes too much antecedent knowledge for the common reader, an uncharacteristic defect. On the other hand the opening chapter on

1. op. cit., p. 167.
2. op. cit., pp. 253 ff.
3. ibid., pp. 32–3.

the Theatre and its publics handles complicated and unfamiliar matter with marvellous lucidity. The last chapter, entitled Mind and Spirit, centres on a fine defence of Francis Bacon. Perhaps the core of his attraction, apart from the force of his style, was the range of his learning and of his sympathetic understanding: 'Bacon was a true Elizabethan in disliking specialization: he appreciated the fruitful cross-fertilization of different subjects, the insights afforded by comparative views.'[1] It is the strength of Rowse that though he certainly was a specialist in various departments of learning his energy and curiosity led him to transcend any such narrow limitations. It is that zest, and the enjoyment it carries with it, that will command readers for the trilogy of the Elizabethan Age when safer, steadier works will be left to a venerated repose in the bibliographies.

1. op. cit., p. 298.

23

Portraits

That acropolis rises from a surrounding diversity of works, some of which are evidently related to it. The biographies of Marlowe (1964), of Shakespeare (1963), of his patron Southampton (1965), of Simon Forman (1974), and of Ralegh and the Throckmortons (1962) all form part of his extended view of the Elizabethan age.

William Shakespeare: A Biography has a delicacy, almost a tentativeness, that disappear from his later writings on the poet. The chapter on the sonnets, it is true, sounds a note that will in time drown all others: the claim to exclusive authority, almost to infallibility, of the historian in the hitherto unresolved difficulties of dating these astonishing compositions. But for the most part the book is a brilliant, even a charming, portrait of one of the most attractive as well as the greatest of all men of genius that England can show. As in his other writings on the age Rowse combines a solid, down to earth, matter of factness (his boyhood experience in his parents' shop had its value) with an imaginative sympathy that owed as much to his own poetic endeavours as it did to his extraordinarily wide reading. If he had only been content to show, silently, how much the historian can contribute to the understanding of literature, how much more telling his testimony would have been. In this book at least he extends the usual courtesies of scholarship to other writers.

Christopher Marlowe: A Biography, published a year later, is in essence an outgrowth of the preceding work, a study reflecting the shared qualities and the antitheses of the two great dramatists. It is bold in its judgments and unqualified in its assertion of the creativity and originality of a mind whose independence had a particular appeal. Both books have a liveliness that makes them hard to put down.

Shakespeare's Southampton, again separated by a year, is less successful. Unlike the other two the subject is not so much interesting in himself as for the people with whom he was connected either as patron or client, Shakespeare, Marlowe, Essex, Burghley, the Queen herself. One could hardly have a more arresting circle. The minor stature of the central figure perhaps tempts an inclination to write of historical personages as though they were, or had been, his pupils. On the other hand his familiarity with the political, dynastic and intellectual aspects of the age and his sense of their interpenetration added to, informed by, his consciousness of locality give the book balance. Awareness of genealogy, so true to and explicative of the Tudor age, does not recommend itself to the general reader of the twentieth century. But the relation of literature to life is vividly illustrated in a fine passage on *Troilus and Cressida*.[1]

Standing apart from these three closely related biographies is *Ralegh and the Throckmortons* (1962). Unlike them it is centred on an entirely new and valuable original source, the diary of Arthur Throckmorton, whose sister Ralegh had married after the close encounter so salaciously described in Aubrey's *Brief Lives*. Sixteenth-century diaries are rarities: the form came into its own in the next century with Pepys and Evelyn its most famous practitioners. Rowse is unstinting in his acknowledgment to this document: 'the fullest, the most extensive and revealing of all Elizabethan diaries that remain.'[2] Unlike Pepys and Evelyn the diarist was not himself a prominent figure, though both his father and his brother-in-law were, so that he was well placed to observe and describe and report without the anxieties and self-justifications of men charged with great responsibilities. He had time too for the travels and amusements as well as the day to day concerns of a well-connected, well-endowed, well-disposed gentleman of the late sixteenth century. 'The main interest of the Diary is social: it provides a clear and candid mirror of Elizabethan social life.'[3]

Yet for Rowse it was really, as he admits in his preface, biographical: 'Only a seasoned Elizabethan scholar can hope to get Ralegh right

1. op. cit., pp. 168 ff.
2. op. cit., p. 58.
3. ibid., p. 59.

... For many years I have ruminated about him without feeling satisfied that I had grasped the problematical, essential nature of this so difficult man. At last I feel, though I know well one is not supposed to say such things, that I have got him ...

'I have made the undreamed-of good fortune of the Diary my setting for Ralegh's life: all one needs to know for a biography is here, with the accent on person and family ...'

All one needs? The Diary, to judge from quotation and from the passages reproduced in facsimile, is jerky, telegraphic, factual. Tone and mood are wholly absent. Sometimes indeed the facts are, though drily related, sensational, for instance Ralegh's hitherto unknown secret marriage to Bess Throckmorton (with Essex, Ralegh's deadliest enemy and rival, as groomsman) and the subsequent birth of a son who then disappears from history. This quality, high as its historical value certainly is, seems to have communicated itself to Rowse's handling of his matter. It is almost as though he was half editing a new document of exceptional importance and half painting a portrait. The title is faithful to the contents: Ralegh and the Throckmortons. The copula is merely associative, as in fish and chips.

Perhaps the author was, for once, too confident in the importance of his new material to pay the attention he usually devoted to the writing. There are infelicities, even vulgarities. The description of the inventory and search made of Cardinal Pole's possessions on his death ends with the sentence: 'Among the papers they found a note of all those who had been frazzled for the faith.'[1] The diary was indeed extraordinary, not only in itself but also in its provenance. It had been found by a chapter workman at Canterbury in an outhouse belonging to the Cathedral and by him handed over to the Chapter Librarian and Archivist. There A. B. Emden spotted it in the course of his research for the medieval register of Oxford University. He told Rowse, who offered to buy it. But the Chapter felt embarrassed at their lack of title. They had no idea, and no record, of how the Diary had come there in the first place. In a letter dated 20 June 1961 Canon F. J. J. Shirley, a friend since 1940 when he had been Headmaster of the King's School evacuated to Cornwall, wrote 'You do understand

1. ibid., p. 25.

that they [the diaries] were never in our archives, but were discovered by one of our carpenters in a box in a wood-shed near our workshops. There were other papers with them, mostly eighteenth-century and relating to the Hales family, and as the Hales were Papists I suppose it is not improbable that these diaries were originally among their papers.' Not for the last time Rowse saw and exploited the useful possibilities of newspaper publicity in this intriguing story. In the academic world the book was extensively noticed by the leading scholars. There were some sharp exchanges with G. R. Elton who had reviewed it in the *Spectator* and had challenged some of its assertions.

Rowse's biography *Simon Forman: Sex and Society in Shakespeare's Age* (1974) is easily the most attractive product of these studies. Few historians could match his combination of appropriate responses, the sensibility of a highly cultivated intelligence and the harshness left by a settled experience of poverty that must, in early life, have seemed interminable. Both enable him to establish a rapport with Forman and to sympathize with his exclusion from the recognized, approved world of the profession he practised. Like Rowse, Forman had felt rejected – and rejected by people he believed to be his intellectual inferiors.

The book is written with evident enjoyment. The speed and comedy of Ben Jonson's *Alchemist* are never far away, both in the vivid and sympathetic account of Elizabethan low life and in the scholarship and wide reading applied to the interpretation of the dreams to which Forman attached such significance. Rowse's agnosticism left him free from the metallic certainties of the know-all twentieth century. On the remarkably accurate forecast of the course and outcome of Essex's attempted coup d'état he remarks 'with Forman there seems to have been an element of the psychic'. 'All this book' he writes, summarizing the contents of Forman's jottings, 'is an exposure of the Elizabethan mentality, its mercurial character, credulity and sense of illimitable possibilities – hence the stimulus to the imagination for its poetry and drama: life itself had the tone of drama.'[1]

Elizabethan subjects were to crop up again and again in Rowse's

1. op. cit., pp. 217, 220.

later publications. *An Elizabethan Garland* (1953) is a collection of miscellaneous essays offered to celebrate the coronation of Elizabeth II but it does contain a characteristically lively piece on Queen Elizabeth I and the historians. Froude, for once, is subjected first almost to barracking, and then to more subtle criticism: and the treatment of Mandell Creighton shows the author at his best. *Eminent Elizabethans*, that work intended to challenge comparison with Lytton Strachey which had been so long contemplated eventually appeared in 1983, dedicated, an appropriately Elizabethan touch, to 'Jacqueline Kennedy Onassis, historic figure, for her love of history'. The team he fields is not quite up to Strachey's: second-rank figures whom he skilfully makes interesting but cannot make memorable: Father Parsons, the Jesuit, Bess of Hardwick, Edward de Vere, seventeenth Earl of Oxford, Elizabeth's godson, Sir John Harington and her cousin Lord Chamberlain Hunsdon. The best is on Father Parsons, the tough, tenacious, rebarbative ex-Oxford don whose feelings of rejection answered to Rowse's own. Bess of Hardwick shows to advantage both his own acute visual sense and his understanding of Elizabethan aesthetics.

A livelier and more rewarding collection is *Court and Country: Studies in Tudor Social History* (1987). This is deutero-Rowse with a vengeance: vigorous, outrageous, sometimes touching, always readable. The people depicted are even less prominent than the earlier quintet but they are fresher. Most of them have not had even walking-on parts in earlier books. For the author at his most gloriously unfair the reader is recommended to the account of English activity in Ireland as part of the background to the exciting career of a soldier of fortune, Sir Peter Carew.[1] The comparison between Queen Elizabeth and Mrs Thatcher on page 232 was no doubt intended to *épater les académiques*. Acute judgments abound: 'England's natural and commercial ally was the Netherlands, where Charles V ruled and Philip was shortly to succeed him. Philip was eleven years younger than Mary, but a serious young man, already a King and always a good Catholic; while Mary on her mother's side was even more of a Spaniard than he was, and a religious fanatic, unlike her father.'[2] Or on Bishop Stephen Gardiner,

1. op. cit., pp. 124–5.
2. ibid., pp. 73–4.

generally represented as a pillar of the Marian régime: 'There could never be complete confidence between him and Mary, for he had been implicated in every move in the divorce of her mother and the breach with Rome. But his political ability and experience were indispensable.'[1] Or this generalization on how Elizabeth's government worked: '. . . the wish at the top to do justice, to do the best for everybody, manoeuvring for a practical solution to an imprecise, contingent problem which yet could have wider repercussions and make future trouble.'[2] The book contains what were in effect valedictory studies of two of the author's favourite Cornishmen with whom he had been at home in imagination for half a century: William Carnsew, a country gentleman and Richard Carew, the great antiquary. The insights and understanding gained in the writing of *Tudor Cornwall* still informed all his best work.

His unashamed eagerness for the acquaintance of the great did not blind him to the interest and charm, often the excitement, of the lives of such people who had not been famous, even in their own time. But he turned with especial pleasure to the study of those who had held the spotlight of history. Above all, to the hero who had, in the nick of time, saved not only his country but European civilization, Winston Churchill. Rowse claims that Churchill was the only man whose personal acquaintance he deliberately set out to make. He has given his own account,[3] drawn largely from his journals written at the time, emphasizing that the great man had expressed a wish to see the first of two volumes that Rowse projected on the Churchill dynasty and that his ukase was necessary to gain access to the family archives at Blenheim, without which the second could not be undertaken.

Rowse did not get to know him well: Churchill was eighty-three when they met and his subsequent letters, much treasured by the recipient, are, to borrow Pepys's expression, letters of civility. The two books, *The Early Churchills* (1956) and *The Later Churchills* (1958) gratified their author by their popular success and by the

1. ibid., p. 69.
2. ibid., p. 250.
3. *Memories of Men and Women* (1980), pp. 1–24. In spite of their common detestation of appeasement, Churchill does not feature in Rowse's journals and letters of the thirties.

approbation accorded even by such a sworn opponent of historical biography as Richard Pares. He was fortunate. Both books exhibit weaknesses unhappily characteristic of deutero-Rowse, tub-thumping rhetoric, banality – 'When all is said in the complexities of politics, the personal issues, the struggles, the feuds and hatreds, it is the simple overriding facts that matter'[1] and slipshod scholarship such as he would have censured in anybody else. On page 41 he has Charles II attending mass in Madrid, a city the King never came near. On page 365 he has John Churchill's brother Charles serving in Tangier from 1682 to 1685, a solitary posting since the place was evacuated in 1684. There are other errors of the kind, trivial perhaps but disquieting evidence of insubstantiality.

There is too an embarrassing servility, almost adulation, towards Churchill, both in his character as historian and biographer of Marlborough and as the national leader of 1940. No one who recalls and understands that last achievement can grudge any measure of praise and gratitude. But in *The Early Churchills* the recitation and interpretation of events is frequently bent out of shape to impose a comparison with those of the 1930s and 1940s or to pay a literary compliment. In spite of this the book succeeds by the qualities of verve, excitement, narrative technique, enjoyment that are always present in Rowse's writing, from his schoolboy letter to the Kaiser to the controversial squibs and vivid recollections of extreme old age. The personalities of the principals, John the first Duke and Sarah his Duchess, are realized with a subtlety that somehow triumphs over the *engouement* that such larger than life figures tended to inspire in him. He interests the reader because he cannot help being interested himself. This is not to deny the art that tells a complicated story with a speed and simplicity that deceives the eye. But the compulsion that drives the book, and so many of his books, along is natural, not contrived.

The Later Churchills shows the same virtues and defects even more conspicuously. Dedicated to Richard Pares and acknowledging the guidance of such scholars as Sir Lewis Namier and Jack Simmons, high expectations are raised. The early pages on Sarah and her grandsons confirm them. But as the book goes on slackness of writing ('It is

1. *The Early Churchills*, p. 277.

unlikely that the Duke got round to being familiar with Mr Pitt'),[1] lack of narrative control and sheer carelessness become distressingly evident. The inequality of the work is exasperating. The prose ranges from a nudging woman's magazine style to the clear, dignified but lively English which the author naturally commands when he stops to think. In treating Sir Winston's own life again the strengths of perception and sympathy are counterbalanced by adulation. The Dardanelles story is told in so partisan, so shrill, a tone that it is hard to understand how so distinguished a scholar could have written it. Even the name of the Admiral commanding is wrongly spelled. Fisher, the First Sea Lord whom Churchill himself had chosen, is described as 'the old bachelor admiral' in spite of the fact that he had married at an exceptionally early age and was, in the opinion of at least one of his biographers, excessively uxorious. The information that Churchill as First Lord spent eight months of every year afloat in the Admiralty yacht *Enchantress*[2] makes the reader rub his eyes. Even the gentlemanly style of Asquith's cabinet hardly allowed so relaxed a conduct of one of the greatest offices of state. The want of critical sense both towards his own work and towards the career and actions of his hero robs the book of its proper effect.

Rowse wrote too much that is well worth reading to waste time on an ungrateful examination of his failures. But they may perhaps help us to understand the difficulties with which he had to contend, particularly those of which he was himself aware if not ready to acknowledge. The conviction that he was rejected begat the defiant solipsism and the scorn for the people who had (as he thought) rejected him. More and more this led him to identify himself with great solitary figures who towered over their age. The obvious danger of such a position is that it leads a man to think of himself more highly than he ought to think. In writing about Churchill Rowse thus comes to assume a common standing with him, and a common self-confidence. Yet their situation in this regard, as obviously enough in others, was by no means comparable. Churchill's self-confidence, enormous, unshakable, impervious, arose from his own nature,

1. op. cit., p. 156.
2. op. cit., p. 394.

Rowse's from reaction to experience, defiant but also defensive.

The theme of rejection by one's inferiors is made yet more explicit in his long-projected biography *Jonathan Swift* (1975). Early in life Swift had fallen in love with a girl who turned him down. She subsequently had second thoughts, to receive, in her turn, a wounding dismissal. 'It is as if this proudest of spirits was fated to be rejected, and by people he justly considered inferior to himself.'[1] Less and less can Rowse stand back from his subjects. Consciousness of his own experience, of his own feelings comes to dominate his understanding of the people he is writing about. Self-identification is not confined to the principal subject:

No wonder he [Swift] was unable to meet the argument of a rationalist Fellow of All Souls, Tindal, that a state church had no separate authority from the state that maintained it, and gave up the attempt to answer Tindal's *Rights of the Christian Church Asserted*. Tindal was an All Souls lawyer who had been a Catholic under James II, and then – seeing through the silliness of both sides – became a deist. He was not popular in college, because he cheated: being a teetotaller, he had no difficulty in answering the other Fellows' arguments after dinner. However Tindal could be attacked as immoral – and was.[2]

That the greatest pamphleteer in our language should have been given no higher preferment than the meagre Deanery of St Patrick's offered only too easy a parallel to the lack of recognition accorded to his biographer. The reader may regret that the book was not written forty years earlier as originally intended, before the buffetings of life had opened this angle of vision. Yet Victor Rothschild, no mean authority, considered it the best book on Swift that he had read. There are qualities in the subject that would at any age have evoked Rowse's eager response, notably sexual equivocation and religious scepticism. Swift's affairs – or non-affairs – with Stella and Vanessa are scrutinized, on the whole approvingly. For what would a man of genius want with the ball and chain of a wife and family? In any case Swift was,

1. op. cit., p. 27.
2. op. cit., p. 53.

in Rowse's view, not at all highly sexed. Yet Rowse's humanity is in the end almost shocked by the egocentricity that determined Swift at all costs to avoid the distress of attending Stella's deathbed, the more so, perhaps, because he has asserted the real tenderness of heart that underlay that often cold and contemptuous exterior.

Swift's daring treatment of the religion he was bound to profess, but did not much, if at all, believe, excites Rowse's keen sympathy. The formularies of Christianity, especially those of the Church of England, were as dear to him as its creeds were impossible. He had always been sure that Swift shared his agnosticism and he was transported when a scholar at the Huntington told him that he had seen in Swift's own hand a marginal note against a reference to the Nicene Creed in the works of Bellarmine: *Confessio fidei digna barbaris*, a confession of faith fit for savages.

There were other characteristics that prompted self-identification:

In company he was usually irresistible, endlessly amusing and vivacious, with the infallible appeal (to the intelligent) of intellectual high spirits. He required only a modicum of intelligence and liveliness in others to set him alight ...

So – another paradox – the great misanthrope, who had no illusions about humanity, was very sociable and a most welcome guest. He had a large circle of friends – may, indeed, be said to have had an exceptional gift for friendship.[1]

The biographer of Rowse feels his work is being done for him.

But it is as the great scourge of humbug, the implacable enemy of fashionable cant, that Rowse, rightly, recognizes a master whom he aspires to follow. All through the sixties and seventies he was tireless and fearless in attacking what is now called political correctness, the submissive acceptance of ideas and attitudes which he saw as counter to good government, common sense and sound learning. In articles, broadcasts, television interviews with the agility of a matador he baited and infuriated men and women who knew that they must be right because fashion told them so. His files bulge with letters of admiration from fellow writers and scholars at his articulacy and

1. op. cit., pp. 42–3.

force. It was at this period that he gained a reputation as an arch-reactionary, a categorization that he denied. Whatever qualities he may have lacked, courage was not one of them. He never played safe as so many of the Great and the Good instinctively did. In the author of *Gulliver's Travels* he recognized a fellow free spirit:

> In Laputa some of their resources went into extracting sun out of cucumbers – but nothing like so much as the Ground-nut Scheme, on which the 1945–51 Labour Government wasted hundreds of millions; or *Concorde*, on which governments of both parties have spent a thousand million. Oh, for a Swift to describe what is happening today! (However George Orwell did very well to point out the end of the road in his *1984*).

It is notable that enthusiasm for Swift extracts Rowse's only admiring acknowledgment of Orwell, whom in his journals he always writes down. Outrage at Orwell's identification with, and claim to interpret the mind of, the working class distorted his judgment of a writer whose straightforward prose and independence of outlook ought, supremely, to have commended him. That this Old Etonian who had been in College with Cyril Connolly should be regarded as the People's Tribune reversed Rowse's role from matador to bull.

24

Shakespeare

Of all the inextricable confusions of good and bad, of brilliant and absurd, of scholarship and shouting to be found in Rowse's writings those of Shakespeare stand by themselves. There is so much that is wonderful: the direct, vivid response of a man who was both a poet and a lifelong familiar of Elizabethan England. There is so much to regret: the spiteful snarling of a wounded pride. Perhaps deepest of all the knowledge, never admitted, that great scholars not only do not need, but could not for a moment accept, descent into abuse and sneers to establish the validity of their contentions.

A biographer, unless he happens also to be a Shakespearean scholar with specialist knowledge in a wide range of subjects such as the Elizabethan techniques of printing and publishing, textual criticism and the massive secondary literature devoted to the tracing of sources and allusions, has no warrant to pronounce on questions to which experts have devoted their lives. No scintilla of such a claim is made here. It does not take much reading to recognize that although a surprising amount can be established about Shakespeare there are enormous gaps in the evidence. Certainty in the dating of the plays cannot in every case be agreed. And that of the Sonnets cannot be agreed at all. Mystery surrounds both their writing and the circumstances of their publication. Even more, once they were published, why were they not at once, and many times, reprinted? Rowse, on this point, admits a debt to the acute suggestion of an American publisher: namely, that there were people, almost certainly including the author, who prevented it. But here too we are in the world of conjecture, as, far more importantly, we are in the whole conception and execution of one of the most extraordinary works in English literature. The only solid incontestable fact is that they were written by the greatest genius that our literature can show.

It is on the Sonnets that Rowse's whole campaign turns: Rowse *contra mundum*. Campaign is not too strong a word. He seems to have wished to establish himself as a Newton or an Einstein, single-handedly overturning what had been the limits of knowledge. The title he gave to his second edition of the Sonnets – *Shakespeare's Sonnets: The Problem Solved* (1973) – leaves no room for dissent and acknowledges no debt to the labours of others. In his earlier edition of the Sonnets (1964) he had asserted proof that Shakespeare's patron, the Earl of Southampton, was the handsome young man to whom the first sequence of one hundred and twenty-six were addressed. The identification was not original. Rowse ascribes it to the great eighteenth-century critic Edmond Malone but the late Samuel Schoenbaum in one of several corrections to Rowse (never acknowledged and fiercely resented) points out that it was in fact first made by Nathan Drake in 1817.[1] Southampton along with his fellow Earl, Pembroke, has long been a favourite candidate. Indeed in the latest Arden Edition of the Sonnets by Katherine Duncan-Jones (1997) the claims of both are fairly set out with no suggestion that the matter is, or is likely to be, closed. What Rowse has done is to put forward a strongly argued case resting on certain assumptions as to date which are in fact incapable of proof on the evidence available. The deficit is made good by frequent assertions of his own pre-eminence as an authority on the period, which, regrettably, lead him into contemptuous comparisons with the work of individual scholars and ultimately into a wholesale dismissal of literary as opposed to historical scholarship.

Between the first and the second editions Rowse's reading of Simon Forman's casebooks preserved in the Bodleian Library led him to an even more daring conjecture concerning the identity of the Dark Lady to whom the last twenty-eight sonnets are addressed. The guess is a fascinating one. In the opinion of many scholars it may well be right. But in the absence of any evidence that she and Shakespeare ever even met it cannot possibly be admitted as proof.

1. *Shakespeare and Others* (1985), p. 58.

Rowse's fury with those who would not accept his claim to proof must surely spring (and this, I hasten to add, is itself a conjecture) from his unadmitted, inadmissible, consciousness that the ground he stood on was not firm. His original statement of claim rested, at least largely, on two simple mis-readings of a not very difficult manuscript. The lady in question, Aemilia Bassano, was said to have been 'somewhat brown in youth', i.e. dark. Q.E.D. But 'brown' turned out, on closer inspection, to read 'brave'. She married a court musician called Lanier: William Lanier, according to Rowse, who made great play with the puns and double-entendres in the Sonnets on the name Will and the substantive 'will', itself heavy with sexual overtones. Unfortunately Lanier's Christian name turned out, from other sources, to be Alphonso. 'William' was a mis-reading for the lady's own name, given in familiar abbreviation as Millia, spelled with two 'l's.[1]

Before taking stock of the repercussions of Rowse's reaction to the refusal of the world of scholarship (historical as well as literary) to accept an ingenious conjecture as proof we should recall the distinguished applause and congratulation with which it was in fact received. No less than three Oxford Professors in the Faculty of English Literature, F. P. Wilson, Nevill Coghill and John Bayley, are recorded by Rowse as having indicated their acceptance. I have found no written evidence of this beyond its regular repetition in Rowse's journals, letters and controversial writings. His account consistently represents their opinion as expressed in speech and although one must allow for the courtesies of private conversation Rowse's extreme sensibility to the faintest tinge of doubt was easily aroused.

It was here that the combination of solipsism and its allied conviction of being doomed to rejection reached their full and fatal effect. Fatal to some of his most valuable and enriching friendships and to his well-earned reputation as a scholar of remarkable quality and a man of letters of generosity and range. His enemies and detractors were offered all the ammunition they could possibly need. Two of his most admiring and admired fellow writers, Veronica Wedgwood and John Buxton, were the first to be sacrificed to this obsession. Rowse had

1. I owe this information to the kindness of Mr Stephen Freer and Miss Mary Edmond. See further on this Appendix C.

actually read his typescript to Buxton, who, deeply impressed, said that he was seventy per cent convinced and thirty per cent reserved for want of clinching evidence, a position from which he does not appear to have resiled. But nothing less than one hundred per cent would do.

Veronica Wedgwood had disagreed with his identification of Southampton as the adored subject of the Sonnets in the first place. In a letter of 20 April 1969 she set out her reasons. She found it impossible to believe that a poet of Shakespeare's modest social standing would have so addressed a nobleman in that age where, as Shakespeare unforgettably argued and Rowse was never tired of emphasizing, degree certified and regulated every relationship. She questioned, too, his interpretation of the meaning of 'beget' in the famous epigraph and dedication to Mr W.H. which Rowse ascribed to the publisher, not to the poet. She had read the Sonnets constantly and pondered them over many years. Her own gifts as a writer and her range of historical and literary reference ought, though she would never have made such a claim, to have entitled her to a respectful hearing. But to Rowse, inflamed by this fever, she was simply his pupil: not even an Elizabethan specialist. She had no right to disagree.

Perhaps he might, if nothing more had exacerbated the issue, in time have simmered down. But three months later she was given the Order of Merit. 'My O.M.!' as he grew, with resentful jealousy, accustomed to exclaim. He sent her a telegram: 'Warmest congratulations, but isn't it *un peu exaggéré*?' She replied by postcard: 'It is no doubt excessive but it's certainly nice.' That so many years of kindness and affection could be torn out of the book of life was perhaps the deepest of his many self-inflicted wounds. No one could have been more charitable, more forgiving, than Veronica. But although he continued, on occasion, to write letters of polite friendship, bitterness and jealousy demeaned his conduct. He contributed, unenthusiastically, to her Festschrift[1] but in conversation, and even in print, he was wounding and offensive. That so essentially ardent, affectionate and generous a nature could be so perverted is an index of the damage it had suffered.

1. *For Veronica Wedgwood These: Studies in Seventeenth Century History* (1986).

The reaction of the wider world to the tone in which Rowse presented his arguments is well summed up in a phrase from a review by Christopher Sykes: 'We should all have followed him like lambs if he had not ordered us about so much, and so offensively.' The same point is made, with greater weight, by Professor Alfred Harbage of the Widener Library in a letter dated 9 October 1970, replying to a complaint from Rowse on the reception of his book:

Was it not a distinct popular success? So far as its scholarly reviewers are concerned, their response was surely predictable. I don't see how you can acknowledge your 'bullying' ways as you do without recognizing that truculence begets truculence.

You make a good point when you say that scholars should have had the 'simple tactical sense to welcome an effective ally in the struggle for sanity in this field.' I had this sense and I did not join in the clamor against the book although parts of it offended me as it did others . . . I consider certain questions still open which you consider closed and I do not like sweeping condemnation of Shakespearean scholars as a class . . .

So temperate, so good-natured a reply was insufficient. Harbage's book *Shakespeare's Audience* was sneeringly dismissed in what Rowse intended as a settling of accounts with his critics, *Discovering Shakespeare* (1989).[1]

Harbage's wise prediction that so fierce an attack would provoke an equivalent reaction was amply borne out. Professor Dover Wilson, one of the main targets, though unnamed, of Rowse's philippics against literary scholars replied immediately in a short book published by the Cambridge University Press. *An Introduction to the Sonnets of Shakespeare for the Use of Historians and Others* (1963). The copy in the Huntington Library, enriched with the sympathetic marginalia of Walter Oakeshott, bears his inscription 'This messy copy of JDW's counterblast to Rowse in *The Times* (if I remember rightly): an article in which ALR most unscrupulously – as JDW felt – borrowed wholesale without acknowledgments from JDW and others, while trouncing them because they were not historians and so could not

1. op. cit., p. 97.

begin to understand the sonnets.' Neither Dover Wilson nor Oakeshott was vain or easily provoked. To list the scholars who were antagonized as much by Rowse's method of disputation as by his arguments would be to pile Pelion on Ossa. Rowse was especially incensed by the unsigned criticisms in *The Times Literary Supplement* which he discovered had been written by an independent scholar called John Crow who had once contributed a column on boxing to the *Daily Mirror* under the headline 'From the Crow's Nest'. Ready as he was to make play with such a detail Rowse had left it a little late to invoke the dignity of scholarship.

Perhaps the most formidable of his critics, who handled the weapons of learned irony with a deadly elegance, was Professor Samuel Schoenbaum, to whose work allusion has already been made. In September 1972 Rowse attempted, unsuccessfully, to involve Harold Macmillan as Chancellor of the University in proceedings against the Oxford University Press for publishing Schoenbaum's remarks which Rowse considered insulting. Macmillan and Agatha Christie were two of the apostles of common sense, as opposed to the priesthood of scholarship, whom Rowse frequently cited in his support. His attempt to recruit T. S. Eliot was firmly rejected:

21 July 1964

My dear Leslie Rowse,

I am sorry to have to disagree with you, but I do not see any compulsive reason for looking into the problem of the Shakespearian sonnets and the identity of the person to whom they were written.

The identification of the lovely boy and the dark lady were not the only questions in the sonnets on which Rowse pronounced. There was also the Rival Poet; Rowse's confident and plausible argument for Marlowe has not found much favour. So much depends upon antecedent assumptions about dating that there is no end to speculation and debate.

Whatever may be the assessment of Rowse's contribution to this, there can be no doubt of his judgment and skill in exploiting the publicity for his contentions. The books sold and sold. Altogether between the first biography in 1963 and the final *My View of Shake-*

speare (1996) there were some fifteen titles, besides the three volume *Annotated Shakespeare* (1978) and the lightly modernized text of the plays *The Contemporary Shakespeare* which began to appear in 1985. The verve and liveliness that the Elizabethan age, especially, inspired in Rowse were communicated to his readers. The two biographies (the second *Shakespeare the Man* was published ten years after the first) take much of their colour from the author's close study of the society and institutions, the landscape, the ideas, the arts, the reading of the world in which his hero moved. In the plays, as in the sonnets, he is forever on the look-out for traces of autobiography, a theme he worked out in *Shakespeare's Self-Portrait* (1984).

One aspect of Shakespeare's genius Rowse time and again illuminates, namely his insistence on a quality, uncommon in that age, his sense of history. He quotes, though he draws back from full endorsement, the judgment of his friend Bruce McFarlane that Shakespeare was our greatest historian. It is an interesting reversal of roles. Rowse as a rule was the one to throw his cap over the windmill, McFarlane to scrutinize and qualify the grounds for such antics.

Perhaps the most surprising feature of his vision of Shakespeare is the emphatic confidence with which he asserts his heterosexuality. The sonnets to the lovely boy have been often taken as obvious evidence to the contrary. Rowse's opinion is the more remarkable because both in his published and his private writings he regards homosexuality as a mark of superior intelligence and sensibility, comprehending both male and female psychological insights. Heterosexuals, on the other hand, are of the earth earthy. Their activities lead, only too infallibly, to domestic ties and the procreation of children who get in the way of the pursuit of truth and beauty. Refinement is the natural characteristic of the homosexual. Such briefly is the deduction to be drawn from the great bulk of his writings.

Yet in the case of Shakespeare this unfortunate orientation towards the opposite sex is not allowed to darken the enjoyment and the admiration that lights up everything Rowse wrote about him. There is a simplicity and strength of feeling that carries the reader, as it carried the author, along. One does not have to be a poet or an

Elizabethan scholar to catch the full meaning of what he has to say. Subtle points are drawn out to a clarity that makes them instantly understandable. Rowse is at ease in Elizabethan England as he never was in the world of his own time. He does not feel himself threatened or open to insult. He hardly feels it necessary to classify people, as he did his own contemporaries, by what degree they obtained or might have been expected to obtain in the Final Honours School of his university. When he is reading Shakespeare or expounding him he is luminous, stimulating, alive. Only when he sees an opportunity of snubbing a rival's interpretation or boasting of the originality of his own, as he does with the sonnets, does the solipsism release its poisons. Even in a work such as *Discovering Shakespeare*, where there is so much self-justification and denigration of others, there are wholly delightful passages such as the chapter entitled 'New Light on the Early Plays' where he loses himself and his preoccupations in enjoyment and fresh recognitions of the text. All this galvanizes the reader. It may, or may not, commend itself to the experts. The present writer does not pretend to be one of them and leaves such questions to those who are.

What is asserted here is that Rowse drew a host of readers to Shakespeare by the vigour, the energy, the excitement with which he wrote about him. Take, for instance, his preface to *Love's Labour's Lost*, not a general favourite among the plays, which he wrote for the *Annotated Shakespeare* and subsequently republished in *Prefaces to Shakespeare's Plays* (1984). Whether his reading of the context of the play and his identification of character and allusion would be accepted by every scholar I am not concerned or qualified to judge. What is at once communicated to the reader is the humour, the immediacy, the *sprezzatura* of the work thus presented. We feel at once inclined to read it and to expect enjoyment.

Rowse's intellect is not a massive one. We do not go to him as we might to Dr Johnson for lapidary judgments founded as much on a general understanding of humanity as on the particulars of text and authorship. What we do find is agility, quickness, sensibility, present-mindedness. In considering a genius as all-embracing as Shakespeare's there is much that these qualities can touch into life. As George Steiner pointed out in an article in the *New Yorker* Rowse's sheer gusto is his special contribution, engendering a corresponding envy and malice among 'the thin grey ones'.[1] The courtesies and the candour of scholarship may not always be present but the zest is.

1. *New Yorker*, 18 March 1974, pp. 142 ff.

25

A Man of Letters

All his life Rowse saw himself as a man of letters. Ready as he was to parade the panoply of scholarship, convinced, too, of his solitary vision as a poet, he never lost the curiosity and excitement, the readiness to champion or to question an established reputation, to encourage a new talent or to scour the horizon for the signs of one. He held strong views about history, about politics, and about much else. Indeed any view of his was likely to be a strong one. But he rarely allowed them to interfere with judgment of literary quality. The most underrated writer of his own time he considered to be the French novelist and dramatist de Montherlant, in spite of the fact that in the great struggle for the preservation of European civilization de Montherlant had hardly played a part that Rowse could approve. Similarly the French historian, Romier, whom he translated was so far removed from Rowse's own understanding of the recent past that he sometimes found it necessary to rewrite his author.

His correspondence with his fellow writers is of the widest scope. To his juniors, and to beginners especially, he was inspiringly generous and encouraging. Nothing in his literary life is more exemplary. He would even take a great deal of time and trouble to help an unpublished author find his way into print. From this sprang many friendships. At least once however it plagued him with an angry correspondent. In his capacity as literary scout for Odhams he recommended the manuscript of an autobiography sent to him by a reader of his own *A Cornish Childhood*. The story it told was that of a childhood and adolescence slightly earlier and far harsher than his own. To quote Rowse's introduction (for the work was published by Odhams in 1954 under the title *A Cornish Waif's Story*) it was 'the autobiography of a Cornish girl – now a woman in her sixties – child of the daughter of a Cornish miner who had been blinded in an accident, with no means of subsistence. Illegitimate, unwanted, she was handed over to an organ-grinder with a hide-out in the slums of Plymouth, with whom she tramped the roads of Cornwall from Plymouth to Penzance and back again all through childhood, singing her way through the years during and after the Boer War at the turn of the century.' It is a terrifying story of misery and degradation – 'the stigma of illegitimacy, the constant feeling of not being wanted, the early years in and out of the workhouse, the searing consciousness of inferiority branded upon a child.'

The work was published anonymously with only Rowse's Foreword. The attention it attracted, far from pleasing the author, led her to write a series of furious letters, even to threaten legal proceedings. Her complaint was that publication in its authentic form made it easy for people to identify her. Rowse, who had done a good deal of editorial work to ensure that its impact was not impaired by minor faults of expression, felt himself unjustly and ungratefully treated. The affair rumbled on for some three years driving him at length to draw up a long statement dated 30 June 1957 of the whole transaction. Silence descended, broken at last by a letter from the author twenty-seven years later in which she apologized for her unreasonableness and celebrated their common love for Cornwall and for cats.

Many of his friendships and encounters with writers of his own or of an older generation are chronicled in the volumes of memoirs or collections of essays. Some, such as Auden and Quiller Couch, have books to themselves. Towards his exact contemporaries there is usually an element of competition. Always there is a degree of egotism. How had these people treated him? What did they think of, or say about, his work? The answer to these questions influenced, sometimes determined, his own estimate of theirs. Repeatedly one is surprised to find an author hitherto commended suddenly relegated to the broad ranks of the second rate. A little further reading generally supplies the explanation: a cool review, a reflection on some weakness of argument or expression reported by a third party or most commonly in later years dissent from Shakespearean conclusions.

Perhaps the most ludicrous instance of such a reversal of opinion is to be found in the copy of his *The Use of History* presented to Lord Berners, the subject of a handsome appreciation in *Friends and Contemporaries* (1989). The author's inscription records 'Admiration, Affection, Homage to the man, writer, musician, painter.' Berners read the book, pencil in hand, underlining various passages of self-approbation and then got rid of it. By all the fates Rowse found it in a second-hand bookshop. He was passionately angry, answering the implied reproof by counter-attacking marginalia and a long pencilled inscription below the original, defining the recipient's qualities in a very different sense '. . . a certain jealousy, a certain snobbery and cattiness'.

The most interesting, because most characteristic, of his oscillating opinions, sometimes weighed down by irritation at excessive praise, sometimes rising through his own unwilling admiration of wit and style, is that of Cyril Connolly. Connolly, his exact contemporary, entered with the stigma of unfair advantage in the race that had been set before them. Scholar of Eton and Brackenbury Exhibitioner of Balliol (Rowse always crossed out 'Scholar' and substituted 'Exhibitioner' in printed references to him) Connolly compounded these offences by throwing away the riches the University had to offer in idleness and dissipation. Worse still, he did the same with the glittering opportunities that life continued to put in his way. His unrestrained hedonism, especially offensive in the pleasure taken and the attention paid to wine, was anathema to the puritanism, that lay, for all his fulminations, so close to the surface of Rowse's nature. Connolly himself paraded all this. Idleness, greed, unscrupulousness in taking money for work he had no intention of doing, evasion of every obligation, were all part of the persona he cultivated and imposed with enviable success on his own and the succeeding generation. Deplorable as this was, there was no denying his obvious gifts, his wide and even assiduous reading, his curious and sometimes minute knowledge of the natural world and his response to its beauties. Why, granted all this talent, opportunity, and real love of literature, did nothing issue beyond collections of reviews and brief flashes of reminiscence and gossip?

Rowse nagged all his life at the question. He received his best answer in a letter from Noel Blakiston, written on 11 April 1976, which also delivered some shrewd criticism of its recipient:

. . . your complicated character which at one moment exults in having 300,000 readers and at the next dismisses the masses as fools. I have just one regret about your character, this 'weather eye' of yours that prevents you from committing yourself, that keeps you as you say on the sidelines, never giving yourself away. What a virginity! Cyril certainly gives himself away in my book,[1] and was indeed Irish and generous of himself. I am so glad that you say that he brought a glow over his and his contemporaries' work . . . It is a pity that he talked so much about writing masterpieces. His gift was that glow you mention which intermittently lasted till his end in his talk and journalism. You say he should have been writing books and then nullify the statement by adding 'that is, if he had had the will power, the discipline, perhaps even the constructive instead of the discursive gift.' Precisely.

What Rowse really objected to was the status granted to Connolly but denied to him. On 15 January 1954 he had written to *The Times Literary Supplement* 'Reading your perceptive and, on the whole, discriminating article on Mr Connolly, I was surprised by your comparing him to Paul Valéry and positively shocked by your roundly declaring Mr Connolly "a great writer . . ."' This was indeed an extraordinary judgment by any serious critical standards. Is Connolly to be ranked with Shakespeare and Milton, or even with Johnson or Hazlitt? But silly as it now seems it did reflect the authority then generally accorded to Connolly's pronouncements in the columns of the week-end press or in his own elegantly produced monthly *Horizon*. Rowse never attained such a position in the fashionable world of letters. He might, he did, outsell Connolly by tens of thousands. But that was not the same thing.

What rankled, what infuriated, was that Connolly achieved this eminence not only without ever doing a proper job or applying himself to the labour of any systematic study but worse, far worse, by sponging and surrendering to every self-indulgence. Rowse had both the generosity and the self-respect in money matters that so often dignifies experience of poverty. He grudged expense, he hated extravagance, he was enraged at having his earnings taxed; but, as we have seen, the minute he had any money at all he helped his friends and parents: with

1. *A Romantic Friendship: The Letters of Cyril Connolly to Noel Blakiston.*

affluence his hospitality and his benefactions were generous. Rowse had worked hard, had done his duty, had discharged his obligations. It was exasperating, not least because, in the last analysis, both writers were born under the same star. For all their reading and knowledge at command, they were aesthetes rather than scholars. Connolly obviously so. But in spite of academic distinctions and the life of learning Rowse never faltered in asserting that literature came first with him. The scholar's aim is to get as near as he can to establishing what can be known. The aesthete's or the artist's to establishing as perfect a form as his material permits.

Rowse read Connolly avidly. His marginalia were often scornful and abusive but frequently admitted admiration for the skill and elegance with which perverse or nihilistic judgments were expressed, deploring only the writer's consistent failure to distinguish between the proper use of 'shall' and 'will'. 'The readableness of this book is a drug' he wrote on the title page of David Pryce-Jones's *Cyril Connolly: Journal and a Memoir*, adding 'C.C. was a Perpetual Adolescent; ALR a Perpetual Don'. Earlier he had written in his copy of Connolly's *The Evening Colonnade* 'Reading C.C. is a succession of chocolate eclairs. C.C.'s *great* quality – he *loved* poetry. A marvellous read. C.C. regarded me as "censorious" – no wonder considering the way he went on!' They rarely corresponded (Connolly's letter about Richard Pares and Evelyn Waugh has been quoted on p. 51), except in the brief period during the War when Connolly acted as Literary Editor of the *Observer*. The proprietors told him that he was giving too much review space to Rowse, whom they suspected, rightly, of unbelief in Christianity. It was certainly a grievance that he was allotted so little space in *Horizon* – only three contributions, of which the most substantial was an article 'Democracy and Democratic Leadership' published in June 1941, only days before the German invasion of Russia altered the character of the War. Its content, outright abolition of the House of Lords, disestablishment of the Church of England, the retention of a degree of the wartime control of the press, is the proto-Rowse of the thirties Labour candidate. Its manner, vigorous, no nonsense, clear the decks, is much more that of the *Political Quarterly* whose Editorial Board he had just been invited to join than the Greenery-Yallery, Grosvenor Gallery approach to world affairs of Connolly's journal.

That the paper only printed one of the many poems Rowse offered was a source of lasting resentment. Here he saw the hand not so much of Connolly of as his assistant editor Stephen Spender. This was another lifelong literary relationship in which periodic scuffles were either narrowly averted (as by Veronica Wedgwood's tactful handling of the *Time and Tide* review already alluded to) or else patched up just enough to avoid embarrassing third parties. Neither really respected the other's work, particularly their poetry. Late in life an *éclaircissement* rather than a reconciliation took place. In a long letter dated 26 April 1982 Spender explains why, though he regrets it, he has not known Rowse better:

I think I've always found it a bit humiliating to be with people who force their opinions on one, because one is faced with the alternative of either having to agree or else quarrel. You are a great forcer of opinions and for that reason I don't think I would ever be easy in your company. It would be too much like having to listen to F. R. Leavis on Virginia Woolf.

He illustrates his feeling by making the point that all the main characters in *King Lear* are, in one way or another, asinine, and speculates how fatal to the play it would have been to have had a Rowsean character telling them so. His parting shot reveals what made so essentially communicative and sociable a man so isolated: 'I do feel that, clever as you are, you do have something to learn.'

This element perhaps coloured Rowse's friendships with T. S. Eliot and with Auden, on both of whom he has written with judgment. Perhaps even better than his own little book *The Poet Auden: A Personal Memoir* (1987) is his review of Charles Osborne's biography.[1] As elsewhere he guesses there, in spite of generous praise, that Mac-Neice, whom he hardly knew, would survive better. As an undergraduate MacNeice had fallen passionately in love with the daughter of J. D. Beazley, herself it would appear as gifted, attractive and uninhibited as her parents. The rapid failure of the marriage had in Rowse's view prevented the poet's talent from fulfilling itself as it should.

Of the other leading poets of his generation Rowse had no contact

1. *Now!*, 7 March 1980.

with Day Lewis and with the younger men whom he admired his encounters were disappointing. Dylan Thomas's drunkenness predictably appalled him as did his readiness to sponge. At the height of austerity in 1941 he and his wife came to lunch in Oxford. For once All Souls was unable to offer hospitality so Rowse took them to the Mitre. 'We will have white wine' said Caitlin as they sat down. Rowse, who was naturally a generous host, never got over his rage. For Philip Larkin, elected to a Visiting Fellowship at All Souls, he felt respect but not sympathy: and he was understandably mortified when in Larkin's *Oxford Book of Modern Verse* his whole poetic output was represented by a minor piece on one of his cats.

These are the well-known names. Of those not so widely recognized he was an admirer of Martyn Skinner's delicate craftsmanship and praised in the highest terms the work of a fellow academic Francis Warner of St Peter's Hall, as it then was. The prose writers with whom he corresponded are so numerous that even a meagre account of each exchange would divert this book from biography and would submerge its bounds under a flood. A list will be printed as an appendix for the convenience of anyone in search of material about a particular author. To select from it is necessarily arbitrary. The principle of selection, however inadequately applied, is that of the importance of the writer to Rowse, how large he or she bulked in his mind, rather than the present writer's estimate of their work, still less any anticipation of that verdict of the common reader to which Johnson refers all claims to literary honours. Naturally it is his own contemporaries who come first to mind.

Peter Quennell had been the editor of *Oxford Verse* in which Rowse had been published while they were both undergraduates. As the founding co-editor of *History Today* he became a frequent correspondent from the 1950s to the 1980s, and was one of the few, the very few, who were permitted to criticize with impunity. On 26 August 1971 he wrote a firm editorial letter about Rowse's review of the new volume of the *Dictionary of National Biography 1951–60* insisting on the removal of offensive remarks about Roger Fry, Cyril Bailey and Desmond MacCarthy. Boldly he went on to criticize Rowse's language in a recent article in *The Times* on Shakespeare, particularly of the use of the word 'sex' in the sentence 'Shakespeare dripped with sex at every pore'. In his reply Rowse accepted the excisions but still defended his choice of words in *The Times*. More surprisingly he invited his critic down to All Souls. Their friendship even survived Quennell's irreverence towards the crucial article in *The Times* in February 1973.

I was of course deeply interested by your article and enjoyed, as I always do, your resounding trumpet-voluntaries! But I must admit that I don't agree that you have *completely* proved your case. Although you've undoubtedly shown that Mrs Lanier *might* have been Shakespeare's mistress, I am not convinced she *must* have been. It's a question, I feel, of possibility – even of probability – but not yet of certainty.

Quennell shared to the full Rowse's disgust at what both felt to be the betrayal of standards in learning and manners in their old University.[1]

Distaste and contempt for fashionable ideas and fashionable reputations were shared with others of his generation with whom he had little else in common, for instance Evelyn Waugh and C. S. Lewis. Their very different forms of Christianity were equally repellent to him, Waugh's especially so, entailing as it did a violently recusant partisanship in the interpretation of the Elizabethan age. Waugh and he had never known each other, or ever had close friends in common except for John Betjeman and Richard Pares. Nonetheless Rowse was deeply interested in him and evidently much admired his writing, again perhaps surprisingly since apart from the bawdy humour of Chaucer and Shakespeare the great English comic writers seem to have made little appeal. Dickens he thought much overrated and I have not found so much as a mention of Thomas Love Peacock or P. G. Wodehouse. Come to that I have found little mention of any of Waugh's novels, but that he was aware of great talent and superb craftsmanship is evident from any mention of his name in the journals.

They met, apparently for the first and only time, at Sunday lunch at Dunster Castle on 27 September 1959.

1. Letter dated 31 December 1988.

We had both clearly made resolutions to be on our best behaviour. We talked about Richard Pares, our great common friend . . . I paid him compliments on the two books, one of which I read and much admired on my last two home-comings across the Atlantic, *A Handful of Dust* and *The Ordeal of Gilbert Pinfold*. He was visibly pleased.

We talked about Oxford and obscure places into which we had penetrated, introduced by John Betjeman. He had been into Skimmery's,[1] St Mary's Hall, of which Newman was Principal, but had not seen the portrait of James Gibbs, nor Oriel Library. He had been in the Senior Common Room to see the Richmond drawing of Newman, but did not know the house where Newman was born in the London street between Southampton Row and the British Museum.

A few of his well-known prejudices peeped diffidently out. We agreed in deploring the fatal Chamberlain influence in English politics – he rather deferring, 'you will know more about that than I'. I deplored the post-ponement of Home Rule for Ireland, with its tragic consequences. He said that Joe Chamberlain was hostile to Christianity – by which he meant Catholicism – with his Masonic and Unitarian affiliations. 'Wasn't he a friend of Gambetta?' This was rather nonsense *à la Belloc*. Chamberlain was really motivated more by pique against Gladstone.

We found a point of accord in mourning the gifted Oxford generation mown down in the First War. They were much in his mind, he said, having been writing about Ronnie Knox,[2] I said that as a young man of twenty-one coming to All Souls I used to hear a great deal about them, and had a kind of *schwärmerei* for them. We talked of Patrick Shaw-Stewart.[3] Evelyn said that, after doing well in the Dardanelles and coming back, he had deliberately gone out to the front again with the idea of being killed – all his friends were already.

I asked did he get the impression that Ronnie Knox was a sad man? He said very, deeply sad. And added that he never got over the loss of all his friends, lived a widowed life thereafter. I registered that another factor must

---

1. The name by which St Mary's Hall was familiarly known before it was absorbed into Oriel College in 1902. See Falconer Madan, *Oxford Outside the Guidebooks* (1923), p. 89.
2. His biography had just been published.
3. Whose biography Ronald Knox had written.

have contributed to that intense sadness, and anyway his religious faith does not seem to have brought him much in the way of happiness.

Waugh came most alive, became himself, querulous, eyebrows alert and puckered up with interest, when describing the eccentricity of the present John Evelyn.[1] *There* was a subject; the eccentric is what stirs his imagination as the seedy Graham Greene's. And John Evelyn is an oddity, a dipsomaniac who, having plenty of money and no need to do so, gave up the Evelyn family house, because he couldn't be bothered with it and went to live in rooms! He handed over his family pictures to Sherman Stonor – nothing whatever to do with the family; they hang or lie about at Stonor. The original John Evelyn's books and presses he handed over to Christ Church – which had nothing to do with Evelyn, a Balliol man.[2] The present John Evelyn writes poetry (unintelligible), Mathematics (ditto), theosophy (equally so) – and now has sent Waugh a drama he can't make head or tail of. This character evidently appeals to him.

I happened to mention Alain-Fournier, and was greatly surprised to find that he had never heard of *Le Grand Meaulnes*. I assured him that, a spiritual allegory, it was very much his book and offered to send it down from Oxford. He said, again almost diffidently, that he would get it.

He was clearly out to behave himself. So was I.

He looked much less irate than in his later photographs, more chubby and boyish; though there was the podginess of too much drink, a slightly alarming look in his eyes. He brought no ear-trumpet and had no difficulty in hearing me.

Eight years later Rowse was commissioned to report on Waugh's letters and papers with a view to their purchase by the Huntington.[3] Accompanied by Robert Dougan of the Huntington and his wife he drove down to Combe Florey from Oxford – an experience no doubt remembered by his passengers:[4]

1. Descendant of the seventeenth-century diarist and connoisseur.
2. A later MS note read, 'Only this last year broken up and dispersed through the idiocy of the will he made – when Evelyn's things would have made an Oxford parallel to the Pepys Library at Cambridge.' Rowse urged his friend Christopher Hill, then Master of Balliol, to secure the collection for the College and was disgusted at the tepid response. Fortunately it has now been bought by the British Library.
3. They were subsequently bought by the University of Texas.
4. He was, by all accounts, an alarmingly impatient, indeed irresponsible, driver.

The house made an impression of sadness on me, of the strong personality that had made it – the interior, all the possessions so characteristic – so recently inhabited it, leaving it now deserted, rather down-at-heel, a bit shabby, not too much money to spare for repairs, or even to keep things ship-shape. In fact the comfortable untidiness of a Catholic household, averse to money values. For all the money Evelyn made – 750,000 of *Brideshead Revisited* sold in America – he lived up to every penny of it, a largeish family, children to educate, nothing spared them, lashings of drink, generous entertaining. Like Belloc, model and mentor (what a model, what a mentor!)

. . . What surprised me was Evelyn's cult of Victorianism – all his life he had collected Victoriana. The walls were covered with pictures by Augustus Egg and Arthur Hughes, Victorian landscapes and *genre* pieces, Victorian chandeliers, carpets and furniture; a stupendous Burgess settle, painted and parapeted, given him by John Betjeman. I had no idea their tastes were so close.

We went into lunch. Fine hall, uglified by Victoriana – I wouldn't have such a collection in a fine Georgian house – Evelyn's bowler hat placed on a marble group above a bookcase filled with treasures of a life-time's collecting. How sensible of him to have bought from undergraduate days lovely books like John Martin's *Illustrated Milton*, landscape books with illustrations by Turner, Daniell, Prout; the Pre-Raphaelite *Tennyson* and so on. Superb books. We passed into the hospitable, family dining-room, also rather the worse for wear. Evelyn's Captain's cap with red band placed firmly on the youthful bust of the Master. His presence was everywhere.

I felt sadder and sadder for Laura, and made myself useful helping her with the waiting. She had cooked the lunch herself – a simple affair of steak-and-kidney pie, no trimmings. I followed her out into the large old-fashioned kitchen, and into the pantry, where the cat had already got at the remains of the pie. I chatted to her as we waited, leaving Robert to his slow-timed conversation with the lawyer . . .

We moved on to the library, with elaborate bookshelves coming out into the room installed by Evelyn (and putting off to inquiring purchasers,[1] I gathered). The atmosphere was discouraging. But the books and papers were fascinating.

Characteristic of Evelyn – a man's books give a portrait of him – were the

1. The house itself was then on the market.

serried ranks of the *Catholic Encyclopaedia*, Burke's *Peerage* and *Landed Gentry* (of whom he fancied himself one). There were earlier books from Arthur[1] Waugh's library and, in a Belloc-inscribed volume, Maurice Bowra's typed verses on Betjeman receiving the Duff Cooper award from the hands of Princess Margaret. Maurice's private verses, brilliant and bawdy, are an extraordinary production ['his best work' crossed out]. His friend Sparrow says what a pity it is that Maurice's genius is intransmissible to posterity, for his verse is unprintable and his prose unreadable.

Evelyn has been *collecting* books all the way along, and I was interested to see the inscriptions of old friends: Harold Acton (in part Anthony Blanche of *Brideshead*), inscribing *Humdrum* in 1928 – 'To dear Evelyn praying it will not bore, with much love from Harold'. Then *Peonies and Ponies* 1941 has 'To gallant Evelyn for a chuckle betwixt commandoes, from his unrepentant old crony Harold'. Quite recently, *Old Lamps for New*, 1965 has 'To my old friend Evelyn who so patiently read some of these chapters and encouraged me to persevere, with much affection from Harold'. Evelyn had fixed his book-plate: *Industria Ditat*[2] with his arms quartered with the Herberts![3]

A life-time's friendships showed up in these inscriptions, since we were all young together at Oxford. Now Evelyn is dead, and Harold has been operated on for cancer. What absorbing lives they had! I had never heard of any of these books by Harold – an ineffective literary career, in contrast to Evelyn's: a triumph. But Evelyn had genius;[4] Harold, just talent.

Quite recently came Edith Sitwell's *Collected Poems* 'For dearest Evelyn with great admiration and much love from his god-daughter Edith'. So he had a hand in her conversion – I don't fancy that he was much of a friend of the Sitwells before. But he was a fanatical proselytizer – responsible for converting Penelope Betjeman away from John . . .

While Robert endlessly chaffered and haggled with the lawyer – I have never seen anyone so slow . . . I looked into [Evelyn's papers]. I was astonished at their richness and at his conscientiousness. The manuscripts of all his novels were in his own hand with corrections all the way through – an

1. His father.
2. Hard work brings home the bacon.
3. His wife's ancient and aristocratic family.
4. Waugh always denied this, claiming only craftsmanship.

accomplished, stylish hand . . . And some unpublished stories. Best of all, were the unpublished Journals, frank and candid, as one would expect. I looked into them here and there, noting a comment on his friend Betjeman's later TV career – showing people over the stately homes of England: was that any better than succeeding to old Ernie Betjeman's business in *papier mâché* objects for the Middle East? Evelyn had to resist – as I have – the temptation to write a letter to *The Times* every day about some new folly. But he complains that his memory is going – too much drink all through life . . .

The house made a deep impression on me – I was overwhelmed by the sense of loss and desertion, the glimpse into the life and mind of the man of genius who had called it into being. I looked for his grave in the churchyard below the house; but of course he wouldn't be there, uncompromising to the last. Where is he buried? At Downside?

This long extract from Rowse's journal for 8 June 1967 is remarkable for the reverence paid to an author who was far from being of his own way of thinking. Was Waugh's solitariness a bond? Or the element of homosexuality which Rowse, always on the look out for any such manifestation, found dominant in *Brideshead*, surfacing once more in the voices heard by Gilbert Pinfold?

No such mitigating qualities could be pleaded in defence of C. S. Lewis, whose overt heterosexuality and hearty enjoyment of beery symposia with the Inklings put him outside the pale. Whenever his name drifts into Rowse's consciousness as he writes his journals, dislike, even venom, is the immediate reaction. Yet when, after his death, he was attacked by John Carey, Rowse was outraged by what seemed to him the sneering, patronizing tone. In a reply, robustly headed 'A Literary Skunk', admitting that 'C. S. Lewis and I were at opposite poles of thought at Oxford' he characterized him as 'the most remarkable man, by far, in the English Literature school there in his time' and quoted, with emphatic endorsement, Kathleen Raine's appreciation of him, celebrating 'the pure joy he found in works of romance, poetry, philosophy'. Delight in literature was the air they breathed in common, different though their perceptions might be. When Lewis's *English Literature in the Sixteenth Century* was published in 1954 Rowse wrote an enthusiastic review. A few days later, finding themselves in the same compartment going up to London, Lewis thanked him and Rowse took the opportunity of pointing out omissions and errors which, as a good reviewer knows, should not be highlighted before the public but communicated to the author. Lewis, like Rowse, did not like admitting he was wrong and a frosty silence ensued. The whole scene together with other interesting details of their relations, is too well described in A. N. Wilson's biography of Lewis[1] to need amplification.

Graham Greene, so often and so oddly bracketed with Evelyn Waugh, had been a personal, though never a close, acquaintance since undergraduate days. The bleak morosity of his view of the world, relieved only by heavy drinking from which Rowse recoiled, could hardly have sorted with the ardent, lyric, passionate temper of the young radical. Rowse's extended sketch of him in *Friends and Contemporaries* (1989), rambling and egocentric though it is, contains some interesting biographical detail coolly observed. Too much of it is taken up with Rowse's already sufficiently advertised inability to understand how anybody of sense could become or remain a Roman Catholic. Yet it is a writer deeply committed to that faith, Flannery O'Connor, whose collected letters Rowse considered the best he had ever read, who expressed most pithily what his essay seems to have been groping after:

What he [Graham Greene] does, I think, is try to make religion respectable to the modern unbeliever by making it seedy. He succeeds so well in making it seedy that he has to save it by the miracle.[2]

The points of contact between the two men were so frequent that nothing but aversion of temperament could have kept them at a distance from each other. Both appeared in *Public School Verse* and again in *Oxford Poetry* in the twenties. The newspaper on which Greene served his apprenticeship was the *Nottingham Journal*, edited by Cecil Roberts, later celebrated and successful as a popular novelist, who became a friend and incessant correspondent of Rowse's later

1. pp. 243–5.
2. *The Habit of Being. Letters*, ed. Sally Fitzgerald (1979), p. 201.

years. Greene's conversion was effected and his beliefs kept in repair by Father Gervase Mathew, one of Rowse's steady Oxford friends. They were in direct contact again when Greene was Literary Editor of the *Spectator*, to which Rowse was a frequent contributor. Yet there was none of the ease and openness in their relations that characterized those with Peter Quennell. Rowse was affronted by his cult of squalor and of violence. In a lurid paragraph he gives chapter and verse for what he had seen of both in his own childhood and youth. 'I suppose it is the charm of the old folk ways of life that attracts people in *A Cornish Childhood*. But I could write an account of it that would give the other side of the coin.'[1] Greene, son of a public school headmaster, connected through his mother with R. L. Stevenson, came, like Orwell, from a background that had protected him from such things.

1. *Friends and Contemporaries*, p. 245.

26

Surplus Energy

Rowse's inexhaustible energy was both a blessing and a curse. A blessing, in that it enabled him to master an infinity of materials and to produce some very remarkable work. A curse, in that he seems to have been incapable of sitting still and keeping quiet, above all of relaxing. The spring was always wound up to a tension that necessitated discharge in speech or writing. There is evidence that he was himself aware of this, though whether he recognized the dangers inherent in such a condition is not so clear.

In an article in the *Week-End Telegraph*,[1] as perceptive as it is entertaining, Charles Nevin gives an account of accompanying Rowse on a visit to Stratford. As the train passes through Slough, Rowse recites Betjeman's poem 'Come, friendly bombs, and fall on Slough' in a penetrating voice without eliciting any reaction from their fellow travellers. Undeterred he chatters on, exclaiming as they change trains at Oxford 'I have too much mental energy. It's exhausting for other people.' More revealingly still: 'A rage upsets other people. It only stimulates me.' Finally 'The Doctor announced that he was so highbrow he was hardly human, dear, and mused, not unkindly, on the ignorance that tried to pigeonhole his talents. "You cannot," he said "pigeonhole genius."'

The sixties and seventies were the heyday of Rowse the Devil's Advocate against consensual progressivism. To hear him attacking fashionable ideas about education and easy human perfectibility often gave the feeling of fresh air suddenly gusting through the air-conditioned corridors of late twentieth-century cant. It was because

1. *Daily Telegraph*, 20 August 1988.

Eloquence Putting to Flight the Forces of Anarchy, MCMLXIX.
Osbert Lancaster, the guest of Sir Michael Howard at Encaenia,
thanks his host with inimitable wit.

he himself was by nature a radical and had fought against entrenched unreason that he was so effective. In Cromwell's imperishable phrase he knew what he fought for and loved what he knew. Perhaps even more powerfully he hated what he fought against. Yet here again the pluses and the minuses of his temperament dissipated the thrust. He spoke and wrote too much and thought too little. Solipsism stifled self-criticism.

With rare exceptions friendly criticism, from which he had profited so much as a young man, simply extinguished a friendship. Peter Quennell, Kenneth Rose and Norman Scarfe are the only instances that come to mind of those who were not summarily exiled for such an offence. For those who could not plead benefit of intimacy harsher measures were attempted. The old trick of lying in wait for a man's book and damning it in a review sometimes served the turn. Rowse himself was ready to take legal action against what he considered an unfair review, a cause from which his lawyers generally dissuaded him. In October 1963, provoked by Malcolm Muggeridge's review of his biography of Shakespeare in the *Evening Standard* he wrote to

Lord Beaverbrook to complain and to threaten. Beaverbrook's reply, notably wise and temperate, calmed him down. In an article in *Tribune*[1] Daniel George, a critic and publisher's editor, had attacked Rowse as 'our pinchbeck Carlyle . . . He complains that when he thunders there is no reverberation. By cohabiting so long with the Virgin Queen he has lost contact with reality.' Ten years later, crossing the Atlantic on the same flight as Veronica Wedgwood, Rowse fulminated against the author of those insults, expressing his intention of taking any vengeance he could. 'If you do that, I shall never speak to you again.' The fierceness of such a reaction from so peaceable a person at the time amused him. But when she dissented from his Shakespearean assertions and, worse still, was given the OM it was no joking matter.

His happiest release of surplus energy was in writing popular history, books that set out to inform and entertain, not to cut rival scholars down to size. Based on wide reading, on an acute visual sense, a keen awareness of place and of the entwining strands of family connexion they were also informed by the experience of original research. To have had to ask oneself, what did the man who wrote this letter mean by such and such a use of words? Why did so shrewd a judge of character employ so unreliable a figure on so important a mission? develops an awareness of how unsure one is of what appears to be plain and obvious simply by virtue of the fact that it actually happened. Working from original sources teaches many lessons and develops unexpected insights as nothing else can. It intensifies the down-to-earth, solid reality of the past and strengthens its relation to the present. But it also sharpens scepticism and caution in drawing conclusions and ascribing motives.

Among the most successful of such books were those that took a place or a building as their point of departure. *Bosworth Field* (1966), *The Tower of London in the History of the Nation* (1972), *Windsor Castle in the History of the Nation* (1974), *Oxford in the History of the Nation* (1975). This last, dedicated to John Sparrow, is a notable performance, shot through with autobiographical insights gained at different stages of his long and sometimes storm-crossed love affair

1. 22 August 1952.

with the place. The range and élan are remarkable. The scientific subjects are accorded their proper importance, not least in the brilliant chapter on the University in the aftermath of the Civil War and the Restoration. There are bold and surprising judgments, such as that on John Wesley: 'No Oxford man has ever accomplished more.' There is a wonderful passage (pp. 156–7) on White's *The Natural History and Antiquities of Selborne*. There are intrusions, such as the thinly veiled analogy between the Wycliffe–John of Gaunt relationship and that between A. J. P. Taylor and Lord Beaverbrook. And the diatribes against the Germans, however understandable in a survivor from the first decade of the twentieth century, do not enhance the quality of the book. But the sure chronological sense, fostered by the emphasis laid on continuity and perspective in the Oxford History School, shows to as much advantage in his account of the rise of the Colleges in the medieval university as in the fair, indeed generous, appraisal of Jowett's influence in the nineteenth century. It is in this connexion that he deplores the loss to society of the idealism that inspired the Workers Educational Association, personified in Gore, Temple, R. H. Tawney and G. D. H. Cole. Altogether it shows how good deutero-Rowse could be. In all these books he was well served by his publishers and his picture researchers.

Simultaneously he was publishing collections of essays, reviews, portrait sketches, memoirs and passages of arms with those who criticized or rejected his Shakespearean conclusions. *Discoveries and Reviews* (1975) devoted a whole section to this topic. The two follow-ing sections took a rather more indulgent but still sufficiently stern line with other historians, mostly of the Tudor and Stuart period. In a surprisingly genial opening to a review of G. R. Elton's collected papers he offers a criticism that might justly be retorted on himself:

Professor Elton is a Good Thing on the academic scene: with his combative energy, his aggressive scholarship inspired by secular commonsense, his sheer enthusiasm, he keeps us alert and on our toes, constantly reminding us of his presence. He has now brought together a mass of his serious studies, along with reviews. Those modest men of genius, Gibbon and Maitland, had their miscellaneous papers collected for them after their deaths: not so the Professor.

I, for one, am glad that he did not wait: though I think it was a mistake to produce two volumes where one would have done.[1]

There are, however, engaging departures from solipsism. On page 164 he admits to having learnt something about Queen Elizabeth from the biographies of her written by Elizabeth Jenkins and Paul Johnson. On page 178 he acknowledges his debt to the help of J. A. Williamson in his own biography of Sir Richard Grenville: 'he was able to read the winds and the currents'. He is tireless in defending the study of history from the sociological technocrats with their gleaming trends and glossy models.

'True historical method means the patient accumulation of concrete detail.'[2] And he is unflinching in resistance to bad, dull writing, especially to that of academics who presume to expound or pronounce on the work of original authors: 'The writing of this book is of an unwearied pedestrianism . . . It is odd that persons of no literary sensitivity should choose to write about literature.'

His next collection *Portraits and Views* (1979) bears the subtitle 'Literary and Historical'. In his preface he writes that 'they have enabled me to portray various figures in our literature as I think of them, or to define my position with regard to significant historical issues, such as those of modern Germany and the two German wars of our time; or of the Russian Revolution, Marxism and Communism.' The literary essays all demonstrate Rowse's splendid talent for enjoyment, even in writers to whom for one reason or another he is markedly unsympathetic, such as Belloc or E. M. Forster. Where there is no obstruction, as with Jane Austen or Flannery O'Connor, the generosity of his nature lights up the subject. 'I regard Flannery O'Connor as comparable with Emily Brontë. Pure genius which, in a short life, achieved absolute expression in art; an unflinching view of life which revealed alike its tragedy and its poetry, penetrated by the sense of the mystery behind it all; disciplined by an uncompromising stoicism. Emily Brontë may have had more poetry; Flannery

1. op. cit., p. 150.
2. op. cit., p. 178.

O'Connor had much more humour.'[1] This fine tribute perhaps takes some colour from his savouring of the *goût du terroir*, so strong in her work as in another Southern author Rowse much admired, William Faulkner.

Of the other pieces in the book that on Goldsworthy Lowes Dickinson's *Autobiography* provides perhaps the most succinct summary of the innumerable statements of Rowse's views on homosexuality. Certainly it is far clearer, far more pointed than anything one could collect from the whole book *Homosexuals in History* (1977) which he devoted to the subject. The interest and pleasure of that work consists chiefly in its lively biographical sketches, its mixture of gossip, speculation and sometimes improbable self-identification with figures who, the reader may feel, would be startled rather than flattered by the compliment. Its reception caused Rowse some amusement, particularly in that a number of homosexuals considered themselves affronted by it. 'Silly fools! Couldn't they see that I was on their side.'[2] Although Rowse characterizes Lowes Dickinson as 'second-rate all through,' he found his book 'most interesting reading, if only for its transparent honesty, a rare quality, especially in an autobiography.' Recognizing homosexuality as the dominant theme, Rowse quotes its author: 'the homosexual temperament must, I think, be regarded as a misfortune, though it is possible with that temperament, to have a better, more passionate and more noble life than most men of normal temperament achieve.'

'In that case,' rejoins Rowse, 'why a misfortune? – better than living the life of a clod anyway, if it makes a man more sensitive, more intuitive, more aware, doubling his gifts so that he has both feminine and masculine within himself.' Lowes Dickinson was a man of the pre-1914 generation, so that both he and Rowse lived under a real threat of punishment, blackmail or disgrace which may have lent the glamour and excitement of belonging to an underground group. There is no mistaking the thrill that Rowse feels when he finds grounds for supposing that some historical character or some new acquaintance shares his own orientation. It is strange that a man of such breadth

1. op. cit., p. 96.
2. Rowse MSS.

of imagination and breadth of reading cannot accept the fact of difference without seeking to apply a competitive qualification. Granted that a variety of sexual orientation may (not must) afford a variety of insights, why should one be superior to another? The idea, constantly reiterated by Rowse, that homosexuality gives one two for the price of one evidently exhilarates him. But it might equally well be asserted that it is a double deprivation.

> To observations which ourselves we make
> We grow more partial for the observer's sake

The three succeeding volumes in this *genre*, *Memories of Men & Women* (1980), *Glimpses of the Great* (1985) and *Friends and Contemporaries* (1989) contain a mélange of the categories defined in the last two titles. Of these the more modest pieces on those whom he had known well, and corresponded with, are much the best. Kenneth Rose, to whom *Friends and Contemporaries* is dedicated, has pointed out to me that a great deal of the book is lifted, without acknowledgment, from the work of others such as his own *The Later Cecils*. The liveliest pieces benefit from the correspondence, both sides of which he retrieved, which is preserved in his archive.

If nothing else from Rowse's pen were to survive but his correspondence the future student of twentieth-century civilization would still have reason for amazement at its energy and range. Cornwall, its houses and churches, Marxism and its exponents, Labour politics in the late twenties and thirties, Publishing, Book Reviewing, Homosexuality, French life and literature, to say nothing of the whole range of English authors from the Renaissance to his own day. His encouragement of young authors, particularly those who like Raleigh Trevelyan, Colin Wilson, William Golding and others who had or came to have a Cornish connection of some sort, was not confined to those whose books he actually read and admired. He was on excellent terms with popular writers whose work he left unsampled, such as Howard Spring. Agatha Christie is another conspicuous example. Perhaps the top-selling author of her day, she read and admired and encouraged Rowse. Exceptionally he did eventually read a number of her books (including the straight works she wrote under the *nom de guerre* of

Mary Westmacott) and admired her gift for dialogue and characterization. But this was in so many respects an unusual relationship. Her
husband, Max Mallowan, a distinguished archaeologist, was for
many years a Professorial colleague at All Souls and their comfortable house near Wallingford became, like the Betjemans' establishment on the Berkshire downs, a favourite retreat within easy reach
of Oxford.

A now forgotten, but in his day highly successful, popular novelist
with whom Rowse conducted an immense correspondence, animated
in equal proportions by shared excitement in homosexuality and grand
acquaintance and a common horror of having to pay income tax, was
Cecil Roberts. Their friendship appears to have originated in an
admiring letter which nonetheless corrected two or three historical
errors in one of Rowse's books. Gossip and snobbery make up the
bulk of it, descending with advancing years to prolonged complaint,
on Roberts's part, of the declining standards of the great European
hotels, in which, for tax reasons, he was generally domiciled. Rowse's
wittiest and best correspondents, as he himself recognized, were
women: Rebecca West, Elizabeth Jenkins, Violet Holdsworth, Honor
Tracy, to name but a few. 'You get me wrong about women' he wrote
to his friend at the Huntington, Andrew Rolle. 'Actually I am rather
a feminist, get on with them and share a good deal of their point of
view. Only I don't want them in bed, and certainly didn't intend to
be "roped" and tied.' Writing to the same correspondent he extended
this to American literature. 'I am not fond of Ezra Pound, etc. I *admire*
the women more – sensible Edith Wharton, Willa Cather, Flann
O'Connor.'[1]

Most of his brilliant women correspondents, Veronica Wedgwood
in earlier life, Violet Holdsworth, Elizabeth Jenkins, Rebecca West
later, understood, perhaps were amused by but certainly allowed for,
the instinctive assumption of male superiority implicit in Rowse's
attitude. Some emphatically did not. Margaret Forster, who got in
touch with him in connexion with her biography of his neighbour
and friend Daphne du Maurier, gave as good as she got. Moreover

1. Letters dated 30 October 1985 and 22 August 1987. I am grateful to Professor Rolle
for allowing me to read and quote from this correspondence.

she could, and did, trump any tricks he tried to take in the matter of early poverty and deprivation.

And what of Daphne du Maurier herself? Rowse's piece on her in *Friends and Contemporaries* tries on the one hand to suggest a tutor–pupil relationship as regards the vivid historical background against which her novels are set while at the same time betraying uncharacteristic signs of nervousness. Is he going too far? He admits that, a fluent French speaker, she had made discoveries of her own in the archives at Montauban. The reader perceives that his suggestions, corrections rather, were not always acted upon or even well received. Raleigh Trevelyan, a neighbour of both, tells me that her polite hearing of Rowse's instruction concealed a certain irritation and a resolve to take little if any notice of what he had to say.

If one is sometimes inclined to feel that the great exert too powerful a pull, whether they be politicians, writers or that indefinable category of those who are well known simply for being well known, a second look at Rowse's archive corrects the balance. He was tireless in maintaining relationships – largely by letter – with homosexuals, often of strong Christian conviction, who seem to have derived as much pleasure, certainly as much thrill, from their sense of guilt as from any carnal satisfaction. And loyalty to old acquaintance, courtesy towards new, involved an expense of time and energy that, for most men, would have left nothing over for the stream of reviews, articles and books that showed no sign of drying up. Obviously the admiration and encouragement of writers such as Kenneth Clark, Maurice Bowra, Elizabeth Bowen, James Lees-Milne, John Summerson refreshed him. And he certainly liked to know that he was read and enjoyed by an enormous public. Several of his correspondents, such as Noel Blakiston already quoted, point out the inconsistency of this with his favourite denunciations of the Idiot People. Some, such as Philip Toynbee, with equal justice criticize his indiscriminate attacks on 'intellectuals' as indistinguishable from mere Blimpish rant.

As early as 1962 John Carter of Sotheby's discussed with him the glittering prospects of selling his archive in the USA. This was at a moment when Rowse's impatience with his own country was at one of its periodic peaks. In March 1967 he was corresponding with the poet W. R. Rodgers about taking Irish citizenship and living in Dublin.

But his passion for Cornwall, like his archive, continued to grow and it was there that he spent the long evening of his life, still reading, still writing books, still corresponding for another thirty years. It is there that we should now join him.

27

Cornwall: In my End
is my Beginning

It was not only in the physical sense that Rowse was born and died in Cornwall. The two books that brought him fame proclaimed its identity in their title. He lived most of his life in Cornwall, and when absent from it it was not absent from him. In his unwise attempts to obtain honours for himself he usually cited Cornwall as the true beneficiary, adding with his engaging lack of humility that he was the most distinguished living Cornishman and as such the proper person to remedy this hitherto shameful neglect. When he was made a Bard he was proud to take the title Lev Kernow, old Cornish for the Voice of Cornwall. Cornwall was the inspiration of some of his best poems in the opinion of John Betjeman, uniquely qualified to judge. Unmistakably it was the source of those which Rowse himself felt to have come most from the heart.

To say that it was a lifelong love affair is both an understatement and an oversimplification. There was bitterness as well as honey, anger as well as calm. When he was young and struggling Cornwall had set its smug, chapel-going, liberal-voting face against him. If it hadn't been for Q., he would never have got to Oxford. When he sacrificed so much of his young manhood to the tedious chores of Parliamentary candidacy, they rejected him. When he had made a name for himself the great people of the county took no notice of him until, at what he considered an insultingly late age, he was invited to join the Cornish Club, a small, exclusive society of the most respected figures in the county. He shewed his anger by instant rejection. Rejection, rejection: the idea that more and more took possession of him had its roots in Cornwall.

At the same time the love of the Cornish countryside, awoken in boyhood when the choirman at St Austell took him for a long walk up the Luxulyan valley, grew into a passion. His excitement as the train crossed the Tamar, reaching a crescendo at Par junction, never diminished. A late motorist, the same thrill of inexplicable anticipation flooded his being as he stopped to eat the sandwiches provided by All Souls at Yarcombe, the Devon village that made a convenient half-way point between Oxford and Trenarren. No Cornish appeal to restore a church, preserve a country-house or save coast or moor from the developer went unheeded. When he died his residuary legatees were the National Trust and the Royal Institution of Cornwall.

This is the impact of Cornwall in its corporate capacity. What of more intimate connexions? We have seen how deeply upset Rowse was by the poison pen letter, questioning his paternity, that a spiteful neighbour sent on his election to All Souls. He burned it: but it smouldered on. If, as many of his close friends thought, lack of self-confidence lay at the root of his often aggressive and boastful behaviour, it seems likely that this anxiety contributed to it. In certain moods it flattered his self-esteem to guess that his intelligence and sensibility were inherited from some more distinguished line. Ambivalence, or as a mere Englishman would put it, having things both ways, was to him a Celtic quality that set him above Anglo-Saxon flatness. And yet in his late age tears poured down his cheeks as he told an old friend that his mother would never tell him who his father was.

Prying into family secrets (of which, anyhow, the key has been lost) is not the highest form of the biographer's art. But this uncertainty, a game of hide and seek almost, played such a large part in Rowse's life and was so often the chief pre-occupation of his journals that it cannot be brushed aside. When Rowse's father died, it seems that his son, though deeply attached to him, doubted their relationship. So, for many years, his view inclined. But during the course of his researches for *The Cornish in America* (1969) he thought he had at last found out the truth.

How deeply the whole question was entwined with his feelings for a Cornish past, for a society in many ways so uncongenial to him and yet so indelibly his own, how vividly it was coloured by the recall of his childhood that had inspired his book, may be seen from his journals. A prefatory word may make the following extracts more easily intelligible. Montana was one of the States to which there had been considerable Cornish emigration; among the emigrants had been Fred May, the butcher at Tregonissey, who was later joined by his wife Hetty and their children, the friends of Rowse's early boyhood.

Sunday, October 18 [1964]. Helena, Montana.

I have attained this strange objective after the years. Shall I find out from it what Fred May really was? I have no doubt that he was my mother's lover. On her death-bed she was firm that she had nothing to tell me. But she was a most inflexible stony woman. I arrived last night after an uncomfortable journey over the mountains, as bumpy as riding the waves, by air from Billings. Met by Professor Clinch, who brought me up the main street, filled in over Last Chance Gulch where was the Placer Hotel.

The first thing that happened to me in Helena was that my hat was filched. I took it off politely at the Registration desk, left it there, took my luggage up to my room, went back for coffee with the professor – and found my hat was not there. Went back to my room to look for it, but only found a humbug book, *The Desire of the Ages*, sponsored by a librarian of Congress: a kind of Dean Farrer's Life of Christ. Back to the hall to inquire. The young lobby assistant said that last week he had lost his sweater. It somehow gave an impoverished impression to this mining town, founded in 1864 – the year of our[1] father's birth – the mines here now ended. Nor is Butte – at its apogee in the First World War – prosperous any longer.

Early I walked out on the eastern side of the Gulch, the working-class area, noticing a Nonconformist chapel now turned into a Dance School, another a Labor Temple. The area is now dominated by the Catholic cathedral, and I went in to the 9 a.m. Mass. The big church, based on the Votiv-Kirche in Vienna, was quite full, plenty of small children with their parents. At the back near me was a distracting youth of sixteen or so, in clean blue shirt and tight jeans: I have rarely seen a more perfect figure. What a disturbing influence he was, with gestures such as one has seen in Renaissance pictures . . .

He did not distract me from the excellent sermon preached about the Novena beginning to-morrow, commemorating the first novena kept by

1. Altered from 'my'. His brother George and his sister Hilda were very much present to his mind.

the Apostles. [There follows a careful, and carefully sceptical though not unkindly, summary of the sermon.]

How well geared the Catholic Church always has been to average humanity: *every* consideration called into play, never a point lost. The sanctus bell rang in the sanctuary at intervals to tell the congregation to be particularly devotional. The Cathedral occupied the dominating site in the town: you couldn't miss it, as you could the little Episcopal church of St Peter's . . .

I reflected that Fred May must have known this building. But what *had* become of all his children in this area? I had been frustrated by finding not a single May in the telephone book. When I came back to my room I asked the elderly cleaning woman. By a stroke of luck she had known Phyllis, the youngest to be born before leaving home. Her first husband, now dead, was called Garvity. His brother was Harold. I called him. He put me on to Beryl, the youngest, born over here, called Mrs Bielen, who knew all about me; said that I had been her old mother's hero (she couldn't bear me as a child). I said I would like to see the old people's graves: Hetty died two years ago at ninety-three. (What a spitfire she was.) But Nora, now a widow, lived in town. I got on to her. She was overjoyed – after fifty years, and after so many years that I have intended to get here and find out. She told me that Alec, Mildred – who wrote my mother that venomous letter – and Phyllis,[1] all live in Seattle. Perhaps I shall see them. I told Nora that I have never forgotten a thing about them and the old days – she said neither had she. She keeps in touch with Hilda,[2] married again: I didn't know her name, Mrs William Higgins. What a name! We laughed a lot. Her son was home for the day, lives at Victorville in Mojave desert, quite near Pasadena, and she hadn't seen him for seven years.

Perhaps all this was the answer to unspoken prayer? I should never have found out if I hadn't happened on that particular cleaning woman. Now, shall I find my hat also?

Monday, 19 October. The important question is answered, the question I came all this way to have answered. No son of Fred May, but of Dick Rowse. Rather disappointing in a way – Fred May was a so much more interesting character, if a less good man. Even so, his characteristics are nearer mine: a gambler, venturesome, stubborn, would try or take on anything, a

1. Fred May's surviving children.
2. Rowse's sister.

vile temper, *his* family always in the wrong. His oldest daughter, Nora, thinks there is no family resemblance; nor does Hilda apparently. (So I have laid down a suggestion of a false trail in *A Cornishman at Oxford*[1] that may create some confusion.) Of course Fred and Annie were lovers; but also Dick played with Hetty, when he took the groceries over late on Saturday evenings to Belmont. Fred and Dick were good friends, Dick accepting the leadership of the younger man, the gambler, who bankrupted himself several times. Last time at sixty-five – and worked his way back again to solvency. Three times his farm buildings burned down, and he would never insure – last time lost $30,000. What an obstinate type.

This morning I went to their graves in the cemetery under Scratch Gravel Hills . . . an avenue of silver spruce, cottonwoods, silver birch, pine and native Montana juniper. No wonder Fred May loved this Montana country. We passed the ranch with the trees Nora and Beryl had planted and watered, now fully grown. A herd of Black Angus were being brought in from summering on the mountains by a couple of cowboys on ponies, dogs keeping the herd together, for winter pasture in the Valley.

In the cemetery two flat slabs. 1872 Fred W. May. Father 1953. 1870 Elizabeth May. Mother 1963. It was very moving to see them and to know their story so closely intermingled with ours in the village. Over here Fred was free with the women, bore no good name; Hetty had a poor time with him, not much love between them, and little affection for the children. Just like ours: too ignorant, too uncultivated. They all had a hard life in coming over and to begin with.

The upshot of it is that I feel more compassion for them all than I ever did before: I appreciate the struggle they had to keep going and feed their families. They were so poor, life was primitive, prospects so few. Primitive! – when I think of May's old 'killin'-'ouse', the terrified cries of the animals, the mess and horror after a killing, the immense Sunday breakfast afterwards – which father tucked into – of animal's entrails, pig's insides, fried liver, whatnot. To think that I have known it all! . . .

In the evening I gave my lecture to a large crowd in the dining room of the college. Afterwards I was driven by a good-looking young seminarist through the mountains to Butte: over the Continental Divide, in moonhaze,

1. op. cit., pp. 14, 17. In the first paragraph of each of these pages there are guarded hints.

shapes of trees advancing and retreating, valleys, precipices. Touching at last to be in Butte, Mecca of so many thousands of poor Cornish miners. Apparently Fred May first went there, butchering I suppose. In those days it was wild and raw, plenty of fighting, drinking and twenty-four brothels – a miners' community. Now a depressing and depressed community, living under the impersonal shadow of the vast Anaconda Company. Three big mines of 5,400 feet deep, work getting unbearably hot as they go deeper, one degree for every hundred feet. Plenty of silicosis about. We looked in the morning at the big Berkeley open pit – like a Leonardo drawing, terrace upon terrace up the gigantic hillside, men and trucks like ants on an ant-hill, the whole thing humming, a cloud of copper dust hanging over it all.

Almost exactly a year later (12 October 1965), again in America, this time at Saratoga Springs, he reverts to the subject. Remembering a house in Cornwall, Trewithen, with its furniture and pictures, he bursts out

Oh, to have inherited something like that, a family, instead of being born to nothing. I have resented that all my life – instead of thinking that I have made a fine thing of it. I never think of that, even gratefully, let alone smugly.

Yet I *ought* to be grateful for the gift of life I have so much enjoyed – like Hazlitt. Whether I have made the most of what I was given, I have tried, though not sufficiently with my defects of character. They are obvious enough to me. One reason why I have not struggled with them more is that the gifts are bound up with defects; that I must above all be natural, to be released into my work. If I tried to achieve the restrained self-control of T.S.E. – anyway to be like that was Eliot's nature, not mine – it would inhibit both what I have to say and how to say it.

A heavy blow befel me this year, which has taken a great deal of adjusting to. It is strange – like so much in my life – that I should have had to wait until my 61st year before the doubt about [substituted for 'true fact of'] my paternity, and that I may be Fred May's son, not dear Dick Rowse's, who fed, clothed, and brought me up.[1] That is why I was so glad – in *A Cornishman at Oxford* – that I was good to him when he was getting old. And I was certainly fonder of him than his own children were and I took care of him

1. This is an accurate transcription of a significantly confused sentence.

. . . He can never have thought that I was not his. His last message was for me. He kept asking for me.

This passage is much altered and revised. A note dated 1990 reads 'Still uncertain. For it is a curious fact that men of genius are apt to suspect their paternity.' He goes on to recapitulate Fred May's characteristics which resemble his own, concluding, as so often, that the heredity of his mother's family, the Vansons, account for much more. There is a horrifyingly vivid moment of recall:

My earliest memory of him is that time when in the slaughter-house at Tregonissey, after a killing, he took me up in his arms and shut me inside the slit carcase of a pig. I remember reacting violently, aged three, kicking him in the stomach and using *all* the swear words I had heard him use . . .

Once, when a boy of nine or ten, I was sent on an errand to the old pursy saddler, Kellow . . . The old red-faced fellow, white moustache under the black bowler, asked me, 'Who's your father?' When I said Richard Rowse, 'Oh, no: he id'n your father.' I was very vexed and told what he said when I got home. [He was never sent on that errand again.] . . .

The next time I came up against the Doubt was as a Labour candidate for Parliament in the Election of 1931. I was canvassing in the village of Polgooth, the Mays' village, when an elderly dark-looking man gave me a scrutinizing look – he may have been one of them – and said 'You're no Rowse' . . . Only now do I know the meaning of the greeting from the riff-raff of Truro women-folk, 'Bring out your love-child.' I thought afterwards, when I learned about Mabel,[1] that it referred to her. The Labour people brought Mother and Father on to the platform for my final meeting in my home-town. I was delighted to see them there, large as life. I was particularly pleased to see poor old Father there, and he was innocently delighted too. We gave each other an affectionate smile – I was afraid he might be nervous, as at the Drapers' Company interview. The affection for him pleased the audience – it must all have worked better than the organisers could have hoped. All through the campaign emphasis was placed on my being a china-clay worker's son. I used to put myself down proudly as such in *Who's Who*.

1. His half-sister. An earlier sentence in this entry reads: 'It was not until I was well into my thirties that I learned the St Michael's Mount story.'

What about the man from whom I *may* get other traits? . . . He evidently had a way with him. Aunt Beat – Mrs Peters – says that he was a superior-looking man with a good manner, whose little wife, Hetty Combe of Polgooth, wasn't up to him . . . She was a school-teacher, ignorant as could be and not at all good-looking . . .

His father was a regrater[1] and farmer. Noreen Sweet remembers him – an old patriarch who dominated Polgooth Chapel, played the organ, ran the choir. This sexy old patriarch was three times married, and Fred must have been a son of the first marriage. Used to help his father selling eggs and butter in St Austell market, always well turned out . . .

So he had larger horizons than village life, and I believe that he had 'large ideas' – i.e. set himself up for more than he could achieve. (*Achtung*!) When he married he set himself up in the butchering business – whether he had any capital I doubt. He certainly did things in style. He not only had a good shop at West End, but he took on the best new house in the village, built by rascally old Bill Rowse, Father's brother. The slaughter-house was on the road to Lane End.

Hence the connexion between the families. Father used to help Fred, who was his junior by five or ten years, in the 'killin'-'ouse' – I well remember those horrible Sunday breakfasts of every kind of fried innards, relished by Father and Mother, not by me . . .

When I at last got to Montana last October, Nora didn't believe that I was Fred's son. When I got to Seattle, Mildred's husband recognized my family looks, and Phyllis was sure that I was. I have at last elicited what Hilda thinks and tried to fit the pattern together. But how much of the story is buried for ever, and how I long to recover it in vain! To think that I might have got in touch with the old couple when I first came to America in 1952! I was surprised when Nora told me that I was a 'hero' with her mother. Hetty must have satisfied herself that I wasn't Fred's after all. Perhaps *he* didn't even know.

This enormous entry, far longer and more repetitive than what is here printed, concludes with a passage which Rowse struck out in 1990:

1. Obsolete word for retailer, with perhaps a bad connotation, as of one who tries to corner a commodity. Its use is additional evidence of the early layers of memory on which Rowse was drawing.

I can only be grateful to them for that, the instinct that brought them together, Fred and my mother in the one love of both their lives, so long and so far disjoined, coming together in me who will carry the story no further.

And yet I follow in his footsteps, all unknown. It should give me a closer stake, make me feel less alien, more at home in this country where my father lies buried, a half-brother and half-sisters unrecognized, where their children – having some of my looks – are alive and have their home.

In 1990 he substituted this conclusion:

There remains uncertainty over it all. And what does it matter? I approve of whatever conjunction of genes produced me – any other mixture, and I should have been a fool like the rest.

This was whistling to keep his spirits up. There is evidence of the distress, serious distress, that this unsolved question continued to cause him. But there we must leave the matter.

Rowse's often repeated axiom that a writer should never cut himself off from his roots was no glib formula. He couldn't have emancipated himself from Cornwall even if he had wanted to. And he didn't want to. Only a month before he had arrived at Saratoga Springs he had, at last, gained admission to one of the grandest of all the grand houses of Cornwall, Boconnoc, which he had only seen at a distance from the hills that surround it. A succession of great families, Mohuns, Pitts, Grenvilles had lived there, leaving their portraits and furniture to be acquired by the next owner until the place was inherited by the Fortescues in the nineteenth century. The royalties from the then unsuspected china-clay deposits brought them fabulous wealth. But the old reclusive couple, who at last had Rowse over for the afternoon, hoping that he would not stay for tea, were misers who would not employ a single servant, let alone workmen to maintain the treasures that lay about in disorder. When Rowse fantasized, he fantasized about what he would have done to revive and enhance so magnificent an inheritance.

A sizable proportion of his enormous correspondence is with Cornish people on Cornish topics. From the far off days with Charles Henderson he had savoured every country house, every church and family chapel to which he could gain admission. From his years as a Labour candidate he had made a number of friends among the party activists and journalists on the West Country papers, with many of whom he continued to correspond after he had resigned the candidacy in 1943. Violet Holdsworth opened her memories of the Cornish Quaker connexion that he knew of through the journals of Caroline Fox. His friendships with the high church Cornish clergy from W. H. Frere down and his association, culminating in an excellent joint picture-book, with John Betjeman were further strands in the cord that bound him.

No wonder that Cornwall inspired so many of his books. The two early masterpieces *Tudor Cornwall* and *A Cornish Childhood* are in a class of their own. But the later works show how even so limited a territory could extend the range of his curiosity and his readiness to explore and to experiment. His prejudices might ossify but his imagination floated free. The earliest, *West Country Stories* (1945), a collection of pieces which had appeared in a variety of journals during the thirties and early forties, includes topographical, historical and anecdotal description ('Cornish Conversation Piece. How Dick Stephens fought the bear') with fiction. As the author explains in his preface 'the stories of invention, even though mostly ghost stories, have a foundation of fact; while the narratives of fact I hope, are not wholly without imagination.' The model for the first category that comes most readily to mind is M. R. James's *Ghost Stories of an Antiquary* which perhaps themselves owe something of their inspiration to Meade Falkner's *The Lost Stradivarius*. The street-lighting of the rationalism that Rowse prided himself on, or the impatience of temper which he admitted to, make it hard for him to achieve the atmosphere of mystery, of fear and awareness of indefinable evil that is the secret of those two masters. The medium is an exceptionally difficult one, perhaps requiring a good deal of unpublished failure before the attainment of publishable success. Rowse was clearly fond of them, even proud of them, reprinting them in a later collection *Cornish Stories* (1967). If they do not quite come off, there is no doubting the genuineness of the romantic impulse that inspired them. Perhaps the author was testing his speculation that if he had not won his way to Oxford he might have established a literary reputation such as V. S. Pritchett or J. B. Priestley had done.

On the purely historical and descriptive side *The Little Land of Cornwall* (1986) gathers a remarkable harvest. The most substantial is the brilliant parish history *St Austell: Church, Town, Parish* which Rowse had written to raise funds for the restoration of the church. 'The Elizabethan Pilchard Fishery', after many years in the deep freeze of the *Economic History Review*, reads like hundreds of such studies, a single fragment that shows what Rowse might have become if he had not listened to his own voices and been true to his own talent. That this was in the highest degree personal a clutch of vivid studies attest. People, not pilchards, were his meat. The essay on Hawker of Morwenstow exemplifies the tenderness and sympathy he could show to men whose opinions were far from his own when he was not carried away by gusts of prejudice or impatience. His address at the unveiling of a monument to Charles Henderson fifty years after his death has a delicacy and a balance that may surprise those who have formed their impression of its author on his better reported utterances. Two pieces specially written for this collection on the Treffry family commemorate Rowse's admiration for their public service and entrepreneurial activity, conspicuous in the late medieval and Tudor period and flowering again in the early nineteenth century, which has left a monument in the splendid house overlooking the town and harbour of Fowey. These traditions were notably upheld by its owner, the close friend of Rowse's later years, whose kindness and hospitality to the present writer have been unfailing.

The Treffrys had intermarried with another Cornish family, the Trevanions, who had been the joint subject of an earlier book *The Byrons and the Trevanions* (1978). A close, rather huddled, family history, diversified by gibes at Puritans or glimpses of landscape and houses, the book has the inequalities of deutero-Rowse. Both families rendered gallant service to the Royalist cause in the Civil War, whose miseries are tellingly brought home. Rowse's own experience of life had made him familiar with the poignancy of gentle, unmilitary people, such as Sidney Godolphin, killed in battle. He is sensitive to both the brutality and the heroism of war, yet cannot resist spoiling the effect of an eloquent letter on the death of Sir Bevil Grenville by punctuating it with his own asides. He hustles and bustles these families through English history, awarding them marks when they have the sense to cash in on some piece of government patronage and wagging his finger at them when they scruple over a principle of politics or religion. On the other hand *The Controversial Colensos* (1989) celebrated the most intellectually daring son of St Austell, the missionary bishop who, taking no thought for his own career, had set the cat among the pigeons by his original and powerful essays in biblical criticism. Colenso had had even stiffer obstacles to overcome in his determination to secure a University education than Rowse had had. In his first job he had had to work from five in the morning till eight at night and still found time for two hours study each day. Entering St John's, Cambridge, as a sizar (by which membership of the university was granted in return for the discharge of menial duties) he triumphed in the Mathematical Tripos and was elected to a Fellowship. Here surely Rowse saw a forerunner. As Bishop of Natal he produced the first Zulu grammar and the first Zulu dictionary as well as, in answer to the questions raised by his converts, prosecuting his studies of the Pentateuch. Again we see the versatility on which Rowse prided himself. The rejection by authority of his pioneering scholarship, the attempt to deprive him of his bishopric and even to excommunicate him, heroically foreshadow the sufferings of his fellow Cornishman.

Cornwall comes into other biographical studies which he published in his later years such as *Matthew Arnold* (1976), an attractive and sympathetic study of the poet emphasizing principally his importance in the history of education – greater, Rowse thought, than that of his more widely acknowledged father – but drawing attention to his Cornish inheritance from his mother. One of his *Four Caroline Portraits* (1993), Hugh Peters, owes his presence largely to the fact that he had been born in Fowey and that his mother was a Treffry. One wonders if so rabid a Puritan would have been so understandingly and kindly handled if he had not had the advantage of this connexion. But the book that Rowse clearly considered the most important of his later contributions to Cornish history was *The Cornish in America* (1969). Essentially a series of topographical essays with a linking theme rather than a book, its strengths are the awareness of geography and understanding of economic history. Wherever there was copper or gold to be mined the Cornish settled. Rowse used his wide-ranging lecture tours to travel in states not often visited by English academics and made the most thorough survey of Cornish surnames surviving in the USA. Emigration to America, South Africa, Australia and New Zealand had been an everyday feature of the Cornwall he had known as a boy. He hoped that his book would lead the way to other studies of the part Cornwall had played in the development of these countries.

This chapter may conclude with a mention of his unpublished book on Trenarren, his home for the last forty years of his life. Undated, but from internal evidence easily datable to 1953, it was written just after he had moved there:[1] in fact the early pages vividly chronicle the obstructions and disasters of moving house while they are irradiated with the joy of possession and the solid gratification of having achieved the ambition of a lifetime. For Trenarren was *das Land wo die Limonen blühmen*, its attraction transcending reason and prejudice. When it stood empty, as it did for years, the young Rowse, climbing up its garden wall, hears in imagination the cheerful noises of the Hext children, the family that built and owned the house, playing in its glorious woods that frame the view of the sea. In real life his reaction would have been anything but entrancement. 'I hate children!'

The book was written, he tells us on the first page, purely for diversion, while he was engaged in the composition of the second volume of the great Elizabethan trilogy. It was to have no shape, no direction. There was to be none of the underlying tension that every writer, every artist, feels when engaged in trying to express a theme. He could toss in ideas, recollections, descriptions as they entered his head or caught his eye. There is a great deal about the furniture and pictures he had acquired and how he has disposed them in the new house. There is a great deal (too much, some may feel) about his cats. He gives free rein to his detestation of relations, one of whom peeled an apple on his polished dining table, marking it indelibly. The trials and unhappinesses of his life are almost entirely absent (nothing about the Wardenship election, then so recent, nothing about his uncertainty of his parentage) except for a glance or two – 'the twenties and the thirties ravaged by pain and sickness', 'I never even began to enjoy life till I was forty and the fifties are even better.' There is a brief, unusually restrained, recollection of his early friendship (never inti-

---

1. He acquired it by lease. On his death it reverted to the Hext family.

mate) with Graham Greene, which is fresher than his later study of him in *Friends and Contemporaries*. There are interesting details of autobiography not, I think, elsewhere recorded. 'The MS of *A Cornish Childhood* has Gerald Berners', Jack Simmons' and my corrections bound in with it.' 'My devoted reading of Virginia Woolf had its effect on my way of seeing and describing things, is reflected in my prose writing, even in my historical work.' 'I simply couldn't make myself learn the language in Germany in 1926 and 1927 until I got on to [Rilke]. I did it partly by translating his prose-ballad *Die Weise von Liebe und Tod von Christoph Rilke*. That was a help. It made the beastly language a bit more congenial.'

It is a sunlit book, and with the light streaming in from the south-facing windows of his study on the piles of notes, opened books and other matter needed for *The Expansion of Elizabethan England*, let us leave him in his armchair where he is writing it before returning to his desk where the serious work awaits him.

28

Sunset

The long evening of Rowse's life saw no diminution in his appetite for reading and writing. His energy outlasted his bodily faculties. Growing, and ultimately severe, deafness put an end to the musical pleasures in which his early and middle life had been so rich and which have been inadequately conveyed in these pages. As travel became harder for him he had less opportunity to look at pictures, but the tenacity of his memory was not less strong for the visual as for the intellectual and the literary. He could not cease to be an aesthete simply because his body was ageing.

In the last decade of his life he spent most of his time in bed, reading and writing with as much ease as when he was up and dressed. When occasion arose, the funeral of a distinguished Cornish figure, the escorting of a friend to admire the beauties of his native county, an interview (in German) for Swiss television, even an invitation to dine at 10 Downing Street, he would rise and perform the necessary function without any appearance of invalidism. He wasn't an invalid. But his years of acute pain and ill-health had given him an exact, particular knowledge of what his physique could sustain and how his energies could best be conserved.

His reading and his writing were to a great extent complementary. The range, as always, was wide but three themes predominated: an onslaught on the Puritans, responsible in his eyes for so much destruction, so much philistinism and for preventing people from enjoying themselves; a retrospect of persons, which found expression in an abundance of biographical sketches, some published and many more written with a freedom that forbade publication; and, related to, indeed intimately involved with this, autobiography and the collection of autobiographical material.

The attack on Puritanism was, at root, religious. For Rowse, rejecting theism in any form, beauty, especially beauty achieved in art, constituted the immortality that sets us above the beasts that perish. Intellectually he was eager to confront the representation of the seventeenth century so persuasively argued by Christopher Hill and the reigning school of post-war historiography that elevated the sectaries into the dayspring of rational civilization. The most powerful of these works were *Milton the Puritan: Portrait of a Mind* (1977) and *Reflections on the Puritan Revolution* (1986). Reaction to the prevalent dismissal of Laud and Charles I as oppressive and intolerant opponents of all that was hopeful and illuminating led Rowse to defend them with a warmth that was easily mistaken for Royalist partisanship. His real hatred of Puritan cant creates the same effect. In his preface to *Milton the Puritan* he states his true position. 'My standpoint is one of scepticism, if of an aggressive scepticism. Imperceptive critics will identify it with a simple Royalist outlook. They will be wrong as usual. My point of view has much more in common with Hobbes, who saw through the fooleries on both sides and was contemptuous of people's delusions.' But Hobbes, after all, knew he had more to fear from militant Puritanism than from Laud and Charles I, little as he might think of their ideas. It was from the Puritan wrath to come that he had fled abroad on the eve of the Civil War, and he did not return home until Cromwell had established a monarchical régime far stronger and far more consonant with *Leviathan* than anything Charles I could have achieved. Like most deutero-Rowse, these two books contain errors (generally minor) and enough overstatements for his critics to dismiss them, and enough learning and zest to stimulate anyone interested in the period and in its great issues. Rowse could draw at will on the recollection of a long life and a wealth of reading to actualize the past:

As a boy in Nonconformist Cornwall I had the advantage of knowing millenarian types straight out of the seventeenth century. One was a club-footed tailor named Freeman, who in the intervals of quarrelling with his wife, spouted interminable confused babble from the Book of Revelation. Another such was an intermittent china-clay worker, with the good Puritan name of Rogers, who varied bouts of drinking with bouts of inspired Biblical trash. His daughter, a schoolteacher who became a Christadelphian, was inspired to assure me as a somewhat apprehensive boy that the world would come to an end in 1920. When the year was safely past, I reminded her of her prophecy (or promise); without turning a hair she assured me that the world would come to an end in 1926.[1]

The retrospect of persons, so closely allied to the recording of his own life, took many forms. The published collections of portrait sketches have already been noticed. Obviously in such works the choice of sitter depends more on how well known he (or she) is to the reader than on how well the author knew him. Rowse was very good at thumbnail sketches: the man who shows him round a country-house; a figure glimpsed for an instant in a historical document. If there is an individualizing trace Rowse will catch it. But the form that pleased him most was that of John Aubrey's *Brief Lives*, leaving as it did the most complete freedom to state or to omit, and achieving its effects by the apparently random selection of trivialities that suggested rather than delineated character. The technique succeeds brilliantly in Aubrey's hands, partly perhaps because the writer appears so totally engaged with his subject as to have no awareness of himself or his own opinions. Such a disembarrassment of self was not open to a solipsist. Rowse is always present in his own portrayals of others, even when separated by several centuries. In fact it is this quality that gives his work its edge, nowhere more so than in the gallery of likenesses, often retouched, sometimes redrawn, of those he had known as colleagues, particularly at All Souls.

'All Souls – too many clever people living at too close quarters' he scribbled above one such draft. No doubt that was one of the troubles. Another, surely, was the want of the everyday discipline that marriage and family life imposes. The growth of personality went unpruned. No one had to go shopping or see about securing the services of a builder or a plumber if anything went wrong. The pattern of life was monastic, with all the restraints and austerities of monasticism removed. Even with these fully enforced the severest trial is still the endurance of one's fellow members of the community.

1. *Milton the Puritan* (US edn. 1985), p. 207.

Grr – there go, my heart's abhorrence!
Water your damned flower-pots, do!
If hate killed men, Brother Lawrence,
God's blood, would not mine kill you!

The weakness of these studies is a self-indulgent voyeurism. Just when a character is beginning to engage our interest we are overwhelmed with personal confidences or pure speculation about his supposed sexual life. Rowse was not without delicate perceptions. It is often in the sketches of people from whom he stood at some distance that these are best seen. G. M. Young and John Sparrow were not close friends of his but he knew them intimately over a long period: the studies are subtler and better balanced than is generally the case where his emotions are involved. They also allow the play of that sense of humour which made his conversation so enjoyable. This quality is notably absent in anything he writes about people who had disparaged his work or, as he thought, obstructed his career. Professor Trevor-Roper, whose early career he had encouraged, was never forgiven for touches, sometimes more than touches, of derision in reviews which, on balance, were by no means hostile. In their repeated exchanges of correspondence his critic consistently maintains that an inability to admire all that Rowse writes or to agree with his Shakespearean contentions does not range him with the large body of academic opinion who refuse to take him seriously: 'I am sorry you think I am inspired by "personal animus". Far from it. I have often said in speech and writing what I believe, namely that you are a very good historian, that I agree with most of your views, and greatly admire much of your work: on the other hand there are certain aspects of it (or rather of its presentation) which I don't like. I find them too personal.'[1] Rowse's piece on him in *Historians I Have Known* (1995) is only too apt an exemplification of the last part of this judgment.

The most carefully considered are of the men whose lives, like his own, were bound up with All Souls, which is not the same thing as being a Fellow. There were Fellows, with whom he got on and about whom he wrote, Quintin Hailsham, Cyril Radcliffe, Penderel Moon

1. Letter dated 2 May 1961.

for example, whose lives had their centres elsewhere. Some of the older men who belong to this special category of college men have been discussed in earlier chapters, Feiling, Lionel Curtis, Grant Robertson. Those nearer his own age, John Sparrow, Richard Pares, Isaiah Berlin, John Foster were, except for Pares, never close to him in affection. Sparrow for most of their time he looked on with a critical eye, as Sparrow certainly did on him. But after the contest for the Wardenship they drew closer together in college politics, even, on Rowse's side, in personal esteem so that Rowse could write to me two years before his own death 'I appreciate what a remarkable man he was, quite under-estimated by Oxford. Also how right All Souls was to elect him for Warden, not me.' The extended estimate of him in the unpublished 'Oxford Lives', clear and firm in its judgments of his weaknesses, procrastination, laziness, self-indulgence, plain shirking of duty (as in his declining the Vice-Chancellorship of the University when it was All Souls' turn), is none the less sympathetic and percipient.

Much of the matter in the 'Oxford Lives' is used in one or other of the books discussed in the previous chapter or in the autobiographical publications to which we shall turn in the conclusion of this one. Much is unpublishable, though by no means unreadable. Rowse loved gossip and had few, if any, inhibitions. It is clear that he learned much about his own nature from his close study of other people's. He closes a notably full and fair account of Sir Charles Grant Robertson, the disappointed rival of Pember in the Wardenship Election of 1913, with the reflection that his eminent services as the first Vice-Chancellor of the University of Birmingham had offered a far more rewarding fulfilment of his talents than he could have obtained as Warden of All Souls. As he looked along the shelves of his own publications he was comforted by a similar reflection.

Not that he allowed any such consolation to appease the grudges and resentments that he found so powerful a stimulus to autobiography. We have seen earlier how the bitterness against Christ Church was carefully preserved even when its injustice was perceived, because it would provide the literary lift-off to propel the successor to *A Cornish Childhood* into orbit. In fact the launching pad was obstructed by unforeseen obstacles until 1965, when *A Cornishman at Oxford* appeared, to be followed eleven years later by *A Cornishman Abroad*.

Both books lack the intensity and force of their predecessor. Although they rest on the documentary foundation of diaries written at the time, their author, by now an established figure, feels impelled to pronounce on a number of topics and persons whose importance belongs to a later period. Sometimes, as in the moving *éloge* on his friend Ralph Fox, an artist and political innocent trapped by the evils of his time into martyrdom for a Communism he was already beginning to doubt, he needs to go beyond his period to round off the story.[1] *A Cornishman at Oxford* presents, on the whole, a temperate and tranquil view of a temperament which he admits to be inclined to passion. Published in 1965, its preface is dated 1963. Rowse was in buoyant mood, to judge from the prologue to its successor *A Cornishman Abroad* dated 1964.[2]

> O the sense of the beauty of life, in this sixtieth year of my age (Picasso: 'At sixty we are young, but it is too late').[3] But not too late – never have I felt it more acutely, more intensely, pressing in upon me at every moment as if this were to be my last! Never have I known a more beautiful summer (except the fatal summers of 1914 and 1940), or Trenarren in greater beauty . . . Hardly ever have I been in such a press of work, such a tight schedule to get *Shakespeare's Southampton* finished, the proofs of *A Cornishman at Oxford* done and various urgent articles, before leaving for America. And all the while there was the summer campaign in the garden – a subtropical jungle when I came down in July . . . Yet tired out every night, limbs aching, never have I had such a sense of enjoyment . . .

He goes on to detail the pleasures of the year: attacking his critics, lecturing at the Sorbonne, the visits to Stratford occasioned by the fourth centenary of Shakespeare's birth, being entertained by Princess Bibesco in her flat in the Ile St Louis and entertaining her in return in Cornwall. He has quite forgotten that the *douceur de vivre* has vanished for ever. The key to Rowse's success as a writer is his

---

1. *A Cornishman at Oxford*, pp. 56–7.
2. The book itself was not published until 1976.
3. A mis-remembering of the phrase, quoted by Connolly in a letter to him in its more poignant form 'At sixty we are young *for the first time* . . .'

readiness to enjoy and his power of communicating enjoyment. He does not bore his readers because he is never bored, except by bad writing, stupidity or failure to observe. It is this alertness that makes him such good company on the page as it did in life. It is even possible (he himself seems to have wondered) that he derived enjoyment from the idea of rejection. Recollecting yet again after nearly half a century the failure of Christ Church to offer him the tutorship he pauses:

... the strange thing was that it set a pattern that recurred again and again all through my life: myself not wanting to be pushed into a position of asking something from my fellow-men, yet exposing myself – only to be denied and rejected. There is a very subtle psychological tie-up which I do not fully understand here. C. P. Snow has a searching phrase somewhere that our fate consists of the things that we really want to happen to us. Can I have wanted always to be denied and rejected by what I have loved most? I fear that this may be true.[1]

Most of the subject matter of *A Cornishman Abroad* (1976) and *A Man of the Thirties* (1979) has been discussed in the early chapters of this book. There are a few points to be added. The shaking of the dust of Christ Church from Rowse's feet, even to the extent of not attending any public or private occasion there, has been repeatedly proclaimed. Yet on page 44 of *A Cornishman Abroad* the author finds on looking through his Engagements Books for the autumn of 1926, only a few months after his rejection, that he has been dining at Christ Church 'with Masterman, Ryle and even Dundas'.[2]

A Man of the Thirties exhibits a characteristic of Rowse's later writings, that of recycling his material. Much of it has already appeared – sometimes in identical words – in *A Cornishman Abroad*. Much of it will re-appear in *All Souls in My Time* (1993) or *Historians I Have Known* (1995). It is none the less extremely readable and often contributes new and interesting information as well as re-adjustments of views already stated: for example the friendship with Maurice

---

1. *A Cornishman at Oxford*, pp. 312–13.
2. Masterman and Dundas have already appeared. Gilbert Ryle, the philosopher, had no obvious connexion with Rowse.

Bowra or his estimate of Christopher Sykes's biography of von Trott. More than the earlier volumes in the autobiographical series it is an essay in self-portraiture, an attempt to interpret and assess the totality of the author's experience of life, rather than to re-capture a particular phase of it. There are piquant details, such as the fact that it was over Suez that he eventually resigned his long membership of the Labour Party.[1] There are strange lapses of memory, such as his assertion that he never heard Bevin (held up to admiration for his undeviating political judgment) speak. Could he have forgotten the very full reports of the Labour Party Conferences that he wrote for the *Political Quarterly* and for *The Nineteenth Century and after*? The account he contributed to the last-named periodical[2] of the Party Conference at Southport in 1934 identifies '. . . three men above all, Arthur Henderson, Ernest Bevin and Herbert Morrison'. He plumped for Morrison (then out of Parliament) as the man to take over the leadership from Attlee, a view he admits in *A Man of the Thirties* to have been a mistake. But of Bevin's performance he wrote that there is 'no man in the Labour Movement whose whole approach to politics . . . is so intellectual in the best sense: it is very little emotional: he thinks the whole thing out in terms of long-range policy.' Reporting the Norwich Conference in 1937 he is again emphatic in Bevin's support, noting 'an entirely irresponsible and mischievous speech by Mr Aneurin Bevan.'[3] Rowse had every reason to congratulate himself on his judgment of affairs and to expose, as he does, the different idiocies of Kingsley Martin, Malcolm Muggeridge, R. H. S. Crossman and A. J. P. Taylor.[4]

He also, in his reporting of the Conferences, shows a striking respect for those who were to be, later, dismissed as the Idiot People: 'I sat among a number of representatives of the smaller trade unions, and it was perfectly evident how they were influenced by good arguments on both sides of the case and made up their minds on the evidence.'[5] But if his recollection of the time he had spent in Labour politics, time

1. Did he know that the same event, interpreted in the opposite sense, caused his old tutor Sir Keith Feiling, historian of the Tory party, to do the same from his?
2. Vol. 116, pp. 478–85.
3. ibid., vol. 122, pp. 596–605.
4. *A Man of the Thirties*, pp. 23–4.
5. *The Nineteenth Century*, vol. 116, pp. 478–85.

he now considered largely wasted, is clear and forceful, the book as a whole is clouded by the sediment of his passion for Adam von Trott. There are quotations from his letters, descriptions of their exploration of the late Kaiser's deserted apartments: but emotional disturbance is all that the reader can discern. What did Rowse ultimately feel about this intense and obviously unsatisfactory relationship? Did he know himself? The compass needle seems to waver.

All Souls in My Time (1993), though largely autobiographical, stands outside the main series. It could equally well be considered as belonging to the genre of *Portraits and Views*. It incorporates material from the unpublished 'Oxford Lives' with several mistakes of detail. How could Rowse ever have thought of John Sparrow's legendary feat of editing Donne while still a schoolboy in the same category as editing Henry King, easiest and simplest of seventeenth-century poets?[1] But the recollection of people is still vivid, the sense of excitement at having been elected to the most exclusive intellectual society in England is as fresh as it had been on that never to be forgotten day in 1925. There is a pleasant play of humour, a self-indulgent enjoyment of having won the highest prize in life, that transcends the jeremiads and the ichabods of the Old Testament Rowse of the late twentieth century. It is an assertion, all the more splendid for being made in his ninetieth year, of the enjoyment that kept breaking through.

That this was nourished by recollection, especially of the people he had known, is abundantly evident from his liberal annotation of his reading. Leonard Woolf's second volume of autobiography *Downhill All the Way* bears on its title-page an ungrudging estimate of the author as a thoroughly good man, while admitting that their personalities were unsympathetic. It seems strange, in view of Rowse's admiration for Virginia Woolf and his acknowledgment of her influence on his own work, that he, apparently, made no use of this connexion to make her acquaintance or to correspond with her as he did with Vita Sackville-West, whose kindly husband, Harold Nicolson, he took such pains to quarrel with.

Rowse not only annotated the books he read, dissenting from or

---

1. op. cit., p. 103. Sparrow did, in fact, edit both. But the Donne is climbing Everest, the King a walking holiday in the Cheviots.

applauding the judgments expressed and amplifying them from his own reading or reflection: he corrected and 'improved' their grammar and syntax. Was this, perhaps, a symptom of that anxious possessiveness that characterized his close friendships? He was making the work in some sense his own. Nowhere is this more evident than in his copy of John Sparrow's *Independent Essays* (1963), inscribed to him by the author. On the flyleaf Rowse records re-reading it, in August 1993 and October 1995, and on the title page under the author's name he has written 'How superior to Lytton Strachey'. Most of us would hesitate before setting about the improvement of John Sparrow's prose, lean, supple, crystalline and forceful, but his admirer (and the margins are liberally adorned with admiring expressions) had no such inhibitions. Sparrow's classical training must have taught him the cumulative effect of a well-cadenced sentence: but Rowse is forever breaking them up, to make points by a declamatory stab which the author had wished to establish by a subtler flow.

What is heart-warming after so many years of competition, rivalry, resentment, is the generous acknowledgment of Sparrow's intellectual courage and distinction of mind. At the end of his Warton Lecture on Great Poetry, he has written 'Very good and remarkable. I could never have done it. I take it all for granted.' He girds, now and then, at the minute exactitude of Sparrow's scholarship, reverting to his favourite phrase for him 'the lawyer in literature'. At the end of the essay on 'Oscar Wilde after Fifty Years' he comments – after a close and often enthusiastic engagement with the piece – 'A perfect lawyer-like summing up – just underestimates Wilde's literary achievement – as Ellman completely *over*-estimates it.' Yet at the beginning he quotes Sparrow's predecessor, Warden Sumner. 'B.H.S. (prig) to J.Sp: "If I were you I would not have written that article." and adds: "But nor would I." J.Sp. was courageous and candid.'

When Sparrow was dying Rowse came to Oxford to say good-bye. He was not in fact able to see him but he went into the chapel at All Souls and sat there alone reflecting on the friendships and remembering the kindnesses of the place. The last and greatest of his self-inflicted wounds had healed.

29

A Life

The circumstances of the last two or three decades of Rowse's life altered little until the disabling stroke in the summer of 1996. In the New Years Honours of 1997 he was made a Companion of Honour. In June the Prince of Wales visited him at Trenarren. In October he died.

The pattern of life at Trenarren has been sketched. Underpinned by the services of his housekeepers, Beryl, succeeded by her sister Phyllis Cundy, both almost his contemporaries, his life was free from the shade of his mother, who had never lived there. When Phyllis, after a gallant struggle against age and infirmity, at last retired she was succeeded by the much younger and more active Valerie Brokenshire. It was a time of unbroken productivity. The real business of life, reading and writing, went on as before. He conducted an enormous correspondence. Although he took no newspaper, never listened to the wireless or watched television, and never ceased to repeat that he had given up the modern world for lost, he continued to voice his criticisms of policies and institutions with a vigour that the most committed controversialist might envy. For all the extremes of his opinions he usually had a well-informed understanding of what was going on and a shrewd judgment of people and issues. Partly no doubt this was because he was always reviewing his own experience of life so intensely and remembering so vividly the people he had known that the interpenetration of past and present was profound. He read and re-read, annotating freely, his journals and the vast accumulation of letters, including his own retrieved from their recipients, which, as he was fond of asserting, would form an archive to keep researchers busy well into the next century.

He was in fact kept in touch with current events not only by his correspondents but by regular intercourse with friends who lived nearby. In spite of the constant repetition of his distaste for the human race and of his preference for solitude he much enjoyed, and was supported by, the constant friendship of David Treffry, living only a few miles away at Fowey, and of Raleigh Trevelyan who had a house almost as close, although generally based in London. In early years at Trenarren he still played a great part in Cornish life, social as well as aesthetic and intellectual. Even in the years when he no longer travelled to Oxford or to London he would accept invitations to lunch or tea, but these were always fraught with concern for his digestion. For a man who had to keep such unsleeping vigilance, Rowse complained little about his health. How much it had ruined the prime of his life his retrospect makes clear, but he doesn't go on about it as he does about the lack of recognition accorded to his work. Many of his readers and his friends might conclude that he had better reason for the first than for the second.

The most considerable publication of this long evening of life was in his view the collection of his poems which appeared in 1981. Its title *A Life* is explained in the Preface:

Looking through it all now, I see that it is an authentic record of my inner life – rather than of the external public life, given to history and (for a time) politics, though it also offers a true commentary on the history of our ruinous, tragic age. Poets are prophets – those savage poems of the thirties offered more truthful witness than the complacent humbug of politicians or the optimistic illusions of the liberal-minded.

Early on I was interested in exploring fear, a rare subject; many poems in those decades were the fruit of long illness, also a subject not much explored in verse. Hopkins wrote of mental anguish – no one that I can think of describes physical pain. Those poems describe both; Hopkins found consolation in religion, I had none – except the beauty of the physical world, natural and human. Then I notice an extraordinary Manichean strain as war was renewed and up to the Second War itself – tragic, but the most heroic period in Britain's long history, in which she went bravely out in fire and flame.

After the War, not during it, the poet transfers himself to America, recovering health and a new inspiration. . . . I observe that these poems portray an enclosed world, an almost solipsistic life, as near as maybe to self-sufficiency . . . a strong position, I have found, from which to confront the ruin and desolation of our time . . .

The publication came as a surprise even to his close friends, not least in appearing under the imprint of Blackwoods, an Edinburgh firm little heard of since its great days in the nineteenth century. 'I know that Fabers had refused to produce a volume of his *Collected Poems*' wrote Jack Simmons in answer to a letter of enquiry, 'and I believe Jonathan Cape also. I had never thought of Blackwoods as publishers since George Eliot's day, when suddenly this book arrived, which at once seemed to me a distillation of all that was best in his mind and spirit – except of course the perception and imagination he applied to his study of history. Directly I ran my eye over the titles of the poems I could see what this volume was going to be: a truly worthy continuation of *A Cornish Childhood* reaching out to old age.' That work had been autobiographical in the truest, fullest sense where its successors, *A Cornishman at Oxford* and the rest, had largely consisted of the *ex post facto* views and comments of the author on the issues and personalities of the day, reinforced from time to time by quotation from his diaries. *A Life* on the other hand belonged to the same category of literature as Wordsworth's *Prelude* in offering an account of the growth of a poet's mind. In this quality its great defect, especially exasperating in a historian, is the almost total absence of date and context. Nearly four hundred poems are printed, most of them short, divided into nine sections, of which the first five are chronological: Earlier Poems, The Thirties, Poems of Wartime, Poems of War and Peace, and American Poems (i.e. written between 1951 and 1972). Section VI is entitled Poems Mainly Cornish though of course there are many poems of purely Cornish inspiration in the first four sections. Section VII contains only one poem, entitled Duporth, the name of the house (now destroyed) built by the Cornish entrepreneur Charles Rashleigh, whose dramatic career and the folklore it inspired, is its theme. In his final revision of the volume with a view to posthumous republication Rowse added this Postscript, dated 1995:

Since writing the poem a few more fragments of Charles Rashleigh's life have surfaced in R. and B. Larn's *Charlestown: The History of a Cornish Seaport*, though they have not been able to penetrate the mystery of this man's remarkable life. Evidences of him – unrecognized by ordinary folk – remain around us in the two neighbouring villages to which he gave his name, Charlestown and Mount Charles. Also, since writing, Duporth, the country house he built has been wantonly pulled down: destruction appropriate to our demotic age.

In an imaginative work – though largely based on historic fact and folklore – I have felt free to conflate *two* affiliations and figures in Rashleigh's personal (and emotional) life. Now all is not buried, though the mystery of it remains.

Section VIII, New Poems, contains twenty or thirty recent pieces and Section IX consists of half a dozen Children's Verses.

In conversation, as in his Preface, Rowse always asserted that those who wished to know him as he really was would find him there better than in any biography that might be written. This may very well be true. But the reader needs Rowse's own specialist equipment, the knowledge of *when* exactly a particular poem was written and *why* (in the sense of what was its inspiration), if he is, like the Ethiopian in the Bible, to understand what he reads. Somewhere in his pocket books, those receptacles of odd thoughts and apothegms that flashed into his mind, Rowse wrote 'Desire and Memory the twin pillars of existence'. One cannot read far in *A Life* without perceiving the truth of this self-analysis. One of the last poems in the book, *Te lucis ante terminum*, written, one gathers from the first line, in his room in the Hotel Wellington in New York at which he always stayed, is a direct recall of his early undergraduate days at Christ Church.

> Reading high up in my New York room,
> My eye falls on the words in Dante,
> *Te lucis ante:*
> The years fall away, and I hear
> The voices of the youths we were
> Lifted up towards the end of the day
> In that same hymn in lighted choir

At Oxford. I sense the spirit we put in
The ancient words for compline
In unison, gallant and surpliced,
Under the vigilant eye of bird-like Dean
And gathered dons – Julian, Tom and I.
Julian, who was to face a charge of treason,
Tom, mathematical and pious, against reason
Would submit to medieval discipline,
And I remain, dedicated to memory.
The day over, full of eager activity,
Night closing down on cloister and hall,
Light reflected in plashing Mercury –
I hear our vanished voices in the room,
Te lucis ante terminum.
And recognise from far away
The closing of our day.

His fellow choristers were Julian Wadleigh, whose involvement in the Alger Hiss case led to the charge of treason, and Tom Lawrenson, the charming, gentle Geordie with whom Rowse enjoyed complete ease and equality of friendship. There they are in the Cathedral at evensong, in the innocence of youth, before undergraduates called themselves students and when the closing of the College gate a few hours later is already implicit, the world physically as well as spiritually excluded. Many times in later years at All Souls Rowse records the same sensation of relief, of release, after he has shewn out a guest into Radcliffe Square and closes the iron gate behind him. His solipsism is partly an attempt to recreate this sense of collegiate insulation within the bounds of his own personality.

Dreams and recollection are here more real than reality. It is this quality of his consciousness that gives Rowse's history and poetry their peculiar power. When reality in the ordinary sense forces itself upon him the vision fades. 'The letter killeth but the spirit giveth life.'

The themes to which Rowse constantly reverts in his journals and letters are all there: his resentment at having been born into a poor and uncultivated home when nature had equipped him to inherit and to cherish beauty; his deep distress at his uncertain paternity; his conviction that the world – and especially the literary and academic world – was against him. His affections for Cornwall, for Oxford, for the towns and landscapes he associates with his friends, and, most of all, for the friends he had lost and the friendships he had mishandled, they are there too, and they inspire the best of his poems.

The homosexuality, of which he was proud in the same way that he was proud of his intellectual ability, also insists itself. As does a certain voyeurism, a prurience which had perhaps developed or even derived from his retreat, under what he considered snubs and rebuffs, into solipsism. 'Solitude' said Dr Johnson 'is the surest nurse of all prurient passions.' His tendency to speculate on the sex lives of acquaintances, to measure (on no discernible evidence) their probable performance and their physical endowments became, in later life, absurd. It even spread (as his critics were quick to point out) to his interpretation of historical characters. And the Oxford Lives, which were the product of his old age, are dominated by assertions of this nature for which his sources are, to say the least, unequal. Sometimes he claims to be repeating what the person concerned has confided in him. Sometimes he appears, from the specificity of his account, to have some source beyond the incessant gossip of a closed society. Sometimes the appetite seems to be providing for its own satisfaction.

Sex was both an amusement and an obsession. An amusement in the sense that he often enlivens his description of some staid respectable figure by mischievous imaginings. An obsession in the sense that he cannot leave the subject alone, that it can always be pressed into service to supply an explanation of what would otherwise be puzzling. Sexual attraction is one of the first observations that he makes on meeting people, both their own and his. Rightly or wrongly he believed a number of women to have been eager to marry him, or to have an affair. This is usually followed by a profession of his feelings of repulsion for any such relations with the opposite sex, much as he enjoyed the sympathy and friendship of many women. Yet there are some rare exceptions, even if distinctly half-hearted. His emotions as he attended Noreen Sweet's wedding have been recorded. That lifelong friendship, happily sustained during her long widowhood, was always graced by Rowse's open admiration for her looks and style. It is possible, though his own journals say nothing, that he may have led the lady who wrote a novel about him to believe that he was seriously attracted to her. There are one or two remarks in letters written by others at the time that imply this. The only direct evidence in his own right of such feelings, and they were evanescent enough, which I have come across is in his diary of a visit to New York in September 1963:

That evening I had rather a new experience for me. Deciding at the last moment to go to the Ballet at the Civil Center, I got a seat in the first row of the stalls with a view into the orchestra. There were the middle-aged men tuning up their fiddles, the pretty harpist conscientiously practising her solo part, all the excitement of tuning instruments, chatter, coming and going. Then came the girl in the corner who was playing a double-bass. Evidently Italian from her appearance, and unmarried – I can't think why, she was so attractive. Really rather beautiful: lovely white skin, swan-throat, black hair with the beginning only of a parting in the middle, drawn straight back in the Italian manner and the way my mother used to do her hair (when I was a small boy I loved brushing it); *petit nez retroussé*, nice lips and white teeth. Perhaps just such a Dark Lady, it only now occurs to me, as gave Shakespeare so much trouble. Above all, it was those lambent eyes that spoke her personality – and her gestures. For she was full of vivacity and humour, laughing like a good comrade with her fellow-bass, making *moues* and talking nineteen to the dozen. She at once woke the corner up, and I was transfixed. I looked at her and watched her and nothing else for twenty minutes, before the curtain went up on *Swan Lake*, and often in the intervals of the ballet.

She must have been aware of my admiring fixation, but never once did she show it or give me a straight look. I suppose there is some Trade Union regulation against communication with the audience.

The moment she came in the whole corner came alive. The middle-aged man, her companion double-bass, lit up: she made him laugh, laughing vivaciously herself, showing those white teeth. Then she went forward to talk to one of the violins: he came alive under the spell of her vivacity. I saw that she was a good sort, popular, rather a card. Not once did she bother to tune up her instrument like the others, merely resined her bow absentmindedly while telling some story to her fellow, ear-rings flashing, everything about her glittering.

I was more than fetched, I was fixed. I played with the thought of an alternative life, making up to her, sending a message, taking her out, making a mistress of her, for one couldn't marry.

The curtain went up. But *Swan Lake* didn't engross my eye and every sense as usual. Nor did I respond, as formerly, to the beautiful young male dancers. In the interval I went back to my mute worshipping. (Could I turn over a new leaf at my age? Might I be a corrected hetero, as Geoffrey H.'s[1] Texan Ph.D. used to say?) My Italian girl came forward to dispense her vivacity to a little group of violins nearer me. She talked too much. She gestured a little too much, made too many *moues*, was a little too expressive. One would tire of it; one couldn't live with it. Not interested in her instrument, was she a trifle careless, not much of a musician? She played with expression and feeling, and occasionally looked up at the stage, white throat gleaming out of black dress, eyes lovely.

I am sure she was a good fellow, a good sort. She certainly compelled my imagination all right, disturbed my mind. But I haven't been back since. Too much business to occupy my mind, and the dream is over: Flaubert's Madame Arnoux. I shall not forget her appearance, her personality, the upward look of her eyes.

By chance he was giving lunch next day to one of the ladies who had, according to him, indicated in no ambiguous terms that he would be well received as her lover. She was also, we are told, among the mistresses of one of his more promiscuous All Souls colleagues. 'Looking quite beautiful – she certainly does know how to dress: a silver-grey silk frock that brought out the nut-brown colour of her hair, done with a charming new American coiffure, with a fringe in front. (I warned her not to let John disarrange it. "How do you know about such things?" she simpered. "You always pretend you don't know about them." Did it not occur to her that translation is an easy art?).'

These passages seem so candid and so revealing as to require no glossing. The reader is as well equipped as the author for interpreting the nature and strength of Rowse's sexuality. Conspicuous as it was

1. Presumably his All Souls friend Geoffrey Hudson.

on the surface of his nature one may doubt its profundity. Other loves, other loyalties, other desires are more powerfully and more clearly reflected in *A Life* which on his own testimony is the true record, the true self-portrait.

30

Bells Across the Water

'Never give up, never give in.' The stern injunction Rowse repeats at each setback, ever more frequently in later life as not only the academic world but even long cherished friends refused to accept his Shakespearean assertions, reminds his biographer that his subject's vitality and energy will always outrun pursuit. The multiplicity of his awareness, the recording and the investigation of so many diverse perceptions, will, as Rowse himself prophesied, afford material enough to satisfy the kind of literary industry at which he himself often liked to scoff. To do justice to what he has left behind would need many volumes. But would they find readers? Readers, that is, in the sense that Rowse desired, the sense that Johnson intended and Virginia Woolf approved in the term the common reader. Perhaps they would. The last three or four decades have seen the successful publication of the correspondence and diaries of many public figures and men and women of letters. But, unlike the Victorians who expected the Life and Letters all together in two or more volumes, the modern reader prefers the two kept apart.

What then are the themes in this long and energetic life? What conclusions may be drawn about the character this book tries to delineate? A biographer is not bound to supply Counsel's opinion for the Day of Judgment. Nor is he, as used to be presumed until Lytton Strachey took pen in hand, retained as counsel for the defence. Rowse anyhow never professed much respect for lawyers and constantly reiterates his scepticism of ethical judgments. Not that that prevents him from passing them on others: it is only in his own case that he professes not to pay much attention to them. Yet even here he was perhaps not so indifferent as he made out. Not long before his death he sent me a letter, written by one of his friends at All Souls, expressing the hope that it might find a place in his biography (see Appendix E). In others, as in the letter to Raleigh Trevelyan already quoted, he sees himself as having struggled ineffectively against public disaster and the defeat of everything he cared for.

It is this vibrancy, this intensity of response, that is his special quality, a quality which animates a life of extraordinary breadth and length. He could remember the world before 1914, when his country was indisputably a first-rate power, and he had been for the rest of the century an agonized spectator of its decline, not least in the standards of behaviour and of respect for what it had inherited. The twentieth century seemed longer, more violent, more destructive than any of its predecessors which he had studied and he had lived through the whole of it. As to breadth, the social, literary, aesthetic, topographical perceptions of this observant sensibility are not easily matched. In the years which he divided between England and America he could not, for all his perfectly sincere, profoundly felt, protestations of complaint at having to leave Oxford or Cornwall, contain the pleasure he experiences in his travels (which were often so crammed with lectures, seminars, interviews and necessary civilities as to have exhausted a much younger man). He had the gift, shared with writers so different as John Betjeman and Samuel Pepys, of communicating freshness of enjoyment in everyday things that the rest of the world takes for granted. One does not have to admire everything about Rowse or think every work of his a masterpiece to be overwhelmingly grateful for the play of his mind, the vigour of his expression, his instinct not to find anything boring. He was aware, of course, of boredom as he was aware of ugliness, slovenliness and stupidity. But, like Walter Pater, he counted the pulses of life and was determined not to waste his time. He was, to borrow Berenson's formulation, life-enhancing.

Nowhere are these qualities more evident than in the journals written in the Anglo-American years. In January 1964, snow-bound in New York with no planes flying, he bursts out:

What a life! When I could be snugly at home at Trenarren – should be now, if it were not for ambition, resentment, money, the desire for penance, to inflict discomfort on myself.

I really regard my spending so much as half the year in America as my annual penance – not many people know that. Three months a year would be enough. But – money to make myself recoup the £15,000 I put down the Rhodesian drain[1] (I have now compensated that in dollars) the desire to turn my back on Oxford, England, etc have led me into this. Almost as if I am impelled, driven.

Nor do I think it, strategically, a mistake. At sixty, England has had enough of me. I have been too much in evidence, too available. Time for another phase, to come away and over here for another career – where I could rectify some of the mistakes of the past, begin all over again.

But only a couple of months later, after several pages of minute and loving description of the gardens of the Huntington in which he walked every day, either by himself or with one or two of the distinguished American scholars who formed a regular group at lunch, he is overcome by the 'divine spring breeze and sun – *how* much I love California in the spring, everything bursting into flower (shall I perhaps come to live there, end my days there, like Aldous Huxley?)' Only a week earlier, down in Arizona, he had written 'This is no joke. I am stuck here in Tucson – about the most southerly place in the US. Just on the Mexican border in *snow*! I don't suppose they have seen snow for a quarter of a century. I came here for warm winter sun, wearing my thinnest summer suit – and the whole place looks like a Christmas card.' However within a mere two hours he was exploring the positive potentialities of his situation. '11 a.m. I want to take the opportunity of this blissful intermission, this solitude, to sum up the year's work over here. On the whole, I have reason to be well content. At the Huntington day by day I have written three quarters or more of my biography of Southampton – ten chapters out of perhaps thirteen.' The Huntington! How it refreshed his spirit and integrated, reconciled, the varieties of experience which he elsewhere found discordant.

What I have liked much more has been the lunch-hour walks by myself around the Huntington grounds . . .

Down there are the original rough tracks of the old rancho, and I *love* the

1. This unfortunate speculation is constantly reverted to.

place: the real California unchanged, the rough bumping lane with its curve at the bottom, a few of the native oaks, a screen of whispering firs, redwoods with beautiful striated barks. I often stand there alone transfixed, in ecstasy, listening to a light breeze in the firs . . . One day last week I had a wonderful experience. At the same time as I was looking, listening, inhaling – old California, the cart-track, green firs and pines, a light breeze whispering under translucent blue sky, memories, whisperings that are not mine but with which I seek to identify myself – behind and amid all this there were other memories and images that *are* mine. It was as if in the ears of memory I could hear the bells of Cornish churches, St Austell church on Sundays, the bells of Lanlivery, the image of Lantyan woods above the river Fowey with the bells of St Winnow coming across the water and up the clearing that bluebell evening there with Geoffrey Hudson in the 1950s. In such a moment I feel how rich my life has been, and is. I ought to be grateful. In a way I am. I suppose those moments, when I steal away from everybody, are moments of worship.

There are moments when the clouds part and Rowse's gifts can be seen at their height. His journals often show a keen awareness of his faults. A recurrent motif is that America would give him a chance to break with mental and moral attitudes that he deplored, especially the cherishing of vindictiveness and resentment, and to make a fresh start. But hardly is the thought formulated before it is overtaken by the reflection that the good and the bad in him are so inextricably entwined that if he did bring himself under control (as T. S. Eliot, whom he so much admired, so evidently did) he would lose his own dynamic:

I should no longer be able to release myself into my work. Other people think the keeping up of grudges a waste of energy. Does it waste mine? I sometimes think it fortifies the iron in my composition: sometimes I think it a stimulant. Salter thinks that I have allowed it to spoil my nature. The funny thing is that it is absolutely under my control: I could switch it off tomorrow, if I wanted to – the fixed attitude towards the House, towards Cornwall, All Souls, Oxford. But I don't intend to do it, I don't quite know why. Partly I enjoy hating people for their folly and rubbing their noses in it; partly I am acting a part, I suppose. I have taken up a position, and it has some advantages in keeping people at bay and preserving my own inner sanctum from their common and fatuous presence. I really don't want to know people – I know too many already; better to keep them off.

And yet as he also makes plain so much of his life had been parched by an absence of the love which he had been denied in childhood. The intensity of his feeling was complemented by, or should one rather say 'competed with', intensity of ambition to fulfil the abilities he knew himself to possess:

> On a deeper level – and what really matters – the writing in and for itself . . . I was caught for and by history, even Tudor history, at a very early age. People are fixed in childhood. I think history got me before poetry, and both long before politics. So perhaps the way it has worked out is the right order of my mind's interests. And, deepest of all, I could not have been a novelist, a creative writer in the D. H. Lawrence sense (a near analogy in our origins and lives), because I am not engaged by the flow of life; I do not like living human beings enough to be interested in the play of life among them. Only when it is all over and done with, only when they are dead and the story is rounded and finished, do I feel with and for them. Then I am sorry for them, then I feel the pathos of their lives, with more inner sympathy.
>
> So it was right that I should be an historian, as my poetry is mainly elegiac.

Like so many of the statements that could be made about Rowse, either by himself or by those who knew him well, the truth of this does not, as it should in logic, preclude the truth of its converse. Rowse *did* mind about the sufferings of others and sympathized with them. One has only to read his letters to the bereaved, or to those whom he knew to be tormented by anxieties, to be convinced of that. And the independent testimony of a large number of his friends and acquaintances would itself be sufficient evidence. Perhaps it was rather that he minded minding: that the solipsism was thrown up as a defence not against the idiocy and folly of the human race but against his own heart.

His conclusion that he was not cut out to be a novelist may be accepted after his many earlier reflections on the might-have-beens of his literary career. But its grounds are not altogether satisfactory. He *was* 'engaged by the flow of life'. His history, his autobiography are incontrovertible evidence. And the eagerness with which he sets down the story of some local Cornish affair, the zeal with which he traces the hidden lives of Oxford colleagues, the observations that he pieces together to establish the characters of the rich Americans in whose houses he stayed, all testify to this appetite. No doubt he was right in concluding, after several experiments with the short story, that he was not a born writer of fiction. But fiction is not the only medium in which the creative power can express itself.

Among the many inconsistencies of this tireless and tirelessly self-aware intelligence the preoccupation with competition sits strangely with the disdain, so frequently expressed, for the opinions of others. Emancipated as he was from class in the social sense he was enslaved to it academically. A first-class degree in the Final Honours of his University was the be-all and end-all. In his case he had thrown everything into the fight for it and he had won. Such an experience must leave its mark. This can be seen, only too clearly, in his subsequent demands that the learned world should acknowledge not just his eminence but his sovereignty as the historian of Elizabethan England. He regarded the OM, particularly that bestowed on Veronica Wedgwood, as his by right. Increasingly he came to think of himself as a genius. It is surprising that so searching, so critical, a mind should attach such importance to labels of such dubious provenance. Certainly it contributed nothing to his own artistic and intellectual achievement or to his standing in the eyes of those who appreciated his rare combination of gifts.

Perhaps – nothing is impossible with this Protean personality – he knew this himself. Perhaps he knew that when he was captivated by beauty or intent on following up the character and circumstance of someone who had caught his eye in history or his own life he was then most himself because self was not present to his consciousness. It is this universal, energetic human curiosity that unifies his work. Like Tennyson's Ulysses he was a part of all that he had met. When he found himself in America he not only opened his mind and sensibility to the new landscapes, the unfamiliar forms of social life, the ideas and the atmosphere of a civilization founded on presuppositions that differed from his own. He still pursued opportunities of extending and deepening the knowledge and understanding he brought with him. In Vermont in 1959 he went to call on the veteran socialist, John Spargo, who had known and been much attracted to Marx's daughter, Eleanor. In New Mexico he sought out survivors who knew Brett (then in her nineties) and the closing scenes of D. H. Lawrence's life (much earlier he had, of course, visited Eastwood and talked to people who had known him as a young man). In California he took trouble to cultivate the friendship of the most retiring, least egocentric, of the great commanders of the Second War, Fleet Admiral Chester Nimitz and his wife. The correspondence that flowed from this relationship shows how much it was valued on both sides.

That is the tuneful note, struck time and again, in all the discords of this long and agitated life. Rowse enjoys, but for all his professed egocentricity the giving of enjoyment is half the fun. In his poetry and in his retrospects, touched into life by the memory of friends, this is often evident. In the prose evocations of present beauty it is sometimes veiled, as in this passage written on a Sunday morning in July 1964 sitting out alone on the terrace at Dunster Castle:

Over the great shoulder of the castle the church bells are ringing for morning service. Here is what one misses in America – nothing that really matches to compensate. Down there on the main road at the mouth of the valley is a reminiscence of America, a piece of modern civilization: the cars that swish by to Minehead and the west, the popping motor-bikes, a squad of them, moving east. Otherwise the landscape is the Luttrells' and as they have made it over the centuries since they came here in Norman times. Below is the rich cultivated valley, one rectangle of golden wheat mouthing to the sea, green meadows and pastures up valley, the noise of the mill-race coming down stream now that the bells have ceased. (The people are in church; my hostess, dowager and chatelaine, doing duty in the family pew.) Here all round are evidences of her life's devotion: the rose-beds down the steep slopes, the urns punctuating the terrace walk brimming with hydrangeas blue and pink, the pots with dripping fuchsias, the island of arums in the fountain pool. In the background the old rose-red walls, the too large Victorian windows opened out by Salvin in place of the classical sash-windows of the 17th century the Victorians could not abide. A scented breeze rises from the steep slopes, compounded of so many things, roses, jasmine, lemony magnolia flowers fully out, aromatic yew and the idiosyncratic odour of box like nothing else. The view extends out to the milky, hazy, Bristol Channel and over rolling broken country to the long ridge of the Quantocks – Coleridge, Southey, Wordsworth country – and the dip where Elizabethan East Quantockshead lies, the other Luttrell house, where Walter, the elder son and heir, lives.

The physical sensation illuminates the history and the people. Just after Christmas 1962 Rowse describes a sharp exchange at the Huntington with a distinguished historian who had been running down a historical biography that he thought well of.

She herself is the author of a quite dead monograph – complete in its kind, tells us all and rather more than all we want to know about the subject. It never comes alive, is perfectly dead, like a still-born infant . . .

This was the way she was brought up, a clever woman, rather barbed, eyes sparkling with suppressed sex, unsuppressed malice. A pity she has never learned to live.

She said, afterwards, to mitigate the effect of what she had said, that she and I disagreed about the principle of how history should be written, that I was an artist, but that it wasn't in everybody's power to set out to be an artist.

I said that this wasn't a personal question. That it was everybody's business to make his book as much of a work of art as he could – even third-rate academics should try.

No utterance could be more characteristic – not least the final flouting. It contains the core of everything he stood for, everything that he was. The interpenetration of his consciousness by sensation, memory, ratiocination, vision, self-knowledge – that was the life of the mind to which as an artist he was dedicated. It is as an artist that he would wish to be remembered.

In July 1996 Rowse had a severe stroke, from which he made only a limited recovery. He died a year later at Trenarren on 3 October 1997. His disabilities, which had already deprived him of much, were gaining on him. When I saw him not long before his stroke he was fearful that his deteriorating eyesight might prevent him from reading. After it he could neither read nor write. All this he bore with a stoicism that was part of his character and with a degree of patience that must have required an effort of will.

Submerged below these icy waters his spirit was still there. When Raleigh Trevelyan came to see him, and his presence was announced by the nurse Rowse broke his then usual silence with: 'Trevelyan is a distinguished name'. When his pillow was smoothed, he murmured:

'Thank you Valerie.'

'It's not Valerie, it's Shirley.'

'Don't contradict ME.'

The public honour so long denied him was hurriedly conferred. In advance of the New Year's list he was given the CH a distinction that prompted him to recall that he shared it with his friend David Cecil. The presentation was made by Lady Mary Holborow, the Lord Lieutenant of Cornwall. A few weeks later he was visited by the Prince of Wales. An earlier recognition that had given him great pleasure was the award of the Benson medal of the Royal Society of Literature in 1982. The University of Exeter had honoured him with a Doctorate as long ago as 1960. Many efforts had been made over the years to secure him the national recognition that was, at the eleventh hour, accorded him. In Cornwall, besides his benefactions to the National Trust and the Royal Institution of Cornwall, he is commemorated by a block of granite on Black Head, almost within sight of Trenarren.

APPENDIX A

Memorandum of Wardenship Election 1952

This extract from Rowse's Pocket Memo Book, written on 27 February 1952 at the house of his friend Wyndham Ketton-Cremer, is referred to on p. 199. It is the earliest extended summary of what he felt after his defeat for the Wardenship.

Back once more at Felbrigg, after eighteen months, in the hall after breakfast, wood fire burning up in the stove making a small semicircle of warmth, outside which all is cold, sharp and East Anglian. A complete whitish-grey blankness shuts off the house: nothing penetrates from outside except the occasional rooks. There in the window embrasure are the busts of Charles Fox and the younger Pitt tutelary deities of the house. William Windham a friend of both, who passed over politely from one to the other.

All round charming pictures of Windhams & Pastons, Stuart ladies, nice comfortable deep chairs covered in rich red. On the plain good Georgian table with horse-hoof feet, a vase of winter sweet, that exquisite scent an element in the general sense of well-being with the wood-fire, the smoke of W's vanishing cigarette just going off about the house on his morning round.

Oh these country houses with their adorable round: going to sleep last night in my frilled and valenced bed with the steady unwinking firelight on the walls, occasionally a settling coal aroused me to enjoy the more the sense of falling asleep; being awakened in the morning with tea-tray, tea pot in wool cosy, thin bread & butter, Rockingham china. The immensely long blue curtains are drawn to let in the white fog-light and reveal a patch of pheasant-trodden lawn. In summer there is night-scented stock growing below the windows.

Oh, to have such a house of my own – not such a large house, nor with

319

such possessions. Here the complete contents of Wm Windham's house bought by those successful merchants the Cremers. But why, O why, wasn't I born into some such succession? The *bloody*, the sickening, luck that has always dogged me: to have been born among the idiot people the first curse, to have endless illness consuming time, money, opportunities the second; to have won through to success and to make enough money to live as I should like to live, just at a time when taxation takes half of it, when the rest goes only half as far, so that one enjoys less than a quarter of what my own efforts earn, and it has been totally impossible to build up what would have been ample for the life and surroundings I always intended to achieve for myself – What sickening luck, Curse and curse again!

Now at 48 no wonder it sours me to think of the chances of Shaw & Wells & John Buchan – or even Arthur Bryant or Charles Morgan had before the War – not with envy of them. I admire & applaud their gifts and their well-earned success. I am merely sick at my own luck, the luck that has always been against me all the way along, so that I have had to wring every small achievement out of fortune with the greatest effort, like a hard-fought engagement; when other people have strokes of good fortune bringing all that I must strive for into their laps, while I have still to wait and wait – tho' I have long ago earned what is still to seek.

And what makes me mad to think of is the half-conviction that it is precisely from the person who tries hardest that things are withheld, that the very fact that one is the kind of person who cares most to work hard and achieve is itself a reason for others to withhold recognition and for things to be made more difficult for one; and the suspicion that if one did not mind so much things would come more easily to one and even be put more easily at one's disposal.

This situation has created a regular pattern in my life, a recurrent rhythm. I work hard for something I wish; it is – *if it depends not on myself* but on either other people or external circumstance – withheld: it never by any chance is given or granted or even rendered for work done or reward for desert. Later, when I have passed beyond this point and no longer value it or any recognition it can confer, the point is yielded, too late: it brings me no pleasure or any satisfaction, nor do I much care any more; and usually I make that clear in my attitude, anyone with half an eye can read the contempt. Too late, too late, it has come too late. Again and again that has been enacted: with people, with Cornwall, in the case of my old college; in literary life; it is now at this moment happening in regard to the greatest devotion in my life All Souls.

I sometimes think it is as if I have to be taught at every stage – with the intensity of my temperament, with its natural loyalties and devotions – that I should not attach myself so strongly to anyone or anything. If I were a religious believer in an earlier century the conclusion would be obvious – one was being gradually taught by experience to withdraw one's hopes from earthly things and being led in God's own way to see that they are of no importance compared with the things of the spirit. (It may be that I am not averse to that conclusion in strictly non-religious terms.) In short the realization that came home to Eliot and which is the theme of 'The Cocktail Party' of being one of those elect to whom these things are brought home. And, as often happens in the lives of the chosen, one revolts against one's fate – until finally one accepts. It is all yet another, though a rare one, of the forms egoism takes.

Yet I often have this sense, with each defeat, with every rejection of what I wish (just *because* I wish it so intensely), of an almost destined course. For I cannot but say that each defeat has been turned to good account: if I had been appointed at Christ Church I should still have been a teaching hack; if I had got in for Penryn and Falmouth it should have killed me; if I had become a Professor, I should never have written my books; if I became [note tense] Warden of All Souls, I should waste my life on the trivial, fritter my life away.

So, I sometimes think, I should be grateful at the way things have turned out; though no-one is grateful for defeat, or to those at whose hands one suffers defeat.

True, too, one may derive some stimulus, some injection of iron from constant rebuffs, from successive reverses, from rejections of fortune (and how I hate being rejected and those who reject, my earliest and deepest complex reaching back to first childhood, so that it is never easy to bear). But I am getting better at bearing it; perhaps I really do not mind as much as I did; perhaps I am learning, being made to learn, as always, the hard way.

Why should I be grateful for being made to learn the hard way? But this is a nonsense question, for there is nobody to be grateful to. The sense of there being something destined, something inevitable about it all, remains – even if it is not external, and is only the destiny involved in one's temperament.

But what is the destiny my temperament involves for me? I sometimes think a shattering, a sensational, fall (that would be in keeping with the niggardliness, the meanness, the hardness I have always found towards me in fortune). Or if not that, then the walling up, the isolation within my own ego – the process I have seen take place in my mother's case – more and more cut off from other people, until in the end no one remains, and not caring even if one inhabits loneliness for one's house, an empty void all round me.

In any case, is it any wonder that though some people see on the surface an affectionate nature, high spirits and gaiety, and even charm – underneath there is a real grimness of spirit, one who believes life to be, at any rate for him, a bloody struggle against adverse odds? Is it any wonder that since fate is so niggard to me, so determined to withhold what I strive so hard for and set much store by, that in the private realm of my own conduct at any rate I am determined to make no sacrifices; that since I cannot *have* what I please from life, I will at any rate and in return, by compensation *do* as I please?

That seems only just.

Then again, one has to remember, there is no justice in *life*.

Feb 27, 1952

APPENDIX B

Letter to Lord Salter

For the significance of this letter see p. 199.

Trenarren House
St Austell
Cornwall
Jan 12 .57

Dear Arthur,

Thank you for your good wishes and for the kind things you say about 'The Early Churchills' – characteristically generous, I may say. Not everyone is so generous – but that does not matter much when one's work is approved of by masters like Trevelyan or Neale, and when a book like 'The Early Churchills' sells out its first edition in a fortnight and has to be reprinted.

I have been working very hard to finish a very long chapter of 'The Later Churchills' – some 14,000 words since coming down and now it is finished have had so much work to do in the garden that, as you see, I can scarcely hold the pen.

Certainly not long enough to comment in full on your letter, as you probably expected me to do. In any case my opinion of you has not much changed: I have already spoken of your generosity as characteristic, I have always recognized a kind nature and know you to be a good man. What more of a tribute can anyone have? – there are not so many good men in the world.

What is the point of going back over what happened in the history of the College now five years ago? I agree with the first Marlborough in thinking that *éclaircissements* of this sort never do any good.

But if you wish me to be perfectly sincere with you, it is rather obtuse and tactless, isn't it, to write me a long screed putting forward all of the arguments for an *impersonal* kind of Warden? Really – as if I were not capable of seeing them all for myself – hadn't in fact seen them all along. (It would not interest me to argue that some people were in favour of an admittedly personal kind as Warden – not, it is true, the entire younger generation, marshalled by Rees (as if such a leader were any guide for anyone as to the future of the College), but such senior people of (I take it) good judgment as Simon and Craster and all the officers of the College whom I had worked with – excepting Rees, I am glad to say.

But I am not interested to reply to such a tactless observation, for there is something far more obtuse: you do not seem to realize that *I never did want to be Warden even at the time*. Of course I could not say that, out of loyalty to the friends who were backing me. But do you suppose that I wasn't aware of what a frittering away of one's very life it would be? That I didn't know all the time – what Archibald, Amery and Faber had the decency to point out as their reason for not wanting me to take it on (though they were not intimate friends of mine) that writing is my real vocation and anything else would be a waste? Archibald went further and wrote warning me in the strongest terms not to – saying 'You might think you'd like it for a year or two, but then you'd find it a terrible imprisonment: one has only one life to live: you must do what you are made to do and follow your true vocation.'

I knew he was right at the time: it exactly chimed with my own view of it all. I treasure his letter, I admire him for his imaginative perception and sympathy, I respect him and am grateful for his opposition to what he considerately urged to be wrong for me.

From more intimate friends not a word came at the most agonizing juncture in my life.

For *me* it would have been fatal to take it on – even my enemy Rees urged that: he said 'You would kill yourself.' I dare say: like Humphrey Sumner, who was too conscientious, cared too much about the College and its place in the world. – It would have been a far greater sacrifice for me – for I could not have fulfilled myself as a writer. The frustration would have driven me mad. And what a waste of a career as a writer really worth having – worth a great deal, a very great deal, more to me in terms of cash – though that is not a *first* consideration with me: fulfilment of one's gifts in one's work is and always has been my real aim. And, as you know, I have made myself completely independent of my job, any attachment, by my work: one of the very few historians, academic historians, in England to have done so. (I can only think of Trevelyan who has.)

So that any discussion of the matter that lies between you and me can only begin on this basis – that I never wished to be Warden. You never seem to have realized that or even bothered to look at it from my point of view – desperately as I needed, at that very bad time in the college's history and for me, sympathy and advice rather than support.

Of course I had to be loyal to those who were supporting me – I know who they were, to a man – and could not let them down by saying what I realized was my own best interest.

I hope you will not fall into the trap of saying – very well then, what have you got to complain of? For I know only too well what the motives of all those young men – almost a majority – were: that war-time generation of Raymond Carr, Quinton, Dummett, Leo Butler, Williams (with Cooper in the background to inspire and Rees in the foreground to lead). I understand the motives of those people very well – they thought I wanted to run the place (and it is true that if I had had to I'd have seen to it that they got their work done. As it is, who has heard of anything they have ever accomplished?); they were, like a lot of people one has to put up with if one is successful in one's work, very anxious to obstruct one all they could. While they were not subtle enough to see that they were doing what really suited one's interest best.

But, of course, that doesn't make one any the more fond of them, or relish the more the humiliation of being turned down by the second-rate, or third-rate.

And as for the institution that witnessed, that was responsible for, the most distressing experience in my life, it is *not* the College that I venerated, that I was so proud to be a member of, that was the College that contained the most influential men in the life of the nation, men whom I found uniformly kind to me: Lang, Henson, Headlam, Alington in the Church; Chelmsford, Geoffrey Dawson, Amery, Curtis in public life; Simon, Wilfrid Greene, Cyril Radcliffe in the Law; Oman, Robertson, Holdsworth in the University. (I never had a cross word with any of these.)

These were all men of eminence and first-class ability. There are very few of them, or such as they were, left. I do not want to tell you in detail or with much candour what I think of the present institution or to speculate on its future. The only point relevant to your letter is your appeal to me in regard to it. There is no point in any appeal to me after the experience I had five years ago from the bulk of its members – either as straight opponents or by friends who failed (*not*, I hope I have made clear, by the way they voted) in the hour of need and who *from that moment* ceased to be my friends and became acquaintances.

So far as obligations to the institution are concerned, I am quit: so long as I work hard at my research and write my books – which is more than some of its Fellows have managed to do – I fulfil my obligations. I am well aware that if there *should* be a University Commission to question its utility and ask what it produces, my published work will be one of its strongest lines of defence. I do not begrudge the College that, though I had to make the point to the Warden last year – who saw the force of it – when I found that he was belittling my last work on Elizabethan Expansion. (I am not complaining about this: I simply put him in his place with a letter from Radcliffe, whom he greatly admires, who might very well be the head of a Labour-appointed University Commission and who is no friend of the College: he had written me one of the warmest commendations of my book I have ever received. In any case, it is only obvious sense for a Warden not to *dénigrer* the work of one of the best known members of the institution, not to weaken its defences.)

I repeat I am not making any complaint against Sparrow; from the moment he became Warden I determined that I would behave far better to him than he would have done had I become Warden. Nor am I making any comment on the institution under his direction. If one cannot help noticing a contrast between the College of today and the College I came into and loved, perhaps that is only to be expected in the general decline of standards and achievements in a society I have no respect for.

I cannot tell you how thankful I am to have *no* responsibility for anything in contemporary society – though when I was younger I was public-spirited enough, and fool enough, for anything. Again and again it has proved fortunate for me that my fellow-men were far more anxious to obstruct my making a contribution than to welcome it or to respond to a fundamental good will. I have confidence enough to think that that was their loss – sometimes, too late, they wake up and think so too. But I am self-sufficient in my work: I have an inner world in which to live, that keeps me going and even gives me warmth and happiness. I do not feel called upon to share that with any who have shown that they do not know how to appreciate or respond.

You may, or may not, have observed that I am pretty rigidly consistent in my views and conduct. What I think about the institution you could have deduced from my consistent line of conduct over the past five years. It is fairly clear that I do not really wish to know these people; these are not the kind of people whom I much wish to know. (If they want to know me, they can read my books.)

I am sorry to have put you to the trouble of reading all this. It should not have been difficult to infer that this was what I thought from my general attitude. (Of course I realize that my behaviour makes the second-rate and third-rate impute it simply to chagrin and pique at my not being Warden. That is what *they* would think: a secret source of amusement to one who clearly doesn't care what they think about anything.)

Where you get into trouble is in trying to put emotional pressure into getting back to the state of things of before five years ago as if nothing had happened. Whereas, as you see, a great deal happened in regard to my relation to that institution in which I was once a live nerve and am now a dead one. There were one or two other rather intimate friends who made a similar mistake – but they accept the fact. They know that it is no use pretending that there was no fact. There is no doing anything about it now.

As I said, my opinion of you has not much changed. I find that the best attitude with which to confront an ill world is one of a solitary and rather grim stoicism. It is best to be independent in all senses, independent of people, free of all ties – an atom in an atomic age. If you think that friendly acquaintance mitigates in any way the grimness of the world around us, I am prepared on a purely individual basis for the acquaintance to be a friendly one.

May I ask you to add to your kindness by asking you to return this?

Yours ever,

Leslie

APPENDIX C

The Dark Lady

The following extracts are from two letters written to the author by Mary Edmond.

Leslie launched his 'identification' of the Dark Lady in a centre-page article in *The Times* of 29 January 1973, closely followed by the book *Shakespeare the Man* in May. Two of his main arguments in favour of Emilia were based on misreadings of Forman: her husband's name was *not* William and her colour was not described as '*browne*' . . . I can claim without immodesty to have read Forman's six casebooks at the Bodleian much more accurately than Rowse did. (There are many other misquotations in his writings which I won't bore you with.) By the time the original article appeared in *The Times* in January 1973 I already knew which London parishes were most favoured by the Italian and French-born Court musicians of the day and it took me only about twenty minutes to find, in the register of St Botolph Aldgate, that Emilia was married in 1592 to *Alphonso* Lanier. I wrote off to *The Times*; silence ensued for some weeks; I demanded the letter back and tried it on Karl Miller, then editor of the *Listener*, who promptly and gleefully published it on 10 May. I don't need to remind you that quantities of letters, articles, etc. on all aspects of the story ensued and continued for months.

The mistakes about the name of Emilia's husband of course appeared in *Shakespeare the Man*. In the following year, 1974, in his book *Simon Forman* A.L.R. just stated that Emilia had married 'a Lanier' (p. 99); further on (p. 116) he mentioned her husband (unnamed) and further on still, on the same page, noted that 'Alfonso' had died. This must have come as a surprise to all who had thought his name was William, and noted the many references to 'Will/will' in the Sonnets.

In the revised *Shakespeare the Man* (1988) on the first page of Forman photocopies in addition to the 'Millia' heading he has had to leave in the next bit where Forman clearly writes in her husband's name 'alfōso Lanier'. All he could do was alter the caption 'William consults . . .' to 'Emilia consults . . .' and hope no one would notice what he had written about Sonnets 135 and 136 in the first version of the book.

For a full statement of the matter the reader is referred to Mary Edmond's letter printed in the *Listener* 10 May 1973. Miss Edmond, a scholar and researcher of a distinction better known to her peers than to the general public, wrote to me (6 October 1997) 'I gave Leslie a good deal of information on other things (unacknowledged) during the whole period: in the last book he just refers to "a good deal" having now been found out about Emilia and her husband, both by others [unnamed, mostly me] and myself.'

Rowse's Finances

This is a pretentious title for the sketch that follows but something must be said on a subject to which Rowse so often adverted. Briefly from the time of his election to All Souls in 1925 he did not have to worry about money, having been trained from early youth in habits of extreme frugality. During the War, as he points out in the diary entry quoted on p. 180, he began to make money from his books. He there reproaches himself for having neglected to do so earlier, since he found that he had plenty of uses for it, and determined to pay more attention to the matter.

It presented itself to him under three aspects: first, earnings from books, lectures, reviewing, broadcasts etc. second, investment of the money so earned and third, retention of it in the face of high taxation. The first gave him grounds for lively satisfaction, even for delight: the second and third for gnashing of teeth. In particular an investment in Rhodesian copper shares was never forgotten. At its first mention the loss was estimated at £13,000 but it grew in recollection. For the last twenty or thirty years of his life he placed most of his capital in the United States with highly satisfactory results.

His efforts to minimize his exposure to taxation amounted to little more than crude avoidance, which led inevitably to a serious confrontation with the authorities, resulting in a payment variously recorded – the lowest £60,000, the highest £100,000. One method by which he hoped to elude taxation was an agreement with his publishers Macmillan by which they should pay him an annuity. As originally agreed in 1949 this provided for the payment of £10,000 in forty quarterly instalments of £250. Whatever advantages this might have in reducing liability to taxation it soon came to mean that the publishers were burdened with the retention of capital which they were not entitled to invest and that the author lost what it would have yielded.

Among Rowse's papers is a summary of his literary earnings for the financial year ended 5 April 1963.

Writings, broadcasts etc.	£2,905. 5s. od.
American royalties & fees	£1,194.12s. od.
	£4,099.17s. od.

To this must be added the generous remuneration of whatever American academic appointment he might be holding, together with expenses of travel and maintenance.

In March 1964 he wrote in his journal:

In England I have my All Souls income, some £1,200 a year . . . £1,000 from Macmillans, £5 or 600 a year from my E.U.P. series,[1] various oddments from publishers, B.B.C. etc., the interest on my (depleted) investments (less than half what it was before my Rhodesian gamble). In England everything turns sour.

In America I have $6000 from the Huntington; I have earned $7 or 8000 more from lectures and articles. I am accepting $6000 a year from Harper, though my *Shakespeare* is earning much more, and so will the other books in the campaign. Doubleday are paying me $20,000 for *The Battle of Bosworth* book of which I am accepting $5000 a year. (I've got to accept some of the money sometime). I must have $60 or $70,000 invested already, accumulated in the past few years – a great deal more than over the past twenty in England.

Earlier he estimates a Book of the Month Club choice at $15,000 but in fact it was worth a great deal more, and he obtained it more than once.

This undeniable prosperity did not prevent him from repeated protests at what he considered confiscatory taxation or from lamenting that he had not scored his successes in the sunnier days enjoyed by pre-war best sellers.

1. *Teach Yourself History.*

In his last years he was proud of meeting all his expenses out of current earnings. His savings from earlier publications and from the royalties that continued to accumulate enabled him to leave a handsome fortune of which the residuary beneficiaries were the National Trust and the Royal Institution of Cornwall.

APPENDIX E

A Colleague's Judgment

A year or so before his death Rowse sent me a letter from his friend and colleague, the Chaplain of All Souls, the Rev. Professor McManners, from which, with its writer's kind permission, the following extract is quoted:

You can look back on a wonderful life of achievement, your scholarly output (and every page of it lively and readable) has been prodigious, you have helped so many of us, myself included; you have added infinitely to the gaiety of the era and to the republic of wit and learning; you are the *doyen* of the Republic of Letters. A vast number appreciate you, and I think that God (about whom you have doubts) will also appreciate what you have done with the life he has given you.

APPENDIX F

Some Dates

1903 4 December. Alfred Leslie Rowse born at Tregonissey
1907 Autumn, starts going to school at Carclaze
1915 Wins minor scholarship to St Austell Grammar School
1921 Elected Douglas Jerrold scholar in English Literature at Christ
Church
1925 First-class Degree in History
Elected Fellow of All Souls
His parents move to council house, 24 Robartes Place, Slades,
St Austell
1926 Travels in Germany
1931–5 Part-time work at London School of Economics. Research at
Public Record Office and British Museum
1931 Fights Penryn and Falmouth as Labour candidate in General
Election
1933 October, death of Charles Henderson
1934 5 March, death of ALR's father, Richard Rowse
1935 Fights Penryn and Falmouth for the second and last time
1938 A serious illness, followed by surgery
1940 Moves from 24 Robartes Place to Polmear Mine on the
outskirts of St Austell
1945 Succeeds Sir Arthur Salter in beautiful rooms in All Souls
1951 First visit to USA (Huntington Library, Pasadena)
Presides as Sub-Warden but does not stand as candidate at
the election of a new Warden of All Souls
1952 New Warden, incapacitated by ill-health, resigns. ALR stands
and is defeated by John Sparrow
1953 August. Moves to Trenarren, his home for the rest of his life

1953   27 Sept. Death of ALR's mother

1958   March. Death of Richard Pares

1960   May. Hon. Doctorate at Exeter University

1966   July. Death of Bruce McFarlane

1972   Elected to Athenaeum under Rule II – a great distinction

1982   Receives Benson Medal of Royal Society of Literature

1996   July. Severe stroke. In autumn made Companion of Honour

1997   3 October. Death

A Chronological Listing of works by
A. L. Rowse mentioned in the text

(*This is* not *a full bibliography.*)

1927 *On History*
1931 *Politics and the Younger Generation*
1936 *Mr Keynes and the Labour Movement*
1937 *Sir Richard Grenville of the Revenge*
1941 *Tudor Cornwall*
      Poems of a Decade 1931–1941
1942 *A Cornish Childhood*
1943 *The Spirit of English History*
1944 *The English Spirit*
      Poems Chiefly Cornish
1945 *West Country Stories*
1946 *The Use of History*
      Poems of Deliverance
1947 *The End of an Epoch*
1950 *The England of Elizabeth*
1951 *The English Past*
1953 *An Elizabethan Garland*
      Romier's History of France (translated and completed)
1955 *The Expansion of Elizabethan England*
1956 *The Early Churchills*
1958 *The Later Churchills*
1959 *The Elizabethans and America*
1960 *St Austell: Church, Town, Parish*
1961 *All Souls and Appeasement*
1962 *Ralegh and the Throckmortons*

1963 *William Shakespeare: A Biography*
1964 *Christopher Marlowe: A Biography*
1965 *Shakespeare's Southampton*
      A Cornishman at Oxford
1966 *Bosworth Field and the Wars of the Roses*
1969 *The Cornish in America*
1971 *The Elizabethan Renaissance: The Life of the Society*
1972 *The Elizabethan Renaissance: The Cultural Achievement*
      The Tower of London in the History of the Nation
      Westminster Abbey in the History of the Nation
1973 *Shakespeare's Sonnets: The Problems Solved*[1]
      Shakespeare the Man
1974 *Simon Forman: Sex and Society in Shakespeare's Age*
      Windsor Castle in the History of the Nation
      Victorian and Edwardian Cornwall in Photographs (with John
      Betjeman)
      Peter, the White Cat of Trenarren
1975 *Oxford in the History of the Nation*
      Robert Stephen Hawker of Morwenstow
      Discoveries and Reviews
      Jonathan Swift: Major Prophet
1976 *A Cornishman Abroad*
      Matthew Arnold: Poet and Prophet
      Brown Buck: A Californian Fantasy
1977 *Shakespeare the Elizabethan*
      Homosexuals in History
      Milton the Puritan
1978 *The Byrons and the Trevanions*
      The Annotated Shakespeare
1979 *A Man of the Thirties*
      Portraits and Views
1980 *Memories of Men and Women*

1. This, the second edition, its title throwing down the gauntlet, contains Rowse's identification of the Dark Lady, fully developed in *Shakespeare the Man*. The first edition, lacking these excitements, had appeared in 1963. A third edition, less provocatively subtitled but otherwise little altered, appeared in 1984, dedicated to President Reagan 'for his professional appreciation of William Shakespeare'.

Shakespeare's Globe
1981 *A Life: Collected Poems*
1983 *Eminent Elizabethans*
1984 *Prefaces to Shakespeare's Plays*
Shakespeare's Self-Portrait
1985 *Glimpses of the Great*
The Contemporary Shakespeare
1986 *Reflections on the Puritan Revolution*
The Little Land of Cornwall
1987 *The Poet Auden: A Personal Memoir*
Court & Country: Studies in Tudor Social History
Froude the Historian
1988 *Quiller Couch: A Portrait of 'Q'*
1989 *Friends and Contemporaries*
The Controversial Colensos
Discovering Shakespeare
1993 *Four Caroline Portraits*
All Souls in My Time
1994 *The Regicides*
1995 *Historians I Have Known*
1996 *My View of Shakespeare*

Guest list for lunch given by ALR for Allan Nevins and Irving Stone in Hall at All Souls, 20 June 1965

Transcribed from ALR; holograph

Lady Salter

Isaiah Berlin	Max Mallowan
Mrs Mowrer	Boies Penrose
Professor Trilling	Lady Franks
Lady Mander	Sir Frank Bowden
Lord Franks	Mrs Trilling
Ruth Emery	Allan Nevins
Arthur Goodhart	Lady Hayter
Lady Bowden	Irving Stone
Robert Rhodes Jones	Mrs Goodhart
Alan Collins	Fred Adams
Raleigh Trevelyan	Mrs Mallowan
Lady Berlin ?	Sir George Harmsworth
Lord Salter	Jack Simmons
Mrs Irving Stone	M. I. Fry
Sir William Hayter	R. Balin
Helen Penrose	Mary Nevins

ALR

Note: Several of the guests are mentioned in the text and can be found in the index. Of the others there are three Heads of House with their wives – Lord and Lady Franks (Worcester College), Mr and Mrs Arthur Goodhart (University College), Sir William and Lady Hayter

(New College). Lionel Trilling was Visiting Professor in American studies. Mrs Mallowan is better known as Agatha Christie. Mary Isobel Fry was a friend from Rowse's circle of intimates at the Huntington.

List of Correspondents

This list, alphabetized but otherwise unaltered, is transcribed from a rough holograph, compiled by Rowse probably in the 1960s with a view to selling his archive to an American library. He made several such approaches about that time.

There are a number of conspicuous omissions, mostly English but some American. Incomplete as it is it does give some idea of the range of his correspondence.

Aberconway, Christabel
Alba, Duke of
Aldrich, Mrs Winthrop
Amery, L. S.
Astor, Lady, also Bill &
    Michael
Attlee, C. R.

Balsan, Consuelo, (Dchss of
    Marlborough)
Beaverbrook, Lord
Berlin, Isaiah
Berners, Lord
Betjeman, John
Bevin, Ernest
Bibesco, Princess
Biddle, Francis
Birkenhead, 2nd Lord
Bodelsen

Bogan, Louise
Boothby, Lord
Bottome, Phyllis
Bowen, Catherine Drinker
Bowra, C. M.
Brett, Dorothy
Buccleugh, Duke of
Buchan, John, Lord
Tweedsmuir

Cary, Joyce
Causley, Charles
Cecil, Lord David
Chapman, Hester
Christie, Agatha
Church, Richard
Churchill, W. S.
Clemo, Jack
Cohen, Harriet

Cole, G. D. H.
Commager, Henry Steele
Coward, Noel

Darwin, Sir Charles
De L'Isle and Dudley, Lord
Devonshire, Duchess of

Eden, Anthony, Lord Avon
Eliot, T. S.

Falls, Cyril
Foot, Michael
Fuller, Roy

Gielgud, Sir John
Graham, Winston
Grigson, Geoffrey

Halifax, Lord
Hill, Christopher
Hudson, G. F.

Jay, Douglas
Jenkins, Elizabeth
John, Augustus

Kelly, Sir Gerald
Kemsley, Lord
Kennedy, Ludovic
Ketton Cremer, Wyndham

Lewis, W. S. ('Lefty')

Macaulay, Rose
Mackenzie, Compton
Maclennan, Hugh

Macmillan, Harold
Mais, S. P. B.
Makins, Sir Roger
Mander, Lady (Rosalie Glynn
    Grylls)
Marlborough, Duke of
Masefield, John
Mathew, David (Abp)
Mattingly, Garrett
Menzies, Robert (PM of
    Australia)
Milner, Lady
Morgan, Charles
Morison, Samuel Eliot
Morrison, Herbert
Mortimer, Raymond

Neale, J. E.
Nevins, Allan
Nimitz, Fleet Admiral and Mrs
    Nimitz

Oman, Carola

Penrose, Boies
Portland, Duke of
Powicke, Sir Maurice
Pratt, Stephen
Pritchett, V. S.

Quayle, Anthony
Quick, D.

Radakrishnan, President of
    India
Rennell, Lord
Roberts, Cecil

Salisbury, Lord
Salter, Lord
Siegfried, Andre
Simon, Lord
Sitwell, Osbert and Edith
Spargo, John
Speaight, Robert
Spender, Stephen
Spring, Howard
Stern, G. B.
Stopes, Marie
Stradbroke, Lord
Strang, Lord
Summerson, Sir John

Tate, Allen (poet)
Tawney, R. H.
Tippett, Sir Michael
Tracy, Honor
Trevelyan, G. M.
Trevor Roper, H. R.
Trilling, Lionel

Vaughan Williams, Ralph

Wedgwood, C. V.
Wilberforce, Lord
Woodward, Llewellyn

Young. G. M.

Index

Note: Works by Rowse (ALR) appear under title; works by others under author's name